Sleep and Developmental Psychopathology

Sleep plays a critical role in child development, with insufficient sleep or sleep disorders linked to poorer physical health, increased weight gain, academic deficits, behavior problems, and difficulties with emotion regulation. This book examines the complex and dynamic relationship between sleep and developmental psychopathology. By focusing on broad topics such as social and emotional development or child well-being, as well as specific disorders including ADHD, anxiety, and bipolar, many different aspects of developmental psychopathology are considered. In addition, a breadth of studies examine different measurement approaches and sleep as an underlying mechanism for the development of behavior, social, and emotional problems. This collection of novel research studies exploring the intersection between sleep and developmental outcomes is essential for clinicians and researchers who work with children and adolescents.

This book was first published as a special issue of the *Journal of Clinical Child and Adolescent Psychology.*

Lisa J. Meltzer is an Associate Professor of Pediatrics at National Jewish Health, USA. She is board certified in Behavioral Sleep Medicine by the American Board of Sleep Medicine and is the co-author of *Pediatric Sleep Problems: A Clinician's Guide to Behavioral Interventions* (2015). She also has a funded program of research examining the impact of sleep on health outcomes in youth with chronic illnesses and their parents, the development and validation of objective and subjective measures of pediatric sleep, and the impact of changing school start times on health outcomes.

Sleep and Developmental Psychopathology

Edited by
Lisa J. Meltzer

Routledge
Taylor & Francis Group
LONDON AND NEW YORK

First published 2018 by Routledge

2 Park Square, Milton Park, Abingdon, Oxon OX14 4RN
605 Third Avenue, New York, NY 10017

Routledge is an imprint of the Taylor & Francis Group, an informa business

First issued in paperback 2021

Publisher's Note

The publisher has gone to great lengths to ensure the quality of this reprint but points out that some imperfections in the original copies may be apparent.

British Library Cataloguing-in-Publication Data
A catalogue record for this book is available from the British Library

ISBN13: 978-1-138-54238-9 (hbk)
ISBN13: 978-0-367-53611-4 (pbk)

Typeset in Times New Roman
by codeMantra

Publisher's Note
The publisher accepts responsibility for any inconsistencies that may have arisen during the conversion of this book from journal articles to book chapters, namely the possible inclusion of journal terminology.

Contents

Citation Information

The chapters in this book were originally published in the *Journal of Clinical Child and Adolescent Psychology*, volume 46, issue 2 (March–April 2017). When citing this material, please use the original page numbering for each article, as follows:

Introduction
Sleep and Developmental Psychopathology: Introduction to the Special Issue
Lisa J. Meltzer
Journal of Clinical Child and Adolescent Psychology, volume 46, issue 2 (March–April 2017) pp. 171–174

Chapter 1
Sleep Architecture Relates to Daytime Affect and Somatic Complaints in Clinically Anxious but Not Healthy Children
Cara A. Palmer and Candice A. Alfano
Journal of Clinical Child and Adolescent Psychology, volume 46, issue 2 (March–April 2017) pp. 175–187

Chapter 2
Stage 2 Sleep EEG Sigma Activity and Motor Learning in Childhood ADHD: A Pilot Study
Jared M. Saletin, William G. Coon, and Mary A. Carskadon
Journal of Clinical Child and Adolescent Psychology, volume 46, issue 2 (March–April 2017) pp. 188–197

Chapter 3
A Preliminary Multimethod Comparison of Sleep Among Adolescents With and Without Generalized Anxiety Disorder
Benjamin C. Mullin, Laura Pyle, Dustin Haraden, Justin Riederer, Natalie Brim, David Kaplan, and Douglas Novins
Journal of Clinical Child and Adolescent Psychology, volume 46, issue 2 (March–April 2017) pp. 198–210

Chapter 4
Does an Online CBT Program for Anxiety Impact Upon Sleep Problems in Anxious Youth?
Caroline L. Donovan, Susan H. Spence, and Sonja March
Journal of Clinical Child and Adolescent Psychology, volume 46, issue 2 (March–April 2017) pp. 211–221

Chapter 5
Sleep Moderates the Association Between Response Inhibition and Self-Regulation in Early Childhood
Allyson M. Schumacher, Alison L. Miller, Sarah E. Watamura, Salome Kurth, Jonathan M. Lassonde, and Monique K. LeBourgeois
Journal of Clinical Child and Adolescent Psychology, volume 46, issue 2 (March–April 2017) pp. 222–235

Chapter 6
Sleep and Social-Emotional Development in Infants and Toddlers
Jodi A. Mindell, Erin S. Leichman, Courtney DuMond, and Avi Sadeh
Journal of Clinical Child and Adolescent Psychology, volume 46, issue 2 (March–April 2017) pp. 236–246

Chapter 7
Sleep in Adolescents With Bipolar I Disorder: Stability and Relation to Symptom Change
Anda Gershon and Manpreet K. Singh
Journal of Clinical Child and Adolescent Psychology, volume 46, issue 2 (March–April 2017) pp. 247–257

Chapter 8
Sleep Duration and Child Well-Being: A Nonlinear Association
Sarah James and Lauren Hale
Journal of Clinical Child and Adolescent Psychology, volume 46, issue 2 (March–April 2017) pp. 258–268

Chapter 9
Tracking Effects of Problematic Social Networking on Adolescent Psychopathology: The Mediating Role of Sleep Disruptions
Lynette Vernon, Kathryn L. Modecki, and Bonnie L. Barber
Journal of Clinical Child and Adolescent Psychology, volume 46, issue 2 (March–April 2017) pp. 269–283

Chapter 10
ADHD and Sleep Quality: Longitudinal Analyses From Childhood to Early Adulthood in a Twin Cohort
Alice M. Gregory, Jessica C. Agnew-Blais, Timothy Matthews, Terrie E. Moffitt, and Louise Arseneault
Journal of Clinical Child and Adolescent Psychology, volume 46, issue 2 (March–April 2017) pp. 284–294

Chapter 11
Future Directions in Sleep and Developmental Psychopathology
Lisa J. Meltzer
Journal of Clinical Child and Adolescent Psychology, volume 46, issue 2 (March–April 2017) pp. 295–301

Notes on Contributors

Jessica C. Agnew-Blais is a Research Fellow at the MRC Social, Genetic & Developmental Psychiatry Centre, King's College London, UK.

Candice A. Alfano is Professor of Psychology and Director of Sleep and Anxiety Center of Houston at the University of Houston, TX, USA.

Louise Arseneault is Professor of Developmental Psychology at King's College London and the Mental Health Leadership Fellow for the UK Economic and Social Resarch Council, London, UK.

Bonnie L. Barber is Professor in the School of Applied Psychology at Griffith University, Brisbane, QLD, Australia.

Natalie Brim is a board-certified physician's assistant at the Monroe Carell Jr. Children's Hospital at Vanderbilt University, USA.

Mary A. Carskadon is Professor of Psychiatry and Human Behavior at Brown University, and Director of the Sleep for Science Research Laboratory at E.P. Bradley Hospital, Providence, RI, USA.

William G. Coon is a Research Fellow in Psychiatry at Harvard Medical School and in the Department of Psychiatry at Massachusetts General Hospital, Boston, MA, USA.

Caroline L. Donovan is Associate Professor in the School of Applied Psychology at Griffith University, Brisbane, QLD, Australia.

Courtney DuMond is a Clinical Psychologist at Lakeside Behavioral Health in Auburn, NY, USA.

Anda Gershon is an Instructor of Psychiatry and Behavioral Sciences – Child and Adolescent Psychiatry at Stanford University, Palo Alto, CA, USA.

Alice M. Gregory is Professor of Psychology at Goldsmiths, University of London, UK.

Lauren Hale is Professor of Family, Population, and Preventive Medicine at Stony Brook University, Stony Brook, NY, USA.

Dustin Haraden is a doctoral candidate in Clinical Psychology at the University of Illinois, Urbana-Champaign, IL, USA.

Sarah James is a graduate student in the Department of Sociology and the Office of Population Research at Princeton University, Princeton, NJ, USA.

David Kaplan is Professor of Pediatrics at the University of Colorado School of Medicine, USA.

Salome Kurth is a Research Group Leader in the CRPP Sleep and Health at the University of Zurich, Switzerland.

Jonathan M. Lassonde is an MA graduate from the Department of Integrative Physiology at the University of Colorado, Boulder, CO, USA.

Monique K. LeBourgeois is Associate Professor of Integrative Physiology at the University of Colorado, Boulder, CO, USA.

Erin S. Leichman is a Senior Research Psychologist in the Department of Psychology at Saint Joseph's University, Philadelphia, PA, USA.

Sonja March is Associate Professor in the School of Psychology and Counselling and Research Program Director in The Institute for Resilient Regions at the University of Southern Queensland, Springfield Central, QLD, Australia.

Timothy Matthews is a Postdoctoral Research Associate at the Institute of Psychiatry, Psychology and Neuroscience at King's College London, UK.

Lisa J. Meltzer is Associate Professor of Pediatrics at National Jewish Health, Denver, CO, USA.

Alison L. Miller is Associate Professor of Health Behavior and Health Education at the University of Michigan School of Public Health, Ann Arbor, MI, USA.

Jodi A. Mindell is Professor and Director of Graduate Psychology at Saint Joseph's University and Associate Director of the Sleep Center at the Children's Hospital of Philadelphia, Philadelphia, PA, USA.

Kathryn L. Modecki is Senior Lecturer in the School of Applied Psychology at Griffith University, Brisbane, QLD, Australia.

Terrie E. Moffitt is Chair in Social Behaviour and Development at King's College London, UK.

Benjamin C. Mullin is Assistant Professor in the Department of Psychiatry at the University of Colorado School of Medicine, Denver, CO, USA.

Douglas Novins is Professor in the Department of Psychiatry at the University of Colorado School of Medicine, Denver, CO, USA.

Cara A. Palmer is a Research Assistant Professor at the Sleep and Anxiety Center of Houston at the University of Houston, TX, USA.

Laura Pyle is Assistant Professor and Associate Director of the Child Health Research Biostatics Core at the University of Colorado, Boulder, CO, USA.

Justin Riederer is a Professional Research Assistant in the Developmental Brain Research Lab at the University of Colorado, Boulder, CO, USA.

Avi Sadeh was Professor of Clinical Psychology and the Director of the Laboratory for Children's Sleep-Wake Disorders at Tel Aviv University, Israel.

Jared M. Saletin is Assistant Professor of Psychiatry and Human Behavior at Brown University, and is based in the Sleep for Science Research Laboratory at E.P. Bradley Hospital, Providence, RI, USA.

Allyson M. Schumacher is an MA graduate from the Department of Integrative Physiology at the University of Colorado, Boulder, CO, USA.

Manpreet K. Singh is Assistant Professor of Psychiatry and Behavioral Sciences and Director of the Pediatric Mood Disorders Program in the Division of Child and Adolescent Psychiatry at Stanford University, Palo Alto, CA, USA.

Susan H. Spence is Professor Emeritus in the School of Applied Psychology and Australian Institute of Suicide Research and Prevention, at Griffith University, Brisbane, QLD, Australia.

Lynette Vernon is a collaborative postdoctoral fellow in the School of Psychology and Exercise Science at Murdoch University, Perth, WA, Australia.

Sarah E. Watamura is Associate Professor of Psychology at the University of Denver, CO, USA.

Sleep and Developmental Psychopathology: Introduction to the Special Issue

Lisa J. Meltzer

Research in the field of pediatric sleep has grown significantly in the past 25 years. However, because much remains to be learned about the complex and dynamic relationship between sleep and developmental psychopathology, this special issue of the *Journal of Clinical Child and Adolescent Psychology* was created to provide an influx of cutting-edge research on this important topic. This introduction provides an overview of the special issue, with articles focusing on what different measurement approaches tells us about the intersection of sleep and developmental psychopathology; the overlap between interventions for sleep and anxiety; sleep as a potential mechanism for the development of social, emotional, and behavioral problems; and how population-based studies can be used to consider the interaction between sleep, well-being, and symptoms of psychopathology.

Sleep is as essential to human functioning as eating, drinking, and breathing. Yet much remains to be learned about how sleep impacts physical and emotional development in children and adolescents. By the age of 18 years, children and adolescents should have spent about 40% of their lives sleeping (Mindell & Owens, 2015), yet insufficient sleep is common across development, in particular during adolescence (Owens, 2014). Beyond insufficient sleep, an estimated 25% of typically developing youth have sleep problems (Owens, 2008), with the prevalence increasing to 80% among children with autism (Johnson, Giannotti, & Cortesi, 2009) and other developmental disorders (Wiggs, 2001). Environmental, behavioral, and genetic factors contribute to both sleep physiology and developmental psychopathology, but the dynamic interaction between sleep and psychopathology in children and adolescents has been understudied. This special issue of the *Journal of Clinical Child and Adolescent Psychology* focuses on the topic of Sleep and Developmental Psychopathology and was created to begin addressing some of these important questions about the dynamic and complex relationship between sleep and developmental psychopathology.

SPECIAL ISSUE OVERVIEW

Sleep and Developmental Psychopathology is a broad topic, and the articles in this special issue reflect this broadness with a range of ages (infants through young adults), disorders/developmental concerns (e.g., anxiety, bipolar, attention deficit/hyperactivity disorder [ADHD], self-regulation, social-emotional problems), and research type (e.g., intervention, experimental design, longitudinal cohorts).

Measuring Sleep: Physiological Characteristics and Subjective Self-Report

There are three primary ways to measure sleep: polysomnography (PSG), wrist actigraphy, and subjective self-report using sleep diaries and questionnaires (Sadeh, 2011). PSG is a multichannel measure of sleep physiology that occurs overnight, most commonly in a sleep lab but also in a child's home. The multiple channels capture data about electrical brain activity, muscle activation, and eye movements. Together these data allow for the classification of sleep architecture or sleep stages (nonrapid eye movement sleep, including Stages N1, N2, and N3; rapid eye movement sleep). Sleep architecture changes across development (Carskadon & Dement, 2010). However, only a handful of studies have examined the relationship between sleep physiology and developmental psychopathology.

In this special issue, Palmer and Alfano (2017) examine the relationship between PSG-measured sleep architecture and measures of affective symptoms (anxiety, depression, and hyperarousal) in children with and without generalized anxiety disorder (GAD). This study found that the amount of time spent in different sleep stages was related to both affective and somatic symptoms, but only for children with GAD. The authors highlight the need to develop a stronger understanding of how sleep physiology and long-term risk for psychopathology are related, as well as ways to address problematic sleep behaviors (e.g., late bedtimes) that may alter sleep architecture.

Also using data collected during overnight PSG, Saletin, Coon, and Carskadon (2017) apply EEG spectral analysis (another way to examine brain activity during sleep) to examine whether overnight motor skill learning in children with and without ADHD is related to sleep spindle frequency (during N2 sleep). Despite finding no differences in general sleep architecture, children with ADHD in this study had reduced sleep spindle activity when examined by spectral analysis. In addition, only children with ADHD (not typically developing controls) demonstrated sleep dependent motor skill learning, with greater improvement related to more preserved sleep spindle activity. Although sleep complaints are common in youth with ADHD (Konofal, Lecendreux, & Cortese, 2010), overnight PSG has yet to find a difference in traditional sleep architecture between children with and without ADHD. However, these pilot study results suggest that additional analyses of sleep EEG (with spectral analysis) may provide more information about why sleep differences are perceived, as well as potentially informing future interventions that target sleep neurophysiology (Saletin et al., 2016).

A third study focuses on the comparison of subjective sleep complaints and objective sleep quantity and quality (measured by wrist actigraphy) in a sample of adolescents with and without GAD (Mullin et al., 2017). Actigraphy is an ambulatory device that estimates sleep–wake patterns based on movement. Validated against overnight polysomnography, actigraphy provides a way to capture sleep patterns in the child's natural sleep environment for multiple days or weeks (Meltzer, Montgomery-Downs, Insana, & Walsh, 2012). Mullin and colleagues (2017) find that youth with GAD report longer sleep onset latency and less satisfaction with their sleep; however, by actigraphy anxious youth had longer sleep duration. Additional analyses show that shorter sleep duration is associated with greater morning anxiety, but only in youth with GAD. Differences between subjective and objective sleep may be a result of reporter bias, underscoring the importance of multimethod sleep assessment in youth with developmental psychopathology. Further, the authors suggest that adolescents with anxiety may be more sensitive to overnight sleep loss and recommend that interventions to improve sleep may be beneficial for adolescents who present with comorbid GAD and sleep problems.

Anxiety Intervention and Sleep Problems

There are a number of common elements in cognitive behavioral therapy (CBT) for anxiety and CBT for insomnia, including relaxation training and cognitive restructuring. Donovan, Spence, and March (2017) examine whether an online CBT intervention shown to reduce anxiety in children and adolescents also reduces sleep-related problems. Children who participated in the online CBT intervention had fewer sleep-related problems immediately posttreatment, as well as 6 months later (Donovan et al., 2017). But for adolescents both the intervention and waitlist control groups showed improvements in sleep-related problems after treatment and at 6-month follow-up. Although more research is clearly needed on interventions to improve sleep in youth with anxiety, the authors conclude that it is important for clinicians to assess for and treat sleep problems in both children and adolescents with anxiety.

Mechanisms and Trajectories

Three studies in this special issue consider whether sleep serves as a mechanism for the development of social, emotional, and behavioral problems, as well as the interaction of sleep and symptoms of psychopathology over time.

Parents will frequently report that young children have difficulties with behavior and emotion regulation following insufficient sleep, although few studies have empirically examined this concern. In this special issue, Schumacher and colleagues (2017) examine the impact of 1 night of sleep restriction (keeping a child up 3 hr past regular bedtime) on response inhibition and self-regulation in healthy, typically developing preschoolers. Sleep restriction was found to moderate the relationship between response inhibition and adaptive self-regulation; specifically, a strong association was found when children were well rested but not when they were sleep deprived (Schumacher et al., 2017). Although examining only acute sleep restriction, this study begins to shed light on the role that sufficient sleep duration plays in the emotional development of young children.

In a cohort of young children, assessed at 6, 12, and 18 months, Mindell, Leichman, Du Mond, and Sadeh (2017) found a relationship between sleep (later bedtimes, longer sleep onset latency, and decreased total sleep) and social-emotional development (internalizing, externalizing, and dysregulation symptoms). In addition, structural equation modeling highlighted that sleep was stable over early development and that sleep duration and bedtimes at 12 months predicted internalizing problems at 18 months; however, internalizing problems at 12 months did not predict sleep at 18 months. The authors suggest that an overtired toddler may appear more socially withdrawn and anxious rather than hyperactive (Mindell et al., 2017). Although more information is needed about the interaction between sleep and social-emotional functioning, this study underscores the importance of providing early intervention to support healthy sleep habits in infants and toddlers.

In adolescents, Gershon and Singh (2017) report that sleep is stable over 1 year for healthy, typically developing youth but not for youth with bipolar disorder. In addition, after controlling for initial depressive symptoms, this study finds that weekend sleep disturbances and wake time predict depressive symptoms 1 year later. The authors highlight the importance of targeting sleep problems in adolescents with bipolar, as sleep disturbances can predict symptom change over time. For adolescents with variable sleep schedules, it may be particularly important to focus on keeping a consistent sleep–wake routine, even on weekends.

Population-Based Studies

Three population-based studies in this special issue also consider the interaction between sleep, well-being, and symptoms of psychopathology.

Using the Fragile Families and Child Wellbeing Study cohort (United States), James and Hale (2017) examine whether short and/or long sleep duration at 5 and 9 years of age was associated with both behavior problems and physical health at 9 years of age. A nonlinear U-shaped association was found at age 9 (controlling for sleep at age 5), with children who slept either too much or too little having more behavior problems and poorer health (James & Hale, 2017). This study further supports the importance of ensuring that children are obtaining sufficient sleep duration. However, this study is among the first to also demonstrate that long sleep duration in children may be of concern and should be carefully evaluated by clinicians.

Vernon, Modecki, and Barber (2017) examine data from the Youth Activity Participation Study (Australia), a large sample of high school students' sleep disruptions, problematic social networking (i.e., heavy investment in and use of social networking), and symptoms of psychopathology were assessed annually over three years. Across time points, sleep disruptions mediated the relationship between problematic social networking and depressed mood. Sleep disruptions also mediated the relationship between problematic social networking and externalizing problems, but this was a bidirectional finding. To minimize the negative effects of social networking on developmental psychopathology, the authors highlight the importance of addressing healthy sleep habits in adolescents, including the reduction and rescheduling of social networking time away from bedtime.

In the final article in this special issue, Gregory, Agnew-Blais, Matthews, Moffitt, and Arsenault (2017) examine 2,232 adolescents who were part of the Environmental Risk Longitudinal Twin Study (United Kingdom). ADHD diagnoses were collected at 5, 7, 10, 12, and 18 years of age, whereas sleep quality was measured at 18 years of age. This study finds that children with ADHD have poorer sleep quality as young adults, even when controlling for a number of confounders (including depression, GAD, conduct disorder, and maternal insomnia). Further, this study shows that the relationship between ADHD and sleep quality was influenced by both genetic and environmental factors. However, the truly novel finding of this study is that for young adults whose ADHD has remitted, sleep quality is no different than for young adults who never had ADHD (Gregory et al., 2016). This finding may be encouraging for families of children with ADHD, as ADHD may resolve for some children, and if it does, families can have hope that concurrent sleep issues will also resolve.

Future Directions

Going beyond the simple question of whether sleep causes developmental psychopathology, or vice versa, the final article in this special issue highlights areas I believe are important for both researchers and clinicians in the fields of pediatric sleep and clinical child and adolescent psychology: what is normal in terms of sleep across development, the role of individual variability in terms of sleep needs and vulnerability to sleep loss, how sleep may serve as a risk or resilience factor for developmental psychopathology, and intervention considerations (Meltzer, 2017).

It is my hope that this collection of cutting-edge research studies will inspire and motivate both researchers and clinicians in the field of clinical child and adolescent psychology to integrate sleep into their own work.

ACKNOWLEDGMENTS

The success of this *JCCAP* special issue would not have been possible without the mentorship of Mitch Prinstein, PhD, and the technical support of Barbara Myers.

REFERENCES

Carskadon, M. A., & Dement, W. C. (2010). Normal human sleep: An overview. In M. Kryger, T. Roth, & W. C. Dement (Eds.), *Principles and practices of sleep medicine* (5th ed., pp. 16–26). Philadelphia, PA: Elsevier.

Donovan, C., Spence, S., & March, S. (2017). Does an online CBT program for anxiety impact upon sleep problems in anxious youth? *Journal of Clinical Child & Adolescent Psychology, 46*, 211–221. doi:10.1080/15374416.2016.1188700

Gershon, A., & Singh, M. (2017). Sleep in adolescents with bipolar I disorder: Stability and relation to symptom change. *Journal of Clinical Child & Adolescent Psychology, 46*, 247–257. doi:10.1080/15374416.2016.1188699

Gregory, A. M., Agnew-Blais, J., Matthews, T., Moffitt, T., & Arsenault, L. (2017). ADHD and sleep quality: Longitudinal analyses from childhood to early adulthood in a twin cohort. *Journal of Clinical Child & Adolescent Psychology, 46*, 284–294. doi:10.1080/15374416.2016.1183499

James, S., & Hale, L. (2017). Sleep duration and child wellbeing: A nonlinear association. *Journal of Clinical Child and Adolescent Psychology, 46*, 258–268. doi:10.1080/15374416.2016.1204920

Johnson, K. P., Giannotti, F., & Cortesi, F. (2009). Sleep patterns in autism spectrum disorders. *Child and Adolescent Psychiatric Clinics of North America*, *18*(4), 917–928. doi:10.1016/j.chc.2009.04.001

Konofal, E., Lecendreux, M., & Cortese, S. (2010). Sleep and ADHD. *Sleep Medicine*, *11*, 652–658. doi:10.1016/j.sleep.2010.02.012

Meltzer, L. J. (2017). Future directions in sleep and developmental psychopathology. *Journal of Clinical Child and Adolescent Psychology*, *46*, 295–301.

Meltzer, L. J., Montgomery-Downs, H. E., Insana, S. P., & Walsh, C. M. (2012). Use of actigraphy for assessment in pediatric sleep research. *Sleep Medicine Reviews*, *16*, 463–475. doi:10.1016/j.smrv.2011.10.002

Mindell, J. A., Leichman, E., Du Mond, C. E., & Sadeh, A. (2017). Sleep and social-emotional development in infants and toddlers. *Journal of Clinical Child & Adolescent Psychology*, *46*, 236–246. doi:10.1080/15374416.2016.1188701

Mindell, J. A., & Owens, J. A. (2015). *A clinical guide to pediatric sleep: Diagnosis and management of sleep problems* (3rd ed.). Philadelphia, PA: Wolters Kluwer.

Mullin, B., Pyle, L., Haraden, D., Riederer, J., Brim, N., Kaplan, D., & D. Novins. (2017). A preliminary multimethod comparison of sleep among adolescents with and without generalized anxiety disorder. *Journal of Clinical Child and Adolescent Psychology*, *46*, 198–210. doi:10.1080/15374416.2016.1220312

Owens, J. (2008). Classification and epidemiology of childhood sleep disorders. *Primary Care: Clinics in Office Practice*, *35*, 533–546. doi:10.1016/j.pop.2008.06.003

Owens, J. (2014). Insufficient sleep in adolescents and young adults: An update on causes and consequences. *Pediatrics*, *134*, e921–e932. doi:10.1542/peds.2014-1696

Palmer, C., & Alfano, C. A. (2017). Sleep architecture relates to daytime affect and somatic complaints in clinically-anxious but not healthy children. *Journal of Clinical Child and Adolescent Psychology*, *46*, 175–187. doi:10.1080/15374416.2016.1188704

Sadeh, A. (2011). Sleep assessment methods. In M. El-Sheikh (Ed.), *Sleep and development: Familial and socio-cultural considerations* (pp. 356–371). New York, NY: Oxford University Press.

Saletin, J., Coon, W., & Carskadon, M. A. (2017). Stage 2 sleep EEG sigma activity and motor learning in childhood ADHD: A pilot study. *Journal of Clinical Child & Adolescent Psychology*, *46*, 188–197. doi:10.1080/15374416.2016.1157756

Schumacher, A. M., Miller, A. L., Watamura, S. E., Kurth, S., Lassonde, J. M. & LeBourgeois, M. K. (2017). Sleep moderates the association between response inhibition and self-regulation in early childhood. *Journal of Clinical Child and Adolescent Psychology*, *46*, 222–235. doi:10.1080/15374416.2016.1204921

Vernon, L., Modecki, K., & Barber, B. (2017). Tracking effects of problematic social networking on adolescent psychopathology: The mediating role of sleep disruptions. *Journal of Clinical Child & Adolescent Psychology*, *46*, 269–283. doi:10.1080/15374416.2016.1188702

Wiggs, L. (2001). Sleep problems in children with developmental disorders. *Journal of the Royal Society of Medicine*, *94*(4), 177–179.

Sleep Architecture Relates to Daytime Affect and Somatic Complaints in Clinically Anxious but Not Healthy Children

Cara A. Palmer and Candice A. Alfano

It is increasingly clear that seminal sleep-affective relationships begin to take root in childhood, yet studies exploring how nighttime sleep characteristics relate to daytime affective symptoms, both in clinical and healthy populations of children, are lacking. The current study sought to explore these relationships by investigating whether trait-like and/or daily reports of affective and somatic symptoms of children with generalized anxiety disorder and matched controls relate to sleep architecture. Sixty-six children (ages 7–11; 54.4% female; 56.1% Caucasian; 18.2% biracial; 6.1% African American; 3% Asian; 16.7% Hispanic) participated including 29 with primary generalized anxiety disorder (without comorbid depression) and 37 healthy controls matched on age and race/ethnicity. Participants underwent structured diagnostic assessments including child-report measures and subsequently reported on their negative affect and somatic symptoms over the course of 1 week. Children also completed 1 night of polysomnography. Among children with generalized anxiety disorder only, greater amounts of slow wave sleep corresponded with less negative affect, and greater amounts of rapid eye movement sleep was related to more somatic complaints across the week. Similarly, for trait-like measures, more rapid eye movement sleep and shorter latency to rapid eye movement sleep were related to greater depressive symptoms in the anxious group only. The current findings suggest that physiologic sleep characteristics may contribute in direct ways to the symptom profiles of clinically anxious children. The functional relevance of such findings (e.g., how specific sleep characteristics serve to either increase or reduce long-term risk) is a vital direction for future research.

Although sleep complaints are prevalent across various types of child internalizing disorders (Alfano & Gamble, 2009) differences in sleep architecture (i.e., the basic structural organization of sleep) as compared to typically developing children are far less commonly observed. For example, during the prepubertal years, youth with anxiety disorders and major depressive disorder exhibit objective sleep patterns largely similar to those of healthy youth (for reviews, see Ivanenko, Crabtree, & Gozal, 2005; McMakin & Alfano, 2015). These findings stand in contrast to reliable evidence of sleep abnormalities in adult patients, particularly those with depression (Palagini, Baglioni, Ciapparelli, Gemignani, & Riemann, 2013). Notwithstanding the fact that child-based studies are fewer overall and often comprised of broad age ranges of youth, lack of sleep-based differences in child patients may well be attributable to maturational differences (e.g., stronger homeostatic sleep pressure) that override sleep-based expression of affective illness (Carskadon, 2002; Dahl, 1996). Still, as the vast majority of children with anxiety disorders and depression complain of poor sleep (Alfano, Ginsburg, & Kingery, 2007; Alfano, Patriquin, & De Los Reyes, 2015; Chorney, Detweiler, Morris, & Kuhn, 2008) and early sleep problems reliably presage the later onset of these disorders (Gregory et al., 2005; Kelly & El-Sheikh, 2014; Ong, Wickramaratne, Tang, & Weissman, 2006), it is clear that critical sleep-affective relationships begin to take root in childhood. Thus, there is need for research to move beyond group-based comparisons of sleep in favor of exploring how nighttime sleep characteristics relate to daytime emotional functioning in both clinical and healthy populations of children.

Sleep and affective functioning are also recognized to share bidirectional associations (see Alvaro, Roberts, &

Harris, 2013), yet differential relationships are evident across clinical and non-clinical samples. Sleep deprivation, particularly loss of rapid eye movement (REM) sleep, produces reliable, albeit transient improvements in mood in a majority of clinically depressed patients, whereas a worsening of mood is typically observed in nondepressed samples (see Giedke & Schwärzler, 2002). Other research has found affective responses to sleep deprivation to be predicted by degree of diurnal mood variation more specifically (Haug, 1992). Sleep deprivation studies are infrequent in child samples, but other research highlights the bidirectionality of nighttime sleep and daytime affect in youth both with and without internalizing psychopathology. For the most part, this growing body of research reveals stronger pathways from sleep to affect/mood than the reverse relationship (McMakin & Alfano, 2015). For example, using three waves of data over a 5-year period (8–13 years) Kelly and El-Sheikh (2014) showed shorter sleep duration and worse sleep quality to predict increased anxiety and depressive symptoms, whereas less robust associations were identified in the opposite direction. Similarly, in a study among youth ages 9–16, subjective sleep complaints predicted a later diagnosis of generalized anxiety disorder (GAD; Shanahan, Copeland, Angold, Bondy, & Costello, 2014). In one of the only studies to include youth with anxiety and depressive disorders as well as healthy children, 1 week of actigraphy and daily affect monitoring revealed more time spent asleep at night to predict greater positive affect the next day in the clinical groups only (Cousins et al., 2011). These findings in particular highlight the presence of differential relationships between nighttime sleep patterns and daytime affect in clinical versus healthy children.

Building on this burgeoning area of research, the current study was interested in whether, irrespective of quantitative differences in sleep, the daytime symptoms of youth with anxiety disorders might show distinct relationships with sleep architecture. Our study focuses on children with GAD specifically for several reasons. Most prominently, the vast majority (up to 90%) of children with GAD and/or their parents report sleep to be problematic (Alfano, Beidel, Turner, & Lewin, 2006; Alfano et al., 2007; Alfano, Pina, Zerr, & Villalta, 2010). Second, defining features of the disorder, including chronic worry and hypervigilance for threat, are inherently counterproductive to achieving and maintaining sleep (Dahl, 1996). A large proportion of children with GAD also eventually develop depressive disorders (Brown & Barlow, 1992; Kessler et al., 1994; Pine, Cohen, & Brook, 2001), vulnerability for which is marked by sleep-related disruptions (Palagini et al., 2013). Third, examinations of sleep architecture in this population, which are notably limited, have produced equivocal findings. In a sleep lab setting, children with GAD evidenced prolonged sleep onset and reduced latency to REM sleep compared to controls (Alfano, Reynolds, Scott, Dahl, & Mellman, 2013), but results were not replicated using home-based polysomnography (PSG; Patriquin, Mellman, Glaze, & Alfano, 2014). Understanding whether and how the underlying structure of sleep maps onto the daytime symptoms of children with GAD may provide greater insight into these discrepancies, early sleep-affective relationships in general, and the role of sleep in the symptom profiles of anxious youth.

We begin with an overview of normal sleep architecture including seminal relationships between specific sleep stages and aspects of affect and psychopathology as a basis for the current investigation, which includes children with a primary GAD diagnosis and a healthy control sample.

SLEEP ARCHITECTURE AND AFFECTIVE LINKS IN CHILDHOOD

PSG, which includes electroencephalography (EEG), electrooculography (EOG), and electromyography (EMG), is considered the "gold standard" for assessing sleep architecture. In general, sleep consists of two main types—REM sleep and non-rapid eye movement (NREM) sleep—each with unique neurobiological and physiological characteristics. NREM sleep is further divided into three stages (N1–N3) corresponding with increasing depth of sleep as determined by progressive dominance of high-voltage, low-frequency EEG activity. NREM sleep stages are also marked by parasympathetic dominance, including decreased muscle tone, reductions in blood pressure/heart rate, and slowed and rhythmic respiration. N1, sometimes referred to as "relaxed wakefulness," characterizes the transition from wake to sleep and occupies the smallest percentage of total sleep time. In contrast, N2 occupies approximately 50% of the nighttime sleep period and is characterized as light sleep. N3 is the deepest and most restorative of all sleep stages, marked by slow, delta brain waves, and thus is referred to as slow wave sleep (SWS).

As compared to other stages of sleep, dramatic changes in N3 are observed in late childhood as children transition into adolescence, including an approximate 40% decrease in SWS (Campbell & Feinberg, 2009; Carskadon & Dement, 2011; Colrain & Baker, 2011). This significant decline primarily accounts for observable reductions in total sleep time during adolescence compared to the childhood years (Karacan, Anch, Thornby, Okawa, & Williams, 1975). Studies experimentally disrupting SWS find increased daytime sleep propensity (Dijk, Groeger, Stanley, & Deacon, 2006) and subsequent increases in SWS (Dijk, Beersma, Daan, Bloem, & Van Den Hoofdakker, 1987; Ferrara, De Gennaro, & Bertini, 1999), highlighting its functional significance. SWS enhances various daytime functions and is believed to be important for learning and memory consolidation (Walker, 2009). During childhood, SWS is theorized to play a critical role in brain maturation and development, including increased synaptic density (Campbell & Feinberg, 2009; Kurth et al., 2010).

A multitude of evidence reveals the presence of decreased N3 sleep in adults with depression as compared to healthy individuals (Berger, Van Calker, & Riemann, 2003; Palagini et al., 2013; Riemann, Berger, & Voderholzer, 2001; Tsuno, Besset, & Ritchie, 2005). This robust finding is also evident in the first-degree relatives of those who are depressed and observed even after a depressive episode has remitted (Lauer, Schreiber, Holsboer, & Krieg, 1995; Pillai, Kalmbach, & Ciesla, 2011). In childhood, N3 sleep may be distinctly protective against the later onset of depression in at-risk children. In a longitudinal study of nondepressed pre-pubertal children (ages 6–11) at genetic risk for depression, participants completed diagnostic assessments annually through early adulthood (18–29 years) to examine risk and protective factors (Silk et al., 2007). Participants who did not develop depressive disorders in adulthood (i.e., resilient at-risk participants) evidenced greater amounts of SWS in childhood.

In contrast to NREM sleep, REM sleep is often referred to as "paradoxical sleep" due to the presence of low-amplitude mixed-frequency EEG activity (e.g., theta and alpha waves) that resembles brain activity during wakefulness. Increased eye movements, irregular respiration, and rapid changes in heart rate and blood pressure are also seen during REM sleep. This is the stage during which most dreaming activity occurs, with concomitant muscle atonia inhibiting motor activity so cortical signals during dreaming do not create bodily responses. REM sleep accounts for approximately 25% of nighttime sleep (Anders, Sadeh, & Appareddy, 1995) with mild decreases observed after the transition to adolescence. Unlike N3 sleep, however, REM sleep percentage does not change significantly in relation to total sleep time (Ohayon, Carskadon, Guilleminault, & Vitiello, 2004). Also, whereas N3 sleep dominates the first half of the night, REM sleep is dominant during the second half, with REM periods becoming progressively longer and denser across the night.

REM sleep shows intimate relations with emotional learning and memory (Goldstein & Walker, 2014; Walker & Van Der Helm, 2009). At a basic neurobiological level, increased activity in emotion-related brain regions are observed during REM sleep, including the amygdala, striatum, hippocampus, insula, and the medial prefrontal cortex, along with reductions in levels of various neurotransmitters (e.g., noradrenaline; Hobson & Pace-Schott, 2002; Walker & Van Der Helm, 2009). During REM, the activation of these emotion-related brain structures in the absence of noradrenergic changes is believed to provide the backdrop for consolidating emotional events experienced during the day into memory while attenuating the intensity of associated emotions (Walker & van der Helm, 2009). For example, in a study that selectively deprived healthy adults of REM sleep, subsequent increases in reactivity to emotional stimuli were found in comparison to an NREM sleep-deprived group (Rosales-Lagarde et al., 2012).

REM sleep is also heavily implicated in depressive symptomology. Among the most reliable sleep alterations observed in depressed patients are decreased latency to the first REM sleep period and increased time spent in REM (Palagini et al., 2013), which have been replicated in some samples of youth (Arana-Lechuga et al., 2008; Dahl et al., 1991; Emslie, Rush, Weinberg, Rintelmann, & Roffwarg, 1990; Lahmeyer, Poznanski, & Bellur, 1983). Several studies among those at risk for depression have found alterations in REM sleep to be present even before onset of the disorder (Giles, Roffwarg, & Rush, 1987). REM sleep abnormalities are therefore considered among the most robust biomarkers for depressive illness (Palagini et al., 2013).

To a lesser extent, REM sleep has been implicated in somatic/physiological hyperarousal processes. Sleep disturbance generally is associated with somatic complaints in youth (e.g., Lewandowski, Ward, & Palermo, 2011; Miller, Palermo, Powers, Scher, & Hershey, 2003), but research among depressed patients suggests relationships between REM sleep specifically and inflammatory markers/disease (Motivala, Sarfatti, Olmos, & Irwin, 2005). For example, greater amounts of REM sleep have been observed in patients with irritable bowel syndrome (Kumar, Thompson, Wingate, & Vesselinova-Jenkins, 1992). Also, dreams (typically occurring during REM sleep) have been found to precipitate migraines in adults (especially when containing negative content) and relate to somatic distress (Heather-Greener, Comstock, & Joyce, 1996; Levin, Lantz, Fireman, & Spendlove, 2009). Our research group has also shown percentage of REM sleep to relate positively to pre-sleep somatic arousal in children with GAD but not controls (Patriquin et al., 2014).

THE CURRENT STUDY

Overall, relationships between sleep and daytime affective functioning are evident throughout the sleep literature, but few studies have focused on children. Studies among clinical populations of youth are especially lacking. The current study examined these relationships among youth with GAD and healthy controls. We focused on a school-age sample (7–11 years of age) in order to examine sleep-affective relationships in children predominantly likely to be prepubescent, as puberty results in significant neurobiological, hormonal, and social changes that impact both affect and sleep–wake regulation (e.g., Carskadon, Acebo, & Jenni, 2004; Darchia & Cervena, 2014). Better understanding of these relationships earlier in development may also serve to alter high-risk trajectories. In the current study, we examined sleep architecture during a night of PSG in relation to trait-based measures of psychopathology symptoms (anxiety, depression, and hyperarousal), as well as daily reports of negative affect and somatic symptoms across 1 week. Based on previous research, we expected less N3 sleep, greater REM sleep, and reduced latency to REM sleep to be related to overall depressive and anxiety symptoms in children with GAD. We also expected less N3 and greater REM sleep to be associated with more daytime affective problems in this group. Conversely, we hypothesized positive relationships between total REM sleep and both overall and daytime somatic/hyperarousal symptoms in the anxious group.

METHOD

Participants

Participants were 66 children ages 7 to 11 (M = 8.79, SD = 1.36) including youth with primary GAD (n = 29) and healthy controls (n = 37) recruited from two large metropolitan cities in the United States (Washington, DC, and Houston, TX). Approximately half of the participants were female (n = 36, 54.5%), most were Caucasian (56.1%; African American, 6.1%; Asian American, 3%; biracial, 18.2%), and 16.7% were Hispanic. About half (51.5%) reported household incomes greater than $100,000, 25.7% were between $60,000 and $100,000, 15.2% were between $20,000 and $60,000, and 6% were less than $20,000. Most children had at least one parent with a college (40.9%) or advanced (48.5%) degree. There were no differences in demographic characteristics by group (see Table 1 for more information). Pubertal status was assessed using the parent-reported Pubertal Development Scale (PDS; Carskadon & Acebo, 1993), and all but one child was considered pre-pubertal.[1] The original study sample from which participants were drawn included 83 children, but 17 were excluded from thc current set of analyses because of missing PSG data. Specifically, seven families opted not to complete the PSG, four were unable to complete the PSG due to scheduling issues, and six participants' data were lost due to technical errors. Comparison of children with and without available PSG data did not reveal significant differences in terms of demographic, clinical, or sleep characteristics.

All children were required to live with a primary caretaker and be enrolled in regular educational classes. Children were excluded if they were taking any medications known to impact anxiety or sleep (e.g., selective serotonin reuptake inhibitors, melatonin), had a chronic medical condition, or had a known or suspected sleep disorder (e.g., sleep-disordered breathing). Also, because the goal of the larger study was to examine sleep problems and patterns associated with childhood GAD specifically, youth could not have a current or lifetime history of depressive disorders. Psychotic, pervasive developmental, or bipolar disorders were also exclusionary. Other exclusion criteria included an IQ of lower than 80, a body mass index of more than 25, or a non-English-speaking parent or child. In addition, control children could not meet diagnostic criteria for any psychiatric or sleep disorder.

Procedure

Children were recruited via community flyers, mailings to local schools and pediatrician offices, and advertising in local publications and at local events for a study about "behavior and emotions." The study protocol was approved by an Institutional Review Board at both locations. Participants were first consented/assented and then completed an initial assessment that included a diagnostic interview to determine clinical diagnoses, abbreviated IQ testing (Wechsler, 1999), and parent and child questionnaires.

Within 1 week of this initial assessment, participants completed 7 days of daily reports. Each evening, a member of the study staff called participants on the phone and asked them to provide reports of their negative affective symptoms and somatic complaints during that day. Some participants (34.8%, n = 23) missed at least one phone call, resulting in a significant amount of missing data on these indicators (9.5%). Specifically, 11 children were missing 1 night, seven children were missing 2 nights, three children were missing 3 nights, and two children were missing 5 nights of data. We examined if children who missed at least one phone call differed from children who completed all reports, and there were no differences on any demographic, clinical, or sleep characteristics. However, children at the Houston location were significantly more likely to have missed at least one phone call during week ($\chi^2 = 13.68, p < .001$) than those from the Washington, DC location.

On the final night of the daily reports (a Friday or Saturday), participants completed 1 night of PSG monitoring. Participants from Washington, DC, completed PSG monitoring in a sleep laboratory in a pediatric hospital (n = 29), and participants from Houston completed unattended PSG monitoring at home (n = 37).[2] Equal proportions of anxious and control children completed at-home

[1] For both boys and girls, an average PDS score of 3 or below indicates pre-pubertal status. In the current sample, PDS scores ranged from 1.00 to 2.60 (M = 1.50, SD = .43), with the exception of one participant (age = 11, female) in the control group who had a PDS score of 3.20. We ran all analyses without this participant, and the pattern and significance of all results remained unchanged. Therefore, we retained this participant for analyses, and all values reported represent the entire sample. We also assessed mean level differences in pubertal status by group, $t(64) = .54, p = .53$; gender, $t(63.89) = -1.50, p = .14$; and the interaction between group and gender, $F(1, 62) = .33, p = .57$, all of which were nonsignificant.

[2] The decision to utilize different PSG procedures across sites allowed us to examine whether different sleep patterns were detectable across the two types of sleep settings. See Alfano et al. (2013) and Patriquin et al. (2014) for more information about specific PSG procedures.

TABLE 1
Demographic Characteristics of Children With GAD and Controls

	GAD[a]	*Control*[b]	t or χ^2 (df)	p
Age: *M* (*SD*)	8.76 (1.46)	8.81 (1.31)	.15 (64)	*ns*
Female: *n* (%)	17 (58.6%)	19 (51.4%)	.35 (1)	*ns*
Race/Ethnicity *n* (%)			1.86 (4)	*ns*
Caucasian	19 (65.5%)	24 (64.9%)		
African American	1 (3.4%)	3 (8.1%)		
Asian American	1 (3.4%)	1 (2.7%)		
Biracial/Other	4 (13.8%)	2 (5.4%)		
Hispanic/Latino	7 (24.1%)	10 (27%)		
Parental Education: *n* (%)			.04 (1)	*ns*
No College or Some College	4 (13.8%)	6 (16.2%)		
At Least One Parent With College Degree	25 (86.2%)	31 (83.7%)		
Household Income: *n* (%)			−.97 (63)	*ns*
< $20K	2 (6.9%)	2 (5.6%)		
$20–40K	1 (3.4%)	4 (11.1%)		
$40–60K	3 (10.3%)	2 (5.6%)		
$60–80K	2 (6.9%)	6 (16.7%)		
$80–100K	3 (10.3%)	6 (16.7%)		
> $100K	18 (62.1%)	16 (44.4%)		

Note: GAD = generalized anxiety disorder.
[a]*n* = 29.
[b]*n* = 37.

and lab-based PSGs. Children wore a wrist actigraph (Ambulatory Monitoring, Inc., Ardsley, NY) during the week prior to the PSG to ensure they were not sleep deprived on the PSG night. During this week, children were not given any specific sleep instructions other than to follow their normal sleep routines. A majority of children participated in the study during the school year (*n* = 54, 81.8%). Families who completed the entire study were compensated $160 for their time and effort and were provided clinical referrals if needed.

Questionnaires and Sleep Measures

Clinical Interview

The Anxiety Disorders Interview Schedule for the *DSM–IV* for Children and Parents (ADIS-C/P; Silverman & Albano, 1996) was administered at the initial assessment. Separate interviews were conducted with the child and parent by a Ph.D.-level psychologist or trained doctoral-level graduate student, and all cases were reviewed with a licensed clinical psychologist prior to assigning final diagnoses. Clinician severity ratings (range = 0–8) are used to determine the severity of each disorder in order to differentiate primary (most severe) from secondary diagnoses. The mean clinician severity ratings for the current sample of children with GAD was 5.66 (*SD* = 1.26, range = 4–8). The ADIS C/P is considered the gold standard for assessing child anxiety, and past studies demonstrate strong inter-rater reliability, test–rest reliability, and concurrent validity (Lyneham, Abbott, & Rapee, 2007; Silverman, Saaverdra, & Pina, 2001). Reliability for a GAD diagnoses in the current study was excellent (κ = 1.0). Some children with GAD (*n* = 15) had secondary diagnoses, including separation anxiety disorder (*n* = 3), social anxiety disorder (*n* = 11), specific phobia (*n* = 6), attention deficit/hyperactivity disorder (*n* = 3), and oppositional defiant disorder (*n* = 1).

Depressive Symptoms

General depressive symptoms were measured using the 27-item Children's Depression Inventory (CDI; Kovacs, 1992) at the initial assessment. For each item, children are presented with three statements and asked to choose which statement most describes how they have been feeling over the last 2 weeks (e.g., *I have fun in many things, I have fun in some things*, or *Nothing is fun at all*). Each item is scored from 0 (not indicating depression) to 2 (indicating higher depression). The CDI is a reliable, well-validated, and widely used assessment to assess depressive symptomology in youth (Kovacs, 1992). Raw scores were converted to *T* scores adjusted for age and gender, and items were totaled so that higher values indicate greater depressive symptoms. Cronbach's alpha indicated good reliability in the current sample (α = .86).

Anxiety Symptoms

At the initial assessment, anxiety symptoms were measured using the child-report version of the Screen for Child Anxiety Related Emotional Disorders (SCARED-C; Birmaher et al., 1999), which has demonstrated good internal consistency, validity, and test–retest reliability in child populations (Birmaher et al., 1997). The SCARED-C is a 41-item questionnaire that asks children to indicate how much each statement (e.g., *I worry about other people liking me*) describes how they have felt for the last 3 months from 0 (*not true or hardly ever true*) to 2 (*very true or often true*). The SCARED-C offers subscale scores for panic disorder/somatic symptoms, generalized anxiety, separation anxiety, social anxiety, and school avoidance. For the current investigation, summed total scores of the anxiety-related subscales were used to represent overall anxiety (α = .93).

Physiological Hyperarousal

During the initial assessment, physiological arousal was examined using the Physiological Hyperarousal Scale for Children (PHS-C; Laurent, Catanzaro, & Joiner, 1995, 2004), a reliable and valid measure of anxiety-related hyperarousal in clinical and nonclinical populations (Laurent, Joiner, & Catanzaro, 2011). The PHS-C is a 18-item self-report scale assessing physiological symptoms over the last 2 weeks (e.g., *How much did you feel like your heart was pounding during the past 2 weeks?*) on a 5-point scale from 1 (*very slightly or not at all*) to 5 (*extremely*). Items were summed to create a total score, with higher scores indicating greater hyperarousal ($\alpha = .85$).

Daily Reports of Negative Affect and Somatic Complaints

After the initial assessment, participants completed 7 days of daily phone calls. During each phone call, participants provided responses to three questions assessing negative affect and three questions assessing somatic complaints that day on a 4-point scale from 0 (*none*) to 3 (*a lot*). For negative affect ($\alpha = .77$), children reported how much they felt (a) *nervous or anxious*, (b) *sad or upset*, and (c) *irritable or angry* that day. For somatic symptoms ($\alpha = .60$), children reported how much they experienced (a) *muscle aches or tight muscles*, (b) *headaches*, and (c) *stomachaches*. To account for missed phone calls, we opted to calculate average symptoms across the week as opposed to total scores. Specially, the three items on each scale were averaged across each day and the averages of each day were averaged across the week, resulting in a total score with higher values indicating greater average symptoms during the 1-week period. The affective and somatic items were developed for the purpose of this study, and previous research suggests that the use of daily diary is feasible to assess symptoms in anxious children (Beidel, Neal, & Lederer, 1991).

Polysomnography

For all participants, PSG monitoring (on a Friday or Saturday night following the seven nightly phone calls and 1 week of actigraphy monitoring) included six channels of EEG (frontal, central, and occipital regions), right and left EOG, submental and right/left tibial EMG, electrocardiogram, respiratory inductance plethysmography, and pulse oximetry. For ambulatory PSGs (conducted using NicoletOne ambulatory equipment), participants were prepared at a pediatric sleep center by a registered technologist and followed their typical bedtime and sleep routine at home that night. PSGs conducted in a sleep lab in a pediatric hospital were performed with Medcare amplifiers and Rembrandt 9.0 Sleep Acquisition Software. For all studies, registered PSG technicians with pediatric experience scored sleep stages in 30-s epochs according to American Academy of Sleep Medicine scoring rules (Iber, Ancoli-Israel, Chesson, & Quan, 2007), and studies were reviewed by a certified sleep medicine specialist before generating a final report. All scoring technicians were masked to child diagnostic status. For the current study, the following sleep architecture variables were of interest: percentage of total sleep time spent in N3 sleep (*N3 %*), percentage of total sleep time spent in REM sleep (*REM %*), and the number of minutes from the first epoch of sleep to the first epoch of REM sleep (*REM Latency*).

RESULTS

Preliminary Analyses

We examined if primary study variables differed as a function of group (GAD vs. control), type of PSG (ambulatory vs. lab-based), or whether children participated during the school year versus the summer using a series of *t*-tests and analyses of variance. There were no differences in sleep architecture or psychopathology symptoms based on the type of PSG participants completed. Across the entire sample, children reported marginally more physical symptoms in the summer compared to the school year, $t(64) = -2.00$, $p = .05$.

Means and standard deviations for primary study variables and other PSG characteristics for both groups, and the total sample are reported in Table 2. As expected, children with GAD reported significantly greater anxiety symptoms, physiological hyperarousal, and depressive symptoms than controls. Across the 1-week assessment, children with GAD reported marginally greater somatic complaints and significantly greater negative affect. There were no differences in sleep architecture variables based on group. We also examined descriptive sleep information from each group from the week prior to the PSG using actigraphy-measured variables. This information is presented in Table 3. A series of independent samples *t*-tests indicated that there were no group differences in any of the actigraphy-measured sleep indicators.

Bivariate correlations among the primary variables of interest are reported in Table 4. As would be expected, longer latency to REM was related to less time spent in REM. Daily reports of negative affect and somatic symptoms, and global physiological hyperarousal, depressive, and anxiety symptoms were all positively related to one another. We also examined if age was related to any variables of interest, given typical developmental changes in sleep architecture across childhood. Age was unrelated to sleep architecture, daily symptoms, or psychopathology symptoms.

Sleep Architecture and Daily Affective and Somatic Reports

To examine if sleep architecture was related to daily reports of negative affect and somatic complaints, we conducted a series of hierarchical regression analyses with each (continuous) sleep architecture variable, diagnostic status, and their interaction term as predictors, and daily negative affect and somatic complaints as outcome variables. We included age, PSG type, and school year/summer participation as covariates. Results are reported in Table 5. The interaction between group and N3% was significant, revealing that greater N3% was related to less negative affect over the course of the week in the GAD (simple slope = $-.27$, $p = .01$) but not control group (simple slope = $.18$, $p = .49$). A significant interaction also emerged between group and REM%, indicating that greater REM sleep was

TABLE 2
Descriptive Statistics for Primary Study Variables and Additional PSG Characteristics

	GAD		*Control*		*Total*			
	M	SD	M	SD	M	SD	*t* (df)	*95% CI*
PSG TST (Minutes)	496.28	45.64	484.33	47.66	489.58	46.81	–1.03 (64)	[–35.13, 11.22]
N2 Minutes (%)	246.83 (49.66)	38.53 (5.42)	242.20 (50.29)	40.37 (8.29)	244.23 (50.01)	39.34 (7.13)	–.47 (64)	[–24.23, 12.98]
N3 Minutes (%)	125.40 (25.40)	26.11 (5.36)	124.39 (25.74)	29.10 (5.79)	124.83 (25.59)	27.62 (5.57)	–.15 (64)	[–14.80, 12.79]
REM Minutes (%)	113.38 (22.81)	21.10 (3.48)	109.20 (22.16)	32.27 (5.26)	111.04 (22.45)	27.80 (4.54)	.55 (64)	[–18.02, 9.67]
REM Latency (Minutes)	134.71	58.33	148.97	54.35	142.70	56.15	1.03 (64)	[–13.54, 42.08]
Daily Negative Affect	.33	.40	.14	.17	.22	.31	–2.56 (36.13)*	[–.36, –.04]
Daily Somatic Complaints	.23	.33	.10	.14	.15	.25	–2.02 (35.89)†	[–.27, .00]
CDI	50.84	10.57	42.60	6.47	46.03	9.29	–3.46 (36.72)**	[–13.06, –3.42]
SCARED-C	27.36	14.44	13.77	9.56	19.81	13.68	–4.47 (61)***	[–19.65, –7.52]
PHS-C	30.90	11.49	25.59	6.04	28.11	9.35	–2.22 (41.41)*	[–10.12, –0.49]

Note: PSG = polysomnography; GAD = generalized anxiety disorder; CI = confidence interval; TST = total sleep time; N2 = Stage 2 sleep; N3 = Stage 3 sleep; REM = rapid eye movement sleep; CDI = Children's Depression Inventory; SCARED-C = Screen for Child Anxiety Related Emotional Disorders; PHS-C = Physiological Hyperarousal Scale for Children.

Significant differences between groups are marked: †$p = .05$. *$p < .05$. **$p < .01$. ***$p < .001$.

TABLE 3
Actigraphy Measured Sleep Variables Prior to the PSG Recording

	GAD		*Control*		*Total*			
	M	SD	M	SD	M	SD	*t* (df)	*95% CI*
TST (Minutes)	510.32	32.31	501.10	43.42	505.15	39.78	–.93 (64)	[–28.95, 10.51]
TIB (Minutes)	593.46	47.92	574.24	51.03	582.57	50.21	–1.48 (58)	[–45.15, 6.70]
SE (%)	86.75	5.79	87.36	5.01	87.10	5.32	.44 (59)	[–2.17, 3.38]
WASO (Minutes)	49.29	29.07	44.61	24.58	46.67	26.54	–.71 (64)	[–17.88, 8.52]
SL (Minutes)	23.43	13.94	21.01	11.13	22.04	12.35	–.75 (59)	[–8.84, 4.01]

Note: Values are averaged across the 7-day pre-polysomnography (PSG) period. Actigraphy variables did not significantly differ between groups. GAD = generalized anxiety disorder; CI = confidence interval; TST = total sleep time; TIB = time in bed; SE = sleep efficiency; WASO = wake after sleep onset; SL = sleep latency.

TABLE 4
Bivariate Correlations for Primary Study Variables in the Full Sample

	1	2	3	4	5	6	7	8
1. Age								
2. N3 %	–.11							
3. REM %	.13	–.03						
4. REM Latency	–.10	–.02	–.30*					
5. Daily Negative Affect	.07	–.16	.18	–.24†				
6. Daily Somatic Complaints	.01	.003	.11	–.09	.61***			
7. CDI	–.13	.15	–.01	–.17	.48***	.46***		
8. SCARED-C	.09	.07	.13	–.13	.43***	.54***	.73***	
9. PHS-C	–.08	.21	–.04	–.08	.44***	.64***	.60***	.67***

Note: N3 = Stage 3 sleep; REM = rapid eye movement sleep; CDI = Children's Depression Inventory; SCARED-C = Screen for Child Anxiety Related Emotional Disorders; PHS-C = Physiological Hyperarousal Scale for Children.

†$p = .05$. *$p < .05$. ***$p < .001$.

TABLE 5
Sleep Architecture and Daily Reports

	Negative Affect		Somatic Complaints	
Variable	*β*	*95% CI*	*β*	*95% CI*
Age	−.01	[−.05, .05]	−.04	[−.05, .04]
School/Summer	.36***	[.12, .45]	.25*	[.01, .32]
PSG Type	.06	[−.10, .18]	.16	[−.05, .21]
Diagnostic Status	.29**	[.05, .31]	.23	[−.01, .23]
N3%	.10	[−.05, .11]	.05	[−.06, .09]
REM%	.03	[−.07, .09]	−.08	[−.09, .06]
Latency to REM	−.04	[−.11, .09]	.06	[−.08, .11]
Group × N3%	−.37*	[−.28, −.01]	.05	[−.10, .14]
Group × REM%	−.24	[−.25, .04]	.36*	[.03, .32]
Group × REM Latency	.13	[−.08, .23]	−.21	[−.20, .06]
Adjusted R^2	.30***		.13	

Note: Diagnostic status is coded as generalized anxiety disorder = 1 and control = 0. Summer is coded as during summer = 1 and during school year = 0. Location is coded as lab-based = 1 and ambulatory = 2. The pattern of significant findings remains unchanged when removing covariates from each model. CI = confidence interval; PSG = polysomnography; N3 = Stage 3 sleep; REM = rapid eye movement sleep.

$^*p < .05$. $^{**}p < .01$. $^{***}p \leq .001$.

related to more somatic complaints, but again, for children with GAD (simple slope = .37, p = .02) and not controls (simple slope = −.08, p = .55). These interactions are displayed in Figures 1a and 1b.

Sleep Architecture and Global Symptom Measures

Similar regression models were used to examine relationships between sleep architecture and trait-like measures of psychopathology symptoms (see Table 6). For the model predicting depressive symptoms, a significant interaction between group and REM latency showed that, for children with GAD only, decreased latency to REM sleep was related to greater depressive symptoms (simple slope = −.45, p = .002). A similar interaction emerged between REM% and group. Increased REM sleep was related to greater depressive symptoms in children with GAD (simple slope = .33, p = .02) but not controls (simple slope = −.33, p = .14). These interactions are displayed in Figures 1c and 1d. Sleep architecture and the interaction between sleep architecture and group in the models predicting anxiety symptoms and physiological hyperarousal were not significant.

DISCUSSION

The current study investigated interactions between aspects of sleep architecture and affective symptoms in both clinically anxious and healthy children toward developing a better understanding of the functional relevance of these relationships for emotional functioning in childhood. We

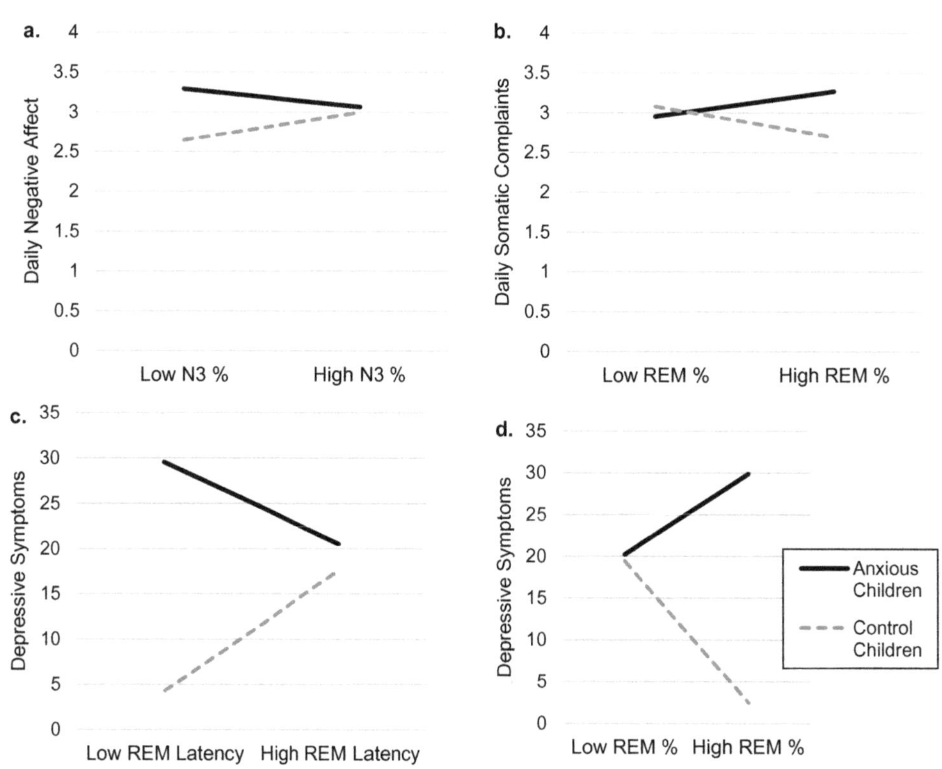

FIGURE 1 **(a–d)** Interactions between group and sleep architecture predicting daily and trait-like psychopathology symptoms. *Note*: High and low values represent ± 1 *SD* from the mean. N3 = Stage 3 sleep; REM = rapid eye movement sleep.

TABLE 6
Sleep Architecture and Psychopathology Symptoms

	Anxiety Symptoms		*Depressive Symptoms*		*Physiological Hyperarousal*	
	β	95% CI	*β*	95% CI	*β*	95% CI
Age	.08	[−1.66, 3.39]	−.05	[−1.93, 1.30]	−.07	[−2.37, 1.43]
School/Summer	−.02	[−8.42, 7.31]	.04	[−4.19, 5.83]	.07	[−4.44, 7.65]
PSG Type	.20	[−1.18, 12.14]	.23	[−.16, 8.47]	.22	[−1.05, 9.27]
Diagnostic Status	.47***	[6.63, 19.05]	.38***	[2.96, 11.13]	.25	[−.25, 9.27]
N3%	.16	[−1.81, 6.28]	.23	[−.45, 4.85]	.24	[−1.02, 5.51]
REM%	−.06	[−4.58, 3.06]	−.21	[−4.29, .62]	−.23	[−5.13, 1.00]
Latency to REM	−.08	[−5.75, 3.64]	.12	[−1.87, 4.03]	−.13	[−4.71, 2.42]
Group × N3%	−.10	[−8.60, 4.25]	−.01	[−4.58, 4.27]	−.01	[−5.14, 4.78]
Group × REM%	.24	[−1.13, 13.97]	.39**	[2.13, 11.85]	.25	[−1.25, 10.14]
Group × REM Latency	−.02	[−7.01, 6.29]	−.43**	[−9.78, −1.37]	.04	[−4.57, 5.52]
Adjusted R^2	.23**		.34***		.05	

Note. Diagnostic status is coded as generalized anxiety disorder = 1 and control = 0. Summer is coded as during summer = 1 and during school year = 0. Location is coded as lab based = 1 and ambulatory = 2. The pattern of significant findings remain unchanged when removing covariates from each model. CI = confidence interval; PSG = polysomnography; N3 = Stage 3 sleep; REM = rapid eye movement sleep.

$^{**}p \leq .01$. $^{***}p \leq .001$.

specifically examined both general measures of psychopathology symptoms and negative affect and somatic complaints across a 1-week period. First, as expected, children with GAD reported greater anxiety symptoms, depressive symptoms, and physiological hyperarousal overall, and experienced greater negative affect and somatic complaints across the 7-day period. Moreover, these group differences were moderated by physiologic sleep characteristics whereby significant relationships were observed for the anxious children only. The implications of these novel findings for developmental models of affective disorders are considered next.

We found a greater percentage of N3 (SWS) sleep to relate significantly to less negative affect across the week among children with GAD but not controls. This finding aligns with emerging experimental research suggesting SWS attenuates the effects of distressing daytime emotional experiences (e.g.,Talamini, Bringmann, De Boer, & Hofman, 2013), as well as evidence for the protective role of SWS in at-risk children. Specifically, in their longitudinal study, Silk and colleagues (2007) found that greater SWS during childhood was protective against the later development of depression in genetically at-risk youth. Of importance, our anxious group was somewhat unique in that children in the current study did not have comorbid depressive disorders. In light of robust genetic and phenomenological overlap between GAD and depression (Kendler, Neale, Kessler, Heath, & Eaves, 1992; Middeldorp, Cath, Van Dyck, & Boomsma, 2005), these children might be conceived of as an at-risk but resilient anxious subgroup. Although we found no differences in the amount of N3 sleep between our two groups, it may be the case that intensity rather than quantity of SWS, as indexed by slow wave activity (EEG power density between 0.5 and 4 Hz) is more germane for understanding this relationship. Specifically, among depressed and at-risk youth, greater negative emotional experiences during the day might accelerate slow wave activity at night as a compensatory response aimed at reprocessing amplified negative emotions (Talamini et al., 2013). The typical daytime emotional experiences of healthy children, comparatively, may not trigger the same accelerations in slow wave activity. Another possibility is that spectral power of SWS may be compromised in those who report sleep problems not corroborated by macrolevel differences in sleep architecture (Krystal, Edinger, Wohlgemuth, & Marsh, 2002).This is a particularly intriguing question for anxious youth who often report sleep problems in the absence of objective sleep alterations (McMakin & Alfano, 2015).

Results from the current study also revealed a positive relationship between percentage of REM sleep and the daytime somatic complaints of anxious children. The mechanisms underlying this relationship require further investigation, but several specific explanations appear worthy of exploration. First, research in adults has linked dream content, specifically negatively valenced dream mentation, with migraines and somatic distress (Heather-Greener et al., 1996; Levin et al., 2009). Anxious/depressed adults and children report more emotionally negative dream content than controls (McNamara, Auerbach, Johnson, Harris, & Doros, 2010; Nielsen et al., 2000), but direct relationships with daytime somatic complaints have yet to be examined. Second, some sleep-related behaviors including bruxism (i.e., involuntary teeth grinding or clenching) have been shown to contribute to daytime somatic symptoms (Shang, Gau, & Soong, 2006) and may occur more frequently during REM sleep in childhood (Herrera et al., 2006; Mahowald & Rosen, 1990). Bruxism is more common in anxious individuals (Ohayon, Li, & Guilleminault, 2001), as well as patients with frequent tension headaches (De Luca Canto, Singh, Bigal, Major, & Flores-Mir, 2014). However, because bruxism occurs outside of conscious awareness and is often imperceptible by others, research utilizing PSG is needed to explore these ostensive links in anxious youth.

It is important to point out that in addition to being a required criterion for the diagnosis of GAD (American Psychiatric Association, 2013), somatic symptoms in anxiety-disordered youth also correspond with a more severe form of anxiety and more impaired functioning (Ginsburg, Riddle, & Davies, 2006), which was evident in the current sample from the positive relationship between somatic symptoms and self-reported anxiety symptoms (a follow-up analysis indicated that this relationship was significant for children with GAD: $r = .63$, $p < .001$). In this way, a positive association between REM sleep and somatic complaints in our anxious group may be driven in part by symptom severity. Further, because high levels of somatization predict the later development of depression (Shanahan et al., 2015; Zwaigenbaum, Szatmari, Boyle, & Offord, 1999), prospective studies examining the potential prognostic value of REM sleep-somatic connections in youth at risk for depression are suggested as an important direction for research.

In terms of more general psychopathology measures, our results converge with a wealth of findings showing reduced latency to and a greater proportion of REM sleep to correspond with depression as well as depression risk (Mendlewicz, Sevy, & De Maertelaer, 1989; Palagini et al., 2013; Riemann et al., 2001; Tsuno et al., 2005). Comparatively, consistent and reliable sleep-based markers of anxious pathology have not been identified, supporting nonsignificant associations between sleep architecture and global anxiety symptoms found in our study. Still, anxiety and depression are highly comorbid across development (Brady & Kendall, 1992; Cummings, Caporino, & Kendall, 2014; Moffit et al., 2007; Pine et al., 2001), and childhood GAD in particular is characterized by hetereotypic more so than homotypic continuity as a majority of affected children lose this diagnosis as adolescents or adults (Bittner et al., 2007; Copeland, Shanahan, Costello, & Angold, 2009). These developmental trajectories are poorly understood at present, but a better understanding of longitudinal relationships between nighttime sleep and daytime affect in clinical and at-risk populations of youth may hold relevance in this regard.

Limitations and Future Directions

Our findings should be viewed in light of several limitations. Only one night of PSG monitoring was conducted, which has been associated with first-night effects (i.e., non-typical sleep patterns due to equipment and/or sleeping in an unfamiliar environment). Our sample also included youth who underwent different types of sleep monitoring procedures (at-home vs. sleep-lab-based studies). Although PSG type was evenly distributed across our two groups and included as a covariate in all analyses, the use of uniform PSG procedures across multiple nights would clearly be more ideal. We are also unable to account for possible differences in sleeping arrangements and environments during ambulatory studies (e.g., co-sleeping) that may have affected sleep patterns (e.g., awakenings). Future research including multiple nights of PSG, and using standardized procedures are therefore needed to replicate our results. In addition, the somatic and negative affect questionnaires in the current study had lower than desirable reliability (though is it important to point out the range of symptoms assessed by both measures). Future studies utilizing validated measures (e.g., Positive and Negative Affect Schedule for Children; Laurent et al., 1999) and/or more distinct components of emotional and physical functioning (e.g., discrete types of negative affect emotion such as sadness or anger, or specific physical symptoms such as inflammation or muscle tension) are needed.

Although racially and ethnically diverse, participants in this sample came from educated and affluent families, and results may therefore not generalize to other populations. The fact that children with primary GAD could not have secondary mood disorders, while providing a novel sample, further limits the generalizability of findings. Given the sample size, we did not explore gender differences in the current study, but Sleep × Gender interactions have been reported in youth with affective disorders (Alfano et al., 2013; Armitage & Hoffmann, 2001). Finally, the directional nature of effects detected cannot be clarified based on these data. Experimental studies that specifically manipulate daytime affective experiences and/or nighttime sleep patterns (e.g., deprivation of REM sleep only) are necessary for deciphering causal relationships between sleep architecture and waking affective symptoms.

Clinical Significance and Implications

These findings contribute to existing knowledge in several ways. First, results build directly on data linking objective sleep characteristics with daytime symptoms in youth with affective disorders (Cousins et al., 2011; Silk et al., 2007) and suggest that for anxious children, aspects of sleep architecture may contribute to symptomatic profiles and possibly longer term outcomes (e.g., depression). Given the sharp increases in depressive disorders in adolescence (e.g., Kessler, Avenevoli, & Merikangas, 2001) and the high rate of comorbidity between depression and anxiety (Brady & Kendall, 1992; Brown & Barlow, 1992), understanding these processes during childhood, before the onset of puberty, is critical for identifying potential targets for prevention and intervention. Furthermore, these findings highlight the potential importance of targeting problematic nighttime behaviors that serve to alter sleep architecture. As an example, late bedtimes during the week become more common and sometimes extreme during the transition to adolescence (Laberge et al., 2001), resulting not only in reduced overall sleep but also in objective sleep alterations (Banks & Dinges, 2007; Banks, Van Dongen, Maislin, & Dinges, 2010). For at-risk youth in particular, these sleep changes could produce or amplify affective risk both in the short term and long term. Future studies aimed at replicating and better delineating these relationships might therefore be harnessed to reduce illness severity and risk.

FUNDING

This research was supported by National Institute of Mental Health grant K23MH081188 award to Dr. Alfano.

REFERENCES

Alfano, C. A., Beidel, D. C., Turner, S. M., & Lewin, D. S. (2006). Preliminary evidence for sleep complaints among children referred for anxiety. *Sleep Medicine*, *7*, 467–473. doi:10.1016/j.sleep.2006.05.002

Alfano, C. A., & Gamble, A. (2009). The role of sleep in childhood psychiatric disorders. *Child Youth Care Forum*, *38*, 327–340. doi:10.1007/s10566-009-9081-y

Alfano, C. A., Ginsburg, G. S., & Kingery, J. N. (2007). Sleep-related problems among children and adolescents with anxiety disorders. *Journal of the American Academy of Child and Adolescent Psychiatry*, *46*, 224–232. doi:10.1097/01.chi.0000242233.06011.8e

Alfano, C. A., Patriquin, M. A., & De Los Reyes, A. (2015). Subjective-objective sleep comparisons and discrepancies among clinically-anxious and healthy children. *Journal of Abnormal Child Psychology*, *43*, 1343–1353. doi:10.1007/s10802-015-0018-7

Alfano, C. A., Pina, A. A., Zerr, A. A., & Villalta, I. K. (2010). Pre-sleep arousal and sleep problems of anxiety-disordered youth. *Child Psychiatry and Human Development*, *41*, 156–167. doi:10.1007/s10578-009-0158-5

Alfano, C. A., Reynolds, K., Scott, N., Dahl, R. E., & Mellman, T. A. (2013). Polysomnographic sleep patterns of non-depressed, non-medicated children with generalized anxiety disorder. *Journal of Affective Disorders*, *147*, 379–384. doi:10.1016/j.jad.2012.08.015

Alvaro, P. K., Roberts, R. M., & Harris, J. K. (2013). A systematic review assessing bidirectionality between sleep disturbances, anxiety, and depression. *Sleep*, *36*, 1059–1068.

American Psychiatric Association. (2013). *Diagnostic and statistical manual of mental disorders* (5th ed.). Arlington, VA: Author.

Anders, T. F., Sadeh, A., & Appareddy, V. (1995). Normal sleep in neonates and children. In R. K. M. Ferber (Ed.), *Principles and practice of sleep medicine in the child* (pp. 7–18). Philadelphia, PA: Saunders.

Arana-Lechuga, Y., Nũnez-Ortiz, R., Terán-Pèrez, G., Castillo-Montoya, C., Jimènez-Anguiano, A., Gonzalez-Robles, R. O., … Velázquez-Moctezuma, J. (2008). Sleep-EEG patterns of school children suffering from symptoms of depression compared to healthy controls. *The World Journal of Biological Psychiatry*, *9*, 115–120. doi:10.1080/15622970701216665

Armitage, R., & Hoffmann, R. F. (2001). Sleep EEG, depression and gender. *Sleep Medicine Reviews*, *5*, 237–246. doi:10.1053/smrv.2000.0144

Banks, S. B., & Dinges, D. F. (2007). Behavioral and physiological consequences of sleep restriction. *Journal of Clinical Sleep Medicine*, *3*, 519–528.

Banks, S. B., Van Dongen, H. P. A., Maislin, G., & Dinges, D. F. (2010). Neurobehavioral dynamics following chronic sleep restriction: Dose-response effects of one night for recovery. *Sleep*, *33*, 1013–1026.

Beidel, D. C., Neal, A. M., & Lederer, A. S. (1991). The feasibility and validity of a daily diary for the assessment of anxiety in children. *Behavior Therapy*, *22*, 505–517. doi:10.1016/S0005-7894(05)80342-9

Berger, M. V., Van Calker, D., & Riemann, D. (2003). Sleep and manipulations of the sleep–wake rhythm in depression. *Acta Psychiatrica Scandinavica*, *108*, 83–91. doi:10.1034/j.1600-0447.108.s418.17.x

Birmaher, B., Brent, D. A., Chiappetta, L., Bridge, J., Monga, S., & Baugher, M. (1999). Psychometric properties of the Screen for Child Anxiety Related Emotional Disorders (SCARED): A replication study. *Journal of the American Academy of Child and Adolescent Psychiatry*, *38*, 1230–1236. doi:10.1097/00004583-199910000-00011

Birmaher, B., Khetarpal, S., Brent, D., Cully, M., Balach, L., Kaufman, J., & Neer, S. M. (1997). The Screen for Child Anxiety Related Emotional Disorders (SCARED): Scale construction and psychometric characteristics. *Journal of the American Academy of Child and Adolescent Psychiatry*, *36*, 545–553. doi:10.1097/00004583-199704000-00018

Bittner, A., Egger, H. L., Erkanli, A., Costello, E. J., Foley, D. L., & Angold, A. (2007). What do child anxiety disorders predict? *Journal of Child Psychology and Psychiatry*, *48*, 1174–1183. doi:10.1111/j.1469-7610.2007.01812.x

Brady, E. U., & Kendall, P. C. (1992). Comorbidity of anxiety and depression in children and adolescents. *Psychological Bulletin*, *111*, 244–255. doi:10.1037/0033-2909.111.2.244

Brown, T. A., & Barlow, D. H. (1992). Comorbidity among anxiety disorders: Implications for treatment and *DSM-IV*. *Journal of Consulting and Clinical Psychology*, *60*, 835–844. doi:10.1037/0022-006X.60.6.835

Campbell, I. G., & Feinberg, I. (2009). Longitudinal trajectories of non-rapid eye movement delta and theta EEG as indicators of adolescent brain maturation. *Proceedings of the National Academy of Sciences of the United States of America*, *106*, 5177–5180. doi:10.1073/pnas.0812947106

Carskadon, M. A. (2002). Factors influencing sleep patterns of adolescents. In M. A. Carskadon (Ed.), *Adolescent sleep patterns: Biological, social, and psychological influences* (pp. 4–26). New York, NY: Cambridge University Press.

Carskadon, M. A., & Acebo, C. (1993). A self-administered rating scale for pubertal development. *Journal of Adolescent Health*, *14*, 190–195. doi:10.1016/1054-139X(93)90004-9

Carskadon, M. A., Acebo, C., & Jenni, O. G. (2004). Regulation of adolescent sleep: Implications for behavior. *Annals of the New York Academy of Sciences*, *1021*, 276–291. doi:10.1196/annals.1308.032

Carskadon, M. A., & Dement, W. C. (2011). Monitoring and staging human sleep. In M. H. Kryger, T. Roth, & W. C. Dement (Eds.), *Principles and practice of sleep medicine* (pp. 16–26). St. Louis, MO: Elsevier Saunders.

Chorney, D. B., Detweiler, M. F., Morris, T. L., & Kuhn, B. R. (2008). The interplay of sleep disturbance, anxiety, and depression in children. *Journal of Pediatric Psychology*, *33*, 339–348. doi:10.1093/jpepsy/jsm105

Colrain, I. M., & Baker, F. C. (2011). Changes in sleep as a function of adolescent development. *Neuropsychology Review*, *21*, 5–21. doi:10.1007/s11065-010-9155-5

Copeland, W. E., Shanahan, L., Costello, E. J., & Angold, A. (2009). Childhood and adolescent psychiatric disorders as predictors of young adult disorders. *Archives of General Psychiatry*, *66*, 764–772. doi:10.1001/archgenpsychiatry.2009.85

Cousins, J. C., Whalen, D. J., Dahl, R. E., Forbes, E. E., Olino, T. M., Ryan, N. D., & Silk, J. S. (2011). The bidirectional association between daytime affect and nighttime sleep in youth with anxiety and depression. *Journal of Pediatric Psychology*, *36*, 969–979. doi:10.1093/jpepsy/jsr036

Cummings, C. M., Caporino, N. E., & Kendall, P. C. (2014). Comorbidity of anxiety and depression in children and adolescents: 20 years after. *Psychological Bulletin*, *140*, 816–845. doi:10.1037/a0034733

Dahl, R. E. (1996). The regulation of sleep and arousal: Development and psychopathology. *Development and Psychopathology*, *8*, 3–27. doi:10.1017/S0954579400006945

Dahl, R. E., Ryan, N. D., Birmaher, B., Al-Shabbout, M., Williamson, D. E., Neidig, M., … Puig-Antich, J. (1991). Electroencephalographic sleep measures in prepubertal depression. *Psychiatry Research*, *38*, 201–214. doi:10.1016/0165-1781(91)90045-Q

Darchia, N., & Cervena, K. (2014). The journey through the world of adolescent sleep. *Reviews in the Neurosciences*, *25*, 585–604. doi:10.1515/revneuro-2013-0065

De Luca Canto, G., Singh, V., Bigal, M. E., Major, P. W., & Flores-Mir, C. (2014). Association between tension-type headache and migraine with sleep bruxism: A systematic review. *Headache*, *54*, 1460–1469. doi:10.1111/head.12446

Dijk, D., Beersma, D. G. M. R., Daan, S., Bloem, G. M., & Van Den Hoofdakker, R. H. (1987). Quantitative analysis of the effects of slow wave sleep deprivation during the first 3 h of sleep on subsequent EEG power density. *European Archives of Psychiatry and Neurological Sciences*, *236*, 323–238. doi:10.1007/BF00377420

Dijk, D., Groeger, J. A., Stanley, N., & Deacon, S. (2006). Age-related reduction in daytime sleep propensity and nocturnal slow wave sleep. *Sleep*, *33*, 211–223.

Emslie, G. J., Rush, J., Weinberg, W. A., Rintelmann, J. W., & Roffwarg, H. P. (1990). Children with major depression show reduced rapid eye movement latencies. *Archives of General Psychiatry*, *47*, 119–124. doi:10.1001/archpsyc.1990.01810140019003

Ferrara, M., De Gennaro, L., & Bertini, M. (1999). Selective slow-wave-sleep (SWS) deprivation and SWS rebound: Do we need a fixed SWS amount per night? *Sleep Research Online*, *2*, 15–19.

Giedke, H., & Schwärzler, F. (2002). Therapeutic use of sleep deprivation in depression. *Sleep Medicine Reviews*, *6*, 361–377. doi:10.1016/S1087-0792(02)90235-2

Giles, D. E., Roffwarg, H. P., & Rush, A. J. (1987). REM latency concordance in depressed family members. *Biological Psychiatry*, *22*, 910–914. doi:10.1016/0006-3223(87)90090-4

Ginsburg, G. S., Riddle, M. A., & Davies, M. (2006). Somatic symptoms in children and adolescents with anxiety disorders. *Journal of the American Academy of Child and Adolescent Psychiatry*, *45*, 1179–1187. doi:10.1097/01.chi.0000231974.43966.6e

Goldstein, A. N., & Walker, M. P. (2014). The role of sleep in emotional brain function. *Annual Review of Clinical Psychology*, *10*, 679–708. doi:10.1146/annurev-clinpsy-032813-153716

Gregory, A. M., Caspi, A., Eley, T. C., Moffitt, T. E., O'Connor, T. G., & Poulton, R. (2005). Prospective longitudinal associations between persistent sleep problems in childhood and anxiety and depression disorders in adulthood. *Journal of Abnormal Clinical Psychology*, *33*, 157–163. doi:10.1007/s10802-005-1824-0

Haug, H. (1992). Prediction of sleep deprivation outcome by diurnal variation of mood. *Biological Psychiatry*, *31*, 271–278. doi:10.1016/0006-3223(92)90050-A

Heather-Greener, G. Q., Comstock, D., & Joyce, R. (1996). An investigation of the manifest dream content associated with migraine headaches: A study of the dreams that precede nocturnal migraines. *Psychotherapy and Psychosomatics*, *65*, 216–221. doi:10.1159/000289078

Herrera, M., Valencia, I., Grant, M., Metroka, D., Chialastri, A., & Kothare, S. V. (2006). Bruxism in children: Effect on sleep architecture and daytime cognitive performance and behavior. *Sleep*, *29*, 1143–1148.

Hobson, J. A., & Pace-Schott, E. F. (2002). The cognitive neuroscience of sleep: Neuronal systems, consciousness and learning. *Nature Reviews Neuroscience*, *3*, 679–693. doi:10.1038/nrn915

Iber, C., Ancoli-Israel, S., Chesson, A., & Quan, S. F. (2007). *For the American Academy of Sleep Medicine. The AASM manual for the scoring of sleep and associated events: Rules, terminology and technical specifications*. Westchester, IL: American Academy of Sleep Medicine.

Ivanenko, A., Crabtree, V. M., & Gozal, D. (2005). Sleep and depression in children and adolescents. *Sleep Medicine Reviews*, *9*, 115–129. doi:10.1016/j.smrv.2004.09.006

Karacan, I., Anch, M., Thornby, J. I., Okawa, M., & Williams, R. L. (1975). Longitudinal sleep patterns during pubertal growth: Four-year follow-up. *Pediatric Research*, *9*, 842–846.

Kelly, R., & El-Sheikh, M. (2014). Reciprocal relations between children's sleep and their adjustment over time. *Developmental Psychology*, *50*, 1137–1147. doi:10.1037/a0034501

Kendler, K. S., Neale, M. C., Kessler, R. C., Heath, A. C., & Eaves, L. J. (1992). Major depression and generalized anxiety disorder. Same genes, (partly) different environments? *Archives of General Psychiatry*, *49*, 716–722. doi:10.1001/archpsyc.1992.01820090044008

Kessler, R. C., Avenevoli, S., & Merikangas, K. (2001). Mood disorders in children and adolescents: An epidemiological perspective. *Biological Psychiatry*, *49*, 1002–1014. doi:10.1016/S0006-3223(01)01129-5

Kessler, R. C., McGonagle, K. A., Zhao, S., Nelson, C. B., Hughes, M., Eshleman, S., … Kendler, K. S. (1994). Lifetime and 12-month prevalence of DSM-III–R psychiatric disorders in the United States: Results from the National Comorbidity Survey. *Archives of General Psychiatry*, *51*, 8–19. doi:10.1001/archpsyc.1994.03950010008002

Kovacs, M. (1992). *The Children's Depression Inventory (CDI) manual*. North Tanawanda, NY: Multi-Health Systems.

Krystal, A. D., Edinger, J. D., Wohlgemuth, W. K., & Marsh, G. R. (2002). NREM sleep EEG frequency spectral correlates of sleep complaints in primary insomnia subtypes. *Sleep*, *25*, 626–636.

Kumar, D., Thompson, P. D., Wingate, D. L., & Vesselinova-Jenkins, C. K. (1992). REM sleep in the irritable bowel. *Gastroenterology*, *103*, 12–17.

Kurth, S., Ringli, M., Geiger, A., LeBourgeois, M., Jenni, O. G., & Huber, R. (2010). Mapping of cortical activity in the first two decades of life: A high-density sleep electroencephalogram study. *Journal of Neuroscience*, *30*, 13211–13219. doi:10.1523/JNEUROSCI.2532-10.2010

Laberge, L., Petit, D., Simard, C., Vitaro, F., Tremblay, R. E., & Montplaisir, J. (2001). Development of sleep patterns in early adolescence. *Journal of Sleep Research*, *10*, 59–67. doi:10.1046/j.1365-2869.2001.00242.x

Lahmeyer, H. W., Poznanski, E. O., & Bellur, S. N. (1983). EEG sleep in depressed adolescents. *American Journal of Psychiatry*, *140*, 1150–1153. doi:10.1176/ajp.140.9.1150

Lauer, C. J., Schreiber, W., Holsboer, F., & Krieg, J. C. (1995). In quest of identifying vulnerability markers for psychiatric disorders by all-night polysomnography. *Archives of General Psychiatry*, *52*, 145–153. doi:10.1001/archpsyc.1995.03950140063009

Laurent, J., Catanzaro, S. J., & Joiner, T. E., Jr. (1995). *Theory-based screening of youth internalizing disorders* (Unpublished manuscript). Department of Psychology, Illinois State University, Normal.

Laurent, J., Catanzaro, S. J., & Joiner, T. E., Jr. (2004). Development and preliminary validation of the Physiological Hyperarousal Scale for Children. *Psychological Assessment*, *16*, 373–380. doi:10.1037/1040-3590.16.4.373

Laurent, J., Catanzaro, S. J., Joiner, T. E., Jr., Thomas, E., Rudolph, K. D., Potter, K., … Gathright, T. (1999). A measure of positive and negative affect for children: Scale development and preliminary validation. *Psychological Assessment*, *11*, 326–338. doi:10.1037/1040-3590.11.3.326

Laurent, J., Joiner, T. E., Jr., & Catanzaro, S. J. (2011). Positive affect, negative affect, and physiological hyperarousal among referred and nonreferred youths. *Psychological Assessment*, *23*, 945–957. doi:10.1037/a0024080

Levin, R., Lantz, E., Fireman, G., & Spendlove, S. (2009). The relationship between disturbed dreaming and somatic distress: A prospective investigation. *The Journal of Nervous and Mental Disease*, *197*, 606–612. doi:10.1097/NMD.0b013e3181b0bd65

Lewandowski, A. S., Ward, T. M., & Palermo, T. M. (2011). Sleep problems in children and adolescents with common medical conditions. *Pediatric Clinics of North America*, *58*, 699–713. doi:10.1016/j.pcl.2011.03.012

Lyneham, H. J., Abbott, M. J., & Rapee, R. M. (2007). Interrater reliability of the Anxiety Disorders Interview Schedule for *DSM-IV*: Child and parent version. *Journal of the American Academy of Child and Adolescent Psychiatry*, *46*, 731–736. doi:10.1097/chi.0b013e3180465a09

Mahowald, M. W., & Rosen, G. M. (1990). Parasomnias in children. *Pediatrician*, *17*, 21–31.

McMakin, D. L., & Alfano, C. A. (2015). Sleep and anxiety in late childhood and early adolescence. *Current Opinion in Psychiatry*, *28*, 483–489. doi:10.1097/YCO.0000000000000204

McNamara, P., Auerbach, S., Johnson, P., Harris, E., & Doros, G. (2010). Impact of REM sleep on distortions of self-concept, mood and memory in depressed/anxious participants. *Journal of Affective Disorders*, *122*, 198–207. doi:10.1016/j.jad.2009.06.030

Mendlewicz, J., Sevy, S., & De Maertelaer, V. (1989). REM sleep latency and morbidity risk of affective disorders. *Neuropsychobiology*, *22*, 14–17. doi:10.1159/000118586

Middeldorp, C. M., Cath, D. C., Van Dyck, R., & Boomsma, D. I. (2005). The co-morbidity of anxiety and depression in the perspective of genetic epidemiology: A review of twin and family studies. *Psychological Medicine*, *35*, 611–624. doi:10.1017/S003329170400412X

Miller, V., Palermo, T. M., Powers, S. W., Scher, M. S., & Hershey, A. D. (2003). Migraine headaches and sleep disturbances in children. *Headache*, *43*, 362–368. doi:10.1046/j.1526-4610.2003.03071.x

Moffit, T. E., Harrington, H., Caspi, A., Kim-Cohen, J., Goldberg, D., Gregory, A. M., & Poulton, R. (2007). Depression and generalized anxiety disorder: Cumulative and sequential comorbidity in a birth cohort followed prospectively to age 32 years. *Archives of General Psychiatry*, *64*, 651–660. doi:10.1001/archpsyc.64.6.651

Motivala, S. J., Sarfatti, A., Olmos, L., & Irwin, M. R. (2005). Inflammatory markers and sleep disturbance in major depression. *Psychosomatic Medicine*, *67*, 187–194. doi:10.1097/01.psy.0000149259.72488.09

Nielsen, T. A., Laberge, L., Paquet, J., Tremblay, R. E., Vitaro, F., & Montplaisir, J. (2000). Development of disturbing dreams during adolescence and their relation to anxiety symptoms. *Sleep*, *23*, 1–10.

Ohayon, M. M., Carskadon, M. A., Guilleminault, C., & Vitiello, M. V. (2004). Meta-analysis of quantitative sleep parameters from childhood to old age in healthy individuals: Developing normative sleep values across the human lifespan. *Sleep*, *27*, 1255–1274.

Ohayon, M. M., Li, K. K., & Guilleminault, C. (2001). Risk factors for sleep bruxism in the general population. *Chest Journal*, *119*, 53–61. doi:10.1378/chest.119.1.53

Ong, S. H., Wickramaratne, P., Tang, M., & Weissman, M. M. (2006). Early childhood sleep and eating problems as predictors of adolescent and adult mood and anxiety disorders. *Journal of Affective Disorders*, *96*, 1–8. doi:10.1016/j.jad.2006.05.025

Palagini, L., Baglioni, C., Ciapparelli, A., Gemignani, A., & Riemann, D. (2013). REM sleep dysregulation in depression: State of the art. *Sleep Medicine Reviews*, *17*, 377–390. doi:10.1016/j.smrv.2012.11.001

Patriquin, M. A., Mellman, T. A., Glaze, D. G., & Alfano, C. A. (2014). Polysomnographic sleep characteristics of generally-anxious and healthy children assessed in the home environment. *Journal of Affective Disorders*, *161*, 79–83. doi:10.1016/j.jad.2014.02.037

Pillai, V., Kalmbach, D. A., & Ciesla, J. A. (2011). A meta-analysis of electroencephalographic sleep in depression: Evidence for genetic biomarkers. *Biological Psychiatry*, *70*, 912–919. doi:10.1016/j.biopsych.2011.07.016

Pine, D. S., Cohen, P., & Brook, J. (2001). Adolescent fears as predictors of depression. *Biological Psychiatry*, *50*, 721–724. doi:10.1016/S0006-3223(01)01238-0

Riemann, D., Berger, M., & Voderholzer, U. (2001). Sleep and depression —Results from psychobiological studies: An overview. *Biological Psychology*, *57*, 67–103. doi:10.1016/S0301-0511(01)00090-4

Rosales-Lagarde, A., Armony, J. L., Del Río-Portilla, Y., Trejo-Martínez, D., Conde, R., & Corsi-Cabrera, M. (2012). Enhanced emotional reactivity after selective REM sleep deprivation in humans: An fMRI study. *Frontiers in Behavioral Neuroscience*, *6*, 1–13. doi:10.3389/fnbeh.2012.00025

Shanahan, L., Copeland, W. E., Angold, A., Bondy, C. L., & Costello, E. J. (2014). Sleep problems predict and are predicted by generalized anxiety/depression and oppositional defiant disorder. *Journal of the American Academy of Child and Adolescent Psychiatry*, *53*, 550–558. doi:10.1016/j.jaac.2013.12.029

Shanahan, L., Zucker, N., Copeland, W. E., Bondy, C. L., Egger, H. L., & Costello, E. J. (2015). Childhood somatic complaints predict generalized anxiety disorder and depressive disorders during young adulthood in a community sample. *Psychological Medicine*, *45*, 1721–1730. doi:10.1017/S0033291714002840

Shang, C. Y., Gau, S. S. F., & Soong, W. T. (2006). Association between childhood sleep problems and perinatal factors, parental mental distress and behavioral problems. *Journal of Sleep Research*, *15*, 63–73. doi:10.1111/j.1365-2869.2006.00492.x

Silk, J. S., Vanderbilt-Adriance, E., Shaw, D. S., Forbes, E. E., Whalen, D. J., Ryan, N. D., & Dahl, R. E. (2007). Resilience among children and adolescents at risk for depression: Mediation and moderation across social and neurobiological contexts. *Development and Psychopathology*, *19*, 841–865. doi:10.1017/S0954579407000417

Silverman, W. K., & Albano, A. (1996). *The Anxiety Disorders Interview Schedule for Children-IV (Child and parent versions)*. San Antonio, TX: Psychological Corporation.

Silverman, W. K., Saaverdra, L. M., & Pina, A. A. (2001). Test-retest reliability of anxiety symptoms and diagnoses with the Anxiety Disorders Interview Schedule for DSM-IV: Child and parent versions. *Adolescent Psychiatry*, *40*, 937–944. doi:10.1097/00004583-200108000-00016

Talamini, L. M., Bringmann, L. F., De Boer, M., & Hofman, W. F. (2013). Sleeping worries away or worrying away sleep? Physiological evidence on sleep-emotion interactions. *PLoS ONE*, *8*, e62480. doi:10.1371/journal.pone.0062480

Tsuno, N., Besset, A., & Ritchie, K. (2005). Sleep and depression. *Journal of Clinical Psychiatry*, *66*, 1254–1269. doi:10.4088/JCP.v66n1008

Walker, M. P. (2009). The role of slow wave sleep in memory processing. *Journal of Clinical Sleep Medicine*, *5*, S20–S26.

Walker, M. P., & Van Der Helm, E. (2009). Overnight therapy? The role of sleep in emotional brain processing. *Psychological Bulletin*, *135*, 731–748. doi:10.1037/a0016570

Wechsler, D. (1999). *Wechsler Abbreviated Scale of Intelligence*. New York, NY: The Psychological Corporation.

Zwaigenbaum, L., Szatmari, P., Boyle, M. H., & Offord, D. R. (1999). Highly somatizing young adolescents and the risk of depression. *Pediatrics*, *103*, 1203–1209. doi:10.1542/peds.103.6.1203

Stage 2 Sleep EEG Sigma Activity and Motor Learning in Childhood ADHD: A Pilot Study

Jared M. Saletin

William G. Coon

Mary A. Carskadon

Attention deficit hyperactivity disorder (ADHD) is associated with deficits in motor learning and sleep. In healthy adults, overnight improvements in motor skills are associated with sleep spindle activity in the sleep electroencephalogram (EEG). This association is poorly characterized in children, particularly in pediatric ADHD. Polysomnographic sleep was monitored in 7 children with ADHD and 14 typically developing controls. All children were trained on a validated motor sequence task (MST) in the evening with retesting the following morning. Analyses focused on MST precision (speed–accuracy trade-off). NREM Stage 2 sleep EEG power spectral analyses focused on spindle-frequency EEG activity in the sigma (12–15 Hz) band. The ADHD group demonstrated a selective decrease in power within the sigma band. Evening MST precision was lower in ADHD, yet no difference in performance was observed following sleep. Moreover, ADHD status moderated the association between slow sleep spindle activity (12–13.5 Hz) and overnight improvement; spindle-frequency EEG activity was positively associated with performance improvements in children with ADHD but not in controls. These data highlight the importance of sleep in supporting next-day behavior in ADHD while indicating that differences in sleep neurophysiology may contribute to deficits in this population.

INTRODUCTION

Attention deficit hyperactivity disorder (ADHD) is associated with simultaneous deficits in daytime learning (Adi-Japha, Fox, & Karni, 2011) and nocturnal sleep (Owens et al., 2013). Whereas sleep supports learning in adults, particularly for motor skills (Walker, Brakefield, Morgan, Hobson, & Stickgold, 2002), this association is less well understood in adolescents, particularly for those with ADHD. This pilot study examines whether distinct profiles of sleep-dependent learning are observed in ADHD and in typically developing children.

The current study focused on a procedural memory paradigm known to demonstrate sleep-dependent improvement in adults. Whereas sleep deprivation impairs overnight improvement in motor skill learning (Fischer, Hallschmid, Elsner, & Born, 2002), both nocturnal sleep (Walker et al., 2002) and daytime naps (Nishida & Walker, 2007) consolidate and stabilize performance. A neural marker of sleep-related overnight improvement is found in the non-rapid eye movement Stage 2 Sleep Electroencephalogram (EEG): the thalamocortical sleep spindle (a synchronous burst in the 12–15 Hz range; Nishida & Walker, 2007). Sleep-spindle-frequency EEG activity in the sigma band (12–15 Hz) over motor cortex predicts overnight gains in motor learning in healthy adults, and indexes the degree of motor skill learning deficits in circumstances such as schizophrenia (Wamsley et al., 2013).

Although one recent study examined sleep-dependent procedural motor skill learning in pediatric ADHD (Prehn-Kristensen et al., 2011), the authors did not perform spectral analysis of the sleep EEG. Indeed, whether sleep spindles are atypical in children with ADHD is unclear. When compared to traditional polysomnography, relatively little is known about the microfeatures of the sleep EEG in this population. Whereas one recent study identified lower slow wave activity and higher spindle-frequency sigma activity in ADHD (Prehn-Kristensen et al., 2013), another group demonstrated a converse increase in slow wave activity over central cortices (Ringli et al., 2013). Neither of these studies involved a motor-learning paradigm. Thus, the current pilot study aimed to add to this growing literature, while testing the hypothesis that overnight motor learning ability in ADHD may be sensitive to spindle-frequency EEG activity expressed during sleep.

MATERIALS AND METHODS

The local Institutional Review Board approved the study. Informed consent was obtained from all parents, with assent from all children. Each child received monetary compensation for participating in the study.

Participants

Twenty-six children (10–12.9 years of age) entered the study. Five children were excluded from analysis for technical issues ($n = 2$) or attrition ($n = 3$), yielding a final sample of seven children with ADHD and 14 typically developing controls (TDC). The sample was primarily male yet was balanced for gender, with two girls in the ADHD group and four girls in the TDC group. Complete demographics are reported in Table 1.

A brief parental telephone interview screened for current past medical/psychiatric conditions, family history of medical/psychiatric conditions, current use of psychoactive agents, and abnormal sleep habits. Diagnosis of ADHD was confirmed using the "ADHD" and "other DSM-IV Diagnostic Categories" of the Diagnostic Interview Schedule for Children, Fourth Edition (Shaffer, Fisher, Lucas, Dulcan, & Schwab-Stone, 2000; Table 1). Exclusion criteria included parental or child report of irregular sleep patterns (e.g., self-reported sleep schedules that

TABLE 1
Demographic Variables

	ADHD[a]	*Controls*[b]	*p*
Gender (No. of Girls)	2	4	1.000
Age (Years)	11.9 ± 0.9	11.7 ± 0.9	.62
DISC-IV			
ADHD Symptoms	11.3 ± 3.4	0.86 ± 1.2	< .001
Behavioral Impairments	6.6 ± 1.9	0.00 ± 0.0	< .001
Symptoms + Impairments	17.9 ± 4.1	0.86 ± 1.2	< .001
BDI			
Raw Score	5.1 ± 4.0	5.00 ± 4.0	.94
T-Score	39.2 ± 4.3	39.15 ± 4.2	.95
WRAML-2			
Verbal Memory	112.3 ± 9.8	116.21 ± 10.5	.42
Visual	98.7 ± 15.1	97.64 ± 11.5	.86
Screening Memory	106.9 ± 11.3	108.86 ± 11.3	.71
KBIT-2			
Verbal	111.6 ± 13.3	119.21 ± 10.6	.17
Nonverbal	105.9 ± 13.3	115.05 ± 9.3	.079
IQ	110.3 ± 14.1	120.07 ± 9.4	.072
WRAT4			
Word Reading	99.2 ± 15.2	115.21 ± 15.9	.067
Spelling	107.0 ± 12.7	116.29 ± 16.3	.31
Math Computation	101.8 ± 18.4	120.20 ± 11.6	.018

Note. Data reported as $M \pm SD$. Significance from two-tailed chi-square tests, or independent samples *t*–tests as appropriate. DISC-IV = Diagnostic Interview Schedule for Children Version IV; WRAML-2 = Wide Range Assessment of Memory and Learning, Second Edition; KBIT-2 = Kaufman Brief Intelligence Test, Second Edition; WRAT4 = Wide Range Achievement Test 4.

[a]$n = 7$.

[b]$n = 14$.

vary by greater than 3 hours across a week, self-reported excessive daytime sleepiness, frequent napping [≥ three times/week], a morningness/eveningness score [Smith, Reilly, & Midkiff, 1989] of greater than 2 standard deviations above or below the mean values of subjects in the same grade [age] and of the same sex, based on our laboratory normative data pool); travel beyond two time zones within 2 months of the study; and diagnosis of a learning disability, mental retardation, dyslexia, pervasive developmental disorder; and a personal and/or family history of narcolepsy.

Neuropsychological assessment characterized children on intelligence/achievement, attention/impulse control, learning/memory, response speed/productivity, and problem solving/cognitive control. Trained staff administered the Kaufman Brief Intelligence Test, Second Edition (Kaufman & Kaufman, 2004), the Wide Range Assessment of Memory and Learning, Second Edition (Sheslow & Adams, 2003), and the Wide Range Achievement Test, Fourth Edition (Wilkinson & Robertson, 2006). Both groups were in normative ranges (Table 1), although TDC children had higher math computation scores compared to ADHD peers ($p = .018$).

PROCEDURES

At-Home Protocol

Participants were monitored by wrist actigraphy (Sadeh, Sharkey, & Carskadon, 1994) and completed a sleep-wake diary for 1 week before and throughout the study. During this time participants were asked to maintain a 10-hr sleep schedule set to habitual rise time (call-ins to a laboratory answering machine ensured compliance) to ensure stable sleep patterns prior to the start of the study for all children. Participants abstained from caffeine 12 hr before bedtime for the entire course of the study. Those in the ADHD group were withdrawn from psychostimulants for 2 weeks before and throughout the in-lab study.

In-Lab Protocol

Participants spent 2 consecutive nights in the laboratory on the same schedule as at home: (a) an adaptation night to acclimate to the laboratory and screen for sleep-disordered breathing; (b) the primary experimental night. On the adaptation night participants arrived approximately 3.5 hr before scheduled bedtime and were monitored overnight using polysomnography (see next). Participants returned the next evening, were provided dinner, and again prepared for polysomnography. Approximately 80 min before bedtime, each participant began a cognitive test battery including a declarative memory assessment (Ellenbogen, Hulbert, Stickgold, Dinges, & Thompson-Schill, 2006) (declarative memory performance not examined in the current report), followed by the Motor Sequence Task (MST) (Nishida & Walker, 2007; Walker et al., 2002; Walker et al., 2003), described in detail next. MST training occurred approximately 60 min before bed; morning testing on the MST began after breakfast, approximately 75 min after waking.

Motor Sequence Task

To assess procedural skill learning, participants completed the MST (Figure 2, upper-panel), well-documented as sleep-dependent in adults (Nishida & Walker, 2007; Walker et al., 2002). The MST required participants to tap a five-element sequence (4–1–3–2–4) on the numeric keys of a computer keyboard with the fingers of their nondominant hand "as quickly and accurately as possible" for 30 s. Participants could see the sequence on the screen; however, no feedback was given with respect to accuracy. Evening training consisted of twelve 30-s trials alternating with 30-s periods of rest. Morning testing consisted of four 30-s trials, with equivalent intervening rest. "MST Precision" was calculated as the proportion of total keystrokes that were not errors. This metric represents a trade-off between speed (number of correct five-digit sequences typed) and accuracy (number of errors made). As in prior studies, evening performance was defined as the average of the final two evening trials; morning performance was defined as the average of the first two trials (Nishida & Walker, 2007; Walker et al., 2002, Walker et al., 2003; Walker & Stickgold, 2005; Walker, Stickgold, Alsop, Gaab, & Schlaug, 2005; Walker, Stickgold, Jolesz, & Yoo, 2005). A within-subject measure of overnight improvement was derived as the absolute difference between morning and evening scores.

Polysomnographic Recording

Sleep on both nights was monitored by polysomnography using a Grass Comet XL system (Astro-Med, Inc., West Warwick, RI) measuring the EEG at central and occipital derivations (C3/A2, C4/A1, O1/A2, and O2/A1), right and left electrooculogram, electromyogram, and electrocardiogram. Sleep stages were visually scored by trained technicians (blind to ADHD condition; interrater reliability ≥ 85%) in 30-s epochs from C3/A2 according to standard criteria (Rechtschaffen & Kales, 1968). Respiratory measures were applied on the adaptation night to screen for sleep-disordered breathing. An Apnea-Hypopnea Index (the number of apnea or hypopnea events per hour of sleep) was derived according to standard criteria (Iber, Ancoli-Israel, Chesson, & Quan, 2007).

Power Spectral Analysis of Sleep EEG

The current analyses focus on sleep spindle frequencies in Stage 2 sleep due to their documented role in supporting overnight MST improvement (Nishida & Walker, 2007; Walker et al., 2002). A power spectral analysis of the Stage 2 NREM sleep EEG was performed following established procedures (Kurth et al., 2010; Mander, Santhanam, Saletin, & Walker, 2011; Ringli et al., 2013; van Der Helm et al., 2011). In short, following semiautomated artifact detection fast fourier transforms on hamming-windowed 5-s segments yielded power spectral densities with 0.2 Hz resolutions. To normalize amplitude differences among individuals, the power spectrum of each channel was divided by the total integrated power (0.6–32 Hz), resulting in relative power spectral densities, which were matched with corresponding sleep stages.

Relative power was assessed for the average of the C3/A2 and C4/A1 derivations, reflecting activity over primary motor cortex, motivated by prior associations with overnight MST improvement (Nishida & Walker, 2007). Group differences in sleep EEG spectra were first examined across the entire frequency range (0.6–32 Hz), and subsequently using a priori defined bands of interest in the sigma band: slow sleep spindle activity (12–13.5 Hz) and fast sleep spindle activity (13.5–15 Hz). Although the primary focus of this analysis was placed on sleep spindle frequency activity, slow wave activity (1–4.6 Hz) was also derived as a comparison and to test prior reports of slow wave activity changes in ADHD (Ringli et al., 2013).

Statistical Analysis

Group differences in the EEG power density spectra were examined using bootstrapped independent-sample *t* tests. This method makes no assumptions regarding the distributional qualities of the EEG frequency spectrum and is described in detail elsewhere (Tarokh & Carskadon, 2010a, 2010b). In short, for each 0.2 Hz frequency bin, 5,000 random group assignments were sampled with replacement from the data, yielding a bootstrapped distribution for each group. A difference distribution, S_2-S_1 was used to test statistical significance of the actual difference between groups. If the true difference exceeded the 97.5th percentile of the bootstrapped distribution, it was considered statistically significant (equivalent to a two-tailed alpha level of .05). To limit erroneous Type 1 errors from testing many frequencies, significant frequencies not surrounded by at least two other significant frequencies were discarded.

Performance data were analyzed in StataSE 13.0 (StataCorp LP, College Station, TX) using mixed-effects models including a within-subjects factor condition (Evening/Morning) and a between-subjects factor group (ADHD/TDC). Primary focus was placed upon the interaction of group and condition: whether ADHD status moderates the impact of sleep. Exploratory simple main effects decomposed the interaction to examine (a) whether the groups differed statistically in the morning or evening conditions and (b) whether overnight changes occurred within-each group independently. Effect sizes are reported as appropriate.

Multiple regression analyses were used to test whether the relationship between prior night sleep EEG activity and overnight behavioral change differed between the ADHD and TDC groups. Each model included three parameters: Relative EEG power, Group (ADHD/TDC), and the interaction of group and EEG power: whether ADHD status moderate the relationship between sleep EEG activity and overnight learning. Simple-slopes decomposed the interaction. Robust standard errors accommodated potential effects of outliers in a heterogeneous and small sample.

RESULTS

Group Sleep Variables

Polysomnographic sleep variables are reported in Table 2. The ADHD group spent less time in bed as evident by a lower Total Dark Time (p = .025). Despite this difference, both groups demonstrated total sleep times of nearly 10 hours, indicating no major differences in sleep opportunity. A nonsignificant trend suggested fewer minutes in REM sleep in the ADHD group (p = .069); however, this trend was eliminated when expressed as a percentage of total sleep time (p = .10). No other differences in sleep were observed. No evidence for sleep-disordered breathing was observed in these participants; AHI was low for both the TDC (1.21 ± 0.22) and ADHD (1.41 ± 0.16) groups; further, AHI did not distinguish the groups (p = .54).

Sleep Power Spectra by Group

Stage 2 EEG analyses revealed a suppression of power in the spindle-related sigma band (12.4–16.4 Hz) in ADHD relative to TDC (Figure 1, bootstrapped ps < .05). Although theta activity (~4–8 Hz) was marginally higher in ADHD, this difference was not statistically significant. No other significant differences in the power spectra occurred between the ADHD and TDC groups. These results were confirmed by examining a priori bands of interest. Slow wave activity did not differentiate groups, $t(19) = -0.01$, $p = .99$, $d = -0.0048$, whereas the ADHD group expressed lower power in the slow, $t(19) = -2.48$, $p = .023$, $d = -1.15$, and fast, $t(19) = -2.11$, $p = .049$, $d = -0.98$, spindle bands, with the greatest deficit observed for slow spindle activity.

MST Behavioral Performance

MST precision—representing the trade-off between speed and accuracy—improved following sleep (Figure 2), as indicated by a main-effect of condition, Wald-χ^2 = 17.56, p < .0001, d = .67. The magnitude of this overnight improvement in precision differed by ADHD status, as

TABLE 2
Polysomnographic Sleep Statistics

	ADHD[a]	*Controls*[b]	*p*
Total Dark Time (min)	590 ± 15	602 ± 9	.025
Sleep Period Time (min)	563 ± 11	579 ± 19	.051
Total Sleep Time (min)	541 ± 21	561 ± 23	.064
Sleep Efficiency (%)	96.0 ± 3.0	96.8 ± 1.7	.44
Latency to Sleep Onset (min)	18 ± 15	17 ± 10	.76
Latency to REM Sleep (min)	144 ± 64	124 ± 55	.48
Wake After Sleep Onset (min)	16 ± 16	10 ± 9	.28
Wake After Final Awakening (min)	8 ± 17	6 ± 16	.76
Wake (min)	42 ± 28	32 ± 18	.33
NREM Stage 1 (min)	35 ± 19	30 ± 9	.38
NREM Stage 2 (min)	205 ± 29	222 ± 41	.36
NREM Stage 3 (min)	74 ± 28	66 ± 22	.56
NREM Stage 4 (min)	125 ± 21	124 ± 30	.95
REM Sleep (min)	108 ± 22	119 ± 18	.069
Slow Wave Sleep (min)	199 ± 41	190 ± 40	.66
Wake (% TST)	9.0 ± 5.7	5.9 ± 3.6	.31
NREM Stage 1 (% TST)	6.5 ± 3.5	5.3 ± 1.5	.28
NREM Stage 2 (% TST)	38.1 ± 6.4	39.5 ± 6.9	.65
NREM Stage 3 (% TST)	13.5 ± 6.8	11.7 ± 3.6	.43
NREM Stage 4 (% TST)	23.2 ± 4.3	22.3 ± 5.9	.72
REM Sleep (% TST)	17.3 ± 3.7	19.8 ± 2.9	.10
Slow Wave Sleep (% TST)	36.7 ± 7.0	34.0 ± 7.3	.43
Stage 2 EEG Spectral Power			
Slow Wave Activity (% μV^2)	.57 ± .058	.57 ± .031	.99
Slow Sleep Spindle Activity (% μV^2)	.024 ± .012	.037 ± .011	.023
Fast Sleep Spindle Activity (% μV^2)	.0059 ± .0014	.011 ± .0062	.049

Note: Data reported as $M \pm SD$. Significance from two-tailed independent-samples *t*–tests. Time in Bed = elapsed time from lights out to lights on; Sleep Period Time = elapsed time from sleep onset to final awakening; Total Sleep Time (TST) = total time scored sleep within SPT; Sleep Efficiency = (TST/SPT) × 100; Slow Wave Sleep = Stages 3 + 4 collapsed. EEG = electroencephalogram.

[a] $n = 7$.

[b] $n = 14$.

shown by an interaction of group and condition, Wald-$\chi^2 = 6.08$, $p = .014$, $d = 1.14$. Specifically, MST precision improved overnight for the ADHD group, Wald-$\chi^2 = 16.61$, $p < .0001$, $d = 1.33$, but not for TDCs, Wald-$\chi^2 = 2.23$, $p = .14$, $d = .079$. As a result, despite the ADHD group having impaired MST precision in the evening vis-à-vis TDC, Wald-$\chi^2 = 3.90$, $p = .048$, $d = 1.33$, this effect was ameliorated in the morning: simple effect, Wald-$\chi^2 = 0.02$, $p = .88$, $d = .34$.

Sleep–Behavior Relationships

We next examined whether the group differences in slow and fast spindle-frequency activity accounted for differential overnight improvement in MST precision in ADHD; these results are illustrated in Figure 3. ADHD status significantly moderated the association between slow spindle EEG frequency activity and overnight improvement in MST precision ($\beta = -8.22$, $p = .023$). Specifically, MST precision was positively associated with slow spindle activity for the ADHD group ($\beta = 8.71$, $p = .003$), but not for TDCs ($\beta = .50$, $p = .82$). Despite having lower slow spindle activity, children with ADHD appear more sensitive than TDCs to the cognitive benefits it supports. These associations were not mirrored for fast spindle activity (*ps* > .05). In light of the potential (albeit not statistically significant) group difference in IQ (ADHD group: 110.3 ± 14.1; TDCs: 120.07 ± 9.4), we repeated this analysis with IQ included as a covariate in the model. Despite controlling for IQ, we confirmed the moderating effect of ADHD status on the association between slow sleep spindle activity and overnight gains in MST precision ($\beta = -8.72$, $p = .026$); thus, a significant effect remained in the ADHD group with no effect for the TDC group ($\beta = .435$, $p = .85$).

DISCUSSION

These initial findings provide a series of novel insights. First, despite no differences in sleep structure, sleep spindle EEG activity appears attenuated in 10- to 13-year-old children with ADHD. Second, despite deficits in motor skill precision present in children with ADHD prior to sleep (Adi-Japha et al., 2011), no group difference was observed

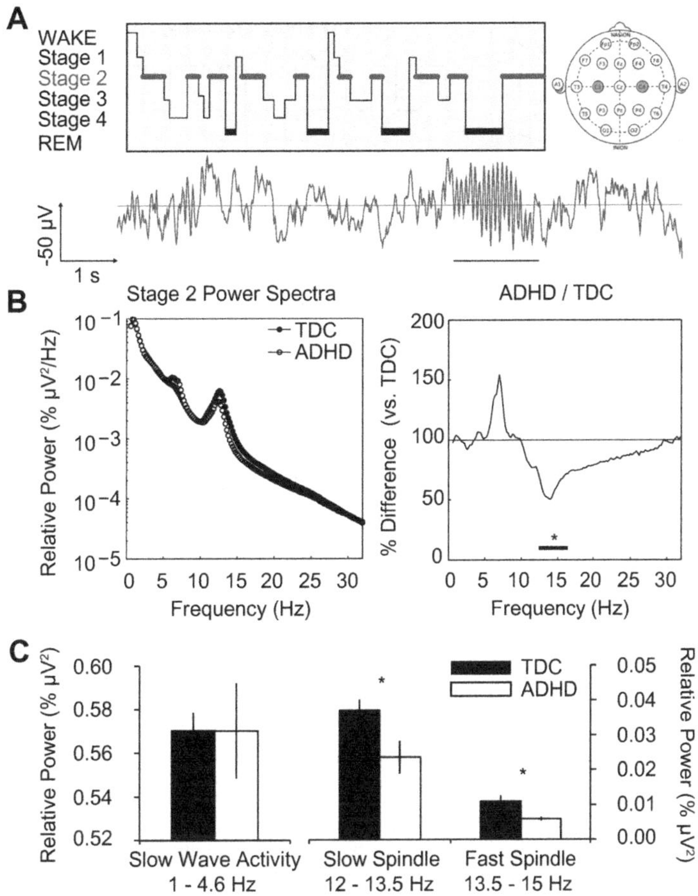

FIGURE 1 All-night NREM Stage 2 power spectra. (**A**) *Top-Left*: A schematic "hypnogram" (adapted, with permission, from Abel, Havekes, Saletin, & Walker, 2013) demonstrating a prototypical night of sleep, as staged by polysomnography. Red highlights NREM Stage 2 sleep, from which all electroencephalogram (EEG) analyses derive. *Top-Right*: A pictorial depiction of the standard electrode placements for EEG. Power spectra are averaged for the left and right central derivations (C3 and C4, labeled in red), respectively, corresponding to primary motor cortex. *Bottom*: Representative 10 s of Stage 2 NREM EEG. Time and amplitude scale as indicated. Underlined portion highlights a prototypical sleep spindle frequency event. (**B**) *Left*: Relative EEG power during Stage 2 sleep for the typically developing controls (black circles) and attention deficit hyperactivity disorder (ADHD) group (white circles), respectively from 0.6 Hz to 32 Hz at 0.2 Hz resolution (frequency on abscissa). Each participant's power spectrum is normalized to his or her total power across this range yielding relative (%) values, plotted here on a base-10 logarithmic scale. *Right*: Stage 2 power in the ADHD group plotted as a percentage of the typically developing group; frequency axis as before. Black bar indicates frequencies of significant difference between groups. (**C**) Integrated Stage 2 power extracted for the slow wave, slow spindle, and fast spindle bands, respectively, using a priori frequency definitions. Significance values are derived from appropriate statistics reported in the text and are indicated as $+p < .10$, $*p < .05$.

in the morning. Third, the degree of successful overnight improvement in ADHD children is associated with the magnitude of sleep spindle EEG frequency activity retained. Together these data underscore a necessity to ensure healthy sleep in this population while indicating a need for future research examining mechanisms underlying these associations.

Traditional polysomnography has yet to reveal a consistent sleep signature of ADHD (Gruber, 2009; Owens et al., 2013). Our finding of reduced spindle-frequency EEG activity adds to recent quantitative spectral analyses (Prehn-Kristensen et al., 2013; Ringli et al., 2013) which demonstrate that microfeatures of the sleep EEG may aid in distinguishing children with ADHD. One limitation of early, inconsistent reports of fewer spindles in ADHD (Khan & Rechtschaffen, 1978; Kiesow & Surwillo, 1987) is that sleep EEG sigma frequencies shift during development (Jenni & Carskadon, 2004; Kurdziel, Duclos, & Spencer, 2013) making automated spindle detection in this age range challenging. The current study examined the entire range of EEG frequencies, circumventing this limitation. Further studies will continue to elucidate how sleep EEG may differentiate children with and without ADHD.

It is intriguing that no associations emerged between overnight gains in MST precision and spindle-frequency EEG activity for the typically developing children—despite

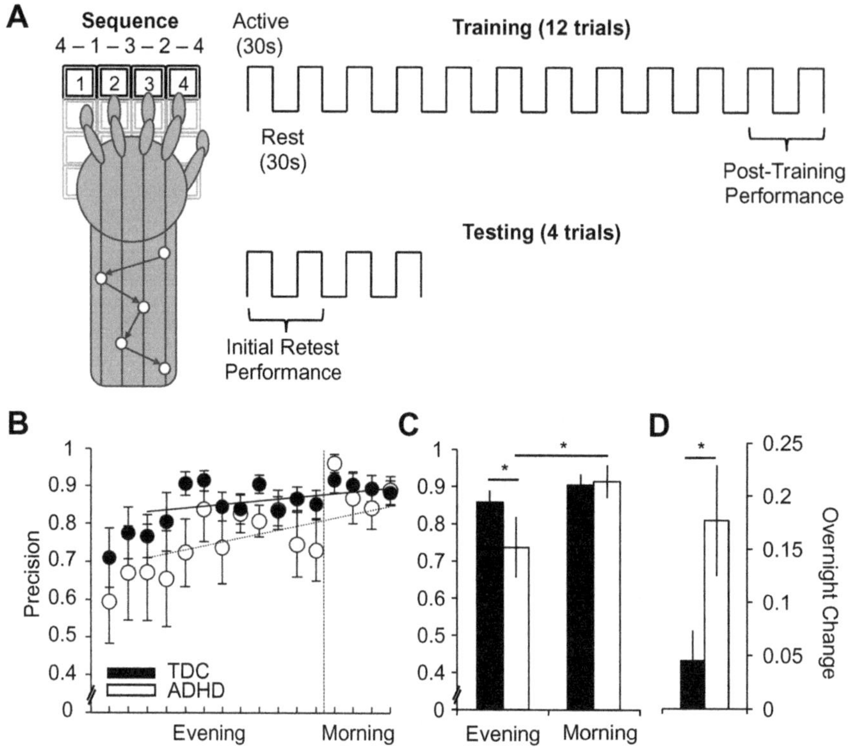

FIGURE 2 Motor Sequence Task (MST) behavior. Motor learning was measured using the Motor Sequence Task (MST). (**A**) MST protocol: Evening training (right-top panel) consisted of 12 rounds of 30-s trials of repeatedly tapping the motor sequence "4–1–3–2–4" on the numeric keys of the keyboard with the nondominant hand (schematic shown in left panel), alternating with 30-s bouts of rest. Morning testing consisted of four rounds of tapping and rest, as before. Evening performance was quantified as the average of the final two training trials, and morning performance as the average of the first two testing trials. MST schematic adapted and redrawn from Walker et al. (2003). (**B**) MST precision is reported trial-by-trial (left panel) and using evening and morning summary scores (right panel) for the typically developing controls (TDC; black-fill) and attention deficit hyperactivity disorder (ADHD; white-fill) groups, respectively. Lines of best fit for ADHD (dotted) and TDC (solid) are fit to the final 10 trials of training, and project forward to predict morning precision gains based on practice alone. (**C-D**) Histograms plotting evening and morning summary scores for each group (**C**), and within-subject overnight change scores (**D**). All error bars indicate standard error of the mean. Significance values are derived from appropriate statistics reported in the text and are indicated as $+p < .10$, $^*p <$ x.05.

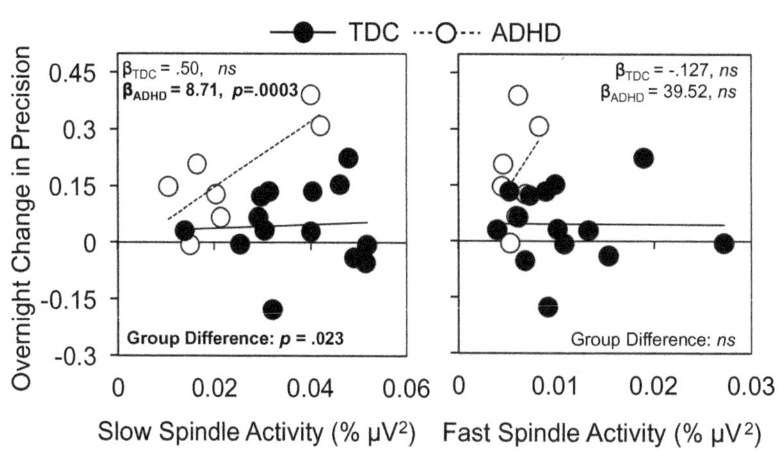

FIGURE 3 Association between electroencephalogram (EEG) spindle activity and overnight precision gains. Scatterplots of the association between individual levels of slow (12–13.5 Hz; left) and fast (13.5–15 Hz; right) spindle activity during NREM Stage 2 sleep and overnight change in Motor Sequence Task (MST) precision (proportion of keystrokes not associated with errors). Lines of best fit for the typically developing controls (TDC) group (black circles) are plotted as solid lines with those for the attention deficit hyperactivity disorder (ADHD) group (white circles) plotted as dotted lines. Groupwise simple slopes and the difference between these slopes are extracted from the regression models reported in the text; *ns* = $p > .05$.

spindle-dependent effects in healthy adults (Nishida & Walker, 2007; Wamsley et al., 2013)—consistent with other sleep-dependent memory studies in children (Wilhelm, Diekelmann, & Born, 2008). Despite this null finding in typically developing children, those with ADHD demonstrated an adultlike relationship despite an overall decrease in sleep spindle activity. Thus, the success of spindle production may be functionally protective in children with ADHD, as those with higher (more TDC-like) spindle activity benefited by exhibiting a concomitantly higher improvement in MST precision the next day. Conversely, those with a greater spindle deficit demonstrated lower overnight improvement in MST precision. The magnitude of the spindle activity deficit in a child with ADHD may therefore provide an index of their behavioral deficits while also providing a mechanistic target within sleep for intervention. For example, noninvasive stimulation of the brain using techniques such as transcranial direct current stimulation (Prehn-Kristensen et al., 2014) or sensorimotor rhythm neurofeedback (Hoedlmoser et al., 2008) can manipulate sleep EEG in a nonpharmacological manner, potentiating slow wave as well as sleep spindle frequency activity above baseline levels. These studies have demonstrated benefits in declarative memory from this modulation of the sleep EEG; however, they have not yet been extended to the motor learning domain described here.

This study is not without limitations. First, as the adaptation night may include EEG-altering first-night effects (Agnew, Webb, & Williams, 1966), the current study cannot preclude the possibility that the differences in sleep EEG reported reflect not a stable difference in ADHD but rather a difference in learning-dependent changes in EEG (Huber, Ghilardi, Massimini, & Tononi, 2004). Second, the current sample was unable to dissociate between symptom presentations of ADHD. To do so will require sample sizes greater than those here or elsewhere (Prehn-Kristensen et al., 2011; Prehn-Kristensen et al., 2014). In the context of the small sample size of the current study, we note that the strength of the effects reported (e.g., $d = 1.14$ with respect to the group difference in overnight performance gains) indicate a potentially powerful difference in sleep-dependent cognition in ADHD, meriting a more robust sample. Specifically, a large within-group effect of sleep was observed in the ADHD group ($d = 1.33$), yet a small effect was observed for TDCs ($d = 0.079$). Third, our subjects were recruited to be free of disordered sleep. Thus, the current study cannot address how sleep disorders in ADHD (e.g., sleep disordered breathing; Sedky, Bennett, & Carvalho, 2014) or atypical Cyclic Alternating Pattern (Akinci et al., 2015)) may impact overnight improvements in motor learning. Fourth, the current study does not replicate a group difference in slow wave activity (Ringli et al., 2013). The lack of frontal EEG derivations limits our present ability to address whether a stable slow wave activity difference is present in ADHD. Slow wave activity transitions from posterior dominance to anterior dominance during adolescence (Kurth et al., 2012); thus, future studies employing denser EEG montages will be necessary to more adequately address this issue. Finally, the current participants were withdrawn from psychostimulants throughout the protocol, limiting the ecological validity of our participants' sleep. Stimulants prescribed for ADHD (e.g., dextroamphetamine) may disrupt sleep (Andersen et al., 2009), although the nature of this disruption, particularly with respect to the frequencies described here, is unclear (Surman & Roth, 2011). More generally, the potential interaction of ADHD medications and sleep in mitigating behavioral deficits in ADHD warrants further examination.

In conclusion, although sleep disturbance is a common complaint in childhood ADHD, traditional polysomnography has been inconclusive in identifying a neurophysiological signature in sleep that indexes cognitive and behavioral deficits. These data join with other recent reports to indicate that microstructural properties of the sleep EEG not commonly examined in a clinical study—here, sleep spindle frequency activity—may, in part, regulate next-day behavioral function in ADHD. Future clinical and basic studies will elucidate the extent to which these sleep EEG oscillations relate to the broader spectrum of symptoms common to ADHD, and, furthermore, whether interventions targeting such sleep neurophysiology may therapeutically aid in the treatment of this and other neurodevelopmental disorders.

ACKNOWLEDGMENTS

We thank Robert Daly of the Periodic Breathing Foundation, as well as Drs. Jeffrey Ellenbogen, Robert Stickgold, and Robert Thomas for their guidance in study design; Drs. Tifenn Raffray, Eliza Van Reen, Bryce Mander, and Matthew Walker for thoughtful discussions in preparation of this manuscript; and laboratory staff—particularly Henry Arantes, Dave Bushnell, Jennifer King, Denise Maceroni, and Erin McInrue—for assistance in collecting the data. We finally offer thanks to the participants in this study and their families for the contribution of their time and effort.

FUNDING

This work was funded by support from the Periodic Breathing Foundation (to MAC), the Johns Hopkins Second Decade Society (to JMS) and NIMH T32MH019927 (to JMS).

ORCID

Jared M. Saletin http://orcid.org/0000-0002-8547-0161
William G. Coon http://orcid.org/0000-0002-2008-8041

REFERENCES

Abel, T., Havekes, R., Saletin, J. M., & Walker, M. P. (2013). Sleep, plasticity and memory from molecules to whole-brain networks. *Current Biology, 23*(17), R774–788. doi:10.1016/j.cub.2013.07.025

Adi-Japha, E., Fox, O., & Karni, A. (2011). Atypical acquisition and atypical expression of memory consolidation gains in a motor skill in young female adults with ADHD. *Research in Developmental Disabilities, 32*(3), 1011–1020. doi:10.1016/j.ridd.2011.01.048

Agnew, H. W., Jr., Webb, W. B., & Williams, R. L. (1966). The first night effect: An EEG study of sleep. *Psychophysiology, 2*(3), 263–266. doi:10.1111/psyp.1966.2.issue-3

Akinci, G., Oztura, I., Hiz, S., Akdogan, O., Karaarslan, D., Ozek, H., & Akay, A. (2015). Sleep structure in children with Attention-Deficit/Hyperactivity disorder. *Journal of Child Neurology, 30*(11), 1520–1525. doi:10.1177/0883073815573318

Andersen, M. L., Margis, R., Frey, B. N., Giglio, L. M., Kapczinski, F., & Tufik, S. (2009). Electrophysiological correlates of sleep disturbance induced by acute and chronic administration of D-amphetamine. *Brain Research, 1249*, 162–172. doi:10.1016/j.brainres.2008.10.023

Ellenbogen, J. M., Hulbert, J. C., Stickgold, R., Dinges, D. F., & Thompson-Schill, S. L. (2006). Interfering with theories of sleep and memory: Sleep, declarative memory, and associative interference. *Current Biology, 16*(13), 1290–1294. doi:10.1016/j.cub.2006.05.024

Fischer, S., Hallschmid, M., Elsner, A. L., & Born, J. (2002). Sleep forms memory for finger skills. *Proceedings of the National Academy of Sciences, 99*(18), 11987–11991. doi:10.1073/pnas.182178199

Gruber, R. (2009). Sleep characteristics of children and adolescents with attention deficit-hyperactivity disorder. *Child and Adolescent Psychiatric Clinics of North America, 18*(4), 863–876. doi:10.1016/j.chc.2009.04.011

Hoedlmoser, K., Pecherstorfer, T., Gruber, G., Anderer, P., Doppelmayr, M., Klimesch, W., & Schabus, M. (2008). Instrumental conditioning of human sensorimotor rhythm (12-15 Hz) and its impact on sleep as well as declarative learning. *Sleep, 31*(10), 1401–1408.

Huber, R., Ghilardi, M. F., Massimini, M., & Tononi, G. (2004). Local sleep and learning. *Nature, 430*(6995), 78–81. doi:10.1038/nature02663

Iber, C., Ancoli-Israel, S., Chesson, A., & Quan, S. (Eds.). (2007). *The AASM manual for the scoring of sleep and associated events: Rules, terminology, and technical specification* (1st ed.). Westchester, IL: American Academy of Sleep Medicine.

Jenni, O. G., & Carskadon, M. A. (2004). Spectral analysis of the sleep electroencephalogram during adolescence. *Sleep, 27*(4), 774–783.

Kaufman, A. S., & Kaufman, N. L. (2004). *Kaufman Brief Intelligence Test* (2nd ed.). Bloomington, MN: Pearson.

Khan, A., & Rechtschaffen, A. (1978). Sleep patterns and sleep spindles in hyperkinetic children. *Sleep Research, 7*, 137.

Kiesow, N. A., & Surwillo, W. W. (1987). Sleep spindles in the EEGs of hyperactive children. *Psychological Reports, 60*(1), 139–144. doi:10.2466/pr0.1987.60.1.139

Kurdziel, L., Duclos, K., & Spencer, R. M. (2013). Sleep spindles in midday naps enhance learning in preschool children. *Proceedings of the National Academy of Sciences, 110*(43), 17267–17272. doi:10.1073/pnas.1306418110

Kurth, S., Jenni, O. G., Riedner, B. A., Tononi, G., Carskadon, M. A., & Huber, R. (2010). Characteristics of sleep slow waves in children and adolescents. *Sleep, 33*(4), 475–480.

Kurth, S., Ringli, M., Lebourgeois, M. K., Geiger, A., Buchmann, A., Jenni, O. G., & Huber, R. (2012). Mapping the electrophysiological marker of sleep depth reveals skill maturation in children and adolescents. *Neuroimage, 63*(2), 959–965. doi:10.1016/j.neuroimage.2012.03.053

Mander, B. A., Santhanam, S., Saletin, J. M., & Walker, M. P. (2011). Wake deterioration and sleep restoration of human learning. *Current Biology, 21*(5), R183–184. doi:10.1016/j.cub.2011.01.019

Nishida, M., & Walker, M. P. (2007). Daytime naps, motor memory consolidation and regionally specific sleep spindles. *PLoS One, 2*(4), e341. doi:10.1371/journal.pone.0000341

Owens, J., Gruber, R., Brown, T., Corkum, P., Cortese, S., O'Brien, L. ... Weiss, M. (2013). Future research directions in sleep and ADHD: Report of a consensus working group. *Journal of Attention Disorders, 17*(7), 550–564. doi:10.1177/1087054712457992

Prehn-Kristensen, A., Molzow, I., Munz, M., Wilhelm, I., Muller, K., Freytag, D. ... Baving, L. (2011). Sleep restores daytime deficits in procedural memory in children with attention-deficit/hyperactivity disorder. *Research in Developmental Disabilities, 32*(6), 2480–2488. doi:10.1016/j.ridd.2011.06.021

Prehn-Kristensen, A., Munz, M., Goder, R., Wilhelm, I., Korr, K., Vahl, W., & Baving, L. (2014). Transcranial oscillatory direct current stimulation during sleep improves declarative memory consolidation in children with attention-deficit/hyperactivity disorder to a level comparable to healthy controls. *Brain Stimulation, 7*(6), 793–799. doi:10.1016/j.brs.2014.07.036

Prehn-Kristensen, A., Munz, M., Molzow, I., Wilhelm, I., Wiesner, C. D., & Baving, L. (2013). Sleep promotes consolidation of emotional memory in healthy children but not in children with attention-deficit hyperactivity disorder. *PLoS One, 8*(5), e65098. doi:10.1371/journal.pone.0065098

Rechtschaffen, A., & Kales, A. (Eds.). (1968). *A manual of standardized terminology, techniques and scoring system for sleep stages of human subjects*. Los Angeles: Brain Information Service/Brain Research Institute, University of California.

Ringli, M., Souissi, S., Kurth, S., Brandeis, D., Jenni, O. G., & Huber, R. (2013). Topography of sleep slow wave activity in children with attention-deficit/hyperactivity disorder. *Cortex, 49*(1), 340–347. doi:10.1016/j.cortex.2012.07.007

Sadeh, A., Sharkey, K. M., & Carskadon, M. A. (1994). Activity-based sleep-wake identification: An empirical test of methodological issues. *Sleep, 17*(3), 201–207.

Sedky, K., Bennett, D. S., & Carvalho, K. S. (2014). Attention deficit hyperactivity disorder and sleep disordered breathing in pediatric populations: A meta-analysis. *Sleep Medicine Reviews, 18*(4), 349–356. doi:10.1016/j.smrv.2013.12.003

Shaffer, D., Fisher, P., Lucas, C. P., Dulcan, M. K., & Schwab-Stone, M. E. (2000). NIMH Diagnostic Interview Schedule for Children Version IV (NIMH DISC-IV): Description, differences from previous versions, and reliability of some common diagnoses. *Journal of the American Academy of Child & Adolescent Psychiatry, 39*(1), 28–38. doi:10.1097/00004583-200001000-00014

Sheslow, D., & Adams, W. (2003). *Wide range assessment of memory and learning, second edition administration and technical manual*. Lutz, FL: Psychological Assessment Resources.

Smith, C. S., Reilly, C., & Midkiff, K. (1989). Evaluation of three circadian rhythm questionnaires with suggestions for an improved measure of morningness. *Journal of Applied Psychology, 74*(5), 728–738. doi:10.1037/0021-9010.74.5.728

Surman, C. B., & Roth, T. (2011). Impact of stimulant pharmacotherapy on sleep quality: Post hoc analyses of 2 large, double-blind, randomized, placebo-controlled trials. *The Journal of Clinical Psychiatry, 72*(7), 903–908. doi:10.4088/JCP.11m06838

Tarokh, L., & Carskadon, M. A. (2010a). Developmental changes in the human sleep EEG during early adolescence. *Sleep, 33*(6), 801–809.

Tarokh, L., & Carskadon, M. A. (2010b). Sleep electroencephalogram in children with a parental history of alcohol abuse/dependence. *Journal of Sleep Research, 19*(1 Pt 2), 165–174. doi:10.1111/j.1365-2869.2009.00763.x

van Der Helm, E., Yao, J., Dutt, S., Rao, V., Saletin, J. M., & Walker, M. P. (2011). REM sleep depotentiates amygdala activity to previous emotional experiences. *Current Biology, 21*(23), 2029–2032. doi:10.1016/j.cub.2011.10.052

Walker, M. P., Brakefield, T., Morgan, A., Hobson, J. A., & Stickgold, R. (2002). Practice with sleep makes perfect: Sleep-dependent motor skill learning. *Neuron*, *35*, 205–211. doi:10.1016/S0896-6273(02)00746-8

Walker, M. P., Brakefield, T., Seidman, J., Morgan, A., Hobson, J. A., & Stickgold, R. (2003). Sleep and the time course of motor skill learning. *Learning & Memory*, *10*(4), 275–284. doi:10.1101/lm.58503

Walker, M. P., & Stickgold, R. (2005). It's practice, with sleep, that makes perfect: Implications of sleep-dependent learning and plasticity for skill performance. *Clinics in Sports Medicine*, *24*(2), 301–317, ix. doi:10.1016/j.csm.2004.11.002

Walker, M. P., Stickgold, R., Alsop, D., Gaab, N., & Schlaug, G. (2005). Sleep-dependent motor memory plasticity in the human brain. *Neuroscience*, *133*(4), 911–917. doi:10.1016/j.neuroscience.2005.04.007

Walker, M. P., Stickgold, R., Jolesz, F. A., & Yoo, S. S. (2005). The functional anatomy of sleep-dependent visual skill learning. *Cerebral Cortex*, *15*(11), 1666–1675. doi:10.1093/cercor/bhi043

Wamsley, E. J., Shinn, A. K., Tucker, M. A., Ono, K. E., McKinley, S. K., Ely, A. V., & Manoach, D. S. (2013). The effects of eszopiclone on sleep spindles and memory consolidation in schizophrenia: A randomized placebo-controlled trial. *Sleep*, *36*(9), 1369–1376. doi:10.5665/sleep.2968

Wilhelm, I., Diekelmann, S., & Born, J. (2008). Sleep in children improves memory performance on declarative but not procedural tasks. *Learning & Memory*, *15*(5), 373–377. doi:10.1101/lm.803708

Wilkinson, G. S., & Robertson, G. J. (2006). *Wide Range Achievement Test 4 professional manual.* Lutz, FL: Psychological Assessment Resources.

A Preliminary Multimethod Comparison of Sleep Among Adolescents With and Without Generalized Anxiety Disorder

Benjamin C. Mullin and Laura Pyle

Dustin Haraden

Justin Riederer

Natalie Brim

David Kaplan and Douglas Novins

Previous studies suggest that youth with anxiety disorders experience their sleep as more disrupted and unsatisfying than their healthy peers. However, it is unclear whether these subjective complaints align with objective measures of sleep quantity and quality. The purpose of this preliminary study was to assess subjective and objective sleep parameters, and their relationships with anxiety symptomatology, among adolescents (62.8% female, 81.4% Caucasian), ages 12 to 18 (M = 15.29 years), with generalized anxiety disorder (n = 26) and controls without any psychopathology (n = 17). We measured sleep over 7 nights using sleep diaries and actigraphy and collected self- and parent-report questionnaires pertaining to sleep, anxiety, and depression. Repeated-measures mixed models were used to examine relationships between nightly sleep duration and morning anxiety. We found a number of differences in sleep between our anxious and healthy participants. Via sleep diary, our anxious participants had longer sleep onset latencies and lower satisfaction with sleep relative to controls, whereas via actigraphy we found longer sleep onset latencies but greater overall sleep duration among anxious versus control participants. Actigraphic measures of sleep disturbance were associated with parent-report of anxiety and depression. Our mixed-model analyses revealed that decreases in nightly sleep duration were associated with increased morning anxiety, but only among our participants with generalized anxiety disorder. Findings suggest that sleep disturbance among anxious adolescents can be detected using both subjective and objective measures and that, for these individuals, fluctuations in sleep duration may have real consequences for daytime anxiety.

INTRODUCTION

Obtaining sufficient sleep is essential to healthy development. However, intermittent sleep disturbance is a common experience for children and adolescents (A. Kahn et al., 1989; Morrison, McGee, & Stanton, 1992; Ohayon, Roberts,

Zulley, Smirne, & Priest, 2000; Owens, Spirito, McGuinn, & Nobile, 2000; Paavonen et al., 2000). Among youth, sleep may be disturbed in a variety of ways, from difficulty initiating or maintaining sleep, to nightmares, to simply obtaining an insufficient quantity of sleep. Correlational studies indicate that reductions in children's sleep quantity or quality are associated with increased daytime sleepiness (Sadeh, Raviv, & Gruber, 2000), diminished school performance (Dewald, Meijer, Oort, Kerkhof, & Bögels, 2010), inattention, impulsivity, and poor behavioral regulation (Paavonen et al., 2009; Sadeh, Gruber, & Raviv, 2002; Steenari et al., 2003). Similarly, youth who have been experimentally deprived of sleep show decrements in attention (Beebe et al., 2008; Fallone, Acebo, Arnedt, Seifer, & Carskadon, 2001) and executive functions (Beebe et al., 2008). Emotional functioning, in particular, may be linked to sleep in a bidirectional fashion (M. Kahn, Sheppes, & Sadeh, 2013). In adults, a growing literature indicates that strong emotions disturb sleep but also that inadequate sleep degrades one's ability to regulate daytime emotions (see review in Walker & van der Helm, 2009). Youth with anxiety disorders, who struggle to regulate high-arousal negative emotions (Suveg & Zeman, 2004), therefore may be especially vulnerable to chronic sleep disturbance.

Sleep disturbance and anxiety appear connected among youth, yet drawing conclusions is challenging given the small number of studies and the variation in methodologies and study findings. In this brief review of literature, we distinguish between *subjective* and *objective* measures of sleep. By subjective, we refer to measures that rely on a child's or parent's judgment regarding the quantity or quality of sleep. This primarily includes questionnaires and prospective sleep diaries. By objective, we refer to measures that estimate sleep without any judgments required by children or parents, such as polysomnography (PSG) and actigraphy (see Table 1 for definitions of key sleep terms). To be clear, these latter methods do not provide unbiased, direct measurements of sleep but do estimate sleep based on physiological data rather than subjective impressions.

Subjective Measures of Sleep Among Youth With Anxiety Disorders

Parents of children with anxiety disorders endorse high rates (up to 85%) of child sleep disturbance (Alfano, Pina, Zerr, & Villalta, 2010), especially trouble sleeping, being overtired, sleeping less than most children (Alfano, Beidel, Turner, & Lewin, 2006; Alfano, Ginsburg, & Kingery, 2007; Alfano et al., 2010; Chase & Pincus, 2011; Kendall & Pimentel, 2003; Masi et al., 2004), and waking throughout the night (Ivanenko, Crabtree, Obrien, & Gozal, 2006). Important to note, the degree of sleep disturbance has been shown to correlate cross-sectionally with overall parent-rated (Alfano et al., 2007) and child-rated (Chase & Pincus, 2011) anxiety severity. However, rates of sleep disturbance are lower (54%) when looking at the self-report of children with anxiety disorders (Alfano et al., 2010). In a study employing a week of sleep diaries, children with anxiety disorders endorsed going to bed later, and obtaining less total sleep than healthy children, but did not endorse more difficulty falling or staying asleep (Hudson, Gradisar, Gamble, Schniering, & Rebelo, 2009).

Although these studies illuminated potential connections between sleep and pediatric anxiety, they relied on parent-report of children's sleep patterns (Alfano et al., 2006; Alfano et al., 2010) or the use of items from general clinical measures, rather than actual sleep questionnaires, to assess sleep (Alfano et al., 2006; Alfano et al., 2007; Alfano, Zakem, Costa, Taylor, & Weems, 2009; Caporino et al., 2015).

Objective Measures of Sleep Among Youth With Anxiety Disorders

Relatively fewer studies have assessed sleep in anxious youth using objective measures. One study employed PSG to compare two subsequent nights of sleep among children and adolescents with a primary anxiety disorder, those with primary depression, and healthy controls (Forbes et al.,

TABLE 1
Definitions of Key Sleep Terms

Term	*Definition*
Polysomnography (PSG)	The "gold standard" method of estimating sleep. PSG involves simultaneous measurement of several physiological channels (brain waves, respiration, heart rate, eye movements, and limb movements) that are analyzed to estimate sleep and wakefulness. PSG allows for the identification of particular sleep stages.
Actigraphy	A method for estimating sleep that typically involves having participants wear a sensitive accelerometer embedded in a watch (actigraph) on his or her nondominant hand. The actigraph measures and stores time-locked data on gross motor movement, which is then downloaded to a computer and converted into estimates of sleep and wake using established algorithms.
Sleep Onset Latency	The number of minutes it takes for an individual to fall asleep at bedtime.
Slow Wave Sleep	A form of non-REM sleep, typically identified as Stage 3 or 4, featuring high-amplitude low frequency brain waves.
Rapid Eye Movement (REM) sleep	A stage of sleep featuring high-frequency brain activity, muscle atonia, and bursts of rapid eye movements. REM sleep is believed to play an important role in emotional memory and emotion regulation.
Sleep Efficiency	The percentage of time in bed during which an individual is actually sleeping (i.e., minutes of sleep/minutes in bed X 100).
Wake After Sleep Onset	The sum total minutes of wakefulness during the night.

2008). Anxious participants had more awakenings than the depressed participants, and less slow-wave sleep and longer sleep onset latencies than the depressed or control participants. That study also found evidence that several objective markers of sleep disturbance were connected to cross-sectional reports of anxiety and depression. Another recent study compared children with and without generalized anxiety disorder (GAD) using PSG, finding longer sleep onset latencies, and reduced latency to rapid eye movement (REM) sleep, among the participants with GAD relative to controls (Alfano, Reynolds, Scott, Dahl, & Mellman, 2013). In contrast, a similar study using home-based PSG found that participants with GAD actually had *higher* sleep efficiency and fewer REM sleep episodes per night than controls (Patriquin, Mellman, Glaze, & Alfano, 2014). These results hinted that perhaps the abnormalities detected in laboratory-based PSG studies actually reflected difficulties that anxious participants might have had adjusting to novel sleep environments, rather than being true markers of chronic sleep dysfunction.

Studies employing actigraphy, which is less intrusive than PSG and allows participants to more easily follow their typical sleep schedules, might help clarify this issue. A recent actigraphy study of children with and without GAD found only marginally longer sleep onset latencies among the GAD participants but no other actigraphic evidence of sleep disturbance despite significant endorsement of sleep disturbance by children with GAD and their parents on questionnaire measures (Alfano, Patriquin, & Reyes, 2015). In another actigraphy study of children and adolescents with a primary anxiety disorder, primary depression, and controls, the anxious youth showed longer sleep onset latencies than controls, and less wake after sleep onset and higher sleep efficiency than depressed participants but not controls (Cousins et al., 2011).

Links Between Sleep Duration and Anxiety

Piecing together the findings from prospective and experimental studies, we can begin to infer potential causal relationships between nighttime sleep and subsequent anxiety. For example, using actigraphy and ecological momentary assessment sampling of mood, Cousins et al. (2011) found that among youth with anxiety disorders, increased wakefulness after sleep onset resulted in higher negative affect ratings the next day. This effect was not present for controls or those with primary depression. Another study of healthy adolescents found that partial sleep restriction (allowing only 6.5 hr in bed per night for 5 consecutive nights) resulted in increased self-ratings of tension/anxiety relative to a "healthy sleep" condition (10 hr in bed per night for 5 nights; Baum et al., 2013). Similarly, adults subjected to 24 hr of sleep deprivation reported higher ratings of anxious arousal and general distress than those who slept normally (Babson, Trainor, Feldner, & Blumenthal, 2010). Two studies have also reported that experimental fragmentation of sleep (i.e., inserting periods of wakefulness throughout the night) produces heightened negative affect the following day (Finan, Quartana, & Smith, 2015; Martin, Engleman, Deary, & Douglas, 1996), suggesting that the continuity of sleep may also be linked to the subsequent expression of anxiety and depression.

In sum, studies employing subjective sleep measures have most consistently reported difficulties falling and staying asleep and shorter overall sleep durations among anxious youth relative to controls, whereas the majority of studies employing objective measures have documented longer sleep onset latencies among anxious youth but few other reliable findings. Interpreting findings is made more difficult due to methodological inconsistencies across studies (use of parent- vs. child-report, composite measures vs. dedicated sleep measures, etc.), and differences in samples (child vs. adolescent, single diagnosis vs. "mixed" anxiety samples). Most existing studies in this area have used either a subjective or objective method to assess sleep but rarely both; thus interpreting subjective-objective discrepancies across studies is difficult due to the use of different samples. The existing literature also focuses primarily on children rather than adolescents, yet adolescents are at a greater risk of developing insomnia than children (Fricke-Oerkermann et al., 2007) and in general have higher rates of insufficient sleep (Gradisar, Gardner, & Dohnt, 2011; McKnight-Eily et al., 2011; Wolfson & Carskadon, 1998). Further studies of anxious adolescents implementing both subjective and objective measurement of sleep, as well as studies evaluating prospective relationships between various forms of sleep disturbance and anxiety symptomatology, are needed. Clarifying the presence and nature of sleep disturbance among anxious youth will assist in the development of appropriate, targeted interventions.

CURRENT STUDY

The overall purpose of this preliminary study was to employ multiple methodologies to characterize the nature of sleep disturbance and its relevance to clinical symptomatology among adolescents with and without GAD. There is some evidence that youth with GAD experience the highest levels of sleep disturbance among the pediatric anxiety disorders (Alfano et al., 2006; Alfano et al., 2010). GAD includes insomnia as a diagnostic symptom (American Psychiatric Association, 2013), as well as other key features such as poorly controlled worry and restlessness that may interfere with sleep. This study had three aims. Our first aim was to investigate differences in sleep among participants using subjective (sleep diary and questionnaire) and objective (actigraphy) measures of sleep collected over a period of 1 week. Based on the existing literature, we anticipated finding evidence of greater sleep disturbance among the GAD participants, primarily increased sleep onset latency, wake after sleep onset, and reduced sleep efficiency via sleep diary, and higher scores on sleep disturbance subscales from the sleep questionnaire. With respect to the actigraphy data, we anticipated finding longer sleep onset latencies among GAD compared to healthy participants but no other significant differences. Our second aim was to investigate relationships between objective sleep parameters and self- and parent-report of anxiety and depression, assessed using questionnaires. Based on previous literature documenting the anxiogenic and depressogenic effects of shortened sleep duration and the fragmentation of sleep, we hypothesized that objective measures of decreased sleep duration and problems with sleep initiation (sleep onset latency) and maintenance (sleep efficiency) would be associated with increased levels of anxiety and depression among the entire sample. Finally, our third aim was to investigate temporal relationships between sleep duration and next-day self-report of anxiety over the course of the recording period. We hypothesized that reduced sleep duration would be predictive of higher levels of morning anxiety, particularly among participants with GAD.

METHOD

Participants

This study utilized a case-control design comparing adolescents with GAD to healthy controls. For both GAD cases and controls, participants needed to be between 12 and 18 years of age. Exclusion criteria included current or lifetime diagnoses of sleep disorders other than insomnia, psychotic disorders, developmental disability, autism spectrum disorders, or current use of hypnotic medications. The adolescents in this study were part of a larger study that included magnetic resonance imaging (MRI), thus all participants were subject to MRI-related exclusion criteria, including having non-removable metallic items on their bodies, having a fear of enclosed spaces, or being pregnant. Controls were also excluded if they met lifetime or current criteria for any *Diagnostic and Statistical Manual of Mental Disorders* (4th ed., text rev.; *DSM-IV-TR*; American Psychiatric Association, 2000) diagnoses. Participants were recruited from the outpatient psychiatry and adolescent medicine clinics of a large, urban pediatric hospital. Potential cases were identified through a medical records search, identifying patients who met age requirements and who had previously received a diagnosis of GAD or who had not received any psychiatric diagnoses. These patients were sent recruitment letters describing the study. Recruitment flyers were also posted in community centers within the Denver Metro area.

Forty-seven adolescents were consented for this study. Of those, participation was discontinued for four individuals following the clinical assessment due to not meeting criteria for GAD (n = 3) or for meeting criteria for a psychiatric diagnosis while in the control group (n = 1). Forty-three adolescents (ages 12–18 years; see Table 2)—26 with a primary diagnosis of GAD and 17 healthy controls without any psychopathology—completed this study. All participants were living with primary caregivers and were currently attending school in a regular classroom setting. The GAD group included participants who met *DSM-IV-TR* criteria for a primary diagnosis of GAD, all of whom were in treatment,

TABLE 2
Participant Characteristics

	GAD[a]	Control[b]	Test Statistic	p
Gender (% Female)	59.26	64.71	χ^2 = .04	.83
Race (% White)	84.62	76.47	χ^2 = 5.68	.22
Ethnicity			χ^2 = .20	.65
Hispanic	2	2		
Non-Hispanic	24	15		
M Age in Years	15.13 (1.92)	15.54 (1.56)	t = –.73	.47
Pubertal Status			χ^2 = 6.86	.23
Pre/Early	3	0		
Mid/Late/Post	17	13		
Missing	6	4		
Body Mass Index	21.09 (4.14)	22.48 (3.90)	t = −1.06	.30
Body Mass Index Percentile	52.2 (31.9)	64.65 (29.68)	t = −1.23	.23
Mean SCARED Total Score–Self-Report	31.57 (16.95)	14.12 (11.30)	t = 5.03	.001
Mean SCARED Total Score–Parent-Report	24.95 (15.01)	5.18 (6.75)	t = 3.64	< .001
Mean MFQ Total Score–Self-Report	19.00 (10.97)	7.59 (5.28)	t = 3.93	< .001
Mean MFQ Total Score–Parent-Report	14.71 (9.25)	3.24 (3.96)	t = 4.77	< .001
% Taking Psychiatric Medication	76.92	6.25	χ^2 = 20.77	< .001

Note: Body mass index was calculated using the Centers for Disease Control and Prevention online calculator (https://nccd.cdc.gov/dnpabmi/calculator.aspx). SCARED = Screen for Child Anxiety Related Emotional Disorders; MFQ = Moods and Feelings Questionnaire.

[a]n = 26.

[b]n = 17.

and 20 of 26 (77%) were taking psychiatric medications. Of those, 17 were taking a selective serotonin reuptake inhibitor (SSRI), three were taking an atypical antipsychotic, two were taking a stimulant, and one a tricyclic antidepressant. We did not inquire about the stability of medication usage for our participants, although no participants had any medication changes during their participation in the study. Secondary diagnoses for the GAD participants included major depressive disorder (n = 9), attention deficit/hyperactivity disorder (n = 5), dysthymic disorder (n = 5), panic disorder (n = 5), social anxiety disorder (n = 5), specific phobia (n = 2), and obsessive-compulsive disorder (n = 1). This high rate of comorbidity among our GAD participants is consistent with previous large epidemiologic samples of adolescents (Merikangas et al., 2010). One healthy participant was taking a stimulant medication for attention but did not meet lifetime or current criteria for any disorder.

Procedure

The Colorado Multiple Institutional Review Board approved this study. Data collection took place only during the school year. The study consisted of two study visits: At the first visit, participants and a parent completed informed assent/consent documents, a joint diagnostic interview, and numerous questionnaire measures. Participants were then asked to complete 7 consecutive nights of sleep monitoring at home, wearing an actigraph and keeping a sleep diary. Each participant completed 5 weeknights and 2 weekend nights, though not always in the same order. Participants then returned 1 week later to return the actigraph and complete MRI scanning (data not described here).

Clinical Assessment

The MINI International Neuropsychiatric Interview for Children and Adolescents version 6.0 (Sheehan et al., 2010) was administered to each adolescent–parent dyad together by a licensed clinical psychologist (the first author) to evaluate the presence or absence of Axis I disorders from the *DSM-IV-TR* (American Psychiatric Association, 2000). The MINI International Neuropsychiatric Interview for Children and Adolescents is a brief, structured interview that has previously shown sensitivity and specificity across diagnoses, comparable to more lengthy diagnostic instruments (Sheehan et al., 2010). Symptoms were considered present when endorsed by either the parent or the adolescent. Adolescents were also interviewed without the parent present, where they were given the opportunity to change any responses that they were not comfortable voicing in front of their parent.

Anxiety symptoms were further assessed using the self- and parent-report versions of the Screen for Child Anxiety Related Emotional Disorders (SCARED) (Birmaher et al., 1997). This widely used 41-item instrument screens for *DSM-IV-TR* anxiety disorders and has excellent psychometric properties across clinical (Birmaher et al., 1999) and community (Hale, Raaijmakers, Muris, & Meeus, 2005) samples, including good discriminant validity between anxiety disorders and other childhood disorders (Birmaher et al., 1999). In this study, we employed the total score as a measure of current anxiety severity. A cutoff score of 25 on the self-report version has been shown to optimally capture youth in the clinically anxious range. (Birmaher et al., 1999). In our study, the SCARED demonstrated high internal consistency for both self-report (α = .96) and parent-report (α = .96). Severity of depressive symptoms was measured using the self- and parent-report Moods and Feelings Questionnaire (MFQ). The MFQ is a 34-item questionnaire that assesses depressive symptoms on a scale from 0 to 2 points (Angold, Costello, Messer, & Pickles, 1995), generating a total score. This measure has been shown to have sensitivity to depression throughout childhood and adolescence (Messer et al., 1995) and adequate ability to discriminate between major depression and anxiety disorders (Daviss et al., 2006). Cutoff scores of 29 on self-report and 25 on parent-report have been found to accurately distinguish between depressed and nondepressed youth (Kent, Vostanis, & Feehan, 1997). The MFQ demonstrated high internal consistency across self-report (α = .92) and parent-report (.93). The SCARED and MFQ were completed during the first study visit.

Pubertal Development

Pubertal maturation was assessed using the Self-Rating Scale of Pubertal Development (Carskadon & Acebo, 1993). Items on the scale assess for external signs of pubertal development, including changes in skin, body hair, voice (male), and menarche. This scale has demonstrated good reliability and reasonable concordance with hormonal indices of pubertal development (Shirtcliff, Dahl, & Pollak, 2009).

Sleep Diary

Each morning, adolescent participants completed an online sleep diary, collected using the secure Research Electronic Data Capture (Harris et al., 2009) web-based application hosted at the University of Colorado, Denver. The diary required participants to report on the previous night's bedtime, sleep onset time, number of awakenings, total time awake during the night, overall quality of sleep on a 6-point scale from 1 (*horrible*) to 6 (*excellent*), and anxiety upon waking in the morning from 1 (*calm, relaxed*) to 6 (*severe*). This online format allowed diary entries to be time stamped, and only entries made before noon each day were included in the data set. To maximize our response rate we sent automated text messages to participants each morning, reminding them to go online and complete their sleep diaries. When study staff noticed that a sleep diary had not been completed, a call was placed to the family reminding them to complete subsequent diaries. Across our 43 participants, we had only 4 nights of missing data (i.e., 98.7% completion rate), with only one participant exceeding more than 1 night of missing data. We had previously decided to exclude from analysis any participant contributing fewer than 5 nights of data, however none of our participants were below this threshold.

Note that the first five participants (all from the GAD group) completed the study using a version of sleep diary that did not include the question assessing morning anxiety, thus those data are missing from analyses involving that variable.

Actigraphy

Nighttime sleep was measured using Actiwatch-2 actigraphs (Philips Respironics, Murrysville, PA) worn over 7 nights on the participant's nondominant wrist. Actigraphs provide an objective estimate of sleep/wake cycles based on the measurement of movement and have the advantage of measuring sleep in an individual's typical sleep environment. Although there is a scarcity of research validating the use of actigraphy with pediatric samples (Meltzer, Montgomery-Downs, Insana, & Walsh, 2012), existing studies of youth and adults have found that when compared to PSG, actigraphs have strong sensitivity to detect sleep but weaker specificity in detecting wake (Meltzer, Walsh, Traylor, & Westin, 2012; Sadeh, Sharkey, & Carskadon, 1994). In the current study, movement data were summed into 1-min epochs, which were analyzed using the "medium sensitivity" setting in the Actiware 6.0 software (Respironics Inc., 2011). This software uses a validated algorithm to classify epochs as either sleep or wake and calculates variables such as sleep duration, sleep onset latency, minutes of wake after sleep onset, and sleep efficiency. Per this algorithm, sleep onset was defined as the first period of 10 consecutive immobile min, and sleep offset as the last 10 consecutive immobile min, between bedtime and wake time. Each actigraph also features an event marker button. Participants were instructed to push this button each night as they were ready to try to fall asleep (i.e., when they turned the lights off) and again in the morning as they got out of bed (i.e., lights on). Each actigraphy record was manually checked. In cases of missing event markers, bedtime or wake time would be imputed from the sleep diary.

Compliance with wearing the actigraphs was also very high, and we had no instances of device failure. We had only 2 nights of missing data across our entire sample (99.3% compliance), thus all participants were included in analyses.

Children's Report of Sleep Patterns

Subjective impressions of sleep were also captured using the Children's Report of Sleep Patterns (CRSP), an instrument that has demonstrated good reliability and validity among both child (Meltzer, Biggs, et al., 2012) and adolescent (Meltzer et al., 2014) samples. Both the self- and parent-report versions were administered. The self-report version contains 62 items and the parent-report version 67 items. The CRSP contains three modules (Sleep Patterns, Sleep Hygiene, and Sleep Disturbance), each with individual subscales. In this study, we focused on the Sleep Disturbance module, which contains the subscales of Bedtime Fears/Worries, Restless Legs, Parasomnias, and Insomnia. We also examined the Sleepiness subscale to assess possible daytime consequences of inadequate or nonrestorative sleep. For all items contributing to the Sleep Disturbance module, respondents were asked to rate the frequency of behaviors for a "regular week" when the adolescent was not sick or on vacation. For the majority of items, a 5-point Likert scale was used. Potential ranges for each subscale were as follows: Bedtime Fears/Worries (2–10), Restless Legs (5–25), Parasomnias (2–10), Insomnia (5–25), and Sleepiness (5–25). Internal consistency was adequate for the Sleepiness scale and all Sleep Disturbance subscales (ranging from $\alpha = .77$ to .89) with the exception of the parent-report Restless Legs subscale ($\alpha = .54$). We did not calculate alpha coefficients for the Bedtime Fears/Worries or Parasomnias subscales, as they each contained only two items.

Data Analysis

For the first study aim, we employed independent samples *t*-tests to address our primary hypotheses regarding group differences across sleep parameters. Mann–Whitney *U* tests were used for all variables with non-normal distributions. We used Pearson correlations to test our hypotheses for the second study aim regarding relationships between sleep parameters and anxiety and depression severity scores. For the third study aim, we employed a repeated measures mixed-effects model, allowing for correlation between repeated measures of sleep duration and sleep-diary-reported morning anxiety made on the same individual, and with an interaction between group and sleep duration, to test whether the two groups differed in the relationship between sleep duration and morning anxiety.

We used independent samples *t*-tests to evaluate whether GAD participants taking versus not taking psychiatric medications differed on any of the sleep parameters measured by actigraphy and sleep diaries. All analyses were performed using SPSS for Windows (version 23.0) with the exception of the mixed-effects analyses, which were performed using SAS.

RESULTS

Sleep Diary

Consistent with hypotheses, sleep onset latencies were longer among participants with GAD than controls (see Table 3). They also reported lower sleep efficiency, although this finding did not quite reach statistical significance ($p = .06$), and both groups endorsed relatively high sleep efficiency (91.5% and 94.7%, respectively). Participants with GAD rated their

TABLE 3
Sleep Diary Comparison Between Groups

	GAD[a]	Control[b]	Test Statistic	*d*	*p*
Total Sleep Time (Min)	484.68 (59.73)	462.01 (57.65)	$t = -1.22$	*.39*	.23
Wake After Sleep Onset (Min)	15.51 (15.97)	10.18 (14.46)		*.35*	.23
Sleep Efficiency (%)	91.55 (6.96)	94.66 (4.94)		.52	.06
Sleep Onset Latency (Min)	30.12 (27.32)	15.26 (12.96)		.70	.01
Sleep Quality Rating (1 = *Horrible*; 6 = *Excellent*)	3.63 (.69)	4.38 (.68)	$t = 3.47$	1.09	< .01
Wake Time Anxiety Rating (1 = *Calm*; 6 = *Relaxed*)[c]	2.71 (.76)	1.74 (.87)		1.19	< .01

Note: Empty cells are Mann–Whitney U test utilized for variables with skewed distributions. GAD = generalized anxiety disorder.
[a]*n* = 26.
[b]*n* = 17.
[c]GAD *n* = 21, control *n* = 17.

sleep as significantly lower quality than controls and endorsed higher ratings of anxiety upon waking.

Children's Report of Sleep Problems

Participants with GAD endorsed widespread problems with sleep. Relative to healthy controls the GAD participants reported higher levels of Bedtime Fears/Worries, Restless Legs, and overall Insomnia symptoms, as well as greater daytime sleepiness (see Figure 1a). Group differences were less consistent via parent report with only the Insomnia and Bedtime Fears/Worries subscales showing greater severity of ratings among the GAD participants (see Figure 1b).

Actigraphy

Significant differences across multiple sleep variables were found using actigraphy (see Table 4). Consistent with our hypothesis, participants with GAD took significantly longer to fall asleep than healthy controls, by an average of nearly 15 min per night. We did not find a significant difference with respect to sleep efficiency or wake after sleep onset. Contrary to hypotheses, participants with GAD slept *longer* each night than controls. This finding appeared to stem primarily from participants with GAD going to bed slightly earlier and waking later than their healthy peers on weekdays and weekends, though group differences on sleep timing did not reach significance thresholds.

Associations Between Actigraphic Sleep Parameters and Clinical Symptoms

We found a significant negative association between sleep efficiency and parent MFQ total score and a positive association between sleep onset latency and parent MFQ total score and parent SCARED total score (see Table 5). There were no significant associations between these sleep variables and self-report of anxiety or depression.

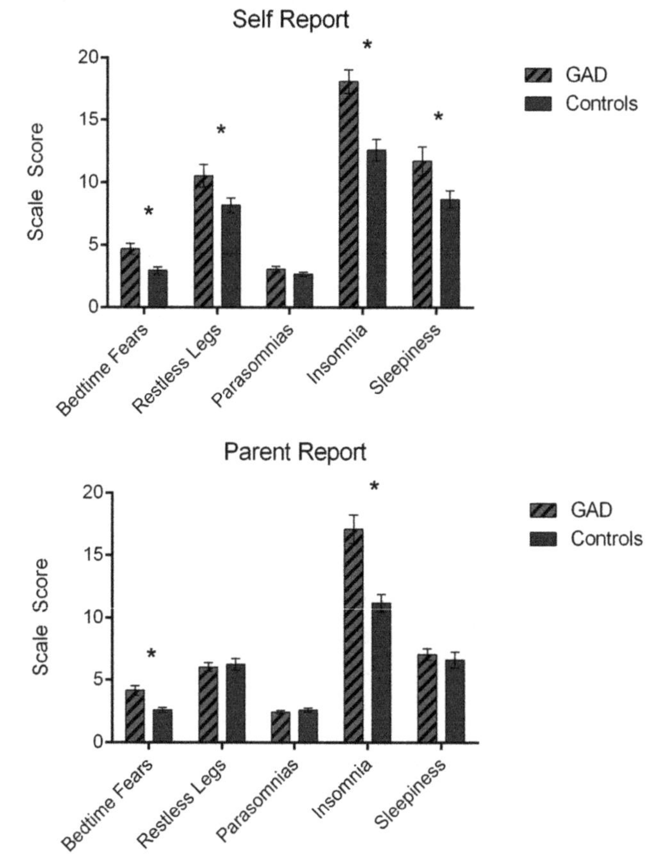

FIGURE 1 Mean subscale scores by group on the Children's Report of Sleep Patterns questionnaire. Error bars indicate standard errors. GAD = generalized anxiety disorder. * = group difference of $p < 0.05$ via independent samples *t*-test.

Prospective Links Between Nightly Sleep Duration and Morning Anxiety

In the entire cohort, there was not a significant relationship between sleep-diary-reported morning anxiety and the previous night's sleep duration (see Table 6). In the model including the interaction of sleep duration and GAD status, each 1-hr increase

TABLE 4
Actigraphic Sleep Comparison Between Groups

	GAD[a]	Control[b]	Test Statistic	*d*	*p*
Total Sleep Time (Min)	425.01 (41.80)	394.51 (40.07)	$t = -2.38$	.75	.02
Wake After Sleep Onset (Min)	61.22 (25.49)			.32	.41
Sleep Efficiency (%)	79.81 (6.34)	82.01 (3.85)		.42	.34
Sleep Onset Latency (Min)	32.46 (24.91)	17.7 (9.50)		.78	.03
Weekday Bedtime	22:43 (00:52)	23:02 (00:56)	$t = 1.74$	.35	.09
Weekday Morning Wake Time	06:30 (00:56)	06:21 (00:50)	$t = -0.49$	.17	.62
Weekend Bedtime	23:44 (01:25)	23:56 (01:21)	$t = 0.46$	.14	.65
Weekend Morning Wake Time	08:27 (01:21)	07:48 (00:50)	$t = -1.81$	.58	.08

Note: Empty cells are Mann–Whitney U test utilized for variables with skewed distributions. GAD = generalized anxiety disorder.
[a]$n = 26$.
[b]$n = 17$.

TABLE 5
Correlations Between Actigraphic Sleep Parameters and Anxiety and Depression Scores

	1	2	3	4	5	6	7
1. Sleep Duration	—						
2. Sleep Efficiency	.19	—					
3. Sleep Onset Latency	−.05	−.69**	—				
4. SCARED Total—Self-Report	.12	.06	.14	—			
5. SCARED Total—Parent-Report	.23	−.26	.38*	.64**	—		
6. MFQ Total—Self-Report	.13	−.10	.24	.74**	.64**	—	
7. MFQ Total—Parent-Report	.05	−.37*	.42**	.59**	.85**	.67**	—

Note: SCARED = Screen for Child Anxiety Related Emotional Disorders; MFQ = Moods and Feelings Questionnaire.
$*p < .05$. $**p < .01$.

TABLE 6
Parameter Estimates From Repeated Measures Mixed-Effects Model

Effect	*Estimate*	*SE*	p
Intercept	1.92	0.47	—
TST	−0.01	0.06	.19
GAD	1.88	0.73	.01
TST × GAD	−0.13	0.09	.13

Note: Beta estimates and standard errors for TST were converted from minutes to hours for this table for ease of interpretation. TST = total sleep time; GAD = generalized anxiety disorder.

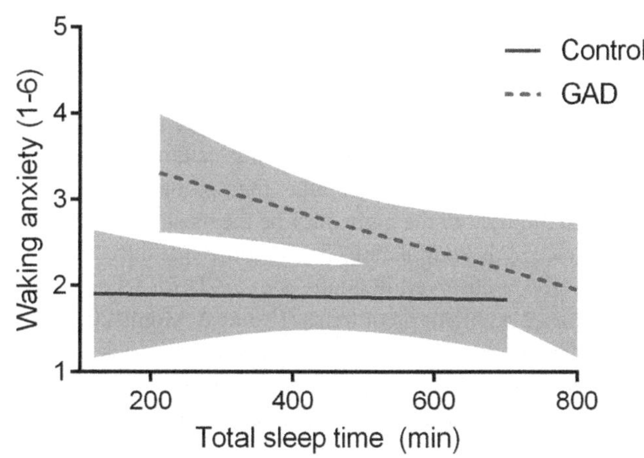

FIGURE 2 Mixed effects model showing the relationship between sleep duration and group status on waking anxiety by group. GAD = generalized anxiety disorder. This figure shows the predicted mean waking anxiety level vs. sleep duration in the two groups across the range of observed sleep duration values in each group, using the results of the mixed-effects model with interaction. The solid line is the predicted mean value of waking anxiety and the shaded regions are 95% confidence intervals for the predicted values.

in sleep duration resulted in a decrease in morning anxiety of 0.13 ± 0.09 additional points for GAD participants relative to controls. Although the interaction of sleep duration and group was not significant ($p = .13$), effect size calculations for each group revealed a very small average effect for sleep duration on morning anxiety in controls (Cohen's $d = 0.08$) but a small to moderate effect for the GAD participants (Cohen's $d = 0.39$). Figure 2 presents the predicted values for each group in this interaction model.

Because these analyses were likely underpowered to detect an interaction, we elected to run a sensitivity analysis with participants stratified by group. Repeated measures mixed-effects models were used to test the association of sleep duration and morning anxiety in each group. There was no significant association in the control group ($p = .68$), but the association in the GAD group was significant ($p = .04$). Each 1-hr increase in sleep duration was associated with a .15 (*SE* = .07) unit decrease in morning anxiety (Figure 2).

Medication Effects

Analyses comparing sleep parameters among GAD participants taking versus not taking psychiatric medications failed to reach significance. These can be found in Supplemental Table 1.

DISCUSSION

This preliminary study sought to evaluate the presence of sleep disturbance and its relationship to clinical symptomatology among adolescents with a primary diagnosis of GAD and healthy controls. We found evidence of sleep disturbance among adolescents with GAD across both subjective and objective measures, as well as evidence for connections between sleep and current anxiety and depression severity. Our prospective data also suggested a significant relationship between nightly sleep duration and subsequent morning anxiety that was specific to the GAD participants.

Sleep Abnormalities Across Subjective and Objective Measures

Our finding of longer sleep onset latencies via actigraphy and sleep diary among our adolescents with GAD was consistent with two previous PSG studies (Alfano et al., 2013; Forbes et al., 2008) and one actigraphy study (Alfano et al., 2015) that focused on clinically anxious youth. We found no evidence to suggest that adolescents with GAD struggle to maintain sleep to a greater degree than controls, using actigraphy or sleep diaries. Sleep-onset insomnia, rather than problems maintaining sleep throughout the night, may be the most defining sleep disturbance in this population. This is somewhat different than what has been observed in adults with GAD for whom sleep maintenance problems predominate (Monti & Monti, 2000) yet is consistent with our questionnaire results in which participants with GAD reported significantly higher levels of bedtime fears than controls. Down-regulating negative emotions at bedtime is a critical aspect of initiating sleep (Baglioni, Spiegelhalder, Lombardo, & Riemann, 2010), thus sleep onset difficulties may reflect a broader deficit in emotion regulation in this disorder. Of interest, one recent study of adults with GAD reported that emotion regulation deficiencies fully mediated the relationship between GAD symptoms and sleep disturbance (Tsypes, Aldao, & Mennin, 2013).

Although we did find the aforementioned evidence of sleep disturbance among our adolescents with GAD using actigraphy, there was a disconnect between our objective and subjective sleep measures, with far greater sleep disturbance in the GAD group revealed in sleep diaries and in the CRSP questionnaire than via actigraphy. For example, unlike some previous studies actigraphy data indicated that our adolescents with GAD actually slept *longer* each night than their healthy peers by a considerable amount, yet these participants endorsed significantly lower sleep satisfaction ratings on sleep diaries and higher ratings of daytime sleepiness on the CRSP than controls. This discrepancy could be attributed to reporter bias, such that anxious individuals are more likely than nonanxious individuals to report problems in a variety of domains due to an influence of negative mood (Dalgleish & Watts, 1990). Another intriguing possibility is that adolescents with chronic anxiety actually have greater sleep *need* than healthy adolescents, thus they chronically wake up feeling unrestored. This hypothesis would be consistent with the observation that anxiety disorders (Hoehn-Saric & McLeod, 1988), and GAD in particular (Lyonfields, Borkovec, & Thayer, 1995; Thayer, Friedman, & Borkovec, 1996), involve an autonomic imbalance with hyperactivity of the sympathetic nervous system relative to the parasympathetic nervous system. Chronic heightened sympathetic activation is linked with excessive energy expenditure (Thayer & Lane, 2007), which may create greater need for restoration through sleep. In addition, there is reason to suspect that the sleep obtained by anxious individuals is less restorative than for healthy individuals given some evidence of reduced slow wave activity in youth (Forbes et al., 2008) and adults with GAD (see review in Papadimitriou & Linkowski, 2005), and findings showing that apprehensive thoughts at bedtime are associated with reduced slow wave sleep throughout the night (Kecklund & Åkerstedt, 2004).

Cross-Sectional and Prospective Links Between Sleep and Anxiety

Our correlational analyses supported the hypothesis that actigraphic measures of disrupted sleep (extended sleep onset latency and poor sleep efficiency) would be cross-sectionally associated with both depression and anxiety; however, this was true only when using parent-report of clinical symptoms. These associations did not reach significance via self-report of symptoms, though the relationships were in the predicted direction, suggesting that this may be due to limited statistical power. Although these analyses do not indicate causality, they reinforce the notion that as severity of internalizing symptoms increases, so too do certain objective measures of sleep disturbance. Forbes et al. (2008) reported similar relationships between PSG sleep parameters and depression and anxiety symptom levels. Our prospective analyses allowed us to explore the temporal relationship between nighttime sleep duration and subsequent morning anxiety. Although we did not find significant relationships across the entire sample or in the interaction analysis, our sensitivity analysis did support our hypothesis of a relationship between decreased sleep duration and increased morning anxiety among our participants with GAD. This effect was statistically significant, but its clinical significance is unclear. We employed a nonstandardized 6-point anxiety rating added to our sleep diary, with the hope of capturing some aspect of morning anxiety but without increasing the burden on participants. The downside of this approach is that scores are difficult to evaluate relative to more thorough, established anxiety measures. Our observed increase in anxiety of .15 points for every hour of sleep below the mean may indicate a rather marginal association. Alternatively, given our small sample size and measurement of anxiety at only a single time point, it may be that more standardized measurement of anxiety several times throughout the day would illuminate a clinically meaningful association between sleep duration and daytime anxiety. These results parallel a recent neuroimaging study of adults, which reported that sleep loss produces intensified activity in neural circuitry responsible for the anticipation of threat (i.e., the amygdala and insula; Goldstein et al., 2013) and that the degree of such vulnerability to sleep loss is related to trait anxiety. Previous studies have also found that sleep deprivation selectively increases amygdala activation to threatening images (Yoo et al., 2007). It may be that anxious individuals are more sensitive to perturbations of sleep, experiencing increasing anxiety as a downstream consequence of the effects of sleep loss on brain regions responsible for threat processing.

The findings of this study indicate the potential utility of intervening directly with sleep among adolescents with GAD who present with sleep disturbance. Promoting good sleep hygiene practices such as maintaining a consistent bedtime, eliminating sleep disrupting electronics (e.g., smartphones, tablets) from the bedroom, and implementing a bedtime relaxation procedure may help these patients establish good sleep habits and reduce the arousal that appears to characterize sleep-onset insomnia (Alfano et al., 2010). Additional cognitive factors such as overestimating the effects of insufficient sleep and excessively attending for signs of sleepiness appear to underlie adult insomnia (Harvey, 2002) and may be treatment targets for adolescents with GAD and chronic sleep disturbance. Treatment protocols aimed at reducing these mechanisms of sleep disturbance among anxious youth are currently being tested (Cowie et al., 2014). Of interest, two recent studies suggest that standard cognitive behavioral therapy and pharmacotherapy for pediatric anxiety may themselves produce improvements in sleep-related problems even without directly targeting sleep symptoms (Caporino et al., 2015; Peterman et al., 2016). Given the interrelatedness of sleep disturbance and anxiety, it is not surprising that interventions that reduce anxiety might confer some benefits in the sleep domain. However, the actual benefits were small in one study (Caporino et al., 2015), and participants continued to report elevated sleep-related problems at posttreatment in the other study (Peterman et al., 2016). Although standard cognitive behavioral therapy for anxiety may prove sufficient for reducing mild sleep disturbance, it may be that patients with more significant or long-standing sleep symptoms require additional sleep-focused intervention.

Limitations and Future Directions

This study has several limitations. Because this is a preliminary study that was intended to gather pilot data, the sample size is relatively small, which left many of our analyses underpowered. For variables on which group differences were quite large, such as "sleep quality" assessed using the sleep diary, the achieved power was excellent (.96). However, for other variables with smaller but potentially significant between-group differences, such as "weekend morning wake time," the achieved power was inadequate (.46). This may have resulted in cases of Type II error. Our sample was also heterogeneous, particularly in terms of age and comorbid conditions. With a small sample it becomes difficult to single out sleep abnormalities that are unique to GAD versus those imparted by comorbid conditions. That said, our findings were for the most part consistent with existing findings in youth with GAD (Alfano et al., 2006; Alfano et al., 2007; Alfano et al., 2015; Alfano et al., 2010; Alfano et al., 2013; Forbes et al., 2008; Kendall & Pimentel, 2003; Masi et al., 2004). In a follow-up study our group has under way, we are pursuing a larger sample and assessing a wider range of variables that may be relevant to understand sleep disturbance in this population, such as dysfunctional beliefs about sleep.

Another possible limitation of the current study is that the majority of our participants with GAD and one of our controls were taking psychiatric medications. When designing this study, we made a deliberate attempt to gather a representative sample of adolescents with GAD, and thus we anticipated that a significant portion would be treated with medication. Of the 20 GAD participants taking medication, 13 were taking SSRIs as monotherapy. Research suggests that the sleep-altering effects of SSRI medications are most consistent in reducing REM sleep and that the effects on sleep initiation and maintenance are inconsistent between agents and typically present only at the early initiation of such treatment (Wilson & Argyropoulos, 2005). Of the other medications taken by our participants, the potential effects on sleep are varied: Atypical antipsychotics often possess sedating properties that may reduce insomnia symptoms but also increase daytime sleepiness (Kane & Sharif, 2008), stimulants are known to cause difficulties with sleep initiation (Greenhill, Pliszka, & Dulcan, 2002), and tricyclic antidepressants do not consistently possess sleep-related side effects (Birmaher et al., 1998; Geller et al., 1993). In this study we did not collect a time line of medication usage and thus cannot rule out the possibility of very recent medication changes that might have been more likely to impact sleep. A previous study of anxious children and adolescents found no differences in the rate of sleep problems among those who were taking versus not taking psychiatric medications (Chase & Pincus, 2011). We did not find any differences among primary sleep parameters for GAD participants who were taking versus not taking medications. However, these analyses were underpowered, and it is certainly possible that medication usage impacted our results. We prioritized the overall representativeness of our sample relative to precluding possible medication effects in this study, but this issue warrants further investigation.

One other potential limitation involves our use of actigraphy. Although actigraphy possesses many important advantages, including allowing researchers to assess sleep unobtrusively while participants sleep in their own environment, its use is not well-established in pediatric populations. It appears to possess high sensitivity with regard to sleep but may overestimate wakefulness after sleep onset (Meltzer, Montgomery-Downs, et al., 2012; Meltzer, Walsh, et al., 2012; Short, Gradisar, Lack, Wright, & Carskadon, 2012). Our data indicated relatively high levels of wakefulness after sleep onset for both groups that was not reflected in sleep diaries, and thus may have been an overestimate. Even with the use of event markers, actigraphy relies heavily on manual entry of the time that participants attempted to fall asleep (i.e., bedtime). Thus, actigraphic measurement of sleep onset latency is of questionable validity. Further validation of actigraphy as a measure of sleep in pediatric and clinical populations is needed.

This study extends previous knowledge on the connections between sleep and anxiety among pediatric populations and suggests several future directions for research in this area. This is now the second study (see also Cousins et al., 2011) to report a prospective temporal relationship between nightly sleep parameters and subsequent mood among anxious youth. However, to make conclusions regarding causality, future studies might choose to employ sleep restriction/extension procedures and identify associated changes in anxiety symptoms and underlying processes (e.g., attentional biases toward threat), as well as examine changes in positive affect. In addition, it will be important for future studies to address whether anxious children and adolescents actually have a greater sleep need than their healthy peers. It may be possible to do this by examining relationships between objective sleep parameters and subjective and objective measures of sleepiness (e.g., multiple sleep latency test; Carskadon et al., 1986) and measures of neurobehavioral impairment (e.g., psychomotor vigilance task; Van Dongen, Maislin, Mullington, & Dinges, 2003). Sleep duration could be carefully manipulated, with examination of changes in these domains among anxious and healthy youth. Also, we would welcome future studies employing behavioral treatment of sleep disturbance among anxious youth, with subjective and objective measurement of sleep outcomes. From such trials, it may be possible to discern which changes across subjective or objective sleep measures are most closely connected with improved overall functioning.

FUNDING

This research was supported by a Research Scholar Award from the Research Institute at Children's Hospital Colorado, pilot funds from the Developmental Psychobiology Research Group at the University of Colorado Denver, and NIMH K23 MH108640. Data collection and management was supported by a Development and Informatics Service Center grant (NIH/NCRR UL1 RR025780) to the Colorado Clinical and Translational Sciences Institute.

REFERENCES

Alfano, C. A., Beidel, D. C., Turner, S. M., & Lewin, D. S. (2006). Preliminary evidence for sleep complaints among children referred for anxiety. *Sleep Medicine*, *7*(6), 467–473. doi:10.1016/j.sleep.2006.05.002

Alfano, C. A., Ginsburg, G. S., & Kingery, J. N. (2007). Sleep-related problems among children and adolescents with anxiety disorders. *Journal of the American Academy of Child and Adolescent Psychiatry*, *46*(2), 224–232. doi:10.1097/01.chi.0000242233.06011.8e

Alfano, C. A., Patriquin, M. A., & Reyes, A. D. L. (2015). Subjective – objective sleep comparisons and discrepancies among clinically-anxious and healthy children. *Journal of Abnormal Child Psychology*, 1–11. doi:10.1007/s10802-015-0018-7

Alfano, C. A., Pina, A. A., Zerr, A. A., & Villalta, I. K. (2010). Pre-sleep arousal and sleep problems of anxiety-disordered youth. *Child Psychiatry & Human Development*, *41*(2), 156–167. doi:10.1007/s10578-009-0158-5

Alfano, C. A., Reynolds, K., Scott, N., Dahl, R. E., & Mellman, T. A. (2013). Polysomnographic sleep patterns of non-depressed, non-medicated children with generalized anxiety disorder. *Journal of Affective Disorders*, *147*(1–3), 379–384. doi:10.1016/j.jad.2012.08.015

Alfano, C. A., Zakem, A. H., Costa, N. M., Taylor, L. K., & Weems, C. F. (2009). Sleep problems and their relation to cognitive factors, anxiety, and depressive symptoms in children and adolescents. *Depression and Anxiety*, *26*(6), 503–512. doi:10.1002/da.20443

American Psychiatric Association. (2000). *Diagnostic and statistical manual of mental disorders* (4th ed., text rev.). Washington, DC: Author.

American Psychiatric Association. (2013). *Diagnostic and statistical manual of mental disorders* (5th ed.). Washington, DC: Author.

Angold, A., Costello, E. J., Messer, S. C., & Pickles, A. (1995). Development of a short questionnaire for use in epidemiological studies of depression in children and adolescents. *International Journal of Methods in Psychiatric Research*, *5*(4), 237–249.

Babson, K. A., Trainor, C. D., Feldner, M. T., & Blumenthal, H. (2010). A test of the effects of acute sleep deprivation on general and specific self-reported anxiety and depressive symptoms: An experimental extension. *Journal of Behavior Therapy and Experimental Psychiatry*, *41*(3), 297–303. doi:10.1016/j.jbtep.2010.02.008

Baglioni, C., Spiegelhalder, K., Lombardo, C., & Riemann, D. (2010). Sleep and emotions: A focus on insomnia. *Sleep Medicine Reviews*, *14*(4), 227–238. doi:10.1016/j.smrv.2009.10.007

Baum, K. T., Desai, A., Field, J., Miller, L. E., Rausch, J., & Beebe, D. W. (2013). Sleep restriction worsens mood and emotion regulation in adolescents. *Journal of Child Psychology and Psychiatry*, *55*(2), 180–190. doi:10.1111/jcpp.12125

Beebe, D. W., Fallone, G., Godiwala, N., Flanigan, M., Martin, D., Schaffner, L., & Amin, R. (2008). Feasibility and behavioral effects of an at-home multi-night sleep restriction protocol for adolescents. *Journal of Child Psychology and Psychiatry*, *49*(9), 915–923. doi:10.1111/jcpp.2008.49.issue-9

Birmaher, B., Brent, D. A., Chiappetta, L., Bridge, J., Monga, S., & Baugher, M. (1999). Psychometric properties of the Screen for Child Anxiety Related Emotional Disorders (SCARED): A replication study. *Journal of the American Academy of Child and Adolescent Psychiatry, 38*(10), 1230–1236. doi:10.1097/00004583-199910000-00011

Birmaher, B., Khetarpal, S., Brent, D., Cully, M., Balach, L., Kaufman, J., & Neer, S. M. (1997). The Screen for Child Anxiety Related Emotional Disorders (SCARED): Scale construction and psychometric characteristics. *Journal of the American Academy of Child and Adolescent Psychiatry, 36*(4), 545–553. doi:10.1097/00004583-199704000-00018

Birmaher, B., Waterman, G. S., Ryan, N. D., Perel, J., McNabb, J., Balach, L., … Rao, U. (1998). Randomized, controlled trial of amitriptyline versus placebo for adolescents with "treatment-resistant" major depression. *Journal of the American Academy of Child and Adolescent Psychiatry, 37*(5), 527–535. doi:10.1097/00004583-199805000-00015

Caporino, N. E., Read, K. L., Shiffrin, N., Settipani, C., Kendall, P. C., Compton, S. N., … Albano, A. M. (2015). Sleep-related problems and the effects of anxiety treatment in children and adolescents. *Journal of Clinical Child & Adolescent Psychology, 0*(0), 1–11. doi:10.1080/15374416.2015.1063429

Carskadon, M. A., & Acebo, C. (1993). A self-administered rating scale for pubertal development. *The Journal of Adolescent Health: Official Publication of the Society for Adolescent Medicine, 14*(3), 190–195. doi:10.1016/1054-139X(93)90004-9

Carskadon, M. A., Dement, W. C., Mitler, M. M., Roth, T., Westbrook, P. R., & Keenan, S. (1986). Guidelines for the multiple sleep latency test (MSLT): A standard measure of sleepiness. *Sleep, 9*(4), 519–524.

Chase, R. M., & Pincus, D. B. (2011). Sleep-related problems in children and adolescents with anxiety disorders. *Behavioral Sleep Medicine, 9*(4), 224–236. doi:10.1080/15402002.2011.606768

Cousins, J. C., Whalen, D. J., Dahl, R. E., Forbes, E. E., Olino, T. M., Ryan, N. D., & Silk, J. S. (2011). The bidirectional association between daytime affect and nighttime sleep in youth with anxiety and depression. *Journal of Pediatric Psychology, 36*(9), 969–979. doi:10.1093/jpepsy/jsr036

Cowie, J., Alfano, C. A., Patriquin, M. A., Reynolds, K. C., Talavera, D., & Clementi, M. A. (2014). Addressing sleep in children with anxiety disorders. *Sleep Medicine Clinics, 9*(2), 137–148. doi:10.1016/j.jsmc.2014.02.001

Dalgleish, T., & Watts, F. N. (1990). Biases of attention and memory in disorders of anxiety and depression. *Clinical Psychology Review, 10*(5), 589–604. doi:10.1016/0272-7358(90)90098-U

Daviss, W. B., Birmaher, B., Melhem, N. A., Axelson, D. A., Michaels, S. M., & Brent, D. A. (2006). Criterion validity of the Mood and Feelings Questionnaire for depressive episodes in clinic and non-clinic subjects. *Journal of Child Psychology and Psychiatry, 47*(9), 927–934. doi:10.1111/j.1469-7610.2006.01646.x

Dewald, J. F., Meijer, A. M., Oort, F. J., Kerkhof, G. A., & Bögels, S. M. (2010). The influence of sleep quality, sleep duration and sleepiness on school performance in children and adolescents: A meta-analytic review. *Sleep Medicine Reviews, 14*(3), 179–189. doi:10.1016/j.smrv.2009.10.004

Fallone, G., Acebo, C., Arnedt, J. T., Seifer, R., & Carskadon, M. A. (2001). Effects of acute sleep restriction on behavior, sustained attention, and response inhibition in children. *Perceptual and Motor Skills, 93*(1), 213–229. doi:10.2466/pms.2001.93.1.213

Finan, P. H., Quartana, P. J., & Smith, M. T. (2015). The effects of sleep continuity disruption on positive mood and sleep architecture in healthy adults. *Sleep, 38*(11), 1735–1742. doi:10.5665/sleep.5154

Forbes, E. E., Bertocci, M. A., Gregory, A. M., Ryan, N. D., Axelson, D. A., Birmaher, B., & Dahl, R. E. (2008). Objective sleep in pediatric anxiety disorders and major depressive disorder. *Journal of the American Academy of Child & Adolescent Psychiatry, 47*(2), 148–155. doi:10.1097/chi.0b013e31815cd9bc

Fricke-Oerkermann, L., Plück, J., Schredl, M., Heinz, K., Mitschke, A., Wiater, A., & Lehmkuhl, G. (2007). Prevalence and course of sleep problems in childhood. *Sleep, 30*(10), 1371–1377.

Geller, B., Cooper, T. B., Graham, D. L., Fetner, H. H., Marsteller, F. A., & Wells, J. M. (1993). Pharmacokinetically designed double-blind placebo-controlled study of nortriptyline in 6- to 12-year-olds with major depressive disorder. *Journal of the American Academy of Child and Adolescent Psychiatry, 31*(1), 32–44. doi:10.1097/00004583-199201000-00007

Goldstein, A. N., Greer, S. M., Saletin, J. M., Harvey, A. G., Nitschke, J. B., & Walker, M. P. (2013). Tired and apprehensive: Anxiety amplifies the impact of sleep loss on aversive brain anticipation. *The Journal of Neuroscience, 33*(26), 10607–10615. doi:10.1523/JNEUROSCI.5578-12.2013

Gradisar, M., Gardner, G., & Dohnt, H. (2011). Recent worldwide sleep patterns and problems during adolescence: A review and meta-analysis of age, region, and sleep. *Sleep Medicine, 12*(2), 110–118. doi:10.1016/j.sleep.2010.11.008

Greenhill, L. L., Pliszka, S., & Dulcan, M. K. (2002). Practice parameter for the use of stimulant medications in the treatment of children, adolescents, and adults. *Journal of the American Academy of Child & Adolescent Psychiatry, 41*(2), 26S–49S. doi:10.1097/00004583-200202001-00003

Hale, W. W.III,, Raaijmakers, Q., Muris, P., & Meeus, W. (2005). Psychometric properties of the Screen for Child Anxiety Related Emotional Disorders (SCARED) in the general adolescent population. *Journal of the American Academy of Child and Adolescent Psychiatry, 44*(3), 283–290. doi:10.1097/00004583-200503000-00013

Harris, P. A., Taylor, R., Theilke, R., Payne, J., Gonzalez, J. G., & Conde, A. (2009). Research electronic data capture (REDCap): A metadata-driven methodology and workflow process for providing translational research informatics support. *Journal of Biomedical Informatics, 42*(2), 377–381. doi:10.1016/j.jbi.2008.08.010

Harvey, A. G. (2002). A cognitive model of insomnia. *Behaviour Research and Therapy, 40*(8), 869–893. doi:10.1016/S0005-7967(01)00061-4

Hoehn-Saric, R., & McLeod, D. R. (1988). The peripheral sympathetic nervous system: Its role in normal and pathologic anxiety. *Psychiatric Clinics of North America, 11*(2), 375–386.

Hudson, J. L., Gradisar, M., Gamble, A., Schniering, C. A., & Rebelo, I. (2009). The sleep patterns and problems of clinically anxious children. *Behaviour Research and Therapy, 47*(4), 339–344. doi:10.1016/j.brat.2009.01.006

Ivanenko, A., Crabtree, V. M., Obrien, L. M., & Gozal, D. (2006). Sleep complaints and psychiatric symptoms in children evaluated at a pediatric mental health clinic. *Journal of Clinical Sleep Medicine, 2*(1), 42–48.

Kahn, A., Van De Merckt, C., Rebuffat, E., Mozin, M. J., Sottiaux, M., Blum, D., & Hennart, P. (1989). Sleep problems in healthy preadolescents. *Pediatrics, 84*(3), 542–546.

Kahn, M., Sheppes, G., & Sadeh, A. (2013). Sleep and emotions: Bidirectional links and underlying mechanisms. *International Journal of Psychophysiology, 89*(2), 218–228. doi:10.1016/j.ijpsycho.2013.05.010

Kane, J. M., & Sharif, Z. A. (2008). Atypical antipsychotics: Sedation versus efficacy. *The Journal of Clinical Psychiatry, 69*(Suppl. 1), 18–31.

Kecklund, G., & Åkerstedt, T. (2004). Apprehension of the subsequent working day is associated with a low amount of slow wave sleep. *Biological Psychology, 66*(2), 169–176. doi:10.1016/j.biopsycho.2003.10.004

Kendall, P. C., & Pimentel, S. S. (2003). On the physiological symptom constellation in youth with Generalized Anxiety Disorder (GAD). *Journal of Anxiety Disorders, 17*(2), 211–221. doi:10.1016/S0887-6185(02)00196-2

Kent, L., Vostanis, P., & Feehan, C. (1997). Detection of major and minor depression in children and adolescents: Evaluation of the Mood and Feelings Questionnaire. *Child Psychology & Psychiatry & Allied Disciplines, 38*(5), 565–573. doi:10.1111/j.1469-7610.1997.tb01543.x

Lyonfields, J. D., Borkovec, T. D., & Thayer, J. F. (1995). Vagal tone in generalized anxiety disorder and the effects of aversive imagery and worrisome thinking. *Behavior Therapy, 26*(3), 457–466. doi:10.1016/S0005-7894(05)80094-2

Martin, S. E., Engleman, H. M., Deary, I. J., & Douglas, N. J. (1996). The effect of sleep fragmentation on daytime function. *American Journal of Respiratory and Critical Care Medicine*, *153*(4), 1328–1332. doi:10.1164/ajrccm.153.4.8616562

Masi, G., Millepiedi, S., Mucci, M., Poli, P., Bertini, N., & Milantoni, L. (2004). Generalized anxiety disorder in referred children and adolescents. *Journal of the American Academy of Child & Adolescent Psychiatry*, *43* (6), 752–760. doi:10.1097/01.chi.0000121065.29744.d3

McKnight-Eily, L. R., Eaton, D. K., Lowry, R., Croft, J. B., Presley-Cantrell, L., & Perry, G. S. (2011). Relationships between hours of sleep and health-risk behaviors in US adolescent students. *Preventive Medicine*, *53*(4–5), 271–273. doi:10.1016/j.ypmed.2011.06.020

Meltzer, L. J., Biggs, S., Reynolds, A., Avis, K. T., Crabtree, V. M., & Bevans, K. B. (2012). The Children's Report of Sleep Patterns–Sleepiness Scale: A self-report measure for school-aged children. *Sleep Medicine*, *13*(4), 385–389. doi:10.1016/j.sleep.2011.12.004

Meltzer, L. J., Brimeyer, C., Russell, K., Avis, K. T., Biggs, S., Reynolds, A. C., & Crabtree, V. M. (2014). The Children's Report of Sleep Patterns: Validity and reliability of the Sleep Hygiene Index and Sleep Disturbance Scale in adolescents. *Sleep Medicine*, *15*(12), 1500–1507. doi:10.1016/j.sleep.2014.08.010

Meltzer, L. J., Montgomery-Downs, H. E., Insana, S. P., & Walsh, C. M. (2012). Use of actigraphy for assessment in pediatric sleep research. *Sleep Medicine Reviews*, *16*(5), 463–475. doi:10.1016/j.smrv.2011.10.002

Meltzer, L. J., Walsh, C. M., Traylor, J., & Westin, A. M. L. (2012). Direct comparison of two new actigraphs and polysomnography in children and adolescents. *Sleep*. doi:10.5665/sleep.1608

Merikangas, K. R., He, J.-P., Burstein, M., Swanson, S. A., Avenevoli, S., Cui, L., … Swendsen, J. (2010). Lifetime prevalence of mental disorders in U.S. adolescents: Results from the National Comorbidity Survey Replication–Adolescent Supplement (NCS-A). *Journal of the American Academy of Child and Adolescent Psychiatry*, *49*(10), 980–989. doi:10.1016/j.jaac.2010.05.017

Messer, S. C., Angold, A., Costello, E. J., Loeber, R., Van Kammen, W., & Stouthamer-Loeber, M. (1995). Development of a short questionnaire for use in epidemiological studies of depression in children and adolescents: Factor composition and structure across development. *International Journal of Methods in Psychiatric Research*, *5*(4), 251–262.

Monti, J. M., & Monti, D. (2000). Sleep disturbance in generalized anxiety disorder and its treatment. *Sleep Medicine Reviews*, *4*(3), 263–276. doi:10.1053/smrv.1999.0096

Morrison, D. N., McGee, R., & Stanton, W. R. (1992). Sleep problems in adolescence. *Journal of the American Academy of Child and Adolescent Psychiatry*, *31*(1), 94–99. doi:10.1097/00004583-199201000-00014

Ohayon, M. M., Roberts, R. E., Zulley, J., Smirne, S., & Priest, R. G. (2000). Prevalence and patterns of problematic sleep among older adolescents. *Journal of the American Academy of Child and Adolescent Psychiatry*, *39*(12), 1549–1556. doi:10.1097/00004583-200012000-00019

Owens, J. A., Spirito, A., McGuinn, M., & Nobile, C. (2000). Sleep habits and sleep disturbance in elementary school-aged children. *Journal of Developmental and Behavioral Pediatrics*, *21*(1), 27–36. doi:10.1097/00004703-200002000-00004

Paavonen, E. J., Aronen, E. T., Moilanen, I., Piha, J., Räsänen, E., Tamminen, T., & Almqvist, F. (2000). Sleep problems of school-aged children: A complementary view. *Acta Paediatrica*, *89*(2), 223–228. doi:10.1111/j.1651-2227.2000.tb01220.x

Paavonen, E. J., Räikkönen, K., Lahti, J., Komsi, N., Heinonen, K., Pesonen, A.-K., … Porkka-Heiskanen, T. (2009). Short sleep duration and behavioral symptoms of attention-deficit/hyperactivity disorder in healthy 7- to 8-year-old children. *Pediatrics*, *123*(5), e857–864. doi:10.1542/peds.2008-2164

Papadimitriou, G. N., & Linkowski, P. (2005). Sleep disturbance in anxiety disorders. *International Review of Psychiatry*, *17*(4), 229–236. doi:10.1080/09540260500104524

Patriquin, M. A., Mellman, T. A., Glaze, D. G., & Alfano, C. A. (2014). Polysomnographic sleep characteristics of generally-anxious and healthy children assessed in the home environment. *Journal of Affective Disorders*, *161*, 79–83. doi:10.1016/j.jad.2014.02.037

Peterman, J. S., Carper, M. M., Elkins, R. M., Comer, J. S., Pincus, D. B., & Kendall, P. C. (2016). The effects of cognitive-behavioral therapy for youth anxiety on sleep problems. *Journal of Anxiety Disorders*, *37*, 78–88. doi:10.1016/j.janxdis.2015.11.006

Respironics Inc. (2011). Actiwatch communication and sleep analysis software. Murrysville, PA: Author.

Sadeh, A., Gruber, R., & Raviv, A. (2002). Sleep, neurobehavioral functioning, and behavior problems in school-age children. *Child Development*, *73*(2), 405–417. doi:10.1111/cdev.2002.73.issue-2

Sadeh, A., Raviv, A., & Gruber, R. (2000). Sleep patterns and sleep disruptions in school-age children. *Developmental Psychology*, *36*(3), 291–301. doi:10.1037/0012-1649.36.3.291

Sadeh, A., Sharkey, K. M., & Carskadon, M. A. (1994). Activity-based sleep-wake identification: An empirical test of methodological issues. *Sleep*, *17*(3), 201–207.

Sheehan, D. V., Sheehan, K. H., Shytle, R. D., Janavs, J., Bannon, Y., Rogers, J. E., … Wilkinson, B. (2010). Reliability and validity of the Mini International Neuropsychiatric Interview for Children and Adolescents (MINI-KID). *The Journal of Clinical Psychiatry*, *71*(3), 313–326. doi:10.4088/JCP.09m05305whi

Shirtcliff, E. A., Dahl, R. E., & Pollak, S. D. (2009). Pubertal development: Correspondence between hormonal and physical development. *Child Development*, *80*(2), 327–337. doi:10.1111/j.1467-8624.2009.01263.x

Short, M. A., Gradisar, M., Lack, L. C., Wright, H., & Carskadon, M. A. (2012). The discrepancy between actigraphic and sleep diary measures of sleep in adolescents. *Sleep Medicine*, *13*(4), 378–384. doi:10.1016/j.sleep.2011.11.005

Steenari, M.-R., Vuontela, V., Paavonen, E. J., Carlson, S., Fjallberg, M., & Aronen, E. (2003). Working memory and sleep in 6- to 13-year-old schoolchildren. *Journal of the American Academy of Child and Adolescent Psychiatry*, *42*(1), 85–92. doi:10.1097/00004583-200301000-00014

Suveg, C., & Zeman, J. (2004). Emotion regulation in children with anxiety disorders. *Journal of Clinical Child & Adolescent Psychology*, *33*(4), 750–759. doi:10.1207/s15374424jccp3304_10

Thayer, J. F., Friedman, B. H., & Borkovec, T. D. (1996). Autonomic characteristics of generalized anxiety disorder and worry. *Biological Psychiatry*, *39*(4), 255–266. doi:10.1016/0006-3223(95)00136-0

Thayer, J., & Lane, R. D. (2007). The role of vagal function in the risk for cardiovascular disease and mortality. *Biological Psychology*, *74*(2), 224–242. doi:10.1016/j.biopsycho.2005.11.013

Tsypes, A., Aldao, A., & Mennin, D. S. (2013). Emotion dysregulation and sleep difficulties in generalized anxiety disorder. *Journal of Anxiety Disorders*, *27*(2), 197–203. doi:10.1016/j.janxdis.2013.01.008

Van Dongen, H. P. A., Maislin, G., Mullington, J. M., & Dinges, D. F. (2003). The cumulative cost of additional wakefulness: Dose-response effects on neurobehavioral functions and sleep physiology from chronic sleep restriction and total sleep deprivation. *Sleep: Journal of Sleep and Sleep Disorders Research*, *26*(2), 117–126.

Walker, M. P., & Van Der Helm, E. (2009). Overnight therapy? The role of sleep in emotional brain processing. *Psychological Bulletin*, *135*(5), 731–748. doi:10.1037/a0016570

Wilson, S., & Argyropoulos, S. (2005). Antidepressants and Sleep: A Qualitative Review of the Literature. *Drugs*, *65*(7), 927–947. doi:10.2165/00003495-200565070-00003

Wolfson, A. R., & Carskadon, M. A. (1998). Sleep schedules and daytime functioning in adolescents. *Child Development*, *69*(4), 875–887. doi:10.1111/j.1467-8624.1998.tb06149.x

Yoo, S. S., Gujar, N., Hu, P., Jolesz, F. A., & Walker, M. P. (2007). The human emotional brain without sleep—A prefrontal amygdala disconnect. *Current Biology*, *23*(17), 88–89.

SUPPLEMENTAL TABLE 1

Sleep Comparison between GAD Participants Taking Versus Not Taking Medications

	Medication+[a]	Medication–[b]	Test Statistic	*d*	*p*
Sleep Diary					
Sleep Duration (min)	489.66 (57.22)	469.21 (70.39)	$t = .72$	.32	.48
Wake After Sleep Onset (min)	15.32 (16.49)	16.10 (15.66)	$t = -.10$	–.05	.92
Sleep Efficiency (%)	92.47 (5.29)	88.61 (10.87)	$t = -1.20$	.46	.24
Sleep Onset Latency (min)	26.09 (19.0)	42.90 (44.95)	$t = -1.34$	–.49	.20
Sleep Quality Rating (1 = Horrible, 6 = Excellent)	3.62 (.64)	3.67 (.89)	$t = -.12$	–.06	.89
Actigraphy					
Sleep Duration (min)	426.91 (34.55)	418.69 (25.23)	$t = .42$	.27	.68
Wake After Sleep Onset (min)	58.01 (23.14)	71.81 (32.27)	$t = -1.17$	–.49	.25
Sleep Efficiency (%)	80.07 (5.73)	78.95 (8.66)	$t = .38$	.15	.71
Sleep Onset Latency (min)	33.21 (25.65)	29.97 (24.33)	$t = .27$	.12	.79

Note: Medication+ = participants taking psychiatric medication; Medication– = participants not taking psychiatric medication.
[a]$n = 20$.
[b]$n = 6$.

SUPPLEMENTAL TABLE 2

Correlations between Sleep Parameters Assessed via Sleep Diary, Actigraphy, and Questionnaire

	Sleep Duration^D	Wake After Sleep Onset^D	Sleep Efficiency^D	Sleep Onset Latency^D	Sleep Duration^A	Wake After Sleep Onset^A	Sleep Efficiency^A	Sleep Onset Latency^A	CRSP Insomnia Score	CRSP Sleepiness Score
Sleep Duration^D	–	.55*	–.36	–.38	.74**	.57*	–.17	.04	.01	.12
Wake After Sleep Onset^D	–.01	–	–.79**	.40	–.31	.22	–.31	.07	.47	.37
Sleep Efficiency^D	.39	–.74**	–	–.86**	.28	.01	.21	–.25	–.31	–.04
Sleep Onset Latency^D	–36	.53**	–.96**	–	–.06	.01	–.21	.35	.14	–.18
Sleep Duration^A	.70**	.40	.01	–.10	–	.31	.24	–.02	–.01	–.13
Wake After Sleep Onset^A	.32	.06	–.10	.19	.13	–	–.71**	–.09	.29	.53*
Sleep Efficiency^A	.06	–.18	.45*	–.56**	.30	.70**	–	–.24	–.28	–.42
Sleep Onset Latency^A	–.27	.50*	–.70**	.72**	–.25	.15	–.74**	–	.09	–.17
CRSP Insomnia Score	–.32	.51*	–.70**	.65**	.04	–.28	.19	.21	–	.40
CRSP Sleepiness Score	.05	.08	–.18	.22	.05	.00	–.03	.12	.26	–

Note: Supplemental Table 1 presents correlations between sleep parameters separately for controls and participants with GAD: correlations presented above the diagonal are for healthy controls, and correlations below the diagonal are for participants with GAD.
^{D} = assessed via sleep diary, ^{A} = assessed via actigraphy, CRSP = Children's Report of Sleep Patterns self-report version. $^*p < .05$ $^{**}p < .01$.

SUPPLEMENTAL TABLE 3

Group Comparisons Across Select CRSP Subscales

	GAD[a]	Control[b]	Test Statistic	*d*	*p*
Adolescent Report					
Bedtime Fears/Worries	4.67 (2.08)	2.94 (1.14)	$t = 3.06$	1.03	<.01
Restless Legs	10.52 (4.08)	8.18 (2.40)	$t = 2.09$	.69	.04
Parasomnias	3.05 (1.12)	2.65 (.70)	$t = 1.29$	.43	.21
Insomnia	18.10 (4.28)	12.59 (3.57)	$t = 4.24$	1.38	<.001
Sleepiness	11.71 (5.16)	8.65 (2.83)	$t = 2.20$	.72	.04
Parent Report					
Bedtime Fears/Worries	4.14 (1.74)	2.59 (.80)	$t = 3.40$	1.11	<.01
Restless Legs	6.05 (1.75)	6.29 (1.90)	$t = -.42$	–.13	.68
Parasomnias	2.43 (.60)	2.59 (.71)	$t = .75$	–.25	.46
Insomnia	17.10 (5.21)	11.18 (2.90)	$t = 4.19$	1.40	<.001
Sleepiness	7.10 (2.12)	6.65 (2.57)	$t = .59$	.17	.56

Note: CRSP = Children's Report of Sleep Patterns; GAD = Generalized anxiety disorder.
[a]$n = 21$.
[b]$n = 17$.

Does an Online CBT Program for Anxiety Impact Upon Sleep Problems in Anxious Youth?

Caroline L. Donovan and Susan H. Spence

Sonja March

This study aimed to assess whether the transdiagnostic therapy elements of an online cognitive behaviour therapy anxiety program also impact on sleep-related problems (SRPs) in anxious youth. Participants were drawn from two previously published studies evaluating online cognitive behaviour therapy for child anxiety (BRAVE-ONLINE). The study included 63 children 7–12 years of age (M = 9.49, SD = 1.37) and 71 adolescents 12–18 years of age (M = 13.90, SD = 1.68). SRPs, severity of anxiety diagnosis, anxiety symptoms, number of diagnoses, depressive symptoms, and global functioning were assessed at pre-, post-, and 6-month follow-up assessment points. SRPs were positively related to anxiety symptoms and severity for children and were positively related to depression for adolescents. SRPs did not differ between male and female participants, between children and adolescents, or between those who had generalised anxiety disorder in their profile and those who did not. Finally, children but not adolescents participating in the online program demonstrated a significantly greater reduction in SRPs from pre- to posttreatment compared to the waitlist group, and these gains were maintained at 6-month follow-up. Treatment focusing on child anxiety alone may reduce SRPs in children but not adolescents. Although further research is clearly needed, clinicians should ensure that they assess for SRPs in their teenage clients and directly target SRPs in treatment where required.

INTRODUCTION

Anxiety in children and adolescents is common, with 12.3% of children and 11% of adolescents meeting criteria for an anxiety disorder (Costello, Egger, Copeland, Erkanli, & Angold, 2011), and 22.7% of youth suffering with an anxiety disorder by the time they reach young adulthood (Copeland, Angold, Shanahan, & Costello, 2014). Along with high prevalence comes a myriad of deleterious consequences for young people with anxiety disorders. Short- and long-term problems associated with academic performance, family relationships, social interaction, substance use, and depression have been found (Ialongo, Edelsohn, Werthamer-Larsson, Crockett, & Kellam, 1994, 1995; Wolitzky-Taylor, Bobova, Zinbarg, Mineka, & Craske, 2012), with childhood anxiety being associated with health, financial and interpersonal problems in adulthood (Copeland et al., 2014).

Fortunately, efficacious treatments exist for youth anxiety disorders, with cognitive behaviour therapy (CBT) being viewed as the treatment of choice (Compton et al., 2004). Despite the efficacy of CBT for anxiety, up to 80% of anxious children do not seek or receive assistance for a variety of reasons, including lack of appropriate services, therapy costs, stigma, and the time-poor nature of busy families (Booth et al., 2004; Lawrence et al., 2015; Merikangas et al., 2011). In recent years, there has been a surge of interest in alternative modes of treatment delivery aimed at overcoming such barriers, with computer and online approaches offering unique benefits. They are extremely flexible, have the potential to reach a greater proportion of the population, offer a sense of anonymity, and have the potential to be cost-effective.

There have been relatively few studies investigating the efficacy of computer-based treatments for child anxiety. In a systematic review of 11 studies examining the efficacy of six computerised CBT programs targeting youth anxiety, Donovan and March (2014a) concluded that programs comprising a variety of CBT anxiety management strategies and that include exposure therapy are able to produce reductions in diagnostic status, severity, and self-reported anxiety symptoms. Of those 11 studies, four were conducted on the BRAVE-ONLINE program, a therapist-mediated, Internet-based CBT program for youth anxiety disorders. There have now been four randomised controlled trials conducted with anxious preschoolers (Donovan & March, 2014b), school-age children (March, Spence, & Donovan, 2009; Spence, Holmes, March, & Lipp, 2006), and adolescents (Spence et al., 2011), with all studies demonstrating signficantly greater improvements in anxiety for treatment versus waitlist control participants from pre- to posttreatment, with treatment gains maintained at follow-up. Furthermore, in two of the studies (Spence et al., 2011; Spence et al., 2006), face-to-face CBT comparison groups were employed, with no differences being found between Internet-based and face-to-face therapy approaches in terms of efficacy. Thus, it would seem that the BRAVE-ONLINE program is effective in treating child and adolescent anxiety disorders.

Sleep Problems in Youth With Anxiety Disorders

Common to youth suffering with anxiety disorders are sleep-related problems (SRPs), with around 90% of clinically anxious children reporting comorbid SRPs (Chase & Pincus, 2011). There appears to be a stronger association between SRPs and anxiety than between SRPs and other psychiatric problems (Gregory, Eley, O'Connor, & Plomin, 2004), and when anxious children have a comorbid SRP, the anxiety disorder tends to be more severe (Chase & Pincus, 2011). Furthermore, it has been found that SRPs tend to predate the onset of child anxiety disorders (Gregory et al., 2004) and that there are bidirectional and cyclical associations between the two disorders, with sleep issues leading to heightened anxiety and anxiety leading to greater sleep problems (Peterman, Carper, & Kendall, 2014).

SRPs themselves are extremely common in young people, with up to 40% of youth reporting issues in this domain (Alfano, Zakem, Costa, Taylor, & Weems, 2009; Gregory & Sadeh, 2012). Like anxiety, SRPs in children and adolescents are associated with numerous problems both in the short and long term, including anxiety, depression, inattention, impulsivity, poor daytime functioning, disruptive behaviour, academic problems, suicidal ideation, overweight and/or obesity status, and substance use (Do, Shin, Bautista, & Foo, 2013; Gregory & O'Connor, 2002; Morrison, McGee, & Stanton, 1992; Shanahan, Copeland, Angold, Bondy, & Costello, 2014; Short, Gradisar, Lack, & Wright, 2013; Short, Gradisar, Lack, Wright, & Dohnt, 2013; Wong & Brower, 2012). Thus, both anxiety and sleep problems are common and problematic in young people, and commonly occur together.

Underpinning the high comorbidy rates of child anxiety disorders and SRPs appears to be a complex interplay of biological, cognitive, and environmental factors (Peterman et al., 2014). In terms of biological factors, the prefrontal cortex is implicated in both sleep regulation and the integration of higher cognitive processing and emotion regulation (e.g., limbic system), with the medial prefrontal cortex in particular being important in the regulation of the amygdala, a section of the brain specficially related to the fear response (Peterman et al., 2014). Underarousal of the prefrontal cortex has been found in those with anxiety and SRPs, lending support for a shared biological pathway (Altena et al., 2008).

With regard to cognitive factors, sleep deprivation has been shown to lead to higher levels of arousal and deficits in emotional processing (Yoo, Gujar, Hu, Jolesz, & Walker, 2007), and similarly high levels of both cognitive (worry and negative thoughts) and somatic (physiological) arousal are associated with limbic system arousal and higher cortisol levels respectively, leading to SRPs (Peterman et al., 2014). In other words, anxious children have many negative thoughts and worries, particularly at bedtime, and are ill-equipped to self-regulate the arousal the thoughts produce. Presleep arousal then activates the limbic system, which might not be well regulated due to the effects of sleep deprivation on the prefrontal cortex. Thus, young people sleep poorly, which leads to further arousal and deficits in emotional processing, and the cycle continues.

In terms of environmental factors, parental accomodation, avoidance, and safety behaviours have all been shown to play a role in both SRPs and anxiety in children (Cowie et al., 2014; Peterman et al., 2014). For instance, parents may allow their anxious child to sleep in their bed and/or to avoid going to sleep by using media. Children may frequently seek reassurance by asking parents to come into their room after lights-out to answer questions. Allowing the child to co-sleep reinforces the child's anxiety around sleep and has been shown to increase sleep problems and separation anxiety (Tikotzky & Sadeh, 2010). Furthermore, parental accommodation, avoidance, and safety behaviours interfere with children learning to reduce their own arousal and to self-soothe (Cowie et al., 2014). Thus, comorbidity between anxiety and sleep problems is high and appears to be due to a number of shared biological, cognitive, and environmental factors.

Whether the association between anxiety and sleep differs depending on type of anxiety disorder, age, and gender has also been of empirical interest. With respect to diagnostic profile, it has generally been found that youth diagnosed with generalised anxiety disorder (GAD) report the highest rate of SRPs (Alfano, Beidel, Turner, & Lewin, 2006;

Alfano, Ginsburg, & Kingery, 2007; Alfano, Pina, Zerr, & Villalta, 2010). In terms of age, the results are somewhat mixed. Some authors have found similar rates of SRPs across anxious children and adolescents (Alfano et al., 2006; Chase & Pincus, 2011), whereas others have suggested that the association between anxiety and SRPs increases as youth become older (Gregory & O'Connor, 2002; Johnson, Chilcoat, & Breslau, 2000). With respect to gender differences, it would seem that the association between anxiety and SRPs does not differ between male and female individuals (Alfano et al., 2007; Alfano et al., 2009; Chase & Pincus, 2011; Hansen, Skirbekk, Oerbeck, Richter, & Kristensen, 2011), although Storch et al. (2008) found that female OCD sufferers reported more SRPs than male sufferers. Furthermore, there may be some gender differences in terms of particular SRPs, with girls being found to demonstrate greater bedtime resistance and sleep anxiety than boys (Alfano et al., 2010).

Given the high comorbidity rates, common underlying maintaining mechanisms, and bidirectional and cyclical associations between youth anxiety disorders and SRPs, it is reasonable to suggest that treating the anxiety disorder may lead to a reduction in SRPs, even if the SRPs themselves are not directly addressed in treatment. This is particularly likely given that CBT treatments for both disorders consist of common therapy elements such as relaxation, cognitive restructuring, self-monitoring, parent management training, psychoeducation, contingency management, guided imagery, and coping self-talk (Peterman et al., 2014). Indeed, a reduction in SRPs following treatment for anxiety has been found to be the case, although the majority of research in this area has been conducted with adults. A meta-analysis of 19 studies examining the effectiveness of CBT for anxiety on SRPs in adults found a moderate effect size (Belleville, Cousineau, Levrier, & St-Pierre-Delorme, 2011). However, only five studies to date have examined the effects of child anxiety treatment on sleep. Kendall and Pimentel (2003) found that CBT for GAD was effective in reducing associated "sleep disturbance" in children 9–11 years of age, and Storch et al. (2008) found that CBT treatment for obsessive-compulsive disorder was effective in reducing secondary SRPs in youth 8–17 years of age. Similarly, Caporino et al. (2015) found that a combination of CBT and sertraline or sertraline alone evidenced the greatest reduction in SRPs, with CBT alone producing the greatest reductions in sleep dysregulation specifically. In a drug trial examining the efficacy of fluvoxamine for anxiety in youth found that those in the drug treatment condition showed a greater reduction in SRPs than those taking a placebo (Alfano et al., 2007). Finally, a very recent study by Peterman et al. (2016) found that anxiety treatment for youth 7–17 years of age resulted in a reduction in SRPs as reported by parents, with treatment responders (in terms of anxiety) demonstrating a greater reduction in SRPs than nonresponders. With respect to specific SRPs, it was found that only parent-reported sleep anxiety and bedtime resistance showed significant reductions from pre- to posttreatment (Peterman et al., 2016).

From the discussion just presented, it is evident that anxiety and sleep problems are highly prevalent in pediatric populations, are associated with numerous problematic consequences, and commonly co-occur. There is preliminary evidence to suggest that pharmocotherapy and CBT for anxiety disorders in youth may have a secondary effect of reducing SRPs in this population. However, to date, the ability of online CBT programs for youth anxiety to reduce SRPs has not been tested in this manner. The present study examined the degree to which CBT for anxious children and adolescents, delivered online, has secondary effects on SRPs. Given that the online programs involved in this study have been shown to produce reductions in anxiety that are equivalent to those found in face-to-face versions of the same program (Spence et al., 2011; Spence et al., 2006), it was expected that they would also produce a reduction in sleep symptoms consistent with prior studies in the area. It was therefore hypothesised that, compared to youth in the waitlist control group, youth receiving the online CBT program would demonstrate a greater reduction in SRPs at posttreatment assessment that would be maintained at 6-month follow-up. The study also examined some subsiduary issues. In particular, the question of whether children with GAD report greater SRPs than children with other disorders, and whether SRPs differ between gender and age groups, were also examined. Consistent with previous research, it was hypothesised that children with GAD in their diagnostic profile would report more SRPs than children without GAD. Given the mixed findings for age and gender in the literature, differences in SRPs for these groups were investigated in an exploratory manner.

METHOD

Participants

Participants were 134 Australian youth from two previously published studies that evaluated Internet delivery of CBT for youth anxiety (March et al., 2009; Spence et al., 2011). The present study included 63 child participants 7–12 years of age ($M = 9.49$, $SD = 1.37$) from the evaluation conducted by March et al. (2009) and 71 adolescent participants 12–18 years of age ($M = 13.90$, $SD = 1.68$) from the study conducted by Spence et al. (2011). Those from the March et al. (2009) study included 34 who received the Internet condition (NET) and 29 who were allocated to waitlist (WLC). Those from the Spence et al. (2011) study included the 44 NET and 27 WLC participants. Figures 1 and 2 outline the number of participants for whom SRP data were available at each time point for children and adolescents, respectively. The flow of participants through each of

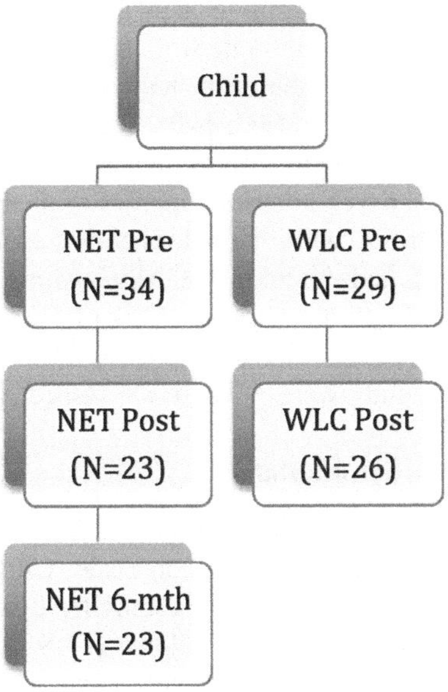

FIGURE 1 The number of child participants for whom sleep-related problem data were available at each time point. *Note*: NET = Internet condition; WLC = waitlist condition.

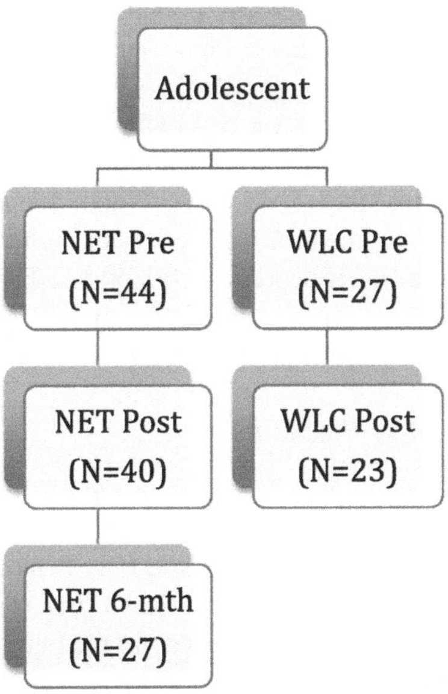

FIGURE 2 The number of adolescent participants for whom sleep-related problem data were available at each time point. *Note*: NET = Internet condition; WLC = waitlist condition.

TABLE 1
Demographic Information for the Sample

	Child Sample N (%)	*Adolescent Sample N (%)*
Gender		
Male	28 (44.4%)	28 (39.4%)
Female	35 (55.6%)	43 (60.6%)
Condition		
NET	34 (54%)	44 (62%)
WLC	29 (46%)	27 (38%)
Primary Diagnosis at Pre		
Separation Anxiety	21 (33.3%)	6 (8.5%)
Social Phobia	24 (38.1%)	26 (36.6%)
Generalised Anxiety	14 (22.2%)	37 (52.1%)
Specific Phobia	4 (6.3%)	2 (2.8%)
Country of Birth		
Australia	60 (95.2%)	66 (93%)
New Zealand	2 (3.2%)	0
Germany	0	1 (1.4%)
Italy	0	1 (1.4%)
United Kingdom	0	2 (2.8%)
United States of America	1 (1.6%)	1 (1.4%)
Living Situation		
Both Biological Parents	57 (90.5%)	56 (78.9%)
Mother Only	4 (6.3%)	10 (14.1%)
Father Only	0	1 (1.4%)
Mother and Stepfather	2 (3.2%)	4 (5.6%)
Education Level of Mother		
Postgraduate University	17 (27%)	14 (19.7%)
Undergraduate	12 (19%)	20 (28.2%)
University		
TAFE or Apprenticeship	15 (23.8%)	9 (12.7%)
Year 12 High School	11 (17.5%)	12 (16.9%)
Year 10 High School	8 (12.7%)	16 (22.5%)
Education Level of Father		
Postgraduate University	17 (27%)	22 (31%)
Undergraduate	11 (17.5%)	14 (19.7%)
University		
TAFE or Apprenticeship	17 (27%)	16 (22.5%)
Year 12 High School	11 (17.5%)	13 (18.3%)
Year 10 High School	7 (11.1%)	6 (8.5%)
Household Income (AUD$)		
< $20,000	3 (4.9%)	3 (4.2%)
$21,000–$40,000	4 (6.6%)	7 (9.9%)
$41,000–60,000	19 (31.1%)	8 (11.3%)
$61,000–$80,000	11 (18%)	11 (15.5%)
$81,000–$100,000	6 (9.8%)	8 (11.3%)
> $100,000	18 (29.5%)	34 (14.9%)

Note: NET = Internet condition; WLC = waitlist condition; TAFE = Technical and Further Education System.

the respective studies, together with the recruitment procedures employed, are outlined in the March et al. (2009) and Spence et al. (2011) studies and therefore are not reported again here.

Table 1 outlines the demographic characteristics of the two samples. Child participants had a mean age of 9.49 years (SD = 1.37), whereas adolescent participants had a mean age of 13.90 years (SD = 1.68). Comorbidity was high in both samples, with children holding between one and six diagnoses (M = 3.05, SD = 1.40) and adolescents holding between one and nine diagnoses (M = 2.54, SD = 1.34) prior to treatment. All youth held a primary anxiety diagnosis of social phobia, specific phobia, GAD, or separation anxiety disorder according to the Anxiety Disorders Interview Schedule for *DSM-IV*–Child and Parent Versions (ADIS-C/P: Silverman & Albano, 1996; see next). As is evident from Table 1, the majority of participants were born in Australia, lived with both biological parents, had relatively educated parents, and came from a range of socioeconomic backgrounds.

Measures

All measures were taken prior to treatment (pretreatment), following treatment (posttreatment), and at 6-month follow-up.

Diagnosis and Diagnostic Severity

Diagnosis and diagnostic severity was determined by a telephone administration of the ADIS-C/P (Silverman & Albano, 1996). The ADIS-C/P comprises both child and parent interviews, each of which take approximately 1 hr to complete. Interviewers assign a clinical severity rating (CSR) for each diagnosis, ranging from 0 (*absent*) to 8 (*severely disabling/disturbing*), with a CSR of 4 indicating clinical-level severity. The combined parent/child diagnosis and CSR was used in accordance with the ADIS-C/P manual. Telephone administration of the ADIS-C/P has shown comparable reliability to face-to-face administration (Cobham, Dadds, & Spence, 1998; Lyneham & Rapee, 2005). A random sample of 15% of interview was chosen for interrater reliability analyses in both the March et al. (2009) and Spence et al. (2011) studies. The interrater reliability for the child sample was high, with a kappa of 1 for the primary diagnosis and a correlation between assessors of .98 for the CSR. Similarly, the interrater reliability for the adolescent sample was high, with a kappa of .94 for the primary diagnosis and a correlation of .92 between the assessors for the CSR.

Global Functioning

Overall level of functioning was measured using the Children's Global Assessment Scale (CGAS; Shaffer et al., 1983) and was determined by the interviewer administering the ADIS-C/P. The CGAS provides a rating from 0 to 100, where scores of 81–100 indicate normal levels of functioning, scores of 61–80 indicate slight disability, scores of 41–60 are indicative of moderate disability, and scores of 1–40 suggest serious disability (Shaffer et al., 1983). The psychometric properties of the CGAS have been found to be strong, with good interrater reliability (r = .84) and test–retest reliability (r = .85; Dyrborg et al., 2000; Rey, Starling, Wever, Dossetor, & Plapp, 1995; Shaffer et al., 1983). An interrater reliability of .91 was found for the CGAS in both the March et al. (2009) and Spence et al. (2011) studies.

Anxiety Symptoms

The Spence Children's Anxiety Scale–Parent (SCAS-P; Nauta et al., 2004) and Child (SCAS-C; Spence, 1998) versions were used to assess anxiety symptoms. The SCAS-P consists of 38 items and the SCAS-C consists of 44 items (of which six are filler items) in response to which participants are required to rate from 0 (*never*) to 3 (*always*) the frequency with which each item applies to themselves (SCAS-C) or their child (SCAS-P). Total scores may range from 0–114, with higher scores indicating greater anxiety symptoms. The psychometric properties of the SCAS-C and SCAS-P are strong, with internal reliability estimates of .89 for the SCAS-P and .92 for the SCAS-C (Muris, Schmidt, & Merckelbach, 2000; Nauta et al., 2004; Spence, 1998). The Cronbach's coefficient alphas for the SCAS-C and SCAS-P in the present study were .92 and .88, respectively.

Depression Symptoms

Depression symptoms were measured using the Center for Epidemiological Studies Depression Scale (CES-D; Radloff, 1977) for the adolescents and the Center for Epidemiological Studies Depression Scale for Children (CES-DC; Faulstich, Carey, Ruggiero, Envart, & Gresham, 1986) for the children. The CES-D consists of 20 items for which youth are required to respond from 0 (*rarely or none of the time, less than 1 day*) to 3 (*most or all of the time, 5–7 days*), the frequency with which they experience each symptom. The CES-D has been shown to be acceptable and to have strong psychometric properties with an adolescent population, with reliabilities of .85 and .86 for junior high school and high school students, respectively (Radloff, 1991). The CES-DC requires children to rate on a 4-point scale from 0 (*not at all*) to 3 (*a lot*), the degree to which they felt the item applied to them during the past week. Total scores for each questionnaire may range from 0–60, with higher scores indicating higher levels of depressive symptoms. The Cronbach's coefficient alphas for the CES-DC and the CES-D in the present study were .84 and .91, respectively.

Sleep-Related Problems

SRPs were measured using a composite of the seven sleep-related items of the Child Behavior Checklist (CBCL; Achenbach & Rescorla, 2001). The CBCL requires parents to rate from 0 (*never*) to 1 (*sometimes*) to 2 (*often*) the frequency with which each item occurs for their child. The seven sleep items are nightmares (Item 47), overtired without good reason (Item 54), sleeps less than most kids (Item 76), sleeps more than most kids during the day and/or night (Item 77), talks or walks in sleep (Item 92), trouble sleeping (Item 100), and wets the bed (Item 108). For the purposes of this study, the seven sleep items were summed to produce a composite sleep score that could vary from 0 to 14, with higher scores indicating more SRPs. Recently, a study by Becker, Ramsey, and Byars (2015) tested this composite and found it to be significantly correlated with the Children's Sleep Habits Questionnaire (Owens, Spirito, & McGuinn, 2000), the Sleep Disorders Inventory for Students (Luginbuehl, Bradley-Klug, Ferron, Anderson, & Benbadis, 2008), and the Adolescent Sleep Wake Scale (LeBourgeois, Giannotti, Cortesi, Wolfson,

& Harsh, 2005). The authors concluded that the composite, although not providing a comprehensive measure of sleep, was adequate in determining overall sleep function (Becker et al., 2015). The reliability of the SRP composite of the CBCL was low (.50) in the current study.

Procedure

The procedures for the March et al. (2009) and Spence et al. (2011) study are outlined in the respective publications and are not repeated in this article. However, it should be noted here that the recruitment for both studies was identical and involved sending information packages to schools, placing advertisements in school newsletters, sending information to general practitioners, and media exposure in the form of newspaper articles, television, and radio interviews. Similarly, the BRAVE-ONLINE programs have been described in detail elsewhere (see March et al., 2009; Spence et al., 2008, 2011; Spence et al., 2006), and therefore only a short description is provided next.

There are both child and adolescent versions of the BRAVE-ONLINE program. The child version comprises 10 child sessions and six parent sessions, whereas the adolescent version includes 10 teen sessions and five parent sessions. Both child and teen versions include two youth and parent booster sessions conducted 1 month and 3 months following the initial 10 sessions. The child and adolescent programs are developmentally appropriate versions of the same content and include identical CBT principles and format. Both programs are highly interactive, incorporating games, graphics, and quizzes to ensure youth engagement and interest.

BRAVE is an acronym for the strategies taught throughout the program. B stands for body signs (identification of the physiological signs of anxiety); R stand for relax (including deep breathing, progressive muscle relaxation, and guided imagery); A stands for activating helpful thoughts (cognitive restructuring); V stands for victory over fears (exposure and problem solving); and E stands for enjoy, reward yourself (positive reinforcement for effort and brave behaviour). The programs are therapist mediated in that each participant is assigned a virtual therapist, who peruses the answers to questions and homework activities provided by the participant and responds with a weekly e-mail to provide encouragement and/or redirection. A telephone call with the therapist is also provided halfway through the program to assist the young person and parent with exposure hierarchy development.

Data Analytic Procedure

Separate analyses were conducted for child and adolescent participants to ensure that any age-related differences were captured. The analyses were divided into two sections. The first section was concerned with examining the association between SRPs and anxiety, and thus for each of the two age groups, SRPs were correlated with CSR of the primary diagnosis, number of diagnoses, CGAS rating, parent and child SCAS, and the CES-D. In addition, for each of the two age groups, an analysis of variance (ANOVA) was conducted to compare participants who had a diagnosis of GAD anywhere in their diagnostic profile with those participants who did not. To determine whether there were any gender differences in SRPs, two between-groups ANOVAs (one for children and one for adolescents) were conducted, with gender as the between-groups variable. Finally, a between-groups ANOVA was conducted to determine whether children and adolescents differed with respect to SRPs.

The second section of the analyses was concerned with determining whether participation in the BRAVE-ONLINE programs resulted in a reduction in SRPs. First, two between-groups ANOVAs (one for children and one for adolescents) were conducted with condition (NET vs. WLC) as the between-subjects variable and SRPs as the outcome variable, to ensure that there were no preexisting differences in SRPs between the two conditions prior to treatment. Subsequently, for both child and teenage participants, linear mixed-model analyses were conducted to determine whether SRPs were reduced as a result of participating in the BRAVE-ONLINE program. Finally, to test for effects on SRPs at 6-month follow-up, only NET participants were available, as the WLC participants ceased to be part of the studies after the postassessment time point. Thus, for each age group, linear mixed-model analyses were conducted to assess for changes in SRPs over time.

RESULTS

Association Between Anxiety and SRPs

The correlations between SRPs and anxiety, depression, and overall functioning are provided in Table 2 (for children) and Table 3 (for adolescents). As is evident from Table 2, sleep issues were correlated with both severity of primary diagnosis and parent-reported, but not child-reported, anxiety symptoms for children. In contrast, Table 3 suggests that sleep issues were strongly related to adolescent-reported depression symptoms and were unrelated to anxiety severity and symptoms.

With respect to the ANOVA comparing SRPs for those participants with a diagnosis of GAD anywhere in their diagnostic profile with those who did not, the results were not significant for either children, $F(1, 61) = .024$, $p = .877$, or adolescents, $F(1, 61) = .045$, $p = .832$. It should be noted, however, than only 19 of the 63 children and 10 of the 71 adolescents were without a diagnosis of GAD somewhere in their profile. In addition, male and female participants were not found to differ on SRPs in

TABLE 2
Correlations, Means, and Standard Deviations for the Child Sample at Preassessment

	SRP	*CSR*	*CGAS*	*Diagnosis No*	*SCAS-P*	*SCAS-C*	*CES-D*
SRP	1						
CSR	.257*	1					
CGAS	−.177	−.518***	1				
Diagnosis No	.101	.361**	−.681***	1			
SCAS-P	.520***	.432***	−.268*	.240	1		
SCAS-C	.074	.210	−.374**	.437***	.298*	1	
CES-D	.007	.060	−.090	.275*	.012	.561***	1
M (SD)	2.78 (2.14)	5.98 (0.61)	51.06 (4.65)	3.05 (1.40)	34.84 (12.81)	41.90 (18.69)	21.78 (10.10)

Note: SRP = sleep-related problem; CSR = clinical severity rating; CGAS = Children's Global Assessment Scale; SCAS-P = Spence Children's Anxiety Scale–Parent; SCAS-C = Spence Children's Anxiety Scale–Child; CES-D = Center for Epidemiological Studies for Depression Scale.
*$p < .05$. **$p < .01$. ***$p < .001$.

TABLE 3
Correlations, Means, and Standard Deviations for the Adolescent Sample at Preassessment

	SRP	*CSR*	*CGAS*	*Diagnosis No*	*SCAS-P*	*SCAS-C*	*CES-D*
SRP	1						
CSR	.072	1					
CGAS	−.163	−.759***	1				
Diagnosis No	−.054	.265*	−.462***	1			
SCAS-P	.180	.307**	−.424***	.371**	1		
SCAS-C	.212	.500***	−.405***	.201	.346**	1	
CES-D	.387**	.225	−.253*	.096	.059	.563***	1
M (SD)	2.58 (1.95)	5.82 (0.76)	50.96 (5.77)	2.54 (1.34)	27.32 (12.36)	39.18 (17.46)	22.41 (12.34)

Note: SRP = sleep-related problem; CSR = clinical severity rating; CGAS = Children's Global Assessment Scale; SCAS-P = Spence Children's Anxiety Scale–Parent; SCAS-C = Spence Children's Anxiety Scale–Child; CES-D = Center for Epidemiological Studies for Depression Scale.
*$p < .05$. **$p < .01$. ***$p < .001$.

either the child sample, $F(1, 61) = .197$, $p = .659$, or the adolescent sample, $F(1, 69) = 2.77$, $p = .101$, and teenagers and children were not found to differ in terms of SRPs either, $F(1, 132) = .321$, $p = .572$,

Changes in SRPs Following the BRAVE-ONLINE Program

At preassessment, there were no significant differences between the NET and WLC conditions for either the child sample, $F(1, 61) = .285$, $p = .595$, $d = .13$, or the adolescent sample, $F(1, 69) = .303$, $p = .584$, $d = .13$, on SRPs, suggesting that there were no preexisting differences in sleep between NET and WLC participants prior to treatment. The estimated marginal means for SRPs for both children and adolescents are presented in Table 4 (pre- to postassessment for NET and WLC groups) and Table 5 (pre- to postassessment and 6-month follow-up for the NET group). The fixed effects for intercept and slopes and effect sizes are presented in Table 6 (pre- to postassessment for NET and WLC groups) and Table 7 (pre- to postassessment and follow-up for the NET group).

TABLE 4
Estimated Marginal Means and Standard Errors for Sleep-Related Problems from Pre- to Postassessment for Children and Adolescents

		NET			*WLC*		
	Time	M	SE	d	M	SE	d
Child	Pre	2.91	0.34		2.62	0.37	
	Post	1.23	0.38	0.59	2.07	0.38	0.18
Teen	Pre	2.48	0.28		2.74	0.36	
	Post	1.64	0.29	0.35	2.06	0.38	0.22

Note: Effect sizes were calculated from pre to post within condition. NET = Internet condition; WLC = waitlist condition.

Children

The analyses conducted on child SRPs revealed a significant effect for time, $F(1, 51.51) = 26.457$, $p < .001$, and a significant Condition × Time interaction, $F(1, 51.51) = 6.69$, $p = .013$. Inspection of Tables 4 and 6 suggests that children in the NET condition demonstrated a greater reduction in SRPs from pre- to postassessment compared to children in the WLC condition. Analyses across preassessment, postassessment, and 6-month

TABLE 5
Estimated Marginal Means and Standard Errors for Sleep-Related Problems from Pre- to Postassessment and 6-Month Follow-Up for Children and Adolescents

		Internet Condition		
	Time	*M*	*SE*	*d*
Child	Pre	2.91	0.33	
	Post	1.29	0.35	
	6 month	0.93	0.36	0.98
Teen	Pre	2.48	0.25	
	Post	1.65	0.26	
	6 month	1.51	0.30	0.53

Note: Effect sizes were calculated from pre to 6-month within condition.

TABLE 6
Effects for NET and WLC for Sleep-Related Problems From Pre- to Postassessment for Sleep-Related Problems for Children and Adolescents

	Children			*Adolescents*		
	B	*SE*	*ES*	*B*	*SE*	*ES*
Intercept						
WLC Baseline	2.91***	0.34	2.24	2.48***	0.28	1.91
NET–WLC	−0.29	0.50	−0.22	0.26	0.46	0.20
Slope Pre to Post						
WLC Slope	−1.68***	0.31	−1.29	−0.84**	0.24	−0.65
NET–WLC Slope	1.12*	0.43	0.86	0.16	0.39	0.12
Random Effects						
Level 1 Residual Variance		1.52			1.42	
Level 2 Residual Variance		0.33			0.26	

Note: Effect sizes were calculated as estimated fixed effects divided by the square root of the sum of the two variance components. NET = Internet condition; WLC = waitlist condition.

*$p < .05$. **$p < .01$. ***$p < .001$.

follow-up revealed a significant effect for time, $F(2, 31.716) = 23.88, p < .001$. Inspection of Tables 5 and 7 suggest that the reduction in SRPs evident at postassessment was maintained at 6-month follow-up.

Adolescents

The analyses conducted on SRPs revealed only a significant effect for time, $F(1, 64.86) = 14.94, p < .001$, suggesting that both WLC and NET participants demonstrated a reduction in SRPs from pre- to postassessment. The Condition × Time effect was not significant, $F(1, 64.86) = 0.147, p = .685$. Analyses across preassessment, postassessment, and 6-month follow-up revealed a significant effect for time, $F(2, 47.78) = 6.68, p = .003$. Inspection of Tables 5 and 7 suggests that the reduction in SRPs evident at postassessment was maintained at 6-month follow-up.

TABLE 7
Effects for NET and Waitlist Condition for Sleep-Related Problems From Pre- to Postassessment and 6-Month Follow-Up for Sleep-Related Problems for Children and Adolescents

	Children			*Adolescents*		
	B	*SE*	*ES*	*B*	*SE*	*ES*
Intercept						
NET Pre	2.91***	0.33	1.49	2.48***	0.25	1.83
Slope						
NET Pre to 6 Month	−1.98***	0.32	−1.02	−0.96**	0.32	−1.36
NET Pre to Post	−1.63***	0.26	−0.84	−0.83**	0.25	−0.52
Random Effects						
Level 1 Residual Variance		1.22				0.10
Level 2 Residual Variance		2.59				1.73

Note: Effect sizes were calculated as estimated fixed effects divided by the square root of the sum of the two variance components. NET = Internet condition.

**$p < .01$. ***$p < .001$.

DISCUSSION

This study examined the relationship between SRPs and anxiety in children and adolescents and assessed whether participation in an online CBT intervention for anxiety disorders led to a subsequent decrease in SRPs despite the program not targeting SRPs per se. It was found that parent-reported SRPs were related to parent-reported anxiety symptoms and severity for children while being related to teen-reported depression for adolescents. It was also found that parent-reported SRPs did not differ between male and female participants, between children and adolescents, or between those who had a diagnosis of GAD in their profile and those who did not. Finally, it was found that (a) for the child sample, those participating in the online program demonstrated a significantly greater reduction in parent-reported SRPs from pre- to posttreatment compared to the waitlist group, and (b) these gains were maintained at 6-month follow-up. With respect to adolescents, parent-reported SRPs were found to reduce equally from pre- to postassessment for the treatment and waitlist participants. Each of these findings is now discussed.

The finding that SRPs were related to anxiety severity and symptoms in children but not adolescents is contrary to previous research where it has generally been found that the association becomes stronger with age (Gregory & O'Connor, 2002; Johnson et al., 2000). Furthermore, the finding cannot be attributed to higher levels of SRPs in children versus adolescents, because consistent with previous research (e.g., Alfano et al., 2006; Chase & Pincus, 2011), frequency of SRPs was not found to differ between the two age groups in this study. The stronger association between SRPs and anxiety in children may be due to the higher rates of bedtime-related anxiety (e.g., separation anxiety, fear of the dark, etc.) experienced by a younger age group. Alternatively, the discrepant results may be due to the use of the CBCL as a measure of sleep. Remembering that the CBCL is parent rated, it may be that although parents are extremely aware of sleep issues in school-age children, they may be less aware of sleep problems in their adolescent offspring. Indeed, there is considerable evidence to suggest that child and parent reports of child sleep do not always align even in school-age children (e.g., Owens, Spirito, McGuinn, & Nobile, 2000). Reliance on parent-report of SRPs is a limitation of the present study, and future research should ensure that youth-rated sleep measures are employed to counteract this potential confound.

The finding that depression symptoms were related to SRPs for adolescents and not children is consistent with previous research (Alfano et al., 2009), and not surprising giving the higher prevalence rates of depression in adolescents versus children generally. Similarly, the finding that SRPs did not differ between male and female participants is also consistent with previous research (Alfano et al., 2007; Alfano et al., 2009; Chase & Pincus, 2011; Hansen et al., 2011). However, the finding that youth diagnosed with GAD were no more likely to experience SRPs than youth not diagnosed with GAD is inconsistent with previous research, where it has frequently been shown that youth with GAD report the most SRPs (Alfano et al, 2006; Alfano et al., 2007; Alfano et al., 2010). However, there was high comorbidity in the current sample, with very few youth being without a diagnosis of GAD somewhere in their profile. Thus, the high rates of GAD in this study may have been responsible for the inconsistent result.

With respect to the assessment of whether BRAVE-ONLINE was able to bring about changes in SRPs despite not directly targeting them, the results were different for children versus adolescents. There was no change in SRPs as a result of engaging in the program for teenagers. However, it would appear that children engaging in treatment were significantly more likely to show a reduction in SRPs following treatment compared to waitlist children. As just noted, a reduction in SRPs following treatment for anxiety is common in adults (Belleville et al., 2011), and there is emerging evidence that this may also be the case for youth engaged in face-to-face CBT (Caporino et al., 2015; Kendall & Pimentel, 2003; Peterman et al., 2016; Storch et al., 2008) and pharmacotherapy (Alfano et al., 2007) for anxiety. Although children and teens are equally likely to have anxiety-related sleep issues that may be reduced by treatment for anxiety, teenagers may require additional sleep-specific strategies due to the developmental period in which they find themselves. Circadian rhythms are thought to slowly change toward an evening phase preference and later circadian phase during adolescence, and there is a slow accumulation of homeostatic sleep pressure during puberty that delays the sleep/wake cycle (Crowley, Acebo, & Carskadon, 2007). In addition, adolescence is a time of increased independence and responsibility coupled with reduced parental control (Moran & Everhart, 2012). Thus, environmental factors such as early school starts, jobs, extracurricular activities, social activities (Wolfson & Carskadon, 1998), more homework, increasing time spent with friends, stress, TV (Noland, Price, Dake, & Telljohann, 2009), video games, instant messaging, surfing the web, and talking on the phone before bed (Moseley & Gradisar, 2009) have all been found to be associated with reduced adolescent sleep. Furthermore, more than 70% of adolescents have been found to have set bedtimes that are later than 10 p.m., disallowing them the 9–10 hr of sleep they require prior to getting up early for school the next day (Moran & Everhart, 2012). Thus, it may well be necessary to incorporate strategies directly targeting sleep within teenage as opposed to child anxiety programs.

Strengths, Limitations, and Suggestions for Future Research

This study had a number of strengths. It employed large sample sizes and psychometrically sound measures, and it was the first of its kind to examine the potential of an online CBT program for youth anxiety to bring about changes in SRPs. However, the study was not without its limitations. Foremost, the measure of sleep employed was really only a proxy for SRPs. This study was conducted in an ad hoc manner, with the CBCL as the only measure of sleep available in studies that were not designed with sleep issues in mind. Thus, although recently found by Becker et al. (2015) to be a reasonable indicator of sleep problems, the CBCL is unlikely to be the most sensitive and informative assessment tool for SRPs, and future research should endeavour to use more targeted, psychometrically sound, and sensitive sleep measures.

In addition to the suggestions for future research to which we just alluded, there are a number of other avenues worthy of investigation. Clearly, research examining the capacity of CBT for youth anxiety to reduce SRPs is in its infancy and more studies are required to shed light on this important topic. In addition, the high comorbidity rates generally found between anxiety and SRPs may warrant investigation of programs designed to address both disorders. To date, only a case series analyses conducted by Clementi and Alfano (2014) examining a CBT treatment for comorbid anxiety and sleep disorders has been conducted with promising results. However, randomised controlled trials are required to better test this idea with youth across the developmental range.

Conclusions

This study suggested that online CBT for youth anxiety disorders may produce changes in SRPs for children but not adolescents. Given the high comorbidity of anxiety and sleep issues, it is suggested that (a) therapists assess for sleep issues as a matter of course in their child and adolescent clients and (b) strategies directly targeting sleep issues are included in the treatment of adolescents. Given the bidirectional and cyclical associations between the two disorders, targeting both disorders in treatment may well bring about enhanced outcomes for both issues.

FUNDING

Funding was provided by the National Health and Medical Research Council, Australia.

REFERENCES

Achenbach, T. M., & Rescorla, L. A. (2001). *Manual of the Achenbach system of empirically based assessment—Child Behavior Checklist, Teacher Report Form, and Youth Report*. Burlington: University of Vermont, Research Center for Children, Youth, and Families.

Alfano, C. A., Beidel, D. C., Turner, S. M., & Lewin, D. S. (2006). Preliminary evidence for sleep complaints among children referred for anxiety. *Sleep Medicine*, *7*(6), 467–473. doi:10.1016/j.sleep.2006.05.002

Alfano, C. A., Ginsburg, G. S., & Kingery, J. N. (2007). Sleep-related problems among children and adolescents with anxiety disorders. *Journal of the American Academy of Child & Adolescent Psychiatry*, *46*(2), 224–232. doi:10.1097/01.chi.0000242233.06011.8e

Alfano, C. A., Pina, A. A., Zerr, A. A., & Villalta, I. K. (2010). Pre-sleep arousal and sleep problems of anxiety-disordered youth. *Child Psychiatry & Human Development*, *41*(2), 156–167. doi:10.1007/s10578-009-0158-5

Alfano, C. A., Zakem, A. H., Costa, N. M., Taylor, L. K., & Weems, C. F. (2009). Sleep problems and their relation to cognitive factors, anxiety, and depressive symptoms in children and adolescents. *Depression and Anxiety*, *26*(6), 503–512.

Altena, E., Van Der Werf, Y. D., Sanz-Arigita, E. J., Voorn, T. A., Rombouts, S., Kuijer, J. P., & Van Someren, E. J. (2008). Prefrontal hypoactivation and recovery in insomnia. *Sleep*, *31*(9), 1271–1276.

Becker, S. P., Ramsey, R. R., & Byars, K. C. (2015). Convergent validity of the child behavior checklist sleep items with validated sleep measures and sleep disorder diagnoses in children and adolescents referred to a sleep disorders center. *Sleep Medicine*, *16*(1), 79–86. doi:10.1016/j.sleep.2014.09.008

Belleville, G., Cousineau, H., Levrier, K., & St-Pierre-Delorme, M. (2011). Meta-analytic review of the impact of cognitive-behavior therapy for insomnia on concomitant anxiety. *Clinical Psychology Review*, *31*(4), 638–652. doi:10.1016/j.cpr.2011.02.004

Booth, M. L., Bernard, D., Quine, S., Kang, M. S., Usherwood, T., Alperstein, G., & Bennett, D. L. (2004). Access to health care among Australian adolescents young people's perspectives and their sociodemographic distribution. *Journal of Adolescent Health*, *34*(1), 97–103. doi:10.1016/S1054-139X(03)00304-5

Caporino, N. E., Read, K. L., Shiffrin, N., Settipani, C., Kendall, P. C., Compton, S. N., & Keeton, C. (2015). Sleep-related problems and the effects of anxiety treatment in children and adolescents. *Journal of Clinical Child & Adolescent Psychology*. doi:10.1080/15374416.2015.1063429

Chase, R. M., & Pincus, D. B. (2011). Sleep-related problems in children and adolescents with anxiety disorders. *Behavioral Sleep Medicine*, *9*(4), 224–236. doi:10.1080/15402002.2011.606768

Clementi, M. A., & Alfano, C. A. (2014). Targeted behavioral therapy for childhood generalized anxiety disorder: A time-series analysis of changes in anxiety and sleep. *Journal of Anxiety Disorders*, *28*(2), 215–222. doi:10.1016/j.janxdis.2013.10.006

Cobham, V. E., Dadds, M. R., & Spence, S. H. (1998). The role of parental anxiety in the treatment of childhood anxiety. *Journal of Consulting and Clinical Psychology*, *66*(6), 893–905. doi:10.1037/0022-006x.66.6.893

Compton, S. N., March, J. S., Brent, D., Albano, A. M., Weersing, V. R., & Curry, J. (2004). Cognitive-behavioral psychotherapy for anxiety and depressive disorders in children and adolescents: An evidence-based medicine review. *Journal of the American Academy of Child & Adolescent Psychiatry*, *43*(8), 930–959. doi:10.1097/01.chi.0000127589.57468.bf

Copeland, W. E., Angold, A., Shanahan, L., & Costello, E. J. (2014). Longitudinal patterns of anxiety from childhood to adulthood: The great smoky mountains study. *Journal of the American Academy of Child & Adolescent Psychiatry*, *53*(1), 21–33. doi:10.1016/j.jaac.2013.09.017

Costello, E. J., Egger, H. L., Copeland, W., Erkanli, A., & Angold, A. (2011). The developmental epidemiology of anxiety disorders: Phenomenology, prevalence, and comorbidity. *Anxiety Disorders in Children and Adolescents: Research, Assessment and Intervention*, *2*, 56–75.

Cowie, J., Alfano, C. A., Patriquin, M. A., Reynolds, K. C., Talavera, D., & Clementi, M. A. (2014). Addressing sleep in children with anxiety disorders. *Sleep Medicine Clinics*, *9*(2), 137–148. doi:10.1016/j.jsmc.2014.02.001

Crowley, S. J., Acebo, C., & Carskadon, M. A. (2007). Sleep, circadian rhythms, and delayed phase in adolescence. *Sleep Medicine*, *8*(6), 602–612. doi:10.1016/j.sleep.2006.12.002

Do, Y. K., Shin, E., Bautista, M., & Foo, K. (2013). The associations between self-reported sleep duration and adolescent health outcomes: What is the role of time spent on Internet use? *Sleep Medicine*, *14*(2), 195–200. doi:10.1016/j.sleep.2012.09.004

Donovan, C. L., & March, S. (2014a). Computer-based treatment programs for youth anxiety: A systematic review. *Psychopathology Review*, *1*(1), 130–156. doi:10.5127/pr.033613

Donovan, C. L., & March, S. (2014b). Online CBT for preschool anxiety disorders: A randomised control trial. *Behaviour Research and Therapy*, *58*, 24–35. doi:10.1016/j.brat.2014.05.001

Dyrborg, J., Larsen, F., Nielsen, S., Byman, J., Buhl Nielsen, B., & Gautre-Delay, F. (2000). The children's global assessment scale (CGAS) and global assessment of psychosocial disability (GAPD) in clinical practice-substance and reliability as judged by intraclass correlations. *European Child & Adolescent Psychiatry*, *9*(3), 195–201. doi:10.1007/s007870070043

Faulstich, M. E., Carey, M. P., Ruggiero, L., Envart, P., & Gresham, F. (1986). Assessment of depression in childhood and adolescence: An evaluation of the Center for Epidemiological Studies Depression Scale for Children (CES-DC). *American Journal of Psychiatry*, *143*, 1024–1027. doi:10.1176/ajp.143.8.1024

Gregory, A. M., Eley, T. C., O'Connor, T. G., & Plomin, R. (2004). Etiologies of associations between childhood sleep and behavioral problems in a large twin sample. *Journal of the American Academy of Child & Adolescent Psychiatry*, *43*(6), 744–751. doi:10.1097/01.chi/0000122798.47863.a5

Gregory, A. M., & O'Connor, T. G. (2002). Sleep problems in childhood: A longitudinal study of developmental change and association with behavioral problems. *Journal of the American Academy of Child & Adolescent Psychiatry*, *41*(8), 964–971. doi:10.1097/00004583-200208000-00015

Gregory, A. M., & Sadeh, A. (2012). Sleep, emotional and behavioral difficulties in children and adolescents. *Sleep Medicine Reviews*, *16*(2), 129–136. doi:10.1016/j.smrv.2011.03.007

Hansen, B. H., Skirbekk, B., Oerbeck, B., Richter, J., & Kristensen, H. (2011). Comparison of sleep problems in children with anxiety and attention deficit/hyperactivity disorders. *European Child & Adolescent Psychiatry*, *20*(6), 321–330. doi:10.1007/s00787-011-0179-z

Ialongo, N., Edelsohn, G., Werthamer-Larsson, L., Crockett, L., & Kellam, S. (1994). The significance of self-reported anxious symptoms in first-grade children. *Journal of Abnormal Child Psychology*, *22*(4), 441–455. doi:10.1007/BF02168084

Ialongo, N., Edelsohn, G., Werthamer-Larsson, L., Crockett, L., & Kellam, S. (1995). The significance of self-reported anxious symptoms in first grade children: Prediction to anxious symptoms and adaptive functioning in fifth grade. *Journal of Child Psychology and Psychiatry*, *36*(3), 427–437. doi:10.1111/jcpp.1995.36.issue-3

Johnson, E. O., Chilcoat, H. D., & Breslau, N. (2000). Trouble sleeping and anxiety/depression in childhood. *Psychiatry Research*, *94*(2), 93–102. doi:10.1016/S0165-1781(00)00145-1

Kendall, P. C., & Pimentel, S. S. (2003). On the physiological symptom constellation in youth with generalized anxiety disorder (GAD). *Journal of Anxiety Disorders*, *17*(2), 211–221. doi:10.1016/S0887-6185(02)00196-2

Lawrence, D., Johnson, S., Hafekost, J. B., De Haan, K., Sawyer, M., Ainley, J., & Zubrick, S. R. (2015). *The mental health of children and adolescents. report on the second Australian child and adolescent survey of mental health and wellbeing*. Canberra, Australia: Department of Health.

LeBourgeois, M. K., Giannotti, F., Cortesi, F., Wolfson, A. R., & Harsh, J. (2005). The relationship between reported sleep quality and sleep hygiene in Italian and American adolescents. *Pediatrics*, *115*(Suppl. 1), 257–265. doi:10.1542/peds.2004-0815H

Luginbuehl, M., Bradley-Klug, K. L., Ferron, J., Anderson, W. M., & Benbadis, S. R. (2008). Pediatric sleep disorders: Validation of the sleep disorders inventory for students. *School Psychology Review*, *37*(3), 409.

Lyneham, H. J., & Rapee, R. M. (2005). Agreement between telephone and in-person delivery of a structured interview for anxiety disorders in children. *Journal of the American Academy of Child & Adolescent Psychiatry*, *44*(3), 274–282. doi:10.1097/00004583-200503000-00012

March, S., Spence, S. H., & Donovan, C. L. (2009). The efficacy of an internet-based cognitive-behavioral therapy intervention for child anxiety disorders. *Journal of Pediatric Psychology*, *34*(5), 474–487. doi:10.1093/jpepsy/jsn099

Merikangas, K. R., He, J. P., Burstein, M., Swendsen, J., Avenevoli, S., Case, B., … Olfson, M. (2011). Service utilization for lifetime mental disorders in US adolescents: Results of the national comorbidity survey–adolescent supplement (NCS-A). *Journal of the American Academy of Child & Adolescent Psychiatry*, *50*(1), 32–45. doi:doi.org/10.1016/j.jaac.2010.10.006

Moran, A., & Everhart, D. (2012). Adolescent sleep: Review of characteristics, consequences, and intervention. *Journal of Sleep Disorders: Treatment and Care*, *1*(2).

Morrison, D. N., McGee, R. O. B., & Stanton, W. R. (1992). Sleep problems in adolescence. *Journal of the American Academy of Child & Adolescent Psychiatry*, *31*(1), 94–99. doi:10.1097/00004583-199201000-00014

Moseley, L., & Gradisar, M. (2009). Evaluation of a school-based intervention for adolescent sleep problems. *Sleep*, *32*(3), 334–341.

Muris, P., Schmidt, H., & Merckelbach, H. (2000). Correlations among two self-report questionnaires for measuring *DSM*-defined anxiety disorder symptoms in children: The screen for child anxiety related emotional disorders and the spence children's anxiety scale. *Personality and Individual Differences*, *28*(2), 333–346. doi:10.1016/S0191-8869(99)00102-6

Nauta, M. H., Scholing, A., Rapee, R. M., Abbott, M., Spence, S. H., & Waters, A. (2004). A parent-report measure of children's anxiety: Psychometric properties and comparison with child-report in a clinic and normal sample. *Behaviour Research and Therapy*, *42*(7), 813–839. doi:10.1016/S0005-7967(03)00200-6

Noland, H., Price, J. H., Dake, J., & Telljohann, S. K. (2009). Adolescents' sleep behaviors and perceptions of sleep. *Journal of School Health*, *79* (5), 224–230. doi:10.1111/josh.2009.79.issue-5

Owens, J. A., Spirito, A., & McGuinn, M. (2000). The Children's Sleep Habits Questionnaire (CSHQ): Psychometric properties of a survey instrument for school-aged children. *Sleep – New York*, *23*(8), 1043–1052.

Owens, J. A., Spirito, A., McGuinn, M. A., & Nobile, C. (2000). Sleep habits and sleep disturbance in elementary school-aged children. *Journal of Developmental & Behavioral Pediatrics*, *21*(1), 27–36. doi:10.1097/00004703-200002000-00005

Peterman, J. S., Carper, M. M., Elkins, R. M., Comer, J. S., Pincus, D. B., & Kendall, P. C. (2016). The effects of cognitive-behavioral therapy for youth anxiety on sleep problems. *Journal of Anxiety Disorders*, *37*, 78–88. doi:10.1016/j.janxdis.2015.11.006

Peterman, J. S., Carper, M. M., & Kendall, P. C. (2014). Anxiety disorders and comorbid sleep problems in school-aged youth: Review and future research directions. *Child Psychiatry & Human Development*, *46*, 376–392.

Radloff, L. S. (1977). The CES-D scale: A self-report depression scale for research in the general population. *Applied Psychological Measurement*, *1*(3), 385–401. doi:10.1177/014662167700100306

Radloff, L. S. (1991). The use of the center for epidemiologic studies depression scale in adolescents and young adults. *Journal of Youth and Adolescence*, *20*(2), 149–166. doi:10.1007/BF01537606

Rey, J. M., Starling, J., Wever, C., Dossetor, D. R., & Plapp, J. M. (1995). Inter-rater reliability of global assessment of functioning in a clinical setting. *Journal of Child Psychology and Psychiatry*, *36*(5), 787–792. doi:10.1111/jcpp.1995.36.issue-5

Shaffer, D., Gould, M. S., Brasic, J., Ambrosini, P., Fisher, P., Bird, H., & Aluwahlia, S. (1983). A children's global assessment scale (CGAS). *Archives of General Psychiatry*, *40*(11), 1228–1231. doi:10.1001/archpsyc.1983.01790100074010

Shanahan, L., Copeland, W. E., Angold, A., Bondy, C. L., & Costello, E. J. (2014). Sleep problems predict and are predicted by generalized anxiety/depression and oppositional defiant disorder. *Journal of the American Academy of Child & Adolescent Psychiatry*, *53*(5), 550–558. doi:10.1016/j.jaac.2013.12.029

Short, M. A., Gradisar, M., Lack, L. C., & Wright, H. R. (2013). The impact of sleep on adolescent depressed mood, alertness and academic performance. *Journal of Adolescence*, *36*(6), 1025–1033. doi:10.1016/j.adolescence.2013.08.007

Short, M. A., Gradisar, M., Lack, L. C., Wright, H. R., & Dohnt, H. (2013). The sleep patterns and well-being of Australian adolescents. *Journal of Adolescence*, *36*(1), 103–110. doi:10.1016/j.adolescence.2012.09.008

Silverman, W. K., & Albano, A. M. (1996). *Anxiety disorders interview schedule for children for DSM-IV: Child and parent versions*. San Antonio, TX: Psychological Corporation.

Spence, S. H. (1998). A measure of anxiety symptoms among children. *Behaviour Research and Therapy*, *36*(5), 545–566. doi:10.1016/S0005-7967(98)00034-5

Spence, S. H., Donovan, C. L., March, S., Gamble, A., Anderson, R. E., Prosser, S., & Kenardy, J. (2008). Online CBT in the treatment of child and adolescent anxiety disorders: Issues in the development of BRAVE–ONLINE and two case illustrations. *Behavioural and Cognitive Psychotherapy*, *36*(4), 411–430. doi:10.1017/S135246580800444X

Spence, S. H., Donovan, C. L., March, S., Gamble, A., Anderson, R. E., Prosser, S., & Kenardy, J. (2011). A randomized controlled trial of online versus clinic-based CBT for adolescent anxiety. *Journal of Consulting and Clinical Psychology*, *79*(5), 629–642. doi:10.1037/a0024512

Spence, S. H., Holmes, J. M., March, S., & Lipp, O. V. (2006). The feasibility and outcome of clinic plus internet delivery of cognitive-behavior therapy for childhood anxiety. *Journal of Consulting and Clinical Psychology*, *74*(3), 614–621. doi:10.1037/0022-006X.74.3.614

Storch, E. A., Murphy, T. K., Lack, C. W., Geffken, G. R., Jacob, M. L., & Goodman, W. K. (2008). Sleep-related problems in pediatric obsessive-compulsive disorder. *Journal of Anxiety Disorders*, *22*(5), 877–885. doi:10.1016/j.janxdis.2007.09.003

Tikotzky, L., & Sadeh, A. (2010). The role of cognitive–behavioral therapy in behavioral childhood insomnia. *Sleep Medicine*, *11*(7), 686–691. doi:10.1016/j.sleep.2009.11.017

Wolfson, A. R., & Carskadon, M. A. (1998). Sleep schedules and daytime functioning in adolescents. *Child Development*, *69*, 875–887. doi:10.1111/j.1467-8624.1998.tb06149.x

Wolitzky-Taylor, K., Bobova, L., Zinbarg, R. E., Mineka, S., & Craske, M. G. (2012). Longitudinal investigation of the impact of anxiety and mood disorders in adolescence on subsequent substance use disorder onset and vice versa. *Addictive Behaviors*, *37*(8), 982–985. doi:10.1016/j.addbeh.2012.03.026

Wong, M. M., & Brower, K. J. (2012). The prospective relationship between sleep problems and suicidal behavior in the national longitudinal study of adolescent health. *Journal of Psychiatric Research*, *46*(7), 953–959. doi:10.1016/j.jpsychires.2012.04.008

Yoo, S., Gujar, N., Hu, P., Jolesz, F. A., & Walker, M. P. (2007). The human emotional brain without sleep—A prefrontal amygdala disconnect. *Current Biology*, *17*(20), R877–R878.

Sleep Moderates the Association Between Response Inhibition and Self-Regulation in Early Childhood

Allyson M. Schumacher

Alison L. Miller

Sarah E. Watamura

Salome Kurth, Jonathan M. Lassonde, and Monique K. LeBourgeois

Early childhood is a time of rapid developmental changes in sleep, cognitive control processes, and the regulation of emotion and behavior. This experimental study examined sleep-dependent effects on response inhibition and self-regulation, as well as whether acute sleep restriction moderated the association between these processes. Preschool children (N = 19; 45.6 ± 2.2 months; 11 female) followed a strict sleep schedule for at least 3 days before each of 2 morning behavior assessments: baseline (habitual nap/night sleep) and sleep restriction (missed nap/delayed bedtime). Response inhibition was evaluated via a go/no-go task. Twelve self-regulation strategies were coded from videotapes of children while attempting an unsolvable puzzle. We then created composite variables representing adaptive and maladaptive self-regulation strategies. Although we found no sleep-dependent effects on response inhibition or self-regulation measures, linear mixed-effects regression showed that acute sleep restriction moderated the relationship between these processes. At baseline, children with better response inhibition were more likely to use adaptive self-regulation strategies (e.g., self-talk, alternate strategies), and those with poorer response inhibition showed increased use of maladaptive self-regulation strategies (e.g., perseveration, fidgeting); however, response inhibition was not related to self-regulation strategies following sleep restriction. Our results showing a sleep-dependent effect on the associations between response inhibition and self-regulation strategies indicate that adequate sleep facilitates synergy between processes supporting optimal social-emotional functioning in early childhood. Although replication studies are needed, findings suggest that sleep may alter connections between maturing emotional and cognitive systems, which have important implications for understanding risk for or resilience to developmental psychopathology.

INTRODUCTION

Early childhood is a sensitive period marked by rapid changes in executive function (EF) and self-regulation (Bell & Deater-Deckard, 2007; Carlson, 2005; Kochanska, Coy, & Murray, 2001; Zelazo et al., 2003), two key underlying processes necessary to achieve key developmental outcomes such as social-emotional adjustment (Riggs, Jahromi, Razza, Dillworth-Bart, & Mueller, 2006) and school readiness (Bierman, Nix, Greenberg, Blair, & Domitrovich, 2008; Blair & Diamond, 2008; McClelland & Cameron, 2012). Self-regulation generally refers to the processes that enable an individual to control one's behavior, attention, and emotion, especially in pursuit of a goal or when posed with a challenge (Raffaelli, Crockett, & Shen, 2005). EF is viewed as an overarching construct encompassing complex cognitions with three core components: working memory, mental flexibility, and response inhibition (Huizinga, Dolan, & Van Der Molen, 2006; Miyake et al., 2000). Although some consider response inhibition an aspect of self-regulation (Kochanska, 1997), we and many others (Blair & Ursache, 2011; Blair, Zelazo, & Greenberg, 2005; Hofmann, Schmeichel, & Baddeley, 2012; Posner & Rothbart, 1998) characterize response inhibition (a component of EF) as a related but distinct process from self-regulation because it is less emotionally charged and more cognitive in nature. Deficits in EF skills and the inability to self-regulate behavior when challenged are hallmarks of many child psychopathologies including externalizing behaviors such as attention deficit/hyperactivity disorder (ADHD) and impulsivity (e.g., if a child cannot inhibit his or her behavior when required in a classroom setting; Barkley, 1997; Gaub & Carlson, 1997), as well as internalizing behaviors such as anxiety (e.g., if a child lacks strategies to manage an emotionally challenging situation; Zahn-Waxler, Klimes-Dougan, & Slattery, 2000).

The relationship between EF and self-regulation is considered bidirectional (Blair & Dennis, 2010; Blair & Ursache, 2011). For example, EF skills facilitate self-regulation strategies by organizing thoughts and behaviors in goal-directed ways (Fuster, 2000; Ochsner & Gross, 2005). Likewise, taxing self-regulation may impair EF by depleting resources for complex cognition, especially during times of high mental "load" (Fuster, 2002). Furthermore, the interplay of EF and self-regulation is increasingly recognized as significant for optimal health outcomes, as the poor integration of emotion and cognitive processes is a risk factor for maladjustment and school failure (Eysenck, Derakshan, Santos, & Calvo, 2007) and has been suggested as a potential pathway contributing to developmental psychopathology (Blair & Dennis, 2010). Finally, an established developmental science literature suggests that both intrinsic child characteristics (e.g., age, sex, stress reactivity, temperament; Carlson & Wang, 2007; Hongwanishkul, Happaney, Lee, & Zelazo, 2005; Hughes & Ensor, 2008; Quas et al., 2014; Rothbart, Posner, & Kieras, 2006) and environmental factors (e.g., socioeconomic status, poverty, quality of caregiving; Blair, 2010; Blair & Raver, 2012) play a role in the development of EF skills and self-regulation, as well as in their association. Data from a number of studies indicate that sleep may also influence the interconnections between these developmental processes (Zohar, Tzischinsky, Epstein, & Lavie, 2005; reviewed in Dahl, 1996; Walker & Harvey, 2010).

Although sleep is increasingly recognized as an important factor in the cognitive and affective dimensions fundamental to EF and self-regulation in older children, adolescents, and adults (Baum et al., 2014; Hagger, 2010; Mauss, Troy, & LeBourgeois, 2013; Sadeh, Gruber, & Raviv, 2002; Talbot, McGlinchey, Kaplan, Dahl, & Harvey, 2010), well-controlled research that "simulates" experimentally how young children lose sleep in the real world is scarce. A few published findings suggest that insufficient sleep may disrupt the behavioral components that enable optimal cognitive and emotional functioning (e.g., response inhibition, self-regulation) during early childhood, the school-age years, and adolescence. For example, experimental and quasi-experimental data indicate that acute daytime sleep loss in regularly napping preschoolers leads to moderate-to-large decrements in objective assessments of self-regulation, emotion processing, and learning (Berger, Miller, Seifer, Cares, & LeBourgeois, 2012; Kurdziel, Duclos, & Spencer, 2013; Miller, Seifer, Crossin, & LeBourgeois, 2015). In addition, kindergarten and primary school-age students experiencing chronic experimental sleep restriction (i.e., multiple nights) show increased impulsivity and emotional lability (Gruber, Cassoff, Frenette, Wiebe, & Carrier, 2012), decreased brain processing under high cognitive "load" (Molfese et al., 2013), and/or impaired neurobehavioral functioning (i.e., attention, working memory, processing speed); however, such effects are not consistent across studies and are commonly task dependent. For example, Vriend et al. (2013) reported reduced emotion regulation and performance on memory tasks but no differences in performance on multiple tasks assessing attention after 4 nights of 1-hr sleep restriction (compared to baseline) in 8- to 12-year-olds. Similarly, in a study of 8- to 15-year-olds, Fallone, Acebo, Arnedt, Seifer, and Carskadon (2001) found increased inattentive behaviors but no change in performance on tasks measuring response inhibition or sustained attention after chronic sleep restriction (5 nights of 4 hr of sleep) as compared to sleep optimization. Finally, in a study by Sadeh, Gruber, and Raviv (2003), 1 hr of sleep restriction across 3 nights led to worse performance on a simple reaction time task but did not significantly change performance on other tasks measuring working memory, attention, or response inhibition in fourth to sixth graders (9–12 years of age). Such variable findings in older children and adolescents suggest that studying the sleep-dependent effects on cognitive and emotional processes (e.g., response inhibition, self-regulation) that are central to healthy development in early childhood is warranted.

Longitudinal and cross-sectional data indicate dramatic shifts in the timing, duration, and quality of sleep between the toddler and kindergarten years: Total 24-hr sleep duration decreases by about 20%, daytime napping declines, and evening behavioral sleep problems (e.g., sleep onset delay, bedtime resistance) commonly emerge (Beltramini & Hertzig, 1983; Iglowstein, Jenni, Molinari, & Largo, 2003; Kataria, Swanson, & Trevathan, 1987; Zuckerman, Stevenson, & Bailey, 1987; reviewed in Honaker & Meltzer, 2014). Insufficient sleep is also prevalent: Approximately 30% of parents report that their toddler or preschooler does not get enough sleep (National Sleep Foundation, 2004), and objective actigraphic data indicate that young children on average obtain less than the recommended 10–13 hr of sleep (Acebo et al., 2005). Further, a number of observational studies suggest links between sleep in early childhood and initial indicators of developmental psychopathology. For example, parent-reported short sleep duration and sleep problems during the preschool years are associated with concurrent reports of behavioral and emotional disturbance, including anxiety, depression, hyperactivity, and impulsivity (Bates, Viken, Alexander, Beyers, & Stockton, 2002; Goodlin-Jones, Tang, Liu, & Anders, 2009; Lavigne et al., 1999; Reid, Hong, & Wade, 2009). Longitudinal data also suggest that the consequences of sleep problems and insufficient sleep in early childhood may persist into the school-age years and adolescence, thus posing a risk for later mood and attentional problems (Gregory & O'Connor, 2002; Touchette et al., 2007; Wong, Brower, & Zucker, 2009).

Although links between poor or insufficient sleep and psychopathology are well documented (Walker & Harvey, 2010), very few studies have focused on the underlying mechanisms contributing to such relationships in childhood. The published data demonstrating sleep-dependent effects on response inhibition and self-regulation have examined them *independent of each other*; however, the cognitive processes involved in response inhibition are intricately bound with the emotional processes involved in self-regulation during a challenge (Bell & Deater-Deckard, 2007; Bell & Wolfe, 2004). Also, poorly connected cognitive and emotional processes have been recognized in psychopathologies during childhood including depression (Blair & Dennis, 2010; Hayden, Klein, Durbin, & Olino, 2006), anxiety disorders (Mennin, Heimberg, Turk, & Fresco, 2002), and ADHD (Barkley, 1997). Further, observational data indicate that sleep moderates the relationship between psychological processes such as emotional insecurity or intelligence and outcomes such as adjustment and academic achievement during childhood (El-Sheikh, Buckhalt, Keller, Cummings, & Acebo, 2007; Erath, Tu, Buckhalt, & El-Sheikh, 2015). Although the literature supports the need for well-controlled experimental research examining the degree to which sleep moderates associations between cognitive and emotional processes underlying developmental psychopathology, such investigations are scarce.

The current study addresses this impetus and several significant gaps in understanding the interplay between sleep, response inhibition, and self-regulation in early childhood. First, as late bedtimes are a risk factor for poor emotional and behavioral outcomes (Asarnow, McGlinchey, & Harvey, 2014; Bates et al., 2002), we utilized an experimental protocol that "mimicked" this type of sleep loss in preschool children by first establishing stable baseline sleep and then introducing sleep loss with randomly assigned timing. With this protocol, our aim was to extend our previously published data showing that nap deprivation resulted in nonadaptive self-regulation strategies in toddlers (Miller et al., 2015). Second, we examined whether acute sleep restriction produced differences in not only self-regulation strategies but also response inhibition. Finally, we utilized an integrative approach supported by the developmental science literature (Bell & Deater-Deckard, 2007; Bell & Wolfe, 2004; Blair, 2002; Gray, 1990; Leventhal & Scherer, 1987) to explore whether acute sleep loss would moderate associations between EF and self-regulation strategies.

METHOD

Participant Recruitment and Screening

Participants were 19 healthy 40- to 48-month-old children (45.6 ± 2.2 months; 11 female; 89% Caucasian, 11% mixed race) who were enrolled in an ongoing longitudinal study of the codevelopment and coregulation of sleep; circadian rhythms; and multiple cognitive, behavioral, and health outcomes. Children entered the study at ages 30–36 months; this within-subjects analysis includes data from the children who completed the 2nd year of the study at ages 40–48 months. Families were recruited from the Boulder, CO, area via community outreach events, flyers, and website advertisements. Parents were 36.3 ± 5.0 years of age (mother) and 39.1 ± 5.5 years (father), attained an education level ranging from high school to graduate degree (for mothers, 50% completed some college or a 4-year college degree, 50% graduate degree; for fathers, 17% completed high school, 44% some college or a 4 year college degree, 39% graduate degree), and average annual family income was $109,444. A telephone-screening interview and questionnaires were used to evaluate study eligibility. Study inclusion required that children were healthy, typically developing, sleeping on a regular sleep–wakefulness schedule, and reportedly napping three times or more per week. Children were excluded based on the following criteria: cosleeping (i.e., bed sharing); travel beyond two time zones within 3 months of the study; regular use of medications affecting sleep or alertness; reported or diagnosed sleep problems; developmental disabilities, neurologic/metabolic disorders, chronic medical conditions, lead poisoning, or head injury involving loss of consciousness; conceptual age < 35 weeks or > 45 weeks; low birth weight (< 5.5 lb); or a family history (first degree) of diagnosed narcolepsy, psychosis, or bipolar disorder. We rescreened children to confirm study criteria before their 40- to 48-month-old assessments; however, because napping naturally declines across early childhood (Iglowstein et al., 2003; Weissbluth, 1995), we expected that some children would be sleeping only at night (i.e., not napping; criteria > 1 month). Thus, for this analysis, participants were not required to take naps (26%; $n = 5$ not napping). Of the 27 children who met criteria at rescreening, 25 completed both behavior assessments. Of these, six were not included in this analysis due to noncompliance ($n = 2$) or failure to demonstrate understanding of the response inhibition task ($n = 4$). Thus, our final sample included 19 preschoolers. Parents signed an informed consent form approved by the University of Colorado Institutional Review Board. Study procedures were performed in accordance with the Declaration of Helsinki. Parents were compensated with cash, and children received a U.S. savings bond and small nonmonetary gifts.

Protocol

Children followed an individualized, strict sleep schedule for at least 3 days based on their habitual sleep–wakefulness pattern (i.e., napping or not napping). This standard lead-in interval is important to promote stabilization of the circadian system and to optimize sleep duration before the experimental sleep protocol. In-home behavior assessments were completed in the morning following two conditions (Figure 1): baseline (children maintained their individual strict sleep schedule) and sleep restriction (16 hr of prior wakefulness; no nap and about a 3-hr bedtime delay; scheduled morning wake time). Conditions were counterbalanced, with an intervening 5 or more days on the sleep schedule between assessments. Both assessments occurred 3 hr after habitual morning wake time (10:01 ± 00:18) to minimize the effects of sleep inertia and to simulate a time when children are likely to be engaging in activities at preschool. The response inhibition task was always administered before the self-regulation task.

Adherence to study rules was monitored through daily correspondence via telephone or e-mail and verified with wrist actigraphy and sleep diaries. In the event of a protocol violation (i.e., accidental nap; sleep patterns deviating > 15 min from set schedule; illness; use of medications affecting sleep and/or alertness; caffeine consumption), assessments were rescheduled after an additional 3 or more days on the sleep schedule. Assessments for eight children (42%) were rescheduled due to protocol violations.

Actigraphy

We utilized standard laboratory procedures for collecting, checking, and scoring actigraphy data, as detailed in our previous publications (Berger et al., 2012; LeBourgeois et al., 2013; Simpkin et al., 2014). Daily sleep diary questions asked about lights-off and wake times for nap and nighttime sleep and intervals when the actigraph was off (Akacem et al., 2015). The actigraph (model AW Spectrum) was worn on the child's nondominant wrist and provided continuous recordings of sleep/wakefulness states by measurement of motor activity (Philips/Respironics, Pittsburg, PA). For each sleep episode, three actigraph variables were derived: (a) *time in bed*—minutes from lights-off to lights-on, (b) *sleep duration*—minutes from sleep start to sleep end, and (c) *sleep efficiency*—% of sleep epochs between sleep start and sleep end time. Although actigraphy measures were not primary outcomes in this study, they were used to verify sleep schedule protocol compliance (Table 2).

Behavior Assessments and Coding

Our experimental protocol included objective assessment of response inhibition and adaptive, as well as maladaptive self-regulation strategies reflecting the ability to cope with a challenge. The setup for behavior tasks included a child-size chair and table with a video camera positioned to capture the child's body from the chest up. The response inhibition task was administered on a touch screen computer.

Response Inhibition

Response inhibition was measured via a standard go/no-go task (Willoughby, Wirth, Blair, & Family Life Project, 2012). In this task, a line drawing of one of seven possible animals appeared on the touch-screen computer. Children were

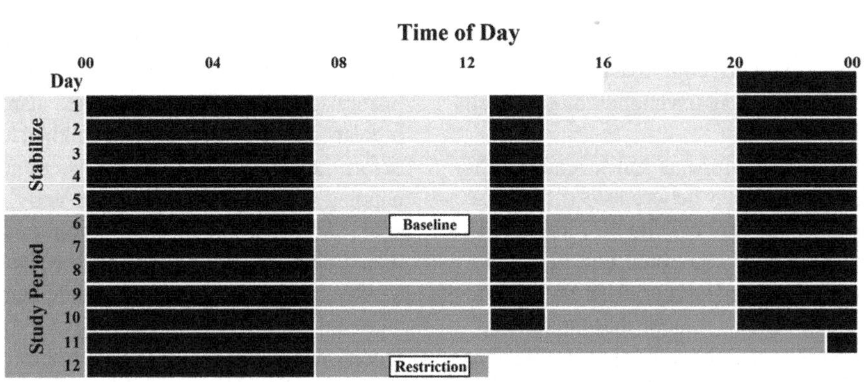

FIGURE 1 Sample protocol for an exemplary child following a stabilization sleep schedule (20:00 bedtime, 07:00 wake time, and 12:30–14:00 afternoon nap opportunity). *Note*. Black bars represent time in bed, gray bars represent time awake, and white boxes indicate the timing of behavior assessments (baseline, sleep restriction). Behavior assessments took place 3 hr after regularly scheduled morning wake time.

instructed to touch a green button on the screen as fast as they could every time an animal appeared, except when the animal was a pig (no-go trials). Up to three training trials were administered first to ensure adequate understanding of task demands. If a child failed all three training trials, the task was discontinued. Eight no-go trials were dispersed among 40 total animal trials. Response inhibition performance was quantified as the % correct inhibitions on no-go trials (out of eight possible; see Table 3).

Self-Regulation

Self-regulation was assessed through administration of our previously published task used to measure young children's behavioral responses to challenge (Berger et al., 2012; Miller et al., 2015) and was adapted from procedures by Smiley and Dweck (1994). The task included an age-appropriate but unsolvable puzzle in which there was a wrong piece that prevented task completion. When all pieces but the misfit piece were successfully placed, children attempted the puzzle for 1 additional min and then were prompted by the examiner to "finish the puzzle" and asked "Why can't you finish the puzzle?" and "What can you do to finish the puzzle?" This task was designed to resemble a challenge that preschoolers may encounter in their daily lives. Children were videotaped during the task, and adaptive and maladaptive self-regulation strategies were later coded as defined in the literature (Berhenke, Miller, Brown, Seifer, & Dickstein, 2011; Smiley & Dweck, 1994) and based on our prior published work (Miller et al., 2015). Self-regulation strategies were coded from videotapes by trained researchers using The Observer XT version 11.0 (Noldus Technologies, Wageningen, The Netherlands). We observed high intercoder correlations for all coded strategies (> 90%). Coders consulted with an expert reviewer (coauthor ALM) for consensus coding as needed.

Twelve self-regulation strategies were coded during the puzzle task (Table 1). The percent time each strategy was used was calculated during the 5 s after the child was prompted to "finish the puzzle," as our previous work indicates that this portion of the task marks the time of most salient challenge and elicits the strongest effects on emotion expression and self-regulation (Berger et al., 2012; Miller et al., 2015). Coded self-regulation strategies were based on and modified from previous work (Berhenke et al., 2011; Miller et al., 2015) and included both adaptive and maladaptive responses to the puzzle challenge. Adaptive self-regulation strategies involved a child attempting to actively address the challenge and problem solve (i.e., healthy skepticism, solicit help, social referencing, self-talk, alternate strategies, cognitive reappraisal). Strategies that reflected a limited ability to effectively cope with the challenge were considered maladaptive (i.e., negative self-appraisal, focusing on the misfit piece, perseveration, fidgeting, insistence on completion). Composite scores of adaptive and maladaptive self-regulation were computed by averaging the z scores of relevant self-regulation strategies based on our theoretical understanding of these adaptive and maladaptive self-regulation strategies and our previously published work (Miller et al., 2015). A negative correlation between adaptive and maladaptive self-regulation composite scores ($r = -.49, p = .03$) indicates that when children use adaptive self-regulation strategies, they are less likely to use maladaptive strategies. This moderate correspondence between adaptive and nonadaptive strategies indicates convergence on the latent construct "self-regulation" yet highlights the importance of distinct self-regulatory dimensions.

Analysis

Descriptive features of the distribution of each behavioral outcome were first inspected for normality (presented as *M, SD*). Because the behavioral data were positively skewed in the sleep restriction condition, we employed Wilcoxon matched-pairs signed-rank tests (two-tailed) to examine sleep-dependent differences in response inhibition and self-regulation composites. In addition, we used Wilcoxon matched-pairs signed-rank tests (two-tailed) to verify that there were no order (learning) effects from one assessment to the other on either the go/no-go task or any of the self-regulation strategies used during the unsolvable puzzle task. Linear mixed-effects regression was then used to determine whether sleep moderated the relationship between response inhibition and adaptive and maladaptive self-regulation. With this analysis, each subject served as his or her own control. We chose to examine one dimension of EF, response inhibition, not only based on the appreciation that inhibitory control is the most elementary aspect of EF (Carlson & Wang, 2007; Jahromi & Stifter, 2008) but also because it is integral to the development of self-regulation in early childhood (Riggs et al., 2006). Although the relationship between EF and self-regulation is bidirectional, cognitive control processes are considered the cornerstone of coping and regulation of behavior; thus, we selected adaptive and maladaptive self-regulation strategies as our outcomes of interest and included composite scores of these as the dependent variables in separate models. Response inhibition, sleep condition, and the interaction between response inhibition and sleep condition were included as independent variables in each model. Finally, Pearson correlations (two-tailed) were computed to examine the association between response inhibition and adaptive and maladaptive self-regulation in each condition (linearity inspected with scatterplots). The alpha level for all analyses was set at .05. All statistical analyses were performed in R version 3.1.1 (R Core Team, Vienna, Austria).

RESULTS

Sleep Schedule and Protocol Verification

We found no significant differences between children's average actigraphic sleep measures (i.e., lights-off time, wake time,

TABLE 1
Coded Self-Regulation Strategies

	Strategy Definition
Adaptive Self-Regulation	
Cognitive Reappraisal	Child attempts to reframe the task to view it in more positive manner (e.g., "It's okay; we can do the other pieces without it.")
Alternate Strategies	Child uses appropriate problem-solving strategies to attempt to fit the wrong piece (e.g., rotating the wrong piece in the spot, trying to put the piece in a different spot, etc.)
Self-Talk	Child talks to himself or herself (any type verbalization not addressed to someone else)
Solicit Help	Child directly asks experimenter for help with the task (e.g., "Can you help me?")
Healthy Skepticism	Child makes comment that indicates that she or he understands something is wrong with the puzzle (e.g., "This piece doesn't go here")
Social Referencing	Child looks to another person for information about how to respond, think or feel about an environmental event or stimuli
Comfort Seeking	Child initiates interaction with another person in the hope of obtaining comfort, not help with the task
Maladaptive Self-Regulation	
Focus on Wrong Piece	Child fixates on the wrong piece and may ignore other pieces
Insistence on Completion	Child insists puzzle is finished—may accept or ignore that the wrong piece does not fit
Negative Self-Appraisal	Child attributes trouble with the task to personal attributes (i.e., "This is too hard for me")
Perseveration	Child is focused on a task element that is no longer (or was never) productive (e.g., attempting to cram the wrong piece into a spot)
Fidgeting	Any repetitive, purposeless motion of the legs, arms, hands, buttocks, or trunk; reflects worry and anxiety
Disruptive Behavior	Child acts in a way that is disruptive or aggressive (yelling, kicking, etc.)

TABLE 2
Actigraphic Sleep Measures for the First 4 Days, and 24 hr Before Each Behavior Assessment

	Baseline		*Sleep Restriction*		*Statistics*		
	M	SD	M	SD	t	d	p
4 Days Before Assessments							
Nap Lights-Off Time	13:13	0:35	13:12	0:23	0.18	0.03	.86
Nap Wake Time	14:52	0:34	14:47	0:32	0.73	0.14	.48
Night Lights-Off Time	20:08	0:24	20:04	0:23	1.28	0.16	.22
Morning Wake Time	06:39	0:22	06:42	0:26	−1.00	−0.16	.33
24 hr Time in Bed (hr)	11.5	0.6	11.7	0.5	−1.49	−0.27	.15
24 hr Sleep Duration (hr)	10.7	0.6	10.9	0.5	−0.95	−0.17	.36
24 hr Sleep Efficiency (%)	88.3	3.5	89.0	3.6	−0.77	−0.19	.45
24 hr Before Assessments							
Nap Lights-Off Time	13:17	0:32	—	—	—	—	—
Nap Wake Time	14:52	0:41	—	—	—	—	—
Nights Lights-Off Time	20:07	0:28	22:34	0:30	−14.50	−5.11	<.01
Morning Wake Time	06:43	0:27	06:54	0:25	−1.47	−0.39	.16
Time in Bed (hr)	11.7	0.9	8.3	0.5	13.71	4.85	<.01
Sleep Duration (hr)	10.9	0.5	8.1	0.5	12.87	4.99	<.01
Sleep Efficiency (%)	89.5	3.2	90.1	4.0	−0.67	−0.17	.51

time in bed, sleep efficiency; Table 2) during the first 4 days before each behavior assessment. Because children did not nap and stayed up late during the sleep restriction condition, we expected differences in sleep during the 24 hr preceding each behavior assessment. Average lights-off time was 2.5 hr later on the night before the sleep restriction condition relative to the baseline condition; however, morning wake time did not differ, as expected by the stipulated experimental protocol. Children spent approximately 3.4 hr less time in bed and had shorter sleep durations of about 2.7 hr during the sleep restriction relative to the baseline condition. Sleep efficiency was similar between conditions ($p > .05$).

We also used actigraphy data to determine whether sleep measures differed between napping ($n = 14$) and non-napping children ($n = 5$). Although 24-hr sleep duration was similar between these two groups ($p > .05$), non-napping children slept 39 min longer at night than those who napped ($t = 2.4$, $d = 1.19$, $p = .03$). The amount of sleep loss in the sleep restriction condition relative to baseline was similar between napping groups ($p > .05$). Thus, our sleep manipulation presented a similar challenge to all participants, whether they were regularly napping or not. We found no differences in response inhibition and self-regulation performance between napping and non-napping children in either condition or in changes between conditions (all $ps > .05$).

Response Inhibition and Self-Regulation

Wilcoxon matched-pairs signed-rank tests showed no significant effect of order on any behavioral measure (response inhibition or self-regulation), indicating that there was no learning effect between assessments (all $ps > .05$). Wilcoxon matched-pairs signed-rank tests revealed no significant effect of sleep restriction on response inhibition or adaptive or maladaptive self-regulation strategies (Table 3). We did observe interindividual differences in children's responses to sleep restriction, with some children performing better in the baseline condition, whereas others improved after sleep restriction. With regard to response inhibition, 26% performed better in baseline and 63% better in sleep restriction. For adaptive self-regulation, 59% used more in baseline and 37% used more in sleep restriction. Finally, with reference to maladaptive self-regulation, 68% used less in baseline and 32% used less in sleep restriction.

Results from the linear mixed-effects regression models are summarized in Table 4. The interaction between response inhibition performance and sleep condition significantly predicted adaptive and maladaptive self-regulation (adaptive: $\beta = -1.35$, $p = .041$; maladaptive: $\beta = 2.60$, $p < .001$), indicating that sleep restriction moderated the association between response inhibition and adaptive and maladaptive self-regulation.

Figure 2 provides scatterplots of the associations between response inhibition performance and self-regulation composites. In the baseline condition, we found a strong correlation between response inhibition performance and adaptive self-regulation ($r = .63$, $p = .004$; Figure 2A), such that children with better response inhibition used more adaptive self-regulation strategies. However, a similar association between response inhibition and adaptive self-regulation in the sleep restriction condition was not observed ($r = -.12$, $p = .63$; Figure 2B). We also found a strong negative association between response inhibition performance and maladaptive self-regulation in the baseline condition ($r = -.63$, $p = .004$; Figure 2C). Children exhibiting poor response inhibition were more likely to use maladaptive self-regulation. Again, this association was not observed following sleep restriction ($r = .22$, $p = .37$; Figure 2D).

TABLE 4
Linear Mixed-Effects Models

	Adaptive SR			*Maladaptive SR*		
Variable	*β*	SE (*β*)	z	*β*	SE (*β*)	z
Response Inhibition	2.63	1.22	2.16*	−4.85	1.26	−3.86***
Sleep Condition	1.01	0.53	1.89	−2.05	0.54	−3.80***
Response Inhibition × Sleep Condition	−1.35	0.66	−2.05*	2.60	0.67	3.87***

Note: SR = self-regulation.
*$p < .05$. ***$p < .001$.

DISCUSSION

This study utilized a well-controlled experimental protocol to examine sleep-dependent effects on response inhibition and self-regulation (i.e., adaptive strategies, nonadaptive strategies) separately, as well as to determine whether acute sleep loss moderated the association between response inhibition and self-regulation in early childhood. In our sample of healthy, good sleeping 40- to 48-month-olds, acute sleep restriction of about 2.7 hr did not reveal a main effect on response inhibition performance or self-regulation strategies during a challenge task. Sleep loss, however, did alter the strength of the interconnection between these measures of cognitive and emotional control. That is, response inhibition was strongly associated with self-regulation when children were well rested but not following sleep restriction. This finding suggests that acute sleep loss across 1 day and night leads to a disconnect between key processes that underlie a number of childhood outcomes, including social-emotional adjustment, school readiness, and mood. The results of this original investigation build upon existing observational, clinical, and other experimental data supporting the importance of sleep for healthy

TABLE 3
Descriptive Statistics of Response Inhibition and Adaptive and Maladaptive Self-Regulation

	Baseline		*Sleep Restriction*		*Statistics*		
Variable	M	SD	M	SD	z	d	p
Response Inhibition (%)	78.29	13.07	81.58	22.96	−0.95	−0.18	.34
Adaptive SR (*z* score)	−0.09	0.33	−0.08	0.44	−1.01	0.15	.31
Maladaptive SR (*z* score)	0.05	0.55	0.05	0.38	−0.56	0.00	.57

Note: SR = self-regulation.

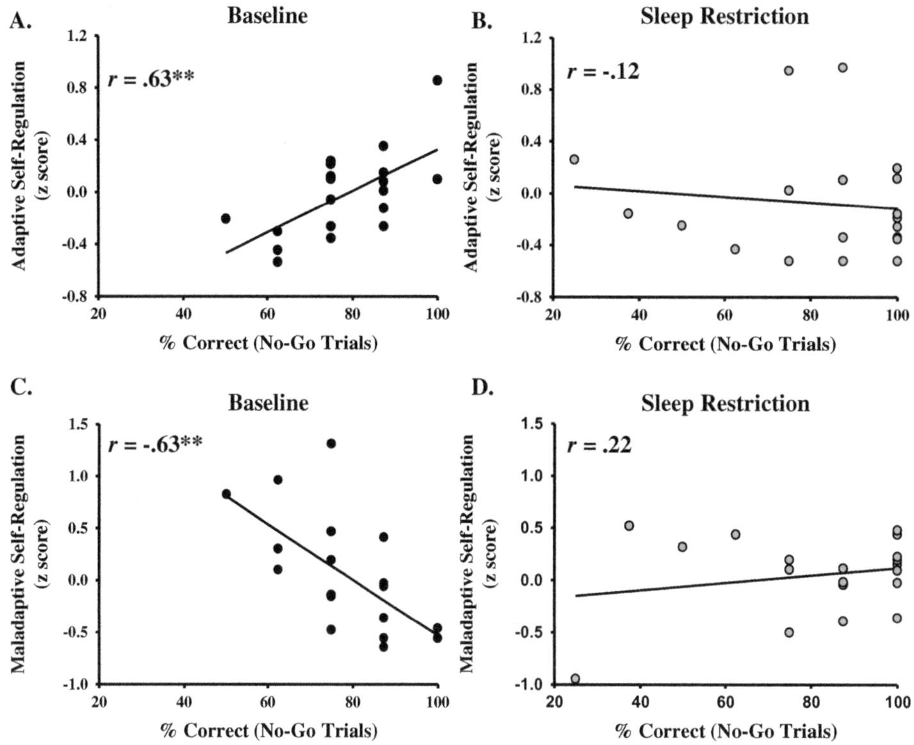

FIGURE 2 Scatterplots of associations between response inhibition performance (% correct on no-go trials) and adaptive and maladaptive self-regulation composite scores in the baseline and sleep restriction conditions. *Note*: $*p < .05$. $**p < .01$.

cognitive and emotional development. They also lay the foundation for additional experimental studies that are needed to replicate and extend our results and thus increase understanding of sleep-related pathways that may promote mood, learning, and attentional disorders. Findings are discussed with regard to the importance of sleep for healthy systemic interactions and risk for developmental psychopathology.

Sleep Moderates the Association Between EF and Self-Regulation

An established literature indicates that cognitive and emotional processes are independent predictors of child functioning in academic and social contexts (Bierman et al., 2008; Blair & Diamond, 2008; Bridgett, Oddi, Laake, Murdock, & Bachmann, 2013; McClelland & Cameron, 2012; Riggs et al., 2006); however, expanding developmental science and theoretical frameworks suggest the importance of studying the predictors of the interconnections across multiple systems (Bauer, Quas, & Boyce, 2002; Bridgett et al., 2013; Quas et al., 2014). Indeed, EF skills are proposed to underlie the capacity to self-regulate in response to stress or challenge (Hofmann et al., 2012). Furthermore, a growing literature shows that interactions among these different stress-response systems together shape child functioning and that patterns of intersystem connection are influenced by environmental variables such as SES (Blair, 2010; Quas et al., 2014). In addition, few observational data suggest that associations between EF and self-regulation during early childhood may be altered by child characteristics. One such study found that verbal ability and age moderated the relationship between inhibitory control and emotion regulation measures (Carlson & Wang, 2007). Others recognize that differing temperaments may influence how recruiting EF skills for cognitive control may contribute to self-regulation (Fox & Calkins, 2003; Hongwanishkul et al., 2005). To date, few published studies have considered how sleep loss as a stressor may disrupt the connections between EF and self-regulation in early childhood, and to our knowledge none have utilized an experimental approach. Thus, our data make an important contribution to both the child development and sleep literatures and suggest that sleep is a significant yet underappreciated state that may be critical for healthy integration of multiple regulatory systems.

In this study, we found no main effects of acute sleep loss on measures of response inhibition and self-regulation; however, we did observe a sleep-dependent moderation of the association between these two performance measures. Although these findings may appear contradictory, they align with propositions made in two theoretical models and neuroimaging findings in adults. First, nearly two decades ago, Dahl (1996) described a developmental framework for studying the interplay between regulatory systems (e.g., sleep, attention, affect, arousal) based on overlap in clinical, behavioral, and physiological domains, as well as the importance of the prefrontal cortex (PFC) in modulating the integration of such processes (Dahl, 1996). According to this model, sleep loss poses a relatively small challenge to cognition in "isolated" conditions; however, when such cognitive demands are presented in the context of demanding emotional or social situations, decrements in self-regulation are more likely. Second, Zohar and colleagues' cognitive-energy model proposes that sleep loss may reduce cognitive energy stores and impair the ability to call upon these resources to promote regulation of emotion and behavior (Zohar et al., 2005).

In addition, data from functional neuroimaging studies performed in the past decade provide strong evidence that sleep plays a significant role in altering interconnections between brain regions involved in the regulation of emotion (reviewed in Goldstein & Walker, 2014). For example, a recent study performed in adults showed that all-night sleep deprivation causes a functional disconnect between the mPFC and amygdala during an emotionally salient task. Such findings suggest that when adults obtain adequate sleep, the PFC is tightly coupled with the amygdala and thus can exert inhibitory control over emotions, whereas without sleep this connectivity and associated cognitive control is diminished (Yoo, Gujar, Hu, Jolesz, & Walker, 2007). Our behavioral data indicating a decoupling between response inhibition and self-regulation with sleep loss map onto these neurophysiological data and suggest that sleep may be especially important for developing connectivity between cognitive and emotion centers of the brain. Indeed, although the neural bases of EF and self-regulation in early childhood are not fully understood, some structural and functional evidence exists. For example, accumulating neuroimaging data indicates that the development of EF and self-regulation is attributed to maturation of the connectivity between cognitive and emotional brain regions (e.g., Belden, Luby, Pagliaccio, & Barch, 2014; Bell & Wolfe, 2004; Cacioppo & Berntson, 1999; Gabard-Durnam et al., 2014; Gee et al., 2013; Luking et al., 2011). The developing functional links between EF and self-regulation are, in part, due to maturation of the PFC, which is reciprocally connected to the amygdala and provides cognitive control of emotion and behavior (Bush, Luu, & Posner, 2000). Of interest, recent resting state functional MRI data indicate that connectivity between the mPFC and amygdala increases between the preschool years and adulthood; however, the functional coupling of such brain regions critical for the regulation of arousal and emotion is not significant in early childhood; adultlike connectivity first emerges at around 10 years of age (Gabard-Durnam et al., 2014). Thus, developmental changes in functional connectivity between regions assumed critical for EF-self-regulation interactions during childhood may make this pathway especially vulnerable to disruption; however, to our knowledge, data on the functional connectivity of emotional and cognitive brain regions after sleep loss do not exist.

Sleep Restriction as a Probe for Understanding Sleep Function in Childhood

Previous experimental studies examining relationships between sleep and aspects of emotion, self-regulation, and neurodevelopment have produced mixed results. For example, Sadeh and colleagues reported that three consecutive nights of 1-hr sleep restriction in kindergarten students impaired tasks measuring simple processing speed, whereas performance on more complex cognitive tasks was preserved (Sadeh et al., 2003). In another study, 5 nights of sleep restriction resulted in increased inattention but no significant decrements in response inhibition in 8- to 15-year-olds (Fallone et al., 2001). Such discrepant findings have been attributed primarily to factors such as the task type or the level of cognitive or emotional load elicited by the task or the specific task type (Drummond et al., 1999; Franzen, Buysse, Dahl, Thompson, & Siegle, 2009; Molfese et al., 2013; Randazzo, Muehlbach, Schweitzer, & Walsh, 1998; Vriend et al., 2013). Such explanations may also apply to our study, as children were older than those in our previous work, thus potentially making the unsolvable puzzle task less challenging.

Our data showing no acute sleep-dependent effects on response inhibition or self-regulation strategies in preschoolers also suggest that the level of "challenge" to the homeostatic sleep system as determined by prescribed experimental protocols may also provide important clues for interpreting mixed results. For instance, quasi-experimental data in preschoolers indicate that napping is important for learning, but only for children who habitually meet part of their 24-hr sleep need with a daytime nap (Kurdziel et al., 2013). We have also shown that nap deprivation of about 90 min in regularly napping toddlers leads to decrements in emotion processing (Berger et al., 2012) and self-regulation strategies (Miller et al., 2015), with effect sizes similar to studies of adults after 1 night of total sleep deprivation. In the current study, however, we utilized a slightly different protocol that simulated another way that children may lose sleep in the real world. We extended their wakefulness by 16 hr, including no napping and a bedtime delay of about 3 hr, and then performed behavioral assessments the following morning when children were likely to be in preschool engaged in social and learning activities. Although we utilized the same challenge task (unsolvable puzzle) as in our previous nap deprivation work (Berger et al., 2012; Miller et al., 2015), our current results differed from these nap-dependent findings. This may imply that nap deprivation poses a robust challenge in regularly napping children when assessed in the afternoon at a time of high homeostatic sleep load (Jenni & LeBourgeois, 2006), whereas our current approach allowed children to obtain some sleep (about 8 hr) and thus potentially "recover" in part from sleep loss. Thus, other protocols such as chronic sleep restriction or sleep promotion in children experiencing insufficient sleep may be warranted to understand the role of sleep in independent aspects of cognition and emotion in early childhood.

Our counterbalanced design produced no order effects ($p > .05$); however, close visual inspection indicated large interindividual variability in children's response to sleep restriction. Some children had better response inhibition and self-regulation in the baseline condition, whereas others showed the opposite response to acute sleep loss. Additional research is necessary to identify potential behavioral, physiological, and social factors that may explain why some children experienced performance decrements after sleep restriction and some did not. The need for understanding individual differences in the sensitivity to acute and chronic sleep loss in adolescence and adulthood is an area of keen interest, with safety, academic, and mental health implications (Leproult et al., 2003; Van Dongen & Belenky, 2009); however, little is known about brain and behavioral markers that differentiate young children's sleep-dependent responses and whether they track susceptibility or resilience to sleep loss across the life span. Data from El-Sheikh and colleagues (2007) suggested that race and socioeconomic status may moderate associations between sleep quality and cognitive functioning during childhood; however, additional research on other factors that may contribute to children's sensitivity to sleep loss (e.g., sex, chronotype) using well-controlled experimental designs is needed, especially given that early childhood is a sensitive period in neurobehavioral development.

Implications for Developmental Psychopathology

Our results indicating that sleep loss alters the behavioral integration between EF and self-regulation in early childhood has important implications for healthy development, as well as developmental psychopathology (Dahl, 1996). EF and self-regulation are considered foundations of school readiness and are independently associated with emotional and behavioral problems. For example, children with difficulties regulating behavior and emotion are more likely to have unhealthy social relationships (Eisenberg et al., 1995) and poor academic outcomes (Blair, 2002). In addition, EF skills are associated with childhood externalizing problems (Lewis, Lamm, Segalowitz, Stieben, & Zelazo, 2006; Riggs et al., 2006) and depression and anxiety. A lack of integration between cognitive and emotional processes has been identified in those with depression (Blair & Dennis, 2010; Hayden et al., 2006). Further, the inability to recruit EF skills to regulate emotions effectively is a key aspect of anxiety disorders (Mennin et al., 2002). Poor EF (inhibitory control and working memory) and the inability to recruit such mechanisms for self-regulation are central to ADHD (Barkley, 1997). The behavioral manifestation of experimental sleep restriction resembles ADHD-like symptoms in healthy children (Fallone et al., 2001). Taken together, we propose that the disruption of neurological and behavioral pathways underlying emotion–cognition links may be mechanisms by which insufficient sleep accelerates the progression of multiple mental health disorders, including anxiety, depression, and ADHD. Furthermore, our data highlight the need for studying multiple systems in tandem and including sleep as part of models for understanding predictors and outcomes of the connectivity between EF and self-regulation as cornerstones of mental health.

Limitations and Future Directions

In this study, we employed a rigorous experimental design and strict study criteria, which increased control of nuisance variables known to influence our outcomes of interest. Although this approach likely diminished the external validity of our findings, it did provide important insights for future research directions. We chose previously published tasks of response inhibition and self-regulation that approximate the situations that children likely encounter in daily life; however, they were administered in a "lab-type" home setting. This approach limits the generalizability of our findings to real-world settings such as preschool, where learning activities present dynamic challenges incorporating EF skills and self-regulation in a social context. We observed a positive skew in the distribution of the response inhibition measure, which may reflect a ceiling effect due to our sample of generally high-functioning children and therefore may have reduced our ability to detect significant sleep-dependent changes due to reduced variability. Experimental sleep studies that utilize observational behavioral assessments of self-regulation in real-world preschool settings are a rich area for future investigation (Ferrier, Bassett, & Denham, 2014; Ponitz, McClelland, Matthews, & Morrison, 2009). Furthermore, we enrolled a sample including only healthy children with no sleep, behavioral, emotional, or developmental problems and whose family context allowed for stable sleep schedules. Our sample was also primarily Caucasian, well educated, and of middle to upper socioeconomic class. Given the high prevalence of sleep and behavior problems in early childhood (Beltramini & Hertzig, 1983; Briggs-Gowan, Carter, Skuban, & Horwitz, 2001; Kataria et al., 1987; Zuckerman et al., 1987), their co-occurrence (Goodlin-Jones et al., 2009; Lavigne et al., 1999; Reid et al., 2009), and disparities in the sleep health of children living in poverty or of minority status (Acebo et al., 2005; Stein, Mendelsohn, Obermeyer, Amromin, & Benca, 2001), we propose the need for additional experimental studies across diverse groups.

Additional areas of fruitful investigation in uncovering the interplay between sleep and developmental substrates are numerous. First, as sleep is a modifiable health-risk behavior, future research could utilize education programs for parents and teachers to promote healthy sleep or behavioral interventions for preschoolers suffering from insufficient sleep (Garrison, 2014). Some intervention programs, such as Head Start REDI (Bierman et al., 2008; Blair & Razza, 2007) or Tools of the Mind (Bodrova & Leong, 2007; Diamond, Barnett, Thomas, & Munro, 2007), seek to improve emotional competence and academic success by targeting EF and self-regulation. Our findings suggest that sleep should be incorporated in these programs in order to promote maximum benefits. Second, we targeted only one aspect of EF (i.e., response inhibition) and did not examine discrete facial measures of emotion expression (Berger et al., 2012). Thus, future sleep-related studies should incorporate additional dimensions of cognitive control (i.e., working memory, mental flexibility) and emotion processing in their interaction with self-regulation (Ferrier et al., 2014). Third, as insufficient sleep is considered a stressor that influences cognitive control, emotion processing, and self-regulation, additional experimental sleep studies that incorporate physiological measures of sympathetic and parasympathetic activation with behavior may provide key insights into how such systems work in tandem. Finally, as previously noted, our behavioral results map onto sleep-dependent functional brain connectivity changes in adults (Yoo et al., 2007), highlighting the need for examining the neurophysiological mechanisms that may account for a behavioral disconnect between EF and self-regulation when children experience insufficient sleep. Such data may also offer novel insights into individual differences in the sensitivity to sleep loss in early childhood and across development.

FUNDING

Funding for this study was provided by the National Institute of Mental Health: K01-MH066139, R01-MH086566.

REFERENCES

Acebo, C., Sadeh, A., Seifer, R., Tzischinsky, O., Hafer, A., & Carskadon, M. A. (2005). Sleep/wake patterns derived from activity monitoring and maternal report for healthy 1- to 5-year-old children. *Sleep*, *28*(12), 1568–1577.

Akacem, L. D., Simpkin, C. T., Carskadon, M. A., Wright, K. P., Jr., Jenni, O. G., Achermann, P., & LeBourgeois, M. K. (2015). The timing of the circadian clock and sleep differ between napping and non-napping toddlers. *PLoS ONE*, *10*(4), e0125181. doi:10.1371/journal.pone.0125181

Asarnow, L. D., McGlinchey, E., & Harvey, A. G. (2014). The effects of bedtime and sleep duration on academic and emotional outcomes in a nationally representative sample of adolescents. *Journal of Adolescent Health*, *54*(3), 350–356. doi:10.1016/j.jadohealth.2013.09.004

Barkley, R. A. (1997). Behavioral inhibition, sustained attention, and executive functions: Constructing a unifying theory of ADHD. *Psychological Bulletin*, *121*(1), 65–94. doi:10.1037/0033-2909.121.1.65

Bates, J. E., Viken, R. J., Alexander, D. B., Beyers, J., & Stockton, L. (2002). Sleep and adjustment in preschool children: Sleep diary reports by mothers relate to behavior reports by teachers. *Child Development*, *73* (1), 62–75. doi:10.1111/1467-8624.00392

Bauer, A. M., Quas, J. A., & Boyce, W. T. (2002). Associations between physiological reactivity and children's behavior: Advantages of a multisystem approach. *Journal of Developmental & Behavioral Pediatrics*, *23*(2), 102–113. doi:10.1097/00004703-200204000-00007

Baum, K. T., Desai, A., Field, J., Miller, L. E., Rausch, J., & Beebe, D. W. (2014). Sleep restriction worsens mood and emotion regulation in adolescents. *Journal of Child Psychology and Psychiatry*, *55*(2), 180–190. doi:10.1111/jcpp.12125

Belden, A. C., Luby, J. L., Pagliaccio, D., & Barch, D. M. (2014). Neural activation associated with the cognitive emotion regulation of sadness in healthy children. *Developmental Cognitive Neuroscience*, *9*, 136–147. doi:10.1016/j.dcn.2014.02.003

Bell, M. A., & Deater-Deckard, K. (2007). Biological systems and the development of self-regulation: Integrating behavior, genetics, and psychophysiology. *Journal of Developmental & Behavioral Pediatrics*, *28*(5), 409–420. doi:10.1097/DBP.0b013e3181131fc7

Bell, M. A., & Wolfe, C. D. (2004). Emotion and cognition: An intricately bound developmental process. *Child Development*, *75*(2), 366–370. doi:10.1111/j.1467-8624.2004.00679.x

Beltramini, A. U., & Hertzig, M. E. (1983). Sleep and bedtime behavior in preschool-aged children. *Pediatrics*, *71*(2), 153–158.

Berger, R. H., Miller, A. L., Seifer, R., Cares, S. R., & LeBourgeois, M. K. (2012). Acute sleep restriction effects on emotion responses in 30- to 36-month-old children. *Journal of Sleep Research*, *21*(3), 235–246. doi:10.1111/jsr.2012.21.issue-3

Berhenke, A., Miller, A. L., Brown, E., Seifer, R., & Dickstein, S. (2011). Observed emotional and behavioral indicators of motivation predict school readiness in Head Start graduates. *Early Childhood Research Quarterly*, *26*(4), 430–441. doi:10.1016/j.ecresq.2011.04.001

Bierman, K. L., Nix, R. L., Greenberg, M. T., Blair, C., & Domitrovich, C. E. (2008). Executive functions and school readiness intervention: Impact, moderation, and mediation in the head start REDI program. *Development and Psychopathology*, *20*(3), 821–843. doi:10.1017/s0954579408000394

Blair, C. (2002). School readiness. Integrating cognition and emotion in a neurobiological conceptualization of children's functioning at school entry. *American Psychologist*, *57*(2), 111–127. doi:10.1037/0003-066X.57.2.111

Blair, C. (2010). Stress and the development of self-regulation in context. *Child Development Perspectives*, *4*(3), 181–188. doi:10.1111/j.1750-8606.2010.00145.x

Blair, C., & Dennis, T. (2010). An optimal balance: The integration of emotion and cognition in context. In S. D. Calkins & M. A. Bell (Eds.), *Child development at the intersection of emotion and cognition* (pp. 17–35). Washington, DC: American Psychological Association.

Blair, C., & Diamond, A. (2008). Biological processes in prevention and intervention: The promotion of self-regulation as a means of preventing school failure. *Development and Psychopathology*, *20*(3), 899–911. doi:10.1017/s0954579408000436

Blair, C., & Raver, C. C. (2012). Child development in the context of adversity: Experiential canalization of brain and behavior. *American Psychologist*, *67*(4), 309–318. doi:10.1037/a0027493

Blair, C., & Razza, R. P. (2007). Relating effortful control, executive function, and false belief understanding to emerging math and literacy ability in kindergarten. *Child Development*, *78*(2), 647–663. doi:10.1111/cdev.2007.78.issue-2

Blair, C., & Ursache, A. (2011). A bidirectional model of executive functions and self-regulation. *Handbook of Self-Regulation: Research, Theory, and Applications*, *2*, 300–320.

Blair, C., Zelazo, P. D., & Greenberg, M. T. (2005). The measurement of executive function in early childhood. *Developmental Neuropsychology, 28* (2), 561–571. doi:10.1207/s15326942dn2802_1

Bodrova, E., & Leong, D. J. (2007). *Tools of the mind*. Upper Saddle River, NJ: Pearson.

Bridgett, D. J., Oddi, K. B., Laake, L. M., Murdock, K. W., & Bachmann, M. N. (2013). Integrating and differentiating aspects of self-regulation: Effortful control, executive functioning, and links to negative affectivity. *Emotion, 13* (1), 47–63. doi:10.1037/a0029536

Briggs-Gowan, M. J., Carter, A. S., Skuban, E. M., & Horwitz, S. M. (2001). Prevalence of social-emotional and behavioral problems in a community sample of 1- and 2-year-old children. *Journal of the American Academy of Child & Adolescent Psychiatry, 40*(7), 811–819. doi:10.1097/00004583-200107000-00016

Bush, G., Luu, P., & Posner, M. I. (2000). Cognitive and emotional influences in anterior cingulate cortex. *Trends in Cognitive Sciences, 4* (6), 215–222. doi:10.1016/S1364-6613(00)01483-2

Cacioppo, J. T., & Berntson, G. G. (1999). The affect system architecture and operating characteristics. *Current Directions in Psychological Science, 8*(5), 133–137. doi:10.1111/1467-8721.00031

Carlson, S. M. (2005). Developmentally sensitive measures of executive function in preschool children. *Developmental Neuropsychology, 28*(2), 595–616. doi:10.1207/s15326942dn2802_3

Carlson, S. M., & Wang, T. S. (2007). Inhibitory control and emotion regulation in preschool children. *Cognitive Development, 22*(4), 489–510. doi:10.1016/j.cogdev.2007.08.002

Dahl, R. E. (1996). The regulation of sleep and arousal: Development and psychopathology. *Development and Psychopathology, 8*(01), 3–27. doi:10.1017/S0954579400006945

Diamond, A., Barnett, W. S., Thomas, J., & Munro, S. (2007). Preschool program improves cognitive control. *Science, 318*(5855), 1387–1388. doi:10.1126/science.1151148

Drummond, S. P., Brown, G. G., Stricker, J. L., Buxton, R. B., Wong, E. C., & Gillin, J. C. (1999). Sleep deprivation-induced reduction in cortical functional response to serial subtraction. *Neuroreport, 10*(18), 3745–3748. doi:10.1097/00001756-199912160-00004

Eisenberg, N., Fabes, R. A., Murphy, B., Maszk, P., Smith, M., & Karbon, M. (1995). The role of emotionality and regulation in children's social functioning: A longitudinal study. *Child Development, 66*(5), 1360–1384. doi:10.2307/1131652

El-Sheikh, M., Buckhalt, J. A., Keller, P. S., Cummings, E. M., & Acebo, C. (2007). Child emotional insecurity and academic achievement: The role of sleep disruptions. *Journal of Family Psychology, 21*(1), 29–38. doi:10.1037/0893-3200.21.1.29

Erath, S. A., Tu, K. M., Buckhalt, J. A., & El-Sheikh, M. (2015). Associations between children's intelligence and academic achievement: The role of sleep. *Journal of Sleep Research, 24*(5), 510–513. doi:10.1111/jsr.12281

Eysenck, M. W., Derakshan, N., Santos, R., & Calvo, M. G. (2007). Anxiety and cognitive performance: Attentional control theory. *Emotion, 7*(2), 336–353. doi:10.1037/1528-3542.7.2.336

Fallone, G., Acebo, C., Arnedt, J. T., Seifer, R., & Carskadon, M. A. (2001). Effects of acute sleep restriction on behavior, sustained attention, and response inhibition in children. *Perceptual and Motor Skills, 93*(1), 213–229. doi:10.2466/pms.2001.93.1.213

Ferrier, D. E., Bassett, H. H., & Denham, S. A. (2014). Relations between executive function and emotionality in preschoolers: Exploring a transitive cognition–emotion linkage. *Frontiers in Psychology, 5*, 487. doi:10.3389/fpsyg.2014.00487

Fox, N. A., & Calkins, S. D. (2003). The development of self-control of emotion: Intrinsic and extrinsic influences. *Motivation and Emotion, 27* (1), 7–26. doi:10.1023/A:1023622324898

Franzen, P. L., Buysse, D. J., Dahl, R. E., Thompson, W., & Siegle, G. J. (2009). Sleep deprivation alters pupillary reactivity to emotional stimuli in healthy young adults. *Biological Psychology, 80*(3), 300–305. doi:10.1016/j.biopsycho.2008.10.010

Fuster, J. M. (2000). Executive frontal functions. *Experimental Brain Research, 133*(1), 66–70. doi:10.1007/s002210000401

Fuster, J. M. (2002). Physiology of executive functions: The perception-action cycle. In D. T. Stuss & R. T. Knight (Eds.), *Principles of frontal lobe function* (pp. 96–108). New York, NY: Oxford University Press.

Gabard-Durnam, L. J., Flannery, J., Goff, B., Gee, D. G., Humphreys, K. L., Telzer, E., & Tottenham, N. (2014). The development of human amygdala functional connectivity at rest from 4 to 23years: A cross-sectional study. *NeuroImage, 95*, 193–207. doi:10.1016/j.neuroimage.2014.03.038

Garrison, M. M. (2014). Predictors of treatment success in behavioral sleep intervention among preschool children. *Sleep, 37*, A303.

Gaub, M., & Carlson, C. L. (1997). Behavioral characteristics of DSM-IV ADHD subtypes in a school-based population. *Journal of Abnormal Child Psychology, 25*(2), 103–111. doi:10.1023/A:1025775311259

Gee, D. G., Humphreys, K. L., Flannery, J., Goff, B., Telzer, E. H., Shapiro, M., & Tottenham, N. (2013). A developmental shift from positive to negative connectivity in human amygdala–prefrontal circuitry. *The Journal of Neuroscience, 33*(10), 4584–4593. doi:10.1523/JNEUROSCI.3446-12.2013

Goldstein, A. N., & Walker, M. P. (2014). The role of sleep in emotional brain function. *Annual Review of Clinical Psychology, 10*, 679–708. doi:10.1146/annurev-clinpsy-032813-153716

Goodlin-Jones, B., Tang, K., Liu, J., & Anders, T. F. (2009). Sleep problems, sleepiness and daytime behavior in preschool-age children. *Journal of Child Psychology and Psychiatry, 50*(12), 1532–1540. doi:10.1111/j.1469-7610.2009.02110.x

Gray, J. A. (1990). Brain systems that mediate both emotion and cognition. *Cognition & Emotion, 4*(3), 269–288. doi:10.1080/02699939008410799

Gregory, A. M., & O'Connor, T. G. (2002). Sleep problems in childhood: A longitudinal study of developmental change and association with behavioral problems. *Journal of the American Academy of Child & Adolescent Psychiatry, 41*(8), 964–971. doi:10.1097/00004583-200208000-00015

Gruber, R., Cassoff, J., Frenette, S., Wiebe, S., & Carrier, J. (2012). Impact of sleep extension and restriction on children's emotional lability and impulsivity. *Pediatrics, 130*(5), e1155–e1161. doi:10.1542/peds.2012-0564

Hagger, M. S. (2010). Sleep, self-regulation, self-control and health. *Stress and Health, 26*(3), 181–185. doi:10.1002/smi.1345

Hayden, E. P., Klein, D. N., Durbin, C. E., & Olino, T. M. (2006). Positive emotionality at age 3 predicts cognitive styles in 7-year-old children. *Development and Psychopathology, 18*(2), 409–423. doi:10.1017/S0954579406060226

Hofmann, W., Schmeichel, B. J., & Baddeley, A. D. (2012). Executive functions and self-regulation. *Trends in Cognitive Sciences, 16*(3), 174–180. doi:10.1016/j.tics.2012.01.006

Honaker, S. M., & Meltzer, L. J. (2014). Bedtime problems and night wakings in young children: An update of the evidence. *Paediatric Respiratory Reviews, 15*(4), 333–339. doi:10.1016/j.prrv.2014.04.011

Hongwanishkul, D., Happaney, K. R., Lee, W. S., & Zelazo, P. D. (2005). Assessment of hot and cool executive function in young children: Age-related changes and individual differences. *Developmental Neuropsychology, 28*(2), 617–644. doi:10.1207/s15326942dn2802_4

Hughes, C., & Ensor, R. (2008). Does executive function matter for preschoolers' problem behaviors? *Journal of Abnormal Child Psychology, 36*(1), 1–14. doi:10.1007/s10802-007-9107-6

Huizinga, M., Dolan, C. V., & Van Der Molen, M. W. (2006). Age-related change in executive function: Developmental trends and a latent variable analysis. *Neuropsychologia, 44*(11), 2017–2036. doi:10.1016/j.neuropsychologia.2006.01.010

Iglowstein, I., Jenni, O. G., Molinari, L., & Largo, R. H. (2003). Sleep duration from infancy to adolescence: Reference values and generational trends. *Pediatrics, 111*(2), 302–307. doi:10.1542/peds.111.2.302

Jahromi, L. B., & Stifter, C. A. (2008). Individual differences in preschoolers' self-regulation and theory of mind. *Merrill-Palmer Quarterly*, *54*(1), 125–150. doi:10.1353/mpq.2008.0007

Jenni, O. G., & LeBourgeois, M. K. (2006). Understanding sleep–wake behavior and sleep disorders in children: The value of a model. *Current Opinion in Psychiatry*, *19*(3), 282–287. doi:10.1097/01.yco.0000218599.32969.03

Kataria, S., Swanson, M. S., & Trevathan, G. E. (1987). Persistence of sleep disturbances in preschool children. *The Journal of Pediatrics*, *110* (4), 642–646. doi:10.1016/S0022-3476(87)80571-1

Kochanska, G. (1997). Mutually responsive orientation between mothers and their young children: Implications for early socialization. *Child Development*, *68*(1), 94–112. doi:10.2307/1131928

Kochanska, G., Coy, K. C., & Murray, K. T. (2001). The development of self-regulation in the first four years of life. *Child Development*, *72*(4), 1091–1111. doi:10.1111/cdev.2001.72.issue-4

Kurdziel, L., Duclos, K., & Spencer, R. M. (2013). Sleep spindles in midday naps enhance learning in preschool children. *Proceedings of the National Academy of Sciences*, *110*(43), 17267–17272. doi:10.1073/pnas.1306418110

Lavigne, J. V., Arend, R., Rosenbaum, D., Smith, A., Weissbluth, M., Binns, H. J., & Christoffel, K. K. (1999). Sleep and behavior problems among preschoolers. *Journal of Developmental & Behavioral Pediatrics*, *20*(3), 164–169. doi:10.1097/00004703-199906000-00005

LeBourgeois, M. K., Carskadon, M. A., Akacem, L. D., Simpkin, C. T., Wright, K. P., Jr., Achermann, P., & Jenni, O. G. (2013). Circadian phase and its relationship to nighttime sleep in toddlers. *Journal of Biological Rhythms*, *28*(5), 322–331. doi:10.1177/0748730413506543

Leproult, R., Colecchia, E. F., Berardi, A. M., Stickgold, R., Kosslyn, S. M., & Van Cauter, E. (2003). Individual differences in subjective and objective alertness during sleep deprivation are stable and unrelated. *American Journal of Physiology - Regulatory, Integrative and Comparative Physiology*, *284*(2), R280–R290. doi:10.1152/ajpregu.00197.2002

Leventhal, H., & Scherer, K. (1987). The relationship of emotion to cognition: A functional approach to a semantic controversy. *Cognition & Emotion*, *1*(1), 3–28. doi:10.1080/02699938708408361

Lewis, M. D., Lamm, C., Segalowitz, S. J., Stieben, J., & Zelazo, P. D. (2006). Neurophysiological correlates of emotion regulation in children and adolescents. *Journal of Cognitive Neuroscience*, *18*(3), 430–443. doi:10.1162/jocn.2006.18.3.430

Luking, K. R., Repovs, G., Belden, A. C., Gaffrey, M. S., Botteron, K. N., Luby, J. L., & Barch, D. M. (2011). Functional connectivity of the amygdala in early-childhood-onset depression. *Journal of the American Academy of Child & Adolescent Psychiatry*, *50*(10), 1027–1041. doi:10.1016/j.jaac.2011.07.019

Mauss, I. B., Troy, A. S., & LeBourgeois, M. K. (2013). Poorer sleep quality is associated with lower emotion-regulation ability in a laboratory paradigm. *Cognition & Emotion*, *27*(3), 567–576. doi:10.1080/02699931.2012.727783

McClelland, M. M., & Cameron, C. E. (2012). Self-regulation in early childhood: Improving conceptual clarity and developing ecologically valid measures. *Child Development Perspectives*, *6*(2), 136–142. doi:10.1111/j.1750-8606.2011.00191.x

Mennin, D. S., Heimberg, R. G., Turk, C. L., & Fresco, D. M. (2002). Applying an emotion regulation framework to integrative approaches to generalized anxiety disorder. *Clinical Psychology: Science and Practice*, *9*(1), 85–90. doi:10.1093/clipsy.9.1.85

Miller, A. L., Seifer, R., Crossin, R., & LeBourgeois, M. K. (2015). Toddler's self-regulation strategies in a challenge context are nap-dependent. *Journal of Sleep Research*, *24*(3), 279–287. doi:10.1111/jsr.12260

Miyake, A., Friedman, N. P., Emerson, M. J., Witzki, A. H., Howerter, A., & Wager, T. D. (2000). The unity and diversity of executive functions and their contributions to complex "Frontal Lobe" tasks: A latent variable analysis. *Cognitive Psychology*, *41*(1), 49–100. doi:10.1006/cogp.1999.0734

Molfese, D. L., Ivanenko, A., Key, A. F., Roman, A., Molfese, V. J., O'Brien, L. M., & Hudac, C. M. (2013). A one-hour sleep restriction impacts brain processing in young children across tasks: Evidence from event-related potentials. *Developmental Neuropsychology*, *38*(5), 317–336. doi:10.1080/87565641.2013.799169

National Sleep Foundation. (2004). *Children and sleep*. Retrieved from https://sleepfoundation.org/sleep-polls-data/sleep-in-america-poll/2004-children-and-sleep

Ochsner, K. N., & Gross, J. J. (2005). The cognitive control of emotion. *Trends in Cognitive Sciences*, *9*(5), 242–249. doi:10.1016/j.tics.2005.03.010

Ponitz, C. C., McClelland, M. M., Matthews, J. S., & Morrison, F. J. (2009). A structured observation of behavioral self-regulation and its contribution to kindergarten outcomes. *Developmental Psychology*, *45* (3), 605–619. doi:10.1037/a0015365

Posner, M. I., & Rothbart, M. K. (1998). Attention, self–regulation and consciousness. *Philosophical Transactions of the Royal Society of London B: Biological Sciences*, *353*(1377), 1915–1927. doi:10.1098/rstb.1998.0344

Quas, J. A., Yim, I. S., Oberlander, T. F., Nordstokke, D., Essex, M. J., Armstrong, J. M., & Boyce, W. T. (2014). The symphonic structure of childhood stress reactivity: Patterns of sympathetic, parasympathetic, and adrenocortical responses to psychological challenge. *Development and Psychopathology*, *26*(4, Pt.1), 963–982. doi:10.1017/S0954579414000480

Raffaelli, M., Crockett, L. J., & Shen, Y.-L. (2005). Developmental stability and change in self-regulation from childhood to adolescence. *The Journal of Genetic Psychology*, *166*(1), 54–76. doi:10.3200/gntp.166.1.54-76

Randazzo, A. C., Muehlbach, M. J., Schweitzer, P. K., & Walsh, J. K. (1998). Cognitive function following acute sleep restriction in children ages 10-14. *Sleep*, *21*(8), 861–868.

Reid, G. J., Hong, R. Y., & Wade, T. J. (2009). The relation between common sleep problems and emotional and behavioral problems among 2- and 3-year-olds in the context of known risk factors for psychopathology. *Journal of Sleep Research*, *18*(1), 49–59. doi:10.1111/j.1365-2869.2008.00692.x

Riggs, N. R., Jahromi, L. B., Razza, R. P., Dillworth-Bart, J. E., & Mueller, U. (2006). Executive function and the promotion of social–emotional competence. *Journal of Applied Developmental Psychology*, *27*(4), 300–309. doi:10.1016/j.appdev.2006.04.002

Rothbart, M. K., Posner, M. I., & Kieras, J. (2006). Temperament, attention, and the development of self-regulation. In K. McCartney & D. Phillips (Eds.), *Blackwell handbook of early childhood development* (pp. 338–357). Malden, MA: Blackwell.

Sadeh, A., Gruber, R., & Raviv, A. (2002). Sleep, neurobehavioral functioning, and behavior problems in school-age children. *Child Development*, *73*(2), 405–417. doi:10.1111/cdev.2002.73.issue-2

Sadeh, A., Gruber, R., & Raviv, A. (2003). The effects of sleep restriction and extension on school-age children: What a difference an hour makes. *Child Development*, *74*(2), 444–455. doi:10.1111/1467-8624.7402008

Simpkin, C. T., Jenni, O. G., Carskadon, M. A., Wright, K. P., Jr., Akacem, L. D., Garlo, K. G., & LeBourgeois, M. K. (2014). Chronotype is associated with the timing of the circadian clock and sleep in toddlers. *Journal of Sleep Research*, *23*(4), 397–405. doi:10.1111/jsr.2014.23.issue-4

Smiley, P. A., & Dweck, C. S. (1994). Individual differences in achievement goals among young children. *Child Development*, *65*(6), 1723–1743. doi:10.2307/1131290

Stein, M. A., Mendelsohn, J., Obermeyer, W. H., Amromin, J., & Benca, R. (2001). Sleep and behavior problems in school-aged children. *Pediatrics*, *107*(4), e60–e60. doi:10.1542/peds.107.4.e60

Talbot, L. S., McGlinchey, E. L., Kaplan, K. A., Dahl, R. E., & Harvey, A. G. (2010). Sleep deprivation in adolescents and adults: Changes in affect. *Emotion*, *10*(6), 831–841. doi:10.1037/a0020138

Touchette, É., Petit, D., Séguin, J. R., Boivin, M., Tremblay, R. E., & Montplaisir, J. Y. (2007). Associations between sleep duration patterns and behavioral/cognitive functioning at school entry. *Sleep*, *30*(9), 1213.

Van Dongen, H. P. A., & Belenky, G. (2009). Individual differences in vulnerability to sleep loss in the work environment. *Industrial Health*, *47* (5), 518–526. doi:10.2486/indhealth.47.518

Vriend, J. L., Davidson, F. D., Corkum, P. V., Rusak, B., Chambers, C. T., & McLaughlin, E. N. (2013). Manipulating sleep duration alters emotional functioning and cognitive performance in children. *Journal of Pediatric Psychology*, *38*(10), 1058–1069. doi:10.1093/jpepsy/jst033

Walker, M. P., & Harvey, A. G. (2010). Obligate symbiosis: Sleep and affect. *Sleep Medicine Reviews*, *14*(4), 215–217. doi:10.1016/j.smrv.2010.02.003

Weissbluth, M. (1995). Naps in children: 6 months–7 years. *Sleep*, *18*(2), 82–87.

Willoughby, M. T., Wirth, R. J., Blair, C. B., & Family Life Project, I. (2012). Executive function in early childhood: Longitudinal measurement invariance and developmental change. *Psychological Assessment*, *24*(2), 418–431. doi:10.1037/a0025779

Wong, M. M., Brower, K. J., & Zucker, R. A. (2009). Childhood sleep problems, early onset of substance use and behavioral problems in adolescence. *Sleep Medicine*, *10*(7), 787–796. doi:10.1016/j.sleep.2008.06.015

Yoo, S.-S., Gujar, N., Hu, P., Jolesz, F. A., & Walker, M. P. (2007). The human emotional brain without sleep—A prefrontal amygdala disconnect. *Current Biology*, *17*(20), R877–R878. doi:10.1016/j.cub.2007.08.007

Zahn-Waxler, C., Klimes-Dougan, B., & Slattery, M. J. (2000). Internalizing problems of childhood and adolescence: Prospects, pitfalls, and progress in understanding the development of anxiety and depression. *Development and Psychopathology*, *12*(03), 443–466. doi:10.1017/S0954579400003102

Zelazo, P. D., Muller, U., Frye, D., Marcovitch, S., Argitis, G., Boseovski, J., & Sutherland, A. (2003). The development of executive function in early childhood. *Monographs of the Society for Research in Child Development*, *68*(3), vii–137. doi:10.1111/j.0037-976X.2003.00260.x

Zohar, D., Tzischinsky, O., Epstein, R., & Lavie, P. (2005). The effects of sleep loss on medical residents' emotional reactions to work events: A cognitive-energy model. *Sleep*, *28*(1), 47–54.

Zuckerman, B., Stevenson, J., & Bailey, V. (1987). Sleep problems in early childhood: Continuities, predictive factors, and behavioral correlates. *Pediatrics*, *80*(5), 664–671.

Sleep and Social-Emotional Development in Infants and Toddlers

Jodi A. Mindell

Erin S. Leichman

Courtney DuMond

Avi Sadeh

The aim of this study was to examine the cross-sectional and longitudinal relationships among variables related to sleep patterns and both social-emotional problems (i.e., internalizing, externalizing, and dysregulation) and healthy social development (i.e., social competence). Assessments were completed at 6, 12, and 18 months across 5 cohorts of children for a total of 117 mother–child dyads. Mothers completed the Brief Infant Sleep Questionnaire at 6, 12, and 18 months, as well as the Infant Toddler Social Emotional Assessment at 12 and 18 months. Later bedtimes and less total sleep across the 24-hr period predicted higher internalizing problem scores, which includes indices of depression/withdrawal, general anxiety, separation distress, and inhibition. In contrast, sleep fragmentation was minimally associated with decreased social competence but not with any negative social-emotional outcomes. These results indicate that sleep patterns, primarily later bedtimes and less total sleep, appear to be associated with and predictive of social-emotional problem areas, namely, internalizing issues, in infants and toddlers. These findings add to the growing literature on the role of sleep in early social-emotional development and suggest that sleep schedule and duration should be addressed in clinical assessment and interventions for infant sleep.

Sleep is an integral component of healthy development in early childhood, affecting multiple developmental outcomes. Associations between both healthy and problematic sleep with developmental factors, including general psychological functioning, cognitive performance, and overall developmental status, have been examined, although primarily in preschool-age children rather than in the first few years of life (Boekamp, Williamson, Martin, Hunter, & Anders, 2015; Hatzinger et al., 2014; Kelly, Kelly, & Sacker, 2013; Lam, Mahone, Mason, & Scharf, 2011; Touchette et al., 2007; Vaughn, Elmore-Staton, Shin, & El-Sheikh, 2015; Yorbik, Mutlu, Koc, & Mutluer, 2014). One area that has been a more recent focus is the concurrent and predictive relationship between sleep and social-emotional functioning (e.g., behavioral functioning, social competence and skills, and psychiatric problems). Several studies have examined these connections during infancy and toddlerhood (e.g., Berger, Miller, Seifer, Cares, & LeBourgeois, 2012; Sadeh et al., 2015; Winsper & Wolke, 2014).

Research on the broader area of regulatory problems (RP), which includes sleeping, crying, and feeding problems, in infants and toddlers as predictors of subsequent behavioral problems has found that behavioral dysregulation in early childhood relates to later difficulties in behavior, cognition, and emotion regulation. For instance, in a sample of more than 6,000 children, Winsper and Wolke (2014) examined infant and toddler RP at approximately 6, 18, and 24 months of age and subsequent behavioral difficulties during childhood (between the ages of 4 and 9.5 years). Latent class analysis revealed that dysregulated behavior was stable from infancy through childhood. Further, all RP, including sleep difficulties (e.g., bedtime refusal, waking early, night wakings, prolonged sleep onset), were significantly related to later behavioral problems (e.g., negative emotionality, conduct problems, and hyperactivity), with multiple regulatory problems increasing the odds of subsequent behavioral problems. Hyde, O'Callaghan, Bor, Williams, and Najman (2012) analyzed data from more than 6,000 infants at 6 months and subsequent behavioral problems at 5, 14, and 21 years of age. Dysregulation (RP including sleep problems) at 6 months was significantly related to mother-reported internalizing and externalizing problems in childhood and adolescence but not to self-reported problems in early adulthood. Relationships between infancy and childhood were stronger than those between infancy and adolescence. Furthermore, Sidor, Fischer, Eickhorst, and Cierpka (2013) assessed approximately 150 mother–child dyads at 4 and 6 months in terms of infant RPs (including sleep problems) and subsequent developmental indicators at 12 months. Results indicated that RPs in early infancy were associated with lower social development scores at 12 months but not other areas of development. Overall, early regulatory problems, including sleep metrics, have been shown to be longitudinally associated with behavioral dysregulation as represented by both negative emotionality and externalizing problems.

Two large Norwegian birth cohort studies have examined sleep in young children and subsequent social-emotional outcomes (Hysing, Siversten, Garthus-Niegel, & Eberhard-Gran, 2016; Sivertsen et al., 2015). Hysing and colleagues (2016) demonstrated that less total sleep, prolonged sleep onset, and frequent night wakings corresponded to greater risk of having concurrent social-emotional problems in toddlerhood, based on a social-emotional subscale of the Ages & Stages Questionnaire. Specifically, children who slept less than 11 hours per night were almost 5 times as likely to have social-emotional problems than those who slept more than 11 hours. Similarly, those who slept between 11 and 12 hr were almost 4 times as likely to demonstrate social-emotional problems. Prolonged sleep onset latency (30 min or more) increased risk for social-emotional problems by more than 3 times, and having three or more night wakings increased that risk by almost 2 times. Finally, considering sleep to be a small to very serious problem increased odds of social-emotional problems by 2 to almost 5 times, respectively. Similarly, Sivertsen and colleagues (2015) found that sleeping for less than 11 hr or having three or more wakings per night at 18 months old was predictive of having emotional regulation difficulties, utilizing the Child Behavior Checklist, both concurrently and at 5 years old. Overall, the relationship between sleep and internalizing problems was stronger than that between sleep and externalizing problems.

In a third cohort study, Jansen et al. (2011) assessed the association between sleep problems at 2 and 24 months and subsequent internalizing problems at 36 months in more than 4,000 children. Results of logistic regression demonstrated that parent presence during sleep and dyssomnia in infants (2 months) and toddlers (24 months) were associated with increased risk for subsequent internalizing problems (36 months). Short sleep, inconsistent bedtime, and presence of parasomnias in toddlers were also associated with risk for later internalizing problems. These associations maintained when internalizing problems in toddlerhood (24 months) were statistically controlled.

Beyond large cohort studies, additional studies have examined sleep and social-emotional outcomes, with some implementing experimental manipulations in order to determine the effects of sleep duration on various aspects of functioning in toddlers. For instance, one study of 43 infants found that lower quality of sleep (i.e., lower sleep efficiency and increased night wakings) at 12 months of age predicted compromised attention regulation and behavior problems at 3 to 4 years of age (Sadeh et al., 2015). In an experimental study, Berger and colleagues (2012) assessed 10 healthy toddlers' (30- to 36-month-olds) emotion expression in response to sleep deprivation. Emotion expression was assessed via video recordings of toddler response to emotion-eliciting images and completing puzzles. After nap restriction, a variety of changes were observed in children, including modified (less) confusion when seeing a neutral image; more negativity to neutral images, negative images, and when solving a challenging or unsolvable puzzle; and less positive responding to positive images and when completing the solvable puzzle. In another experimental study, sleep (nap) restriction in 12 toddlers (30–36 months) was also associated with difficulties in self-regulation during the day (i.e., more skepticism, lowered ability to self-soothe, increased perseveration, more negative self-appraisal, and insistence on completion despite the task being impossible or unsolvable; Miller, Seifer, Crossin, & LeBourgeois, 2015). These experimental studies in addition to the population cohort studies demonstrate clear associations between sleep-specific variables (e.g., sleep duration and restricted sleep, night wakings, sleep-onset latency) and social-emotional problems as measured by parent-reported rating scales and difficulties with social-emotional tasks. It is important to note that these findings were not always consistent with regard to the specific sleep variables (e.g., sleep quality vs. sleep quantity) that were found to be associated with social-emotional factors.

In contrast, other studies failed to find or found mixed associations between sleep and social-emotional development, especially related to competence. For instance, a study of approximately 50 infants (12 months) found that sleep efficiency and percentage of overnight sleep were related to fine motor development, problem solving, and communication but not social development at the same age (Gibson, Elder, & Gander, 2012). Similarly, a study of high-risk infants found no relationship between sleep at 12 and 18 months with IQ and social-emotional outcomes at 5 year of age (Sheridan et al., 2013). Mindell and Lee (2015) assessed a group of approximately 1,300 parent–child dyads (3–13 months) in terms of multiple sleep variables, mood, and developmental domains. Although sleep variables did not demonstrate significant associations with global developmental outcomes, low but significant relations were found among all sleep variables (except sleep onset latency) and at least one mood rating during the day. In sum, although research has demonstrated concurrent and predictive associations between aspects of bedtime behavior, as well as elements of sleep itself and social-emotional regulation, results have been mixed overall in terms of their relation to social-emotional competence.

Current Aim

Considering the importance of sleep, paired with inconclusive evidence of early and predictive relations among sleep and social-emotional variables (e.g., metrics of social competence), additional research is thus warranted to better establish and understand the specific associations among these variables in infancy and toddlerhood. Furthermore, various aspects of sleep have been measured and utilized in these studies, including sleep duration (night, day, and combination for total sleep per 24-hr period), sleep consolidation (i.e., uninterrupted stretches of sleep), bedtime, sleep onset latency (time between putting a child to bed and when a child falls asleep), night wakings (frequency and duration), and bedtime routines. Thus, the aim of this study was to examine the cross-sectional and longitudinal relationships among variables related to sleep (i.e., bedtime factors, overnight sleep, and total sleep) and both social-emotional problems (i.e., internalizing, externalizing, and dysregulation) and healthy social development (i.e., social competence). Based on the existing literature, it was hypothesized that late bedtimes, prolonged sleep onset latency, decreased sleep duration, and sleep fragmentation would be concurrently and predictively associated with both social-emotional problems and social competence.

METHOD

Participants

Participants included a subsample (n = 117) from a larger study of healthy, typically developing mother–child dyads across five cohorts ranging in child age from 3 to 18 months at initial data collection and 18 to 36 months at final data collection (n = 164). Participants were screened for inclusion via phone interview and initial meeting. Maternal–child dyads were excluded or later disqualified based on the following: chronic and significant health or developmental problems of child, infant prematurity, or maternal-identified psychiatric issues or psychotropic medication use. Of the original 164 participants across five cohorts, 71% (117) were retained for analysis; 8.5% (n = 14) were initially disqualified due to maternal depressive symptoms or concerns about child development. Between the second and final data collection waves, an additional 33 participants were disqualified based on maternal depressive symptoms (n = 1) or withdrew due to having moved or failing to respond (n = 28) from study participation. Four additional participants had missing data. Disqualified participants based on maternal psychiatric problems, primarily depressive symptoms, were assessed with the Beck Depression Inventory–Second Edition (Beck, Steer, & Brown, 1996), Edinburgh Postnatal Depression Questionnaire (Cox & Holden, 2003) and Brief Symptom Inventory (Derogatis, 2001). Child-level factors that led to disqualification included concerns identified by the Bayley Scales of Infant Development–Third Edition (Robins, Fein, Barton, & Green, 2001) and/or the Modified Checklist for Autism in Toddlers (Bayley, 2006). Participants in the current sample included all infants with available data who were assessed at any one of the following three time points (i.e., 6, 12, and 18 months old). Table 1 represents the assessment schedule of retained participants in the current study (n = 117). Withdrawn and disqualified participants were not statistically different from those who completed the study based on demographic factors with the exception of maternal education, in that completers were more highly educated (χ^2 = 4.96, p = .026).

TABLE 1
Infant Visit and Assessment Schedule

		Age in Months		
		6	*12*	*18*
Cohort 1	ITSEA	—	x	x
	BISQ	x	x	x
Cohort 2	ITSEA	—	x	x
	BISQ	x	x	x
Cohort 3	ITSEA		x	x
	BISQ		x	x
Cohort 4	ITSEA		x	x
	BISQ		x	x
Cohort 5	ITSEA			x
	BISQ			x

Note: ITSEA = Infant Toddler Social Emotional Assessment; BISQ = Brief Infant Sleep Questionnaire.

Procedure

This prospective, longitudinal study was approved by an Institutional Review Board. All mothers provided written informed consent. In the broader study, information related to child sleep, general child development, child health status and nutrition, maternal and family factors, and mother–child factors was collected. Families were assessed approximately every 3 months across 12 to 18 months (four to five time points per cohort). Families were recruited from the community in the southeastern region of the United States and asked to participate in a longitudinal study about infant development when children were 3–18 months old. Data collection was completed by trained evaluators at a research site, as well as in the family home. Visit length ranged from approximately 45 min to 3 hr. Families were compensated $30 for each meeting and an additional $50 for completing all five meetings. Results reported here pertain to child sleep and social-emotional development.

Measures

Brief Infant Sleep Questionnaire

All mothers completed an expanded version of the Brief Infant Sleep Questionnaire (BISQ; Sadeh, 2004). The BISQ has been validated against actigraphy and daily logs, and its sensitivity in documenting expected developmental trends in young children's sleep and the effects of environmental factors have been established. Test–retest reliability for individual sleep measures on the BISQ was high (r = .81–.95), and comparisons between the BISQ and actigraphy (r = .23–.54) were low to moderate (Sadeh, 2004). The expanded version of the BISQ (current version), as described previously (Sadeh, Mindell, Luedtke, & Wiegand, 2009), includes questions about the child's daytime and nighttime sleep patterns, sleep-related behaviors, and maternal perceptions. The BISQ was completed at 6, 12, and 18 months. At each time point, five items from the BISQ were utilized in current analytic procedures (bedtime, sleep onset latency, number of night wakings, longest continuous sleep period, and total sleep time per 24-hr period). The items selected for use were those most commonly used in the infant sleep literature to track developmental changes in sleep quantity, quality, and timing and to predict sleep problems (e.g., Mindell, Sadeh, Kohyama, & How, 2010; Sadeh et al., 2009). These measures have also demonstrated sensitivity to the effects of behavioral interventions for infant sleep problems (e.g., Mindell et al., 2011; Mindell, Telofski, Wiegand, & Kurtz, 2009).

Infant Toddler Social Emotional Assessment

The Infant Toddler Social Emotional Assessment (ITSEA; Carter & Briggs-Gowan, 2006) is a parent questionnaire that assesses the social-emotional development of children ranging in age from 12 to 36 months. Parents or caregivers indicate their level of agreement to a particular item as 0 (*rarely/not true*), 1 (*somewhat/sometimes true*), or 2 (*very true or often true*). The assessment yields four domain scores (i.e., Externalizing, Internalizing, Dysregulation, and Competence) and 17 subscale scores. Aggression/Defiance, Activity/Impulsivity, and Peer Aggression compose the Externalizing problems composite; Depression/Withdrawal, General Anxiety, Separation Distress, and Inhibition to Novelty compose the Internalizing problems composite; and Sleep, Negative Emotionality, Eating, and Sensory Sensitivity compose the Dysregulation composite score. Competence consists of Compliance, Attention, Imitation/Pretend Play, Mastery Motivation, Empathy, and Prosocial Peer relations. For the purposes of the current analyses, a modified Dysregulation score was constructed that removed the Sleep subdomain.

Based on a sample of more than 1,000 parents of toddlers (12–36 months old), confirmatory factor analysis supported the structure for all scales within the ITSEA (Carter, Briggs-Gowan, Jones, & Little, 2003). ITSEA problem domains showed moderate to high correlations with other well-established measures of young child behavior such as the Child Behavior Checklist (CBCL; Achenbach & Rescorla, 2000). On average, girls scored higher on Competence and Internalizing domains and lower on the Externalizing domain. No gender differences were observed on the Dysregulation domain. Social competence demonstrated increase with age, and internalizing problems peaked at 18–23 months of age. The ITSEA problem domains showed moderate to high correlations with other well-established measures of young child behavior such as the CBCL (Achenbach & Rescorla, 2000): Internalizing ITSEA (r = .47 Total Problems, r = .57 Internalizing, and r = .33 Externalizing), Externalizing ITSEA (r = .67 Total Problems, r = .46 Internalizing, and r = .73 Externalizing), and Dysregulation ITSEA (r = .62 Total Problems, r = .57 Internalizing, and r = .52 Externalizing). The Social Competence domain of the ITSEA resulted in low to moderate negative correlations with Problem scales of the CBCL (r = -.30 Total Problems, r = –.21 Internalizing, and r = –.33 Externalizing).

Statistical Analyses

Two-tailed Pearson product–moment correlations among four of five sleep variables at three time points (i.e., 6, 12, and 18 months) and ITSEA domain scores (i.e., Externalizing, Internalizing, modified Dysregulation, and Competence at 12 and 18 months) were conducted using SPSS Version 22 (IBM Corp., 2013). Spearman's rho correlations were utilized to assess relationships between night wakings and ITSEA domain scores given that night wakings demonstrated skewness in its distribution. A significance level of alpha less than .05 was utilized to determine statistical significance for all correlations. To further understand the relationships between sleep and social-emotional development, structural equation modeling (SEM) was used to assess models describing the relationships between infant sleep and behavior measures at the ages of 12 and 18 months ($n = 80$). These two ages (12 and 18 months) had the largest sample sizes with corresponding longitudinal data and sufficient statistical power to evaluate crossed-lagged prediction models (Kelly & El-Sheikh, 2014; Tikotzky & Sadeh, 2009). A latent sleep measure was derived and separate analyses for each discrete social-emotional scale as observed measures were conducted. SEM analyses were conducted via the AMOS program (Version 21) using the Maximum Likelihood estimation method. The underlying assumption behind the model testing was that child sleep and emotional problems potentially have bidirectional links (see review: Sadeh, Tikotzky, & Kahn, 2014) and that cross-lagged analysis may clarify which predictive link is stronger (sleep predicting emotional problems or vice versa). Missing data were handled using pairwise deletion.

RESULTS

Participant Demographics and Sleep Characteristics

Demographic information collected at the initial assessment period from retained participants is presented in Table 2. Maternal age ranged from 20 to 52 at intake (M = 31.8 years), and approximately 57% of families earned $25,000–$75,000 per year. Approximately 20% of families reported earning less than $25,000 or more than $75,000 per year, respectively. The majority of children were Caucasian (83.8%), with the remaining children representing African American families (8.5%), Asian/Pacific Islander families (4.3%), and mixed-race families (3.4%). Participants who did not complete all scheduled assessment periods in the larger study either withdrew of their own accord (25.6%) or were disqualified (15.2%) due to evidence of maternal psychopathology or child developmental issues and were referred for additional evaluation.

Complete information on sleep and ITSEA scores at each assessment point are provided in Table 3. *T*-scores are provided for the Internalizing, Externalizing, and Competence domains. Unstandardized scores are presented for the modified Dysregulation subscale, as the sleep items were removed from this subscale. Overall, ITSEA scores at 12 and 18 months were moderately to highly correlated within domains. Externalizing ($r = .67$, $p < .01$) and Competence ($r = .73$ $p < .01$) scores demonstrated somewhat more stability over time than did Internalizing ($r = .52$, $p < .01$) and modified Dysregulation ($r = .49$, $p < .01$) scores. The number of participants for each set of correlational analyses described next is provided in Table 4, which also includes all correlations.

ITSEA (12 Months)

Correlations among sleep variables (i.e., bedtime, sleep onset latency, frequency of night wakings, and total sleep time per 24-hr period) at 6, 12, and 18 months and ITSEA domains (i.e., Externalizing, Internalizing, modified Dysregulation, and Competence) at 12 months old were calculated.

Sleep at 6 Months Old

At 6 months of age, total sleep time was moderately correlated with Externalizing ($r = -.42$, $p < .01$), Internalizing ($r = -.42$, $p < .01$), and modified Dysregulation ($r = -.33$, $p < .05$), indicating that more reported sleep at 6 months of age was related to lower levels of social-emotional problems at 12 months of age. Competence at 12 months was not significantly related to sleep at 6 months.

Sleep at 12 Months Old

Concurrent correlations among sleep and social-emotional variables at 12 months of age resulted in low to moderate correlations between indicators of sleep consolidation (i.e., night wakings [$r = -.29$, $p < .01$] and longest sleep period [$r = .34$, $p < .01$]) and Competence. Bedtime and sleep onset latency demonstrated significant positive relations with social-emotional problems (r = .30–.34, $p < .01$) but not with Competence, indicating that later bedtimes and taking longer to fall asleep were related to higher social-emotional problem scores. Total sleep time was negatively correlated with Internalizing problems ($r = -.22$, $p < .05$) and modified Dysregulation ($r = -.23$, $p < .05$), indicating that more total sleep was associated with fewer problems.

Sleep at 18 Months Old

Social-emotional problems at 12 months old were correlated at low to moderate levels with bedtime and sleep onset latency at 18 months. Specifically, later bedtimes were associated with higher reported Internalizing ($r = .33$, $p < .01$) and modified Dysregulation ($r = .24$, $p < .05$) problems. Sleep at 18 months was not correlated with Competence at 12 months.

ITSEA (18 Months)

Similarly, correlations were conducted between sleep variables (i.e., bedtime, sleep onset latency, frequency of night wakings, and total sleep time per 24-hr period) at 6, 12, and 18 months and ITSEA domains (i.e., Externalizing, Internalizing, modified Dysregulation, and Competence) at 18 months of age.

Sleep at 6 Months Old

At 6 months, only one statistically significant correlation was found. Bedtime was negatively correlated with

TABLE 2
Demographics

Participants at Intake	*Total %*	*n*
Sex of Child		113
Boy	41.0	48
Girl	55.6	65
Child Race		117
American Indian/Alaskan Native	0	0
Asian/Pacific Islander	4.3	5
African American/Black	8.5	10
Caucasian/White (Caucasian, non-Hispanic)	83.8 (71.8)	98 (84)
Mixed Race	3.4	4
Child Ethnicity		117
Hispanic	13.7	16
Non-Hispanic	86.3	101
Maternal Marital Status		117
Single, Never Married	13.7	16
Married	70.9	83
Divorced	4.3	5
Separated	3.4	4
Lives With Partner	7.7	9
Other	0	0
Household Income		117
< $5,000 to $24,999	16.2	19
$25,000 to $49,999	32.5	38
$50,000 to $74,999	16.2	19
$75,000 to > $100,000	17.1	20
Missing	17.9	21
Maternal Education		116
Less Than High School	9.5	11
High School Completion	21.5	25
More Than High School	69.0	80
Years of Education	14.3 *M* years (9–20 years) (*SD* = 2.34)	
Maternal Age	31.8 years (20–52 years) (*SD* = 5.66)	

Note: $N = 117$.

modified Dysregulation ($r = -.36$, $p < .05$), indicating later bedtimes were associated with lower Dysregulation scores 1 year later.

Sleep at 12 Months Old

The majority of statistically significant relations among sleep variables at 12 months and social-emotional development at 18 months involved Internalizing problems. Later bedtimes ($r = .35$, $p < .05$) and longer sleep onset latency ($r = .29$, $p < .01$) were associated with higher Internalizing scores, and more total sleep ($r = -.41$, $p < .01$) was related to lower Internalizing scores. Sleep onset latency at 12 months was significantly related to Externalizing problems at 18 months ($r = .23$, $p < .05$). Sleep at 12 months was not related to Competence at 18 months.

Sleep at 18 Months Old

Concurrent correlations at 18 months resulted in statistically significant relations between Externalizing problems and sleep onset latency ($r = .32$, $p < .01$); Internalizing problems with bedtime ($r = .26$, $p < .01$), sleep onset latency ($r = .29$, $p < .01$), and total sleep time ($r = -.29$, $p < .05$); and modified Dysregulation and sleep onset latency ($r = .27$, $p < .01$). Overall, later bedtime and taking longer to fall asleep were associated with higher scores on social-emotional problem scales, and more total sleep was related to lower Internalizing problems. Sleep at 18 months was not related to Competence at 18 months.

Structural Equation Modeling

Model fit was tested using observed sleep and psychosocial indicators (Externalizing, Internalizing, Modified Dysregulation, Competence). The latent sleep measures were derived based on initial examination of the simple correlation matrix between sleep and social-emotional variables. Sleep onset latency was also considered, but models including this variable failed to converge. Only one model, relating sleep and internalizing problems, provided good fit indices as well as significant prediction between sleep and emotional development (see Figure 1). Acceptable fit indices were found for

TABLE 3
Descriptive Statistics—Sleep and ITSEA

	M	*Range*	*SD*
Sleep (6 Months, *n* = 39)			
Bedtime	8:30 p.m.	6.00–11.00 p.m.	1.20
Sleep Onset Latency	0.37	0.03–4.00	0.69
Night Wakings (Frequency)	1.45	0–3.00	0.96
Longest Sleep Period (Night)	6.74	3.50–12.00	2.01
Total Sleep Time (per 24 hr)	13.34	10.00–18.00	1.74
Sleep (12 Months, *n* = 91)			
Bedtime	8:23 p.m.	5:30–11:00 p.m.	0.99
Sleep Onset Latency	0.25	0–0.75	0.16
Night Wakings (Frequency)	1.02	0–5.00	1.01
Longest Sleep Period (Night)	8.52	1.00–14.50	2.67
Total Sleep Time (per 24 hr)	13.09	9.00–19.00	1.43
Sleep (18 Months, *n* = 114)			
Bedtime	8:29 p.m.	5:45 p.m.–12:00 a.m.	1.10
Sleep Onset Latency	0.28	0.03–1.00	0.19
Night Wakings (Frequency)	0.78	0–5.50	0.96
Longest Sleep Period (Night)	9.14	1.00–13.00	2.62
Total Sleep Time (per 24 hr)	12.61	9.00–16.00	1.42
ITSEA (12 Months, *n* = 91)			
Externalizing	48.36	34–73	8.91
Internalizing	43.69	26–76	9.47
Dysregulation[a]	1.02	0.22–3.00	0.58
Competence	47.22	26–70	8.16
ITSEA (18 Months, *n* = 114)			
Externalizing	48.36	33–70	8.86
Internalizing	43.84	23–64	8.77
Dysregulation[a]	1.07	0–2.80	.56
Competence	51.03	20–79	9.88

Note: ITSEA = Infant Toddler Social Emotional Assessment.

[a]Dysregulation with sleep items removed.

TABLE 4
Correlations of ITSEA and Sleep

	ITSEA (12 Mth)					*ITSEA (18 Mth)*			
	Ext.	*Int.*	*Dys.[a]*	*Comp.*		*Ext.*	*Int.*	*Dys.[a]*	*Comp.*
Sleep 6 mth (*n* = 38–39)					Sleep 6 mth (*n* = 33–34)				
BT	−.163	−.202	−.220	.215	BT	−.226	.141	−.359*	.265
SOL	−.006	−.076	−.034	−.205	SOL	−.111	−.152	.233	−.065
NW[b]	−.046	.196	−.002	−.186	NW[b]	.056	−.032	−.068	−.220
LSP	.063	−.116	−.032	.135	LSP	.252	.207	.245	.149
TST24	−.420**	−.423**	−.333*	.020	TST24	−.114	−.254	.061	.030
Sleep 12 mth (*n* = 89–94)					Sleep 12 mth (*n* = 79–81)				
BT	.113	.302**	.179	.013	BT	.140	.348*	.116	−.054
SOL	.303**	.079	.335**	.064	SOL	.230*	.288**	.217	−.005
NW[b]	−.053	−.018	.099	−.230*	NW[b]	−.040	.135	.154	−.186
LSP	.025	.010	−.152	.336**	LSP	.057	−.218	−.118	.207
TST24	−.111	−.215*	−.232*	.001	TST24	−.062	−.409**	.106	−.009
Sleep 18 mth (*n* = 77–80)					Sleep 18 mth (*n* = 116–117)				
BT	.165	.338**	.239**	.072	BT	.107	.264**	.097	−.093
SOL	.170	.024	.267*	.071	SOL	.316**	.293**	.272**	−.077
NW[b]	−.030	−.017	−.024	.004	NW[b]	−.117	.065	.001	.142
LSP	.012	.074	−.097	.093	LSPn	.065	−.049	.025	−.062
TST24	−.023	−.043	−.120	−.091	TST24	−.175	−.292*	−.141	.013

Note: ITSEA = Infant Toddler Social Emotional Assessment; mth = months; Ext. = Externalizing; Int. = Internalizing; Dys. = Dysregulation; Comp. = Competence; BT = bedtime; SOL = sleep onset latency; NW = number of night wakings; LSP = longest sleep period during the night; TST24 = total sleep time in 24 hr.

[a]Dysregulation with sleep items removed. [b]Spearman's rho.

*$p < .05$ (two-tailed). **$p < .01$ (two-tailed).

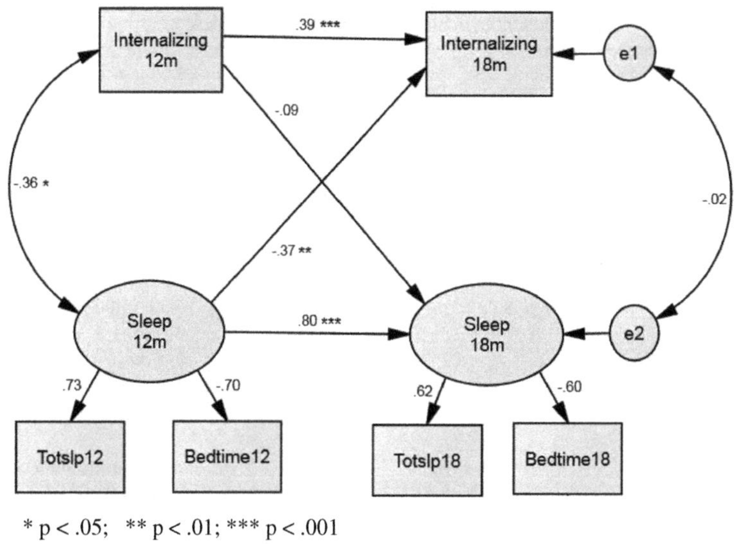

FIGURE 1 Sleep and Internalizing behaviors at 12 and 18 months of age: Structural equation model of concomitant and predictive relations (standardized regression weights). Totslp = total sleep.*$p < .05$. **$p < .01$. ***$p < .001$.

this model: $\chi^2 = 5.68$, $p = .22$; normed fit index = .967, comparative fit index = .989, root mean square error of approximation = .073. The model reflects significant stability in sleep and internalizing behaviors, as well as significant negative correlations between the concomitant sleep and internalizing behavior measures at the 12 months. Furthermore, a significant predictive link from sleep at 12 months to Internalizing at 18 months was found. Other tested models between sleep and Externalizing, Modified Dysregulation, or Competence failed to provide acceptable fit indices or significant predictions.

DISCUSSION

Overall, significant relationships were found between sleep patterns and problem areas in social-emotional development across infancy and toddlerhood. These relationships were evident both concurrently and longitudinally and were more likely for social-emotional problem domains, including externalizing, internalizing, and dysregulation symptoms, than for social competence. It was hypothesized that late bedtimes, prolonged sleep onset latency, decreased sleep duration, and sleep fragmentation would be concurrently associated and predictive of both social-emotional problems and social competence. These hypotheses were partially supported. Overall, later bedtimes, longer sleep onset latency, and reduced total sleep time were associated with social-emotional problems (i.e., internalizing, externalizing, and dysregulation), although they were predominately associated with internalizing problems, both concurrently and longitudinally. Longitudinal prediction, demonstrated through SEM, indicated that less total sleep and later bedtimes at 12 months predicted higher levels of internalizing problems at 18 months. In contrast, only sleep fragmentation (i.e., longest stretch asleep and night wakings) was associated with social competence. This relationship was only demonstrated concurrently at 12 months.

Of interest, predictive analyses revealed that parent-reported sleep was more stable from 12 to 18 months than parent-reported internalizing problems across the same period. A latent sleep variable at 12 months of age, which included total sleep across the 24-hr day and bedtime, was found to predict internalizing problems at 18 months almost equally as well as by the ITSEA at 12 months of age. In contrast, internalizing problems did not predict sleep.

With the exception of the longitudinal association between total sleep time at 6 months and social-emotional outcomes at 12 months (i.e., more total sleep related to lower levels of externalizing, internalizing, and dysregulation problems), relationships among sleep variables and externalizing problems, dysregulation, and competence demonstrated weaker associations and fewer significant relationships. Furthermore, these predictive relationships did not exist between sleep and other areas of social-emotional development, including externalizing problems, dysregulation, and social competence.

These results are similar to results of previous research that demonstrated connections between sleep and internalizing problems in young children. Zaidman-Zait and Hall (2015), for example, assessed more than 1,000 infants and toddlers across three time points between 5 and 29 months of age with regard to sleep (i.e., night wakings), parent behaviors and self-efficacy, and toddler social-emotional problems (externalizing and internalizing). In their study, results indicated that a high frequency of night wakings was associated with higher levels of externalizing (i.e., aggression, hyperactivity, and opposition) and internalizing (shyness/inhibition, anxiety/depression, and separation anxiety) problems. Of note, the strongest effect was found in internalizing problems (i.e., separation anxiety). Scher, Hall, Zaidman-Zait, and Weinberg (2009) found associations between fragmented sleep, cortisol levels, and daycare teacher-reported internalizing problems and negative emotionality in 12- to 36-month-olds. Finally, Reid, Hong, and Wade (2009) also found that sleep problems (bedtime problems and night wakings) predicted both externalizing and internalizing problems in a large sample of 2- and 3-year-olds, with a stronger association between sleep and internalizing problems than between sleep and externalizing problems.

The results presented in the current article align with the results of two previously mentioned studies (i.e., Scher et al., 2009; Zaidman-Zait & Hall, 2015) in that they provide support for a stronger connection between sleep variables and internalizing outcomes, than with externalizing or dysregulation issues. However, rather than sleep fragmentation, reduced total sleep and later bedtimes were associated with increased symptoms of depression, anxiety, and withdrawal, rather than with noncompliance, aggression, and dysregulation in the current study. These findings are in contrast to a common perception that a child who is "overtired" is overactive and noncompliant. Rather, these findings suggest that an "overtired" toddler is more likely to be socially withdrawn and anxious. It is also interesting to note, in this context, that although bidirectional links have been documented between sleep and psychopathology, similar to the results in this study, longitudinal studies in adolescents and adults also suggest that sleep is a better predictor of psychopathology than vice versa, particularly when it relates to depression (Sadeh et al., 2014).

Across time points, associations between sleep and social competence (compliance, attention, imitation/pretend play, mastery motivation, empathy, and prosocial peer relations) resulted in very few statistically significant relationships. Only sleep-consolidation-related variables (i.e., night wakings and longest stretch of sleep overnight) were associated with social competence, and not with any problem scores (e.g., self-regulation) at a single point in time (i.e., 12 months). This result is consistent with previous research indicating that overnight sleep consolidation in infancy and toddlerhood relate to elements of cognitive competence (e.g., Bernier, Carlson, Bordeleau, & Carrier, 2010; Montgomery-Downs & Gozal, 2006; Sadeh et al., 2015). Mixed results of the extant literature regarding social competence and sleep may be at least partially related to how social competence itself is measured across studies. Future research should include various measures of social competence in a single research design during infancy and toddlerhood to compare social competence constructs and their relationship with sleep.

Strengths and Limitations

The current study strengthens the current literature base by meeting several gaps. First, the current study addressed development longitudinally, pertinent to a framework of developmental psychopathology. The results of this study support the need to address sleep issues early on to prevent possible development of social-emotional issues, as well as the need to assess possible social-emotional issues in young children presenting with sleep problems. Second, approximately 36% of the U.S. population belongs to a racial or ethnic minority group (Centers for Disease Control and Prevention, 2012). Collectively, 16.2% of the current sample identified as being part of a racial minority group (i.e., Asian/Pacific Islander, African American/Black, or mixed race), with an additional 13.7% identifying as Hispanic, suggesting comparable minority rates and appropriate generalizability of results. This study utilized a social-emotional measure developed specifically for very young children as opposed to use of a measure assessing general cognitive abilities or global developmental domains. Achieving social-emotional development is important to societal success and must be addressed appropriately through valid and specific research, assessment, prevention, and intervention procedures. Fourth, the current study is one of few that assessed children 18 months and younger with a focus primarily on social-emotional development, examining both problem behavior and healthy, competent trajectories.

There are several limitations inherent to the current investigation. First, overall disqualification of participants based on maternal psychopathology, primarily depression symptomatology, may have limited the number of children with social-emotional problems thus restricting the effects. Additional research including participants with a history of child- or parent-level behavioral or health risk may allow for a broader understanding of potential indirect relationships among sleep, social-emotional variables, and other risk factors. Second, low sample size at certain time points may have resulted in limited power to detect statistical significance among variables. Third, these results relied on maternal report of sleep indicators and indirect behavioral measurement. Future research would benefit from multiple informants (e.g., multiple home caregivers, daycare providers) and more objective data collection through use of tools such as actigraphy, video recording of bedtime routines and infant sleep, and/or direct behavioral observation, enabling a multimethod, multisource assessment paradigm. Fourth, it is possible that there was threat to statistical conclusion validity specific to the correlational results considering the multiple comparisons made (i.e., possible spurious correlations); however, the pattern of correlations, particularly that between internalizing problems and sleep, appear to be quite robust as manifested also in the SEM model. Finally, parents may have engaged in a sleep intervention over time, potentially affecting the relationship and trajectory of both sleep and more general behavior and social competence.

Conclusions

The current study provides additional information in the evolving literature base supporting the connection between sleep and social-emotional development in very young children. Overall, there was evidence for associations between sleep and problematic social-emotional developmental factors, particularly in the area of internalizing problems, with minimal support for a relationship between sleep and social competence. Later bedtimes and less total sleep across the 24-hr period predicted higher internalizing problem scores, which includes indices of depression/withdrawal, general anxiety, separation distress, and inhibition. In contrast, sleep fragmentation was minimally associated with decreased social competence but not with any negative social-emotional outcomes. Clinically, it is important to note that total sleep time, which appears to be at least partially driven by bedtime (Mindell, Meltzer, Carskadon, & Chervin, 2009; Mindell et al., 2010), is a parent-directed behavior that may be modifiable through psychoeducation or other types of behavioral prevention or intervention programming, although it may be a response to more difficulties at bedtime. Another striking finding was the indication that sleep and internalizing problems at 12 months predicted internalizing problems at 18 months with almost equal weight.

Clinically, these results may suggest that implementing intervention or secondary prevention strategies to support healthy sleep habits in infancy may also affect the developmental trajectory of parent-perceived internalizing problems. More well-developed information related to how aspects of sleep early in life affect later social-emotional functioning (e.g., emotion regulation and understanding, affect, mood, competence, psychopathology) is important. This information, in terms of sleep's status as a risk and/or protective factor, has potential to be a critical step in preventing clinical levels of psychopathology from emerging, as may occur through developmental cascades across a lifespan (Masten & Cicchetti, 2010).

CONFLICT OF INTERESTS

Each of the authors has served as a consultant for Johnson & Johnson Consumer, Inc.

FUNDING

This study was sponsored by Johnson & Johnson Consumer, Inc.

REFERENCES

Achenbach, T. M., & Rescorla, L. A. (2000). *Manual for the ASEBA preschool forms and profiles*. Burlington: University of Vermont.

Bayley, N. (2006). *Bayley Scales of Infant and Toddler Development– third edition*. San Antonio, TX: Harcourt Assessment.

Beck, A. T., Steer, R. A., & Brown, G. K. (1996). *Manual for the beck depression inventory-II*. San Antonio, TX: Psychological Corporation.

Berger, R. H., Miller, A. L., Seifer, R., Cares, S. R., & LeBourgeois, M. K. (2012). Acute sleep restriction effects on emotion responses in 30- to 36-month-old children. *Journal of Sleep Research*, *21*, 235–246. doi:10.1111/j.1365-2869.2011.00962.x

Bernier, A., Carlson, S. M., Bordeleau, S., & Carrier, J. (2010). Relations between physiological and cognitive regulatory systems: Infant sleep regulation and subsequent executive functioning. *Child Development*, *81*, 1739–1752. doi:10.1111/cdev.2010.81.issue-6

Boekamp, J. R., Williamson, L. R., Martin, S. E., Hunter, H. L., & Anders, T. F. (2015). Sleep onset and night waking insomnias in preschoolers with psychiatric disorders. *Child Psychiatry & Human Development*, *46*, 622–631. doi:10.1007/s10578-014-0505-z

Carter, A. S., & Briggs-Gowan, M. J. (2006). *Manual for the infant-toddler social & emotional assessment ITSEA - Version 2*. San Antonio, TX: Psychological Corporation, Harcourt Press.

Carter, A. S., Briggs-Gowan, M. J., Jones, S. M., & Little, T. D. (2003). The Infant-Toddler Social and Emotional Assessment (ITSEA): Factor structure, reliability, and validity. *Journal of Abnormal Child Psychology*, *31*, 495–514. doi:10.1023/A:1025449031360

Centers for Disease Control and Prevention. (2012). *Racial & ethnic minority populations*. Retrieved from http://www.cdc.gov/minorityhealth/populations/remp.html

Cox, J., & Holden, J. (2003). *Perinatal mental health: A guide to the Edinburgh Postnatal Depression Scale (EPDS)*. London, UK: Gaskell.

Derogatis, L. R. (2001). *Brief Symptom Inventory (BSI)-18*. Administration, scoring and procedures manual. Minneapolis, MN: NCS Pearson, Inc.

Gibson, R., Elder, D., & Gander, P. (2012). Actigraphic sleep and developmental progress of one-year-old infants. *Sleep and Biological Rhythms*, *10*, 77–83. doi:10.1111/sbr.2012.10.issue-2

Hatzinger, M., Brand, S., Perren, S., Von Wyl, A., Stadelmann, S., Von Klitzing, K., & Holsboer-Trachsler, E. (2014). In pre-school children, sleep objectively assessed via sleep-EEGs remains stable over 12 months and is related to psychological functioning, but not to cortisol secretion. *Journal of Psychiatric Research*, *47*, 1809–1814. doi:10.1016/j.jpsychires.2013.08.007

Hyde, R., O'Callaghan, M. J., Bor, W., Williams, G. M., & Najman, J. M. (2012). Long-term outcomes of infant behavioral dysregulation. *Pediatrics*, *130*, e1243–e1251. doi:10.1542/peds.2010-3517

Hysing, M., Siversten, B., Garthus-Niegel, S., & Eberhard-Gran, M. (2016). Pediatric sleep problems and social-emotional problems. A population-based study. *Infant Behavior & Development*, *42*, 111–118. doi:10.1016/j.infbeh.2015.12.005

IBM Corp. (Released 2013). *IBM SPSS statistics for Macintosh, version 22.0*. Armonk, NY: Author.

Jansen, P. W., Saridjan, N. S., Hofman, A., Jaddoe, V. W. V., Verhulst, F. C., & Tiemeier, H. (2011). Does disturbed sleep precede symptoms of anxiety or depression in toddlers? The Generation R study. *Psychosomatic Medicine*, *73*, 242–249. doi:10.1097/PSY.0b013e31820a4abb

Kelly, R. J., & El-Sheikh, M. (2014). Reciprocal relations between children's sleep and their adjustment over time. *Developmental Psychology*, *50*, 1137–1147. doi:10.1037/a0034501

Kelly, Y., Kelly, J., & Sacker, A. (2013). Time for bed: Associations with cognitive performance in 7-year-old children: A longitudinal population-based study. *Journal of Epidemiology & Community Health*, *67*, 926–931. doi:10.1136/jech-2012-202024

Lam, J. C., Mahone, E. M., Mason, T. B. A., & Scharf, S. M. (2011). The effects of napping on cognitive function in preschoolers. *Journal of Developmental & Behavioral Pediatrics*, *32*, 90–97. doi:10.1097/DBP.0b013e318207ecc7

Masten, A. S., & Cicchetti, D. (2010). Developmental cascades. *Development and Psychopathology.*, *22*, 491–495. doi:10.1017/S0954579410000222

Miller, A. L., Seifer, R., Crossin, R., & LeBourgeois, M. K. (2015). Toddler's self-regulation strategies in a challenge context are nap-dependent. *Journal of Sleep Research*, *24*, 279–287. doi:10.1111/jsr.12260

Mindell, J. A., Johnson, C., Sadeh, A., Telofski, L., Kulkarni, N., & Gunn, E. (2011). Efficacy of an internet-based intervention for infant and toddler sleep disturbances. *Sleep*, *34*, 451–458.

Mindell, J. A., & Lee, C. (2015). Sleep, mood, and development in infants. *Infant Behavior & Development*, *41*, 102–107. doi:10.1016/j.infbeh.2015.08.004

Mindell, J. A., Meltzer, L. J., Carskadon, M. A., & Chervin, R. (2009). Developmental aspects of sleep hygiene: Findings from the 2004 national sleep foundation sleep in America Poll. *Sleep Medicine*, *10*, 771–779. doi:10.1016/j.sleep.2008.07.016

Mindell, J. A., Sadeh, A., Kohyama, J., & How, T. H. (2010). Sleep ecology and predictors of sleep outcomes in infants and toddlers: A cross-cultural comparison. *Sleep Medicine*, *11*, 393–399. doi:10.1016/j.sleep.2009.11.011

Mindell, J. A., Telofski, L. S., Wiegand, B., & Kurtz, E. S. (2009). A nightly bedtime routine: Impact on sleep in young children and maternal mood. *Sleep*, *32*, 599–606.

Montgomery-Downs, H. E., & Gozal, D. (2006). Snore-associated sleep fragmentation in infancy: Mental development effects and contribution of secondhand cigarette smoke exposure. *Pediatrics*, *117*, e495–e502. doi:10.1542/peds.2005-1785

Reid, G. J., Hong, R. Y., & Wade, T. J. (2009). The relation between common sleep problems and emotional and behavioral problems among 2- and 3-year-olds in the context of known risk factors for psychopathology. *Journal of Sleep Research*, *18*(1), 49–59. doi:10.1111/jsr.2009.18.issue-1

Robins, D., Fein, D., Barton, M., & Green, J. A. (2001). The Modified-Checklist for Autism in Toddlers (M-CHAT): An initial investigation in the early detection of autism and pervasive developmental disorders. *Journal of Autism and Developmental Disorders*, *31*, 131–144. doi:10.1023/A:1010738829569

Sadeh, A. (2004). A brief infant sleep questionnaire for infant sleep problems: Validation and findings for an internet sample. *Pediatrics*, *113*, e570– e577. doi:10.1542/peds.113.6.e570

Sadeh, A., De Marcas, G., Guri, Y., Berger, A., Tikotsky, L., & Bar-Haim, Y. (2015). Sleep predicts attention regulation and behavior problems at 3-4 years of age. *Developmental Neuropsychology*, *40*, 122–137. doi:10.1080/87565641.2014.973498

Sadeh, A., Mindell, J. A., Luedtke, K., & Wiegand, B. (2009). Sleep and sleep ecology in the first 3 years: A web-based study. *Journal of Sleep Research*, *18* (1), 60–73. doi:10.1111/jsr.2009.18.issue-1

Sadeh, A., Tikotzky, L., & Kahn, M. (2014). Sleep in infancy and childhood: Implications for emotional and behavioral difficulties in adolescence and beyond. *Current Opinion in Psychiatry*, *27*(6), 453–459. doi:10.1097/YCO.0000000000000109

Scher, A., Hall, W. A., Zaidman-Zait, A., & Weinberg, J. (2009). Sleep quality, cortisol levels, and behavioral regulation in toddlers. *Developmental Psychobiology*, *52*(1), 44–53.

Sheridan, A., Murray, L., Cooper, P. J., Evangeli, M., Byram, V., & Halligan, S. L. (2013). A longitudinal study of child sleep in high and low risk families: Relationship to early maternal settling strategies and child psychological functioning. *Sleep Medicine*, *14*(3), 266–273. doi:10.1016/j.sleep.2012.11.006

Sidor, A., Fischer, C., Eickhorst, A., & Cierpka, M. (2013). Influence of early regulatory problems in infants on their development at 12 months: A longitudinal study in a high-risk sample. *Child and Adolescent Psychiatry and Mental Health*, *7*, 35. doi:10.1186/1753-2000-7-35

Sivertsen, B., Harvey, A. G., Reichborn-Kjennerud, T., Torgersen, L., Ystrom, E., & Hysing, M. (2015). Later emotional and behavioral problems associated with sleep problems in toddlers: A longitudinal study. *JAMA Pediatrics*, *169*, 575–582. doi:10.1001/jamapediatrics.2015.0187

Tikotzky, L., & Sadeh, A. (2009). Maternal sleep-related cognitions and infant sleep: A longitudinal study from pregnancy through the first year. *Child Development*, *80*, 860–874. doi:10.1111/j.1467-8624.2009.01302.x

Touchette, É., Petit, D., Séguin, J. R., Boivin, M., Tremblay, R. E., & Montplaisir, J. Y. (2007). Associations between sleep duration patterns and behavioral/cognitive functioning at school entry. *Sleep*, *30*, 1213–1219.

Vaughn, B. E., Elmore-Staton, L., Shin, N., & El-Sheikh, M. (2015). Sleep as a support for social competence, peer relations, and cognitive functioning in preschool children. *Behavioral Sleep Medicine*, *13*(2), 92–106. doi:10.1080/15402002.2013.845778

Winsper, C., & Wolke, D. (2014). Infant and toddler crying, sleeping and feeding problems and trajectories of dysregulated behavior across childhood. *Journal of Abnormal Child Psychology*, *42*(5), 831–843. doi:10.1007/s10802-013-9813-1

Yorbik, O., Mutlu, C., Koc, D., & Mutluer, T. (2014). Possible negative effects of snoring and increased sleep fragmentation on developmental status of preschool children. *Sleep and Biological Rhythms*, *12*(1), 30–36. doi:10.1111/sbr.12042

Zaidman-Zait, A., & Hall, W. A. (2015). Children's night waking among toddlers: Relationships with mothers' and fathers' parenting approaches and children's behavioural difficulties. *Journal of Advanced Nursing*, *71*(7), 1639–1649. doi:10.1111/jan.12636

Sleep in Adolescents With Bipolar I Disorder: Stability and Relation to Symptom Change

Anda Gershon and Manpreet K. Singh

Sleep disturbances are common features of bipolar disorder (BD), yet little is known about trajectories of sleep disturbances in youth with BD. Using longitudinal data, this study assessed the stability of sleep disturbances and their ability to predict symptom progression in adolescents diagnosed with BD compared to controls. Thirteen- to 19-year-olds meeting diagnostic criteria for BD I (n = 19, 16.2 ± 1.75 years, 57.9 % female, 68.4% Caucasian) and psychiatrically healthy age-comparable controls (n = 21, 15.7 ± 1.48 years. 52.4% female, 57.1% Caucasian) were assessed for sleep onset latency, number of awakenings, and wake time, separately for weekdays and weekends using a self-report questionnaire. Sleep indices and symptoms of mania (Young Mania Rating Scale) and depression (Children's Depression Rating Scale) were assessed at two time points, T1 and T2, approximately 12 months apart. Correlations were used to examine stability of sleep indices across time points and regression models to examine the effects of T1 sleep on T2 symptoms. Adolescents with BD showed low stability on most sleep indices, whereas controls showed high stability on all sleep indices. After controlling for T1 depression symptoms, more T1 weekend awakenings and weekend wake time predicted significantly greater T2 depression symptoms in youth with BD but not in controls. No significant associations were found between T1 sleep and T2 mania symptoms. These findings suggest that increased awakenings and wakefulness on weekends may represent an important therapeutic target for reducing depression in adolescents with BD.

INTRODUCTION

Sleep and circadian disturbances are central features of bipolar disorder (BD). Episodes of mania or hypomania are characterized by either a reduced need for sleep or an inability to get adequate sleep (insomnia; American Psychiatric Association, 2013) and an *earlier* timing of the circadian sleep–wake cycle (phase advance; Salvatore et al., 2008). Depressive episodes, which are frequently present in the course of BD, are often characterized by insomnia or hypersomnia (American Psychiatric Association, 2013), a delay (latening) of circadian timing and a preference for "eveningness" (Robillard et al., 2013). Studies of individuals with BD who are currently between mood episodes demonstrate that sleep and circadian disturbances, including longer onset latencies and wake periods during the night, and a more fragmented sleep/wake rhythm and less day-to-day stability, persist even outside of acute mood episodes in BD (Brill, Penagaluri, Roberts, Gao, & El-Mallakh, 2011; Gershon et al., 2012; Harvey, Schmidt, Scarna, Semler, & Goodwin, 2005; Jones, Hare, & Evershed, 2005; Millar, Espie, & Scott, 2004). Evidence that sleep and circadian disturbances persist outside of acute mood episodes in BD suggests that these may be trait-like features of the disorder.

Given their chronic and persistent nature, sleep and circadian disturbances may have value for understanding the course of BD. Few longitudinal studies have examined the relation between sleep/circadian disturbances and illness course in BD. In one study of 54 adults diagnosed with bipolar I disorder, shorter sleep duration predicted a worsening in depression symptoms, but not mania symptoms, across a 6-month follow-up period (Perlman, Johnson, & Mellman, 2006). Another study of adults with bipolar spectrum disorders (N = 196) found that more variability in sleep duration was associated with increases in both mania and depression symptoms over a 12-month follow-up (Gruber et al., 2011). Less regularity in social rhythms, or daily routines that help entrain natural circadian rhythms, has been found to predict faster relapse among adults with bipolar spectrum disorders (Shen, Alloy, Abramson, & Sylvia, 2008). In a study in which 11 adults with rapid cycling BD provided daily self-ratings of mood and sleep over the course of 18 months, shorter sleep duration was found to be predictive next-day manic or hypomanic onset (Leibenluft, Albert, Rosenthal, & Wehr, 1996). Similarly, a prospective study in which 59 adults with BD provided daily reports of their mood and sleep over the course of 5 months found that shorter sleep duration predicted increased next-day mania and longer sleep duration predicted increased next-day depression (Bauer et al., 2006). Taken together, these findings suggest that sleep and circadian rhythms may be important short-term and long-term predictors of mood symptoms in BD.

Current evidence for sleep disturbances in BD comes primarily from studies of adults. Little research is available on the presentation or effects of sleep disturbances in youth with BD. Studies assessing the symptom presentation of BD in pediatric patients using medical record reviews, self-reports, and/or parent reports have documented that, as is found with adults, a reduced need for sleep typically occurs during manic periods in youth with bipolar symptomatology (Ballenger, Reus, & Post, 1982; Ferreira Maia, Boarati, Kleinman, & Fu, 2007; Findling et al., 2001; Geller et al., 2002; Holtmann et al., 2007; Jerrell & Shugart, 2004). Some studies have also documented that in comparison to age-matched controls, youth with symptoms of BD have more difficulty falling asleep, experience more awakenings throughout the night, and spend more time awake during these awakenings (Lofthouse, Fristad, Splaingard, & Kelleher, 2007; Mehl et al., 2006; Roybal et al., 2011), whereas other studies have not demonstrated such differences (Mullin, Harvey, & Hinshaw, 2011). Although there is some evidence that specific sleep disruptions, such as difficulty falling asleep, occur primarily during depressive phases (Lofthouse et al., 2007), information on the correspondence of specific sleep disturbances to phases of illness is not yet available, possibly because youth with BD tend to display a less episodic pattern of illness than do adults (Biederman et al., 2004).

Whereas studies conducted with adults with BD suggest that disturbances in sleep and circadian rhythms are reliable predictors of symptom change (Perlman et al., 2006; Shen et al., 2008), there has been limited investigation of the contribution of these disturbances to illness course in youth with BD. The few available studies have provided mixed findings. In one study, a clinical record review of 82 children diagnosed with BD (*M* age = 10.6 years, *SD* = 3.6 years) showed that insomnia and parasomnias, a category of sleep disorders that includes sleepwalking and nightmares, were frequently reported by parents as the initial symptoms they retrospectively observed in their children long before the initial onset of the disorder, usually prior to age 3, suggesting that sleep disturbances may precede first episode onset in BD (Faedda, Baldessarini, Glovinsky, & Austin, 2004).

Another study examined the longitudinal impact of self-reported sleep on mood symptoms in 12- to 17-year-olds ($N = 53$) diagnosed with bipolar spectrum disorders. This study found that sleep difficulties, and particularly irregular sleep rhythms and more awakenings, were significantly associated with symptoms over a 2-year follow-up period (Lunsford-Avery, Judd, Axelson, & Miklowitz, 2012). In a longitudinal study of 6- to 18-year-old offspring of parents with BD, subjective sleep difficulties such as frequent nighttime awakenings were associated with higher rates of development of the disorder in at-risk youth (Levenson et al., 2015). By contrast, a study of 13- to 19-year-old youth offspring of parents with BD ($n = 25$) found that although these youth had significantly shorter sleep onset latency and less variable sleep fragmentation by actigraphy than controls, symptomatic bipolar offspring reported more subjective sleep disturbances than asymptomatic bipolar offspring, suggesting that in these high-risk offspring, sleep disturbances co-occur with mood symptoms rather than precede them (Jones, Tai, Evershed, Knowles, & Bentall, 2006).

There are several possible reasons why findings vary across studies. First, studies differ in sample selection (children with BD vs. children of parents with BD) and the measures used to assess sleep disturbances (actigrapy vs. self-reported sleep vs. parent-reported symptoms). Second, while measuring sleep in adolescents, it is important to account for the developmental stage of the adolescent and the day of the week sleep is assessed. Bedtimes become increasingly delayed over the course of development, coinciding with pubertal changes that occur across late childhood and adolescence (Carskadon, Vieira, & Acebo, 1993; Crowley, Acebo, & Carskadon, 2007; Russo, Bruni, Lucidi, Ferri, & Violani, 2007). A delayed bedtime is likely to result in shorter sleep durations on weekday nights relative to weekend nights due to early rise time on school days (Carskadon, 1990). To our knowledge, only one study has separately measured weekday versus weekend sleep in postpubertal youth with BD (Roybal et al., 2011). The findings of this study indicated that adolescents with BD sleep significantly longer on weekends relative to weekdays and that the duration of their weekend sleep is comparable to that of healthy controls (Roybal et al., 2011).

In summary, there is preliminary evidence that sleep disturbances are common among youth with BD, characterized principally by more wake time during the night compared to healthy controls, and may precede the onset of a mood episode. Few studies in BD have directly examined the persistence of sleep disturbances in youth with BD, or the longitudinal impact of sleep disturbances on mood symptoms. Additional studies in this area are clearly needed to gain a better understanding of disturbed sleep in the development and progression of BD in youth.

The current study has two aims. First, in a sample of adolescents diagnosed with BD I, and age-matched adolescent controls, we examine the stability of sleep as assessed across two time points (T1 and T2) approximately twelve months apart. Adolescence represents an important period in which to examine sleep in relation to BD symptoms because it is a period both of high risk for the development of BD and of significant sleep changes. Given that sleep disruption has been identified as a reliable prodrome for mood onset in adults, better understanding of the contribution of sleep disruption to early development or progression of BD is needed. We assess sleep using a self-report measure administered separately for weekdays and weekends. A previous study examined T1 sleep in this sample and showed that adolescents with BD experienced longer sleep onset latency, more awakenings throughout the night, and more time spent awake during these awakenings, relative to age-matched controls (Roybal et al., 2011). We therefore focus on these specific sleep deficits, rather than a general sleep disturbance. We hypothesized that these sleep disturbances would persist at T2 for youth with BD relative to controls.

Second, we examine whether sleep indices assessed at T1 predict mood symptom severity at T2. Roybal et al. (2011) found cross-sectional associations at T1 between mood symptoms, assessed using structured diagnostic interview, and sleep indices. For example, at T1, a longer period of worsening of evening mood and higher levels of excessive guilt were found to be associated with longer sleep onset latency among youth with BD, and increased pacing, greater psychomotor retardation, and increased productivity were each associated with a greater number of awakenings and longer wake time during the night (Roybal et al., 2011). Based on these findings, we hypothesized that sleep disturbances at T1 would contribute to more severe symptoms of depression and mania at T2 for youth with BD but not in controls.

METHOD

Participants

Thirty-three postpubertal adolescents diagnosed with bipolar I disorder (bipolar group = 16.2 ± 1.66 years old) and 27 adolescents with no personal or family history of psychiatric disorders (control group = 15.5 ± 1.45 years old) were recruited from the Stanford University Pediatric Bipolar Disorders Program or the surrounding San Francisco Bay Area community. Participants in the bipolar group had experienced a single episode of mania within 6 to 12 months of research participation, based on *Diagnostic and Statistical Manual of Mental Disorders* (4th ed., text rev. [*DSM-IV-TR*]; American Psychiatric Association, 2000) diagnostic criteria. Mania in this group was not precipitated by exposure to recreational drugs, antidepressants, stimulants, or other medications or medical conditions. Given the potential risk for mood destabilization, youth in the bipolar group were not excluded on thc basis of current psychotropic medication treatment. In addition, BD commonly co-occurs with other psychiatric disorders (Kessler, Chiu, Demler, & Walters, 2005), so participants in the bipolar group were not excluded on the basis of current comorbid psychiatric diagnoses other than alcohol or substance abuse or dependence in the previous 6 months.

Control group participants were required to have neither a lifetime history of psychiatric diagnoses, based on *DSM-IV-TR* diagnostic criteria, nor a family history of any mood or psychotic disorders. Control group participants were also excluded if they had been exposed to psychotropic medications. Participants were excluded if they had metal in their body or braces for a concurrent MRI study, head injury with loss of consciousness for longer than 5 min, IQ lower than 80, seizures, or a developmental disorder.

Measures

Demographic information. Participants and their parents were asked to report on age, gender, and ethnicity. Socioeconomic status was assessed using the Hollingshead Four Factor Index (Hollingshead, 1975).

Psychiatric disorders. The Washington University in St. Louis Kiddie-Schedule for Affective Disorders and Schizophrenia (Geller, Williams, Zimerman, & Frazier, 1996) was used to assess for the presence or absence of lifetime and current psychiatric disorders among all participants. The interview was administered separately to youth and their parents. The interview has demonstrated high interrater reliability for mania diagnosis and individual mania items (Geller et al., 2001), high 6-month stability for mania diagnoses and individual mania items (Geller et al., 2000), and high validity against parental and teacher reports (Geller, Warner, Williams, & Zimerman, 1998). Diagnoses for the present study were determined by a consensus conference attended by a board-certified child and adolescent psychiatrist (MKS) and at minimum master's-level researchers ($K > 0.90$ for all diagnoses). The Family History-Research Diagnostic Criteria (FH-RDC; Andreasen, Endicott, Spitzer, & Winokur, 1977) was administered to parents of control group adolescents to confirm absence of mood and psychosis in first-degree relatives. The FH-RDC specifies criteria required for endorsing psychiatric disorders such as schizophrenia, depression, and BD. The FH-RDC has demonstrated excellent interrater reliability and good reliability against a diagnostic standard (68%–75%; Andreasen et al., 1977).

Depression and mania symptoms. Depression symptom severity was measured using the Children's Depression Rating Scale–Revised (CDRS-R; Poznanski & Mokros, 1995), a widely used 17-item clinician-administered scale. Items assess core symptom domains including depressed mood, impairment in schoolwork, social withdrawal, anhedonia, irritability, sleep, appetite, suicidal ideation, and physical complaints and fatigue. In addition, the scale measures nonverbal expressions depression such as depressed appearance and slowed tempo of language. Items are scored on a 1–5 or 1–7 scale. Total scores range from 17 to 113, with higher scores indicating greater symptom severity. A score of 28 or lower indicates minimal or no symptoms, and a score of 40 or higher is indicative of depression. The scale has demonstrated good reliability and validity in adolescents 7 to 18 years old (Mayes, Bernstein, Haley, Kennard, & Emslie, 2010). Mania symptom severity was assessed using the Young Mania Rating Scale (YMRS; Young, Biggs, Ziegler, & Meyer, 1978), a widely used 11-item clinician administered scale of mania symptom severity. Items assess core symptom domains including elevated mood, motor activity and energy, sexual interest, sleep, irritability, pressured speech, distractibility, racing thoughts, and disruptive or aggressive behavior. Scores range from 0 to 60, with higher scores indicating greater symptom severity. A score lower than 12 indicates asymptomatic to mild symptom severity (e.g., Suppes et al., 2005). The YMRS has demonstrated good psychometric properties (Young et al., 1978).

Pubertal development. The Pubertal Development Scale (Petersen, Crockett, Richards, & Boxer, 1988) is a five-item self-report scale that assessed pubertal status without using picture representations of developmental stages. Items assess for changes in body hair, changes in voice (for boys) or breast development (for girls), skin change, growth spurts, facial hair (for boys), and menarche (for girls). In a large sample of sixth- and seventh-grade boys and girls ($N = 253$), the measure was shown to have good reliability (α = 0.68–0.87) and high correlations between a questionnaire version and physician ratings (r = .61–.67; Petersen et al., 1988).

Sleep. A self-report questionnaire was administered to youth to assess sleep onset latency, number of awakenings, and wake time during the night in the past week, separately for weekdays and weekends. Specifically, to assess for weekday sleep onset latency, adolescents were asked, "On school days in the past week, after you have gone to bed at night, about how long has it usually taken you to fall asleep?" To assess for weekday number of awakenings, adolescents were asked, "On school days in the past week, how many times have you usually woken up?" To assess for weekday wake time during the night, adolescents were asked, "How much time awake during a school night over past week?" These three questions were repeated to assess for weekend sleep.

Procedure

Stanford University's Institutional Review Board approved all study procedures. Potential participants for the bipolar group were recruited by referral to a Pediatric Bipolar Disorders Clinic and from the surrounding community. After parents and adolescents were explained the purpose and procedures of the study fully, written informed consent was obtained from the parents and written assent was obtained from youth younger than age 18. Adolescents and their parents completed a demographic questionnaire, the PDS, and were interviewed using the Kiddie-Schedule for Affective Disorders and Schizophrenia, FH-RDC, YMRS, and CDRS-R. A child and adolescent psychiatrist (MKS) or master's-level researchers administered all interviews. Names, dosages, frequency, and duration of use for each currently prescribed medication were recorded. Eligible participants were administered a sleep questionnaire. Participants returned for a second lab visit 1 year later. During this visit, the sleep questionnaire was readministered. Participants were compensated $125 for completing the study.

Analysis

We conducted preliminary analyses to verify that the BD group and the control group did not differ significantly in demographic composition, including age, gender, ethnicity, socioeconomic status, or pubertal development. Group differences in age, socioeconomic status, and pubertal development score were evaluated using *t* tests, and differences in gender and ethnicity were evaluated using chi-square tests. We examined means, standard deviations, and range of each sleep index. Levene's test of heterogeneity was used to examine whether the variability of sleep indices was significantly different between the groups at either time point.

We tested hypotheses by conducting two sets of analyses. First, bivariate correlations were used to examine the stability in sleep indices between T1 and T2 within each group. Second, separate linear regression models were used to test the effects of each T1 sleep variable (sleep onset latency, number of awakenings, or wake time) on T2 symptom severity while controlling for the effects of T1 symptom severity. That is, for each regression model, we entered T1 symptom severity, group, and T1 sleep (sleep onset latency, number of awakenings, or wake time) as predictors of T2 symptom severity. We separately considered depressive and manic symptom severity. All tests were completed using SPSS for Windows (version 22.0).

RESULTS

Study Attrition and Sample Characteristics

Sixty participants (33 BD group participants and 27 control group participants) completed T1 clinical and sleep assessments and were enrolled in the study. At T2, some people declined participation ($n = 8$), moved ($n = 5$), or were unable to complete the T2 assessment ($n = 6$), yielding a final sample size of 19 bipolar group participants and 22 control group participants.

Given the rate of attrition in the BD group, we conducted within-group comparisons of those who did and did not complete the study on demographic, clinical, and sleep characteristics. Within the BD group, those who did not complete T2 assessment did not differ significantly from BD sample in age, $t(31) = -.397$, $p = .694$; gender, $\chi^2(1) = .203$, $p = .653$; ethnicity, $\chi^2(4) = 2.162$, $p = .706$; socioeconomic status, $t(31) = -.552$ $p = .585$; pubertal development score, $t(31) = 1.139$, $p = .263$; YMRS score, $t(31) = .004$, $p = .997$; or CDRS-R score, $t(31) = .187$, $p = .853$. Those who did not complete T2 had *near* significantly greater sleep onset latency on weekdays, $t(31) = 1.966$, $p = .06$. No other sleep-related differences were found between BD group participants who completed T2 and those who did not. For control group participants, no significant differences were found between those who did not complete the T2 assessment and study participants in age, $t(25) = 1.574$, $p = .128$; gender, $\chi^2(1) = .386$, $p = .535$; socioeconomic status, $t(25) = .609$, $p = .549$; pubertal development score, $t(25) = -.209$, $p = .836$; YMRS score, $t(25) = .387$, $p = .702$; and CDRS-R score, $t(25) = .526$, $p = .604$. On the other hand, control group participants who did not complete T2 showed a trend level difference in ethnicity from control group study participants, $\chi^2(4) = 9.257$, $p = .055$. No sleep-related differences were found between control group participants who completed T2 and those who did not.

The demographic and clinical characteristics of the 41 study participants who completed both T1 and T2 time points are presented in Table 1. There were no significant differences between BD and control groups in age at T1 ($p = .075$) or T2 ($p = .411$), gender ($p = .839$), ethnicity ($p = .126$), socioeconomic status ($p = 1.0$), or pubertal development at T1 ($p = .168$) or T2 ($p = .356$). Ten of 19

TABLE 1
Demographic and Clinical Characteristics of 41 Study Participants Across Study Time Points

	T1		*T2*	
	BD[a]	*Control*[b]	*BD*[a]	*Control*[b]
Demographic Characteristics				
Age in Years, *M* (*SD*)	16.1 (1.75)	15.7 (1.48)	17.3 (1.86)	16.8 (1.40)
Female, *n* (%)	11 (57.9)	11 (52.4)	11 (57.9)	11 (52.4)
Caucasian, *n* (%)	13 (68.4)	12 (57.1)	13 (68.4)	12 (57.1)
Socioeconomic Status, *M* (*SD*)	4.68 (0.58)	4.68 (0.58)	—	—
Pubertal Development Score, *M* (*SD*)	3.41 (0.33)	3.14 (0.62)	3.53 (0.36)	3.39 (0.48)
Clinical Characteristics				
Current Episode				
Manic/Hypomanic, *n* (%)	2 (10.5)	—	1 (5.3)	—
Depressed, *n* (%)	6 (31.6)	—	5 (26.2)	—
Mixed, *n* (%)	3 (15.8)	—	1 (5.3)	—
Interepisode, *n* (%)	8 (42.1)	—	12 (63.2)	—
C-GAS Score, *M* (*SD*)	55.5 (10.5)	93.7 (3.31)	61.1 (9.7)	91.1 (4.87)
YMRS Score, *M* (*SD*)	18.4 (8.15)	0.26 (0.56)	14.3 (9.06)	0.75 (1.12)
CDRS-R Score, *M* (*SD*)	45.6 (16.5)	18.2 (1.51)	37.4 (13.3)	19.0 (1.81)
Medications, *n* (%)				
Antipsychotics	13 (68.4)	—	16 (84.2)	—
Anticonvulsants	9 (47.4)	—	10 (52.6)	—
SSRIs	8 (42.1)	—	7 (36.8)	—
Stimulants	7 (36.8)	—	8 (42.1)	—
Lithium	3 (15.8)	—	7 (36.8)	—
Wellbutrin	2 (10.5)	—	3 (15.8)	—
SARIs	2 (10.5)	—	0 (0)	—
TCAs	1 (5.3)	—	1 (5.3)	—
TeCAs	0 (0)	—	3 (15.8)	—
Two or More Classes of Medications	12 (63.2)	—	15 (78.9)	—

Note: Pubertal development score based on Pubertal Development Scale. Valid percents are reported. Two control group participants were missing YMRS scores. T1 = Time 1; T2 = Time 2; BD = bipolar disorder; C-GAS = Children's Global Assessment Scale; YMRS = Young Mania Rating Scale. CDRS-R = Child Depression Rating Scale–Revised; SSRI = selective serotonin reuptake inhibitor; SARI = serotonin antagonist reuptake inhibitor; TCA = tricyclic antidepressant; TeCA = tetracyclic antidepressant.

[a]$n = 19$.

[b]$n = 22$.

TABLE 2
Means, Standard Deviations, and Ranges for Sleep Variables of 41 Study Participants Across Study Time Points

	T1		*T2*	
	BD[a]	*Control*[b]	*BD*[a]	*Control*[b]
Weekday Sleep				
Sleep Onset Latency (min)				
M (SD)	23.9 (16.7)	20.0 (18.7)	29.2 (37.9)	20.6 (17.1)
Range	5–60	0–60	0–120	5–60
No. Awakenings				
M (SD)	1.05 (1.18)	0.50 (0.76)	0.47 (0.77)	0.65 (0.81)
Range	0–4	0–2	0–2	0–3
Wake Time (Min)				
M (SD)	11.7 (18.9)	1.35 (2.52)	26.0 (77.0)	7.72 (10.9)
Range	0–75	0–10	0–300	0–30
Weekend Sleep				
Sleep Onset Latency (Min)				
M (SD)	34.1 (68.0)	14.1 (17.4)	19.6 (22.1)	17.6 (18.0)
Range	0–300	0–60	0–75	0–60
No. Awakenings				
M (SD)	0.88 (1.17)	0.45 (0.76)	0.39 (0.61)	0.35 (0.75)
Range	0–4	0–2	0–2	0–3
Wake Time (Min)				
M (SD)	10.6 (22.7)	1.58 (2.76)	3.25 (5.69)	3.06 (6.10)
Range	0–90	0–10	0–20	0–20

Note: Two control group participants were missing weekday onset latency and weekday number of awakenings at T1. One bipolar group participant was missing weekday wake time and weekend sleep onset latency at T1. T1 = Time 1; T2 = Time 2; BD = bipolar disorder.

[a]$n = 19$.

[b]$n = 22$.

BD group participants (52.6%) had at least one comorbid psychiatric diagnosis. These diagnoses included attention deficit/hyperactivity disorder ($n = 6$), anxiety disorders ($n = 4$), substance abuse or dependence (past only; $n = 4$), oppositional defiant disorder ($n = 3$), dysthymia (n = 2), conduct disorder ($n = 1$), and bulimia nervosa ($n = 1$).

Group Differences in Means and Variances of Sleep Characteristics Over Time

Table 2 presents the means, standard deviations, and ranges of values for sleep indices at T1 and T2 for study participants. At T2, group comparisons showed no significant differences in sleep onset latency, number of awakenings, or wake time on weekdays or weekends (all *ps* >.30).[1] Levene's test of equality variances indicated that the groups differed significantly at T1 in the variance of wake time on weekdays ($F = 13.595$, $p = .001$, $n = 38$) and on weekends ($F = 8.555$, $p = .006$, $n = 39$), with the BD group showing significantly higher variance on both these indices than controls. At T2, Levene's test of equality of variances indicated that the groups differed significantly in the variance of sleep onset latency on weekdays ($F = 5.523$, $p = .024$, $n = 39$) but not on weekends ($F = 0.545$, $p = .47$, $n = 39$) and the variance of wake time on weekdays ($F = 4.229$, $p = .048$, $n = 39$) but not weekends ($F = 0.028$, $p = .87$, $n = 39$). The BD group, again, showed significantly higher variance on both these indices than controls. The variance in number of awakenings at T2 did not differ significantly between groups for either weekday or weekend measures (both *ps* > .96).

Stability of Sleep in Adolescents With BD Compared to Age-Matched Controls

The within-group bivariate correlations of sleep across T1 and T2 time points are presented in Table 3. Within the BD group, the number of weekday awakenings reported at T1 was significantly correlated with number of weekday awakenings reported at T2 ($r = .46$, $p = .048$), but no other index of sleep disturbance was significantly correlated between T1 and T2 time points (*ps* = .074–.92). By contrast, within the age-matched control group, each sleep variable was significantly correlated between the T1 and T2 time points, suggesting high stability in sleep measures over time for the control group: sleep onset latency on weekdays ($r = .56$, $p = .013$) and on weekends ($r = .61$, $p = .004$), the number of awakenings on weekdays ($r = .54$, $p = .017$) and weekends ($r = .69$, $p = .001$), and the duration of wake time on weekdays ($r = .74$, $p = .001$) and weekends ($r = .53$, $p = .041$).

[1]As reported in Roybal et al. (2011), at T1, youth with BD-I experienced significantly longer wake time on weekdays than did controls, $t(39) = 2.292$, $p = .034$.

TABLE 3
Pearson's Product–Moment Correlations for T1–T2 Sleep Variables by Group

	BD[a]	*Controls*[b]
Weekdays		
Sleep Onset Latency	0.19	0.56*
No. Awakenings	0.46*	0.54*
Wake Time	0.10	0.74**
Weekends		
Sleep Onset Latency	0.03	0.61**
No. Awakenings	0.29	0.69**
Wake Time	−0.03	0.53*

Note: BD = bipolar disorder.
[a]n = 19.
[b]n = 22.
*$p < .05$. **$p < .01$.

Long-Term Effects of Sleep on Symptoms in Adolescents With BD Compared to Age-Matched Controls

After controlling for depressive symptom severity at T1, the number of awakenings on *weekends* at T1 related to depressive symptom severity at T2 ($\beta = .297$, $t = 2.897$, $p = .006$, CI for β = 1.158, 6.564). The final model accounted for 66.1% of explained variance (Table 4). Follow-up correlations indicated that, after controlling for depressive symptom severity at T1, the number of awakenings on weekends at T1 was significantly related to depressive symptom severity at T2 in the BD group ($r = .475$, $p = .040$, $n = 16$) but not in the control group ($r = .283$, $p = .241$, $n = 19$).

After controlling for depressive symptom severity at T1, wake time on *weekends* at T1 related to depressive symptom severity at T2 ($\beta = .310$, $t = 2.941$, $p = .006$, CI for β = .047, .255). The final model accounted for 63.2% of explained variance (Table 5). Follow-up correlations indicated that, after controlling for depressive symptom severity at T1, wake time on weekends at T1 was significantly related to depressive symptom severity at T2 in the bipolar group ($r = .462$, $p = .047$, $n = 16$) but not in the control group ($r = -.185$, $p = .462$, $n = 19$).[2,3]

[2]Results were retained after removal of the sleep items from the CDRS-R for both weekend number of awakenings—overall model, $F(3, 37) = 19.384$, $p < .001$, β for weekend awakenings = .277, $t = 2.551$, $p = .016$, CI for β [.769, 6.828]—and weekend wake time: overall model, $F(3, 37) = 16.280$, $p < .001$, β for weekend wake time = .276, $t = 2.378$, $p = .024$, CI for β [.031, .401].

[3]Given a trend-level difference between BD and control groups in age at T1 ($p = .075$), regression models were rerun with age included in the model. Results were retained for both weekend number of awakenings—overall model, $F(4, 36) = 21.816$, $p < .001$, β for weekend awakenings = .307, $t = 3.076$, $p = .004$, CI for β [1.361, 6.628]— and weekend wake time: overall model, $F(4, 36) = 17.647$, $p < .001$, β for weekend wake time = .299, $t = 2.797$, $p = .008$, CI for β [.040, .253].

No significant effects were found for sleep onset latency on depressive symptom severity at T2 or for sleep onset latency, number of awakenings, or wake time at T1 on mania symptom severity at T2.

DISCUSSION

Despite evidence for sleep disturbances in youth with BD, few longitudinal studies have examined the stability or long-term effects of these disturbances on symptom progression in youth with BD. Our findings indicate that, whereas control adolescents exhibit stability in all sleep variables measured across the T1 and T2 time points, adolescents with BD exhibit stability solely in the number of weekday awakenings. Despite this unstable presentation of sleep among BD youth, we found that sleep disturbances at T1 have long-term implications for symptom progression. Specifically, a greater number of awakenings and longer wake time on weekend nights predicted depression symptom severity 1 year later for adolescents diagnosed with BD. Effects were retained after controlling for T1 depression symptom severity. These results mirror findings in the adult BD literature showing that sleep disturbances are capable of predicting symptom change over time, representing important treatment targets.

We hypothesized that group differences in sleep disturbances identified at T1 would persist at T2. However, our findings revealed no significant group differences in sleep indices at T2. Although at T2 group comparisons did not reach significance, it is interesting to note that the BD group had significantly greater variability in weekday sleep onset latency and weekday wake time than controls, suggesting that youth with BD may experience a more variable sleep presentation on weekdays relative to control adolescents.

Furthermore, our findings show that whereas control adolescents display stability in sleep indices across study time points, adolescents with BD did not. Poor stability and increased variability in sleep measures has been previously reported with samples of adults diagnosed with BD. Relative to controls, adults with BD have been found to exhibit more variability and less day-to-day stability in both self-reported and actigraphy-assessed sleep, including wake time during the night (Eidelman, Talbot, Gruber, & Harvey, 2010; Jones et al., 2005; Millar et al., 2004). In adults, more variable sleep, and particularly more variable wake time during the night, has been found to relate to greater number of lifetime depressive episodes and more depressive symptoms concurrently (Eidelman et al., 2010). Similarly, more variability in sleep duration has been found to predict more severe mood symptoms at a 12-month follow-up (Gruber et al., 2011). Thus, the adult literature suggests that variability in sleep has implications for short-term and long-term illness course in BD.

TABLE 4
Multiple Regression Using T1 Weekend Number of Awakenings to Predict T2 Depressive Symptoms While Controlling for T1 Depressive Symptoms

	t	p	β	95% CIs for β	F	df	p	Adjusted R^2
Overall Model					26.292	3, 37	.000	.661
T1 CDRS-R	1.296	.203	.204	[−.089, .404]				
Group	−3.182	.003	−.490	[−22.720, −5.032]				
T1 Weekend No. of Awakenings	2.897	.006	.297	[1.158, 6.564]				

Note: T1 = Time 1; T2 = Time 2; CI = confidence interval; CDRS-R = Child Depression Rating Scale–Revised.

TABLE 5
Multiple Regression Using T1 Weekend Wake Time to Predict T2 Depressive Symptoms While Controlling for T1 Depressive Symptoms

	t	p	β	95% CIs for β	F	df	p	Adjusted R^2
Overall Model					22.758	3,37	.000	.632
T1 CDRS-R	1.363	.182	.217	[−.081, .412]				
Group	−2.937	.006	−.466	[−21.415, −3.910]				
T1 Weekend Wake Time	2.941	.006	.310	[.047, .255]				

Note: T1 = Time 1; T2 = Time 2; CI = confidence interval; CDRS-R = Child Depression Rating Scale–Revised.

Poor stability and increased variability in sleep measures among BD adolescents relative to controls may be, in part, due to the effects of an irregular sleep schedule. One study showed that going to bed at different times each night was longitudinally related to greater depressive symptoms in a sample of adolescents diagnosed with bipolar spectrum disorders (Lunsford-Avery et al., 2012). Future studies should aim to incorporate indices of the regularity of sleep and daily routines, using indices such as the Social Rhythm Metric (Monk, Kupfer, Frank, & Ritenour, 1991) to characterize the daily context in which sleep instability and variability occur. This type of assessment may help to identify the triggers of unstable rhythms in youth with BD, thereby aiding in treatment development. Future studies should also consider the potential irregularity of parental schedules and the impact this may have on household rules or structure surrounding the adolescent's bedtime and wake time. Given the large genetic contribution to risk for BD (McGuffin et al., 2003), it may be the case that the adolescent's parent is also affected with BD and experiencing sleep and circadian difficulties. Treatments that aim to improve unstable rhythms among adolescents with BD may be most beneficial when applied as a family intervention.

The importance of keeping regular daily routines and sleep–wake cycles to manage mood is the focus of Interpersonal and Social Rhythm Therapy (IPSRT; Frank et al., 2005). Results from clinical trials of IPSRT have shown that increasing regularization of daily rhythms has a preventative impact on relapse in adults (Frank et al., 2005). IPSRT has also been adapted for youth with BD (Hlastala & Frank, 2006) and evidence is accruing to show that IPSRT improves sleep in youth at risk for BD (Goldstein et al., 2014) and reduces symptoms in adolescents and young adults with BD (Inder et al., 2015).

Poor sleep stability and increased sleep variability in the present sample may also be due to the effects of medications. In this study, all of the BD group participants and none of the control group participants were taking psychotropic medications, including antipsychotics, stimulants, and antidepressants. These medications are known to have sedating and activating properties. It is therefore possible that variation in medication regimen could have contributed to the sleep variability and instability observed among this sample of youth with BD. Subgroup analyses would be required to examine effects of classes of medications on sleep. The small size of the current sample limits the statistical power available for such analyses. Nevertheless, our results echo those from previous studies indicating that adolescents with BD experience more unstable and variable sleep relative to controls, suggesting that sleep stability may be an important feature of BD even early in the course of illness.

With regard to the effects of sleep disturbance on symptom progression, we hypothesized that sleep disturbances at T1 would contribute to more severe mood symptoms at T2 among youth with BD. Our findings provide polarity-specific support for this hypothesis. That is, we found that weekend awakenings and weekend wake time at T1 predicted depressive, but not manic, symptoms at T2 among youth with BD. A significant correlation between sleep and depression symptoms was not observed among controls, likely due to a very restricted range of mood symptoms in the control group.

It is notable that awakenings and wake time occurring specifically on the weekends were associated with increased follow-up depressive severity for those with BD. The current study is among few studies to provide a developmentally appropriate assessment of sleep by separating weekdays from weekends. Adolescents are known to keep different schedules on weekdays versus weekends, with weekdays representing typically restricted sleep schedules and weekends representing unrestricted sleep. If replicated, our finding that sleep loss on weekends is predictive of increased depression symptoms over time suggests that sleep disruptions during unrestricted sleep may represent a more enduring, trait-like sleep issue. It may be the case that youth who experience weekend sleep disruption would benefit most from IPSRT, which focuses on sleep–wake regularization for the purpose of increasing stability in circadian rhythms and sleep and, in turn, protecting against the risk of relapse (Ehlers, Frank, & Kupfer, 1988).

Although weekend sleep at T1 was predictive of depressive symptoms at T2 in this sample, it is also the case that there was a trend for mood symptoms to improve between T1 and T2 for the BD group, perhaps owing to the cumulative effects of treatment. Participants were enrolled in the study within 6–12 months of their first manic episode and, as such, had been receiving treatment for less than 1 year at the T1 assessment. By T2, 1 year later, a greater proportion of the BD sample was being treated with medications relative to T1. Although our findings are suggestive of a predictive relationship between sleep and mood, due to our measurement of sleep and symptoms at only two time points and 1 year apart, it is not possible to delineate the temporal sequence between sleep and symptom change. Future studies employing prospective longitudinal designs, with frequent assessments of sleep and symptoms, would help to clarify if sleep precedes symptom change or if sleep disturbance is concurrent to symptoms.

In a previous report on this sample, which focused exclusively on T1 data, cross-sectional associations were found between sleep loss and mania symptoms. Specifically, a greater number of awakenings was found to be associated with elevated and expansive mood and an increase in productivity, whereas more time spent awake during the night was related to a decreased need for sleep, increased goal-directed activity, and increased productivity. In the current study, we found no effect of sleep disturbances on mania at a 1-year follow-up. The absence of mania-specific effects may be because most youth in this sample spent more time depressed than they did manic or because by T2, a greater percentage of the BD sample was being treated with medications relative to T1. Follow-ups during acute mania may be needed to observe the effect of sleep disturbances on mania.

Several limitations of this study should be acknowledged. First, the sample size was small, particularly given the attrition between T1 and T2. The small sample may have limited statistical power to detect group differences in sleep indices at T2. Replication with a larger sample and more frequent assessments of sleep and symptoms is warranted. Second, sleep was assessed using only self-report and with a non-standardized sleep questionnaire. As such, the information obtained is subject to the biases of retrospective reporting, which may have contributed to between-group differences. Future studies should employ both subjective and objective measures of sleep (e.g., actigraphy). Third, half of our bipolar group had a lifetime comorbid diagnosis, whereas none of control group had psychiatric comorbidities. Similarly, the majority of the BD group was taking medications (73.7% at T1 and 94.7% at T2), whereas none of the control group participants were taking any medications. Both psychiatric comorbidities and medication use may have confounded our sleep findings. Replication with a larger sample would allow for subgroup analysis to examine effects of comorbid psychiatric disorders and individual medications (or classes of medications) on sleep. Finally, as the sample was predominantly Caucasian and female, our results may have limited generalizability to a more diverse sample.

Despite these limitations, our findings suggest that weekend wakefulness is associated with long-term increases in depressive symptoms for youth with BD. Given that sleep loss is known to have adverse effects on illness course in adult BD, this study informs treatments in suggesting that treating wakefulness, particularly when it occurs during unrestricted sleep time on the weekends, may be an important therapeutic target for the alleviation and reduction of depression in youth with BD.

FUNDING

This research was supported by the National Institute of Mental Health (NIMH) Research Scientist Development Award K01MH100433 to AG and an NIMH R01MH106581, K23MH085919, the Klingenstein Third Generation Foundation, and the American Psychiatric Association to MKS.

REFERENCES

American Psychiatric Association. (2000). *Diagnostic and statistical manual of mental disorders* (4th ed., text rev.). Washington, DC: Author.

American Psychiatric Association. (2013). *Diagnostic and statistical manual of mental disorders* (5th ed.). Washington, DC: Author.

Andreasen, N. C., Endicott, J., Spitzer, R. L., & Winokur, G. (1977). The family history method using diagnostic criteria. Reliability and validity. *Archives of General Psychiatry, 34*, 1229–1235. doi:10.1001/archpsyc.1977.01770220111013

Ballenger, J. C., Reus, V. I., & Post, R. M. (1982). The "atypical" clinical picture of adolescent mania. *American Journal of Psychiatry, 139*, 602–606. doi:10.1176/ajp.139.5.602

Bauer, M., Grof, P., Rasgon, N., Bschor, T., Glenn, T., & Whybrow, P. C. (2006). Temporal relation between sleep and mood in patients with bipolar disorder. *Bipolar Disorders, 8*, 160–167. doi:10.1111/j.1399-5618.2006.00294.x

Biederman, J., Mick, E., Faraone, S. V., Van Patten, S., Burback, M., & Wozniak, J. (2004). A prospective follow-up study of pediatric bipolar disorder in boys with attention-deficit/hyperactivity disorder. *Journal of Affective Disorders*, *82*(Suppl. 1), S17–23. doi:10.1016/j.jad.2004.05.012

Brill, S., Penagaluri, P., Roberts, R. J., Gao, Y., & El-Mallakh, R. S. (2011). Sleep disturbances in euthymic bipolar patients. *Annals of Clinical Psychiatry*, *23*(2), 113–116.

Carskadon, M. A. (1990). Patterns of sleep and sleepiness in adolescents. *Pediatrician*, *17*(1), 5–12.

Carskadon, M. A., Vieira, C., & Acebo, C. (1993). Association between puberty and delayed phase preference. *Sleep*, *16*(3), 258–262.

Crowley, S. J., Acebo, C., & Carskadon, M. A. (2007). Sleep, circadian rhythms, and delayed phase in adolescence. *Sleep Medicine*, *8*(6), 602–612. doi:10.1016/j.sleep.2006.12.002

Ehlers, C. L., Frank, E., & Kupfer, D. J. (1988). Social zeitgebers and biological rhythms. A unified approach to understanding the etiology of depression. *Archives of General Psychiatry*, *45*(10), 948–952. doi:10.1001/archpsyc.1988.01800340076012

Eidelman, P., Talbot, L. S., Gruber, J., & Harvey, A. G. (2010). Sleep, illness course, and concurrent symptoms in inter-episode bipolar disorder. *Journal of Behavior Therapy and Experimental Psychiatry*, *41*(2), 145–149. doi:10.1016/j.jbtep.2009.11.007

Faedda, G. L., Baldessarini, R. J., Glovinsky, I. P., & Austin, N. B. (2004). Pediatric bipolar disorder: Phenomenology and course of illness. *Bipolar Disorders*, *6*(4), 305–313. doi:10.1111/j.1399-5618.2004.00128.x

Ferreira Maia, A. P., Boarati, M. A., Kleinman, A., & Fu, I. L. (2007). Preschool Bipolar Disorder: Brazilian children case reports. *Journal of Affective Disorders*, *104*, 237–243. doi:10.1016/j.jad.2007.04.003

Findling, R. L., Gracious, B. L., McNamara, N. K., Youngstrom, E. A., Demeter, C. A., Branicky, L. A., & Calabrese, J. R. (2001). Rapid, continuous cycling and psychiatric co-morbidity in pediatric bipolar I disorder. *Bipolar Disorders*, *3*(4), 202–210. doi:10.1034/j.1399-5618.2001.30405.x

Frank, E., Kupfer, D. J., Thase, M. E., Mallinger, A. G., Swartz, H. A., Fagiolini, A. M., … Monk, T. (2005). Two-year outcomes for interpersonal and social rhythm therapy in individuals with bipolar I disorder. *Archives of General Psychiatry*, *62*(9), 996–1004. doi:10.1001/archpsyc.62.9.996

Geller, B., Warner, K., Williams, M., & Zimerman, B. (1998). Prepubertal and young adolescent bipolarity versus ADHD: Assessment and validity using the WASH-U-KSADS, CBCL and TRF. *Journal of Affective Disorders*, *51*(2), 93–100. doi:10.1016/S0165-0327(98)00176-1

Geller, B., Williams, M., Zimerman, B., & Frazier, J. (1996). *Washington University in St Louis Kiddie Schedule for affective disorders and schizophrenia (WASH-U-KSADS)*. St. Louis, MO: Washington University.

Geller, B., Zimerman, B., Williams, M., Bolhofner, K., Craney, J. L., Delbello, M. P., & Soutullo, C. A. (2000). Six-month stability and outcome of a prepubertal and early adolescent bipolar disorder phenotype. *Journal of Child and Adolescent Psychopharmacology*, *10*(3), 165–173. doi:10.1089/10445460050167278

Geller, B., Zimerman, B., Williams, M., Bolhofner, K., Craney, J. L., DelBello, M. P., & Soutullo, C. (2001). Reliability of the Washington University in St. Louis Kiddie Schedule for Affective Disorders and Schizophrenia (WASH-U-KSADS) mania and rapid cycling sections. *Journal of the American Academy of Child and Adolescent Psychiatry*, *40*(4), 450–455. doi:10.1097/00004583-200104000-00014

Geller, B., Zimerman, B., Williams, M., Delbello, M. P., Bolhofner, K., Craney, J. L., … Nickelsburg, M. J. (2002). DSM-IV mania symptoms in a prepubertal and early adolescent bipolar disorder phenotype compared to attention-deficit hyperactive and normal controls. *Journal of Child and Adolescent Psychopharmacology*, *12*(1), 11–25. doi:10.1089/10445460252943533

Gershon, A., Thompson, W. K., Eidelman, P., McGlinchey, E. L., Kaplan, K. A., & Harvey, A. G. (2012). Restless pillow, ruffled mind: Sleep and affect coupling in interepisode bipolar disorder. *Journal of Abnormal Psychology*, *121*(4), 863–873. doi:10.1037/a0028233

Goldstein, T. R., Fersch-Podrat, R., Axelson, D. A., Gilbert, A., Hlastala, S. A., Birmaher, B., & Frank, E. (2014). Early intervention for adolescents at high risk for the development of bipolar disorder: Pilot study of Interpersonal and Social Rhythm Therapy (IPSRT). *Psychotherapy (Chicago, Ill.)*, *51*(1), 180–189. doi:10.1037/a0034396

Gruber, J., Miklowitz, D. J., Harvey, A. G., Frank, E., Kupfer, D., Thase, M. E., … Ketter, T. A. (2011). Sleep matters: Sleep functioning and course of illness in bipolar disorder. *Journal of Affective Disorders*, *134* (1–3), 416–420. doi:10.1016/j.jad.2011.05.016

Harvey, A. G., Schmidt, D. A., Scarna, A., Semler, C. N., & Goodwin, G. M. (2005). Sleep-related functioning in euthymic patients with bipolar disorder, patients with insomnia, and subjects without sleep problems. *American Journal of Psychiatry*, *162*(1), 50–57. doi:10.1176/appi.ajp.162.1.50

Hlastala, S. A., & Frank, E. (2006). Adapting interpersonal and social rhythm therapy to the developmental needs of adolescents with bipolar disorder. *Development and Psychopathology*, *18*(4), 1267–1288. doi:10.1017/S0954579406060615

Hollingshead, A. (1975). *Four Factor Index of Social Status*. New Haven, CT: Yale University Press.

Holtmann, M., Bolte, S., Goth, K., Dopfner, M., Pluck, J., Huss, M.,… Poustka, F. (2007). Prevalence of the Child Behavior Checklist-pediatric bipolar disorder phenotype in a German general population sample. *Bipolar Disorders*, *9*(8), 895–900. doi:10.1111/j.1399-5618.2007.00463.x

Inder, M. L., Crowe, M. T., Luty, S. E., Carter, J. D., Moor, S., Frampton, C. M., & Joyce, P. R. (2015). Randomized, controlled trial of Interpersonal and Social Rhythm Therapy for young people with bipolar disorder. *Bipolar Disorders*, *17*(2), 128–138. doi:10.1111/bdi.12273

Jerrell, J. M., & Shugart, M. A. (2004). Community-based care for youths with early and very-early onset bipolar I disorder. *Bipolar Disorders*, *6* (4), 299–304. doi:10.1111/j.1399-5618.2004.00129.x

Jones, S. H., Hare, D. J., & Evershed, K. (2005). Actigraphic assessment of circadian activity and sleep patterns in bipolar disorder. *Bipolar Disorders*, *7*(2), 176–186. doi:10.1111/j.1399-5618.2005.00187.x

Jones, S. H., Tai, S., Evershed, K., Knowles, R., & Bentall, R. (2006). Early detection of bipolar disorder: A pilot familial high-risk study of parents with bipolar disorder and their adolescent children. *Bipolar Disorders*, *8*(4), 362–372. doi:10.1111/j.1399-5618.2006.00329.x

Kessler, R. C., Chiu, W., Demler, O., & Walters, E. E. (2005). Prevalence, severity, and comorbidity of 12-month DSM-IV disorders in the National Comorbidity Survey Replication. *Archives of General Psychiatry*, *62*(6), 617–627. doi:10.1001/archpsyc.62.6.617

Leibenluft, E., Albert, P. S., Rosenthal, N. E., & Wehr, T. A. (1996). Relationship between sleep and mood in patients with rapid-cycling bipolar disorder. *Psychiatry Research*, *63*(2–3), 161–168. doi:10.1016/0165-1781(96)02854-5

Levenson, J., Axelson, D., Merranko, J., Angulo, M., Goldstein, T., Goldstein, B., … Birmaher, B. (2015). Differences in sleep disturbances among offspring of parents with and without bipolar disorder: Association with conversion to bipolar disorder. *Bipolar Disorders*, (17), 836–848. doi:10.1111/bdi.12345

Lofthouse, N., Fristad, M., Splaingard, M., & Kelleher, K. (2007). Parent and child reports of sleep problems associated with early-onset bipolar spectrum disorders. *Journal of Family Psychology*, *21*(1), 114–123. doi:10.1037/0893-3200.21.1.114

Lunsford-Avery, J. R., Judd, C. M., Axelson, D. A., & Miklowitz, D. J. (2012). Sleep impairment, mood symptoms, and psychosocial functioning in adolescent bipolar disorder. *Psychiatry Research*, *200*(2–3), 265–271. doi:10.1016/j.psychres.2012.07.037

Mayes, T. L., Bernstein, I. H., Haley, C. L., Kennard, B. D., & Emslie, G. J. (2010). Psychometric properties of the Children's Depression Rating Scale-Revised in adolescents. *Journal of Child and Adolescent Psychopharmacology*, *20*(6), 513–516. doi:10.1089/cap.2010.0063

McGuffin, P., Rijsdijk, F., Andrew, M., Sham, P., Katz, R., & Cardno, A. (2003). The heritability of bipolar affective disorder and the genetic relationship to unipolar depression. [Research Support, Non-U.S. Gov't

Research Support, U.S. Gov't, P.H.S. Twin Study]. *Archives of General Psychiatry, 60*(5), 497–502. doi:10.1001/archpsyc.60.5.497

Mehl, R. C., O'Brien, L. M., Jones, J. H., Dreisbach, J. K., Mervis, C. B., & Gozal, D. (2006). Correlates of sleep and pediatric bipolar disorder. *Sleep, 29*(2), 193–197.

Millar, A., Espie, C. A., & Scott, J. (2004). The sleep of remitted bipolar outpatients: A controlled naturalistic study using actigraphy. *Journal of Affective Disorders, 80*(2–3), 145–153. doi:10.1016/S0165-0327(03)00055-7

Monk, T. H., Kupfer, D. J., Frank, E., & Ritenour, A. M. (1991). The Social Rhythm Metric (SRM): Measuring daily social rhythms over 12 weeks. *Psychiatry Research, 36*(2), 195–207. doi:10.1016/0165-1781(91)90131-8

Mullin, B. C., Harvey, A. G., & Hinshaw, S. P. (2011). A preliminary study of sleep in adolescents with bipolar disorder, ADHD, and non-patient controls. *Bipolar Disorders, 13*(4), 425–432. doi:10.1111/j.1399-5618.2011.00933.x

Perlman, C. A., Johnson, S. L., & Mellman, T. A. (2006). The prospective impact of sleep duration on depression and mania. *Bipolar Disorders, 8* (3), 271–274. doi:10.1111/j.1399-5618.2006.00330.x

Petersen, A. C., Crockett, L., Richards, M., & Boxer, A. (1988). A self-report measure of pubertal status: Reliability, validity, and initial norms. *Journal of Youth and Adolescence, 17*(2), 117–133. doi:10.1007/BF01537962

Poznanski, E. O., & Mokros, H. B. (1995). *Children's Depression Rating Scale, Revised (CDRS-R) Manual.* Los Angeles, CA: California Western Psychological Services.

Robillard, R., Naismith, S. L., Rogers, N. L., Ip, T. K., Hermens, D. F., Scott, E. M., & Hickie, I. B. (2013). Delayed sleep phase in young people with unipolar or bipolar affective disorders. *Journal of Affective Disorders, 145*(2), 260–263. doi:10.1016/j.jad.2012.06.006

Roybal, D. J., Chang, K. D., Chen, M. C., Howe, M. E., Gotlib, I. H., & Singh, M. K. (2011). Characterization and factors associated with sleep quality in adolescents with bipolar I disorder. *Child Psychiatry and Human Development, 42*(6), 724–740. doi:10.1007/s10578-011-0239-0

Russo, P. M., Bruni, O., Lucidi, F., Ferri, R., & Violani, C. (2007). Sleep habits and circadian preference in Italian children and adolescents. *Journal of Sleep Research, 16*(2), 163–169. doi:10.1111/j.1365-2869.2007.00584.x

Salvatore, P., Ghidini, S., Zita, G., De Panfilis, C., Lambertino, S., Maggini, C., & Baldessarini, R. J. (2008). Circadian activity rhythm abnormalities in ill and recovered bipolar I disorder patients. *Bipolar Disorders, 10*(2), 256–265. doi:10.1111/j.1399-5618.2007.00505.x

Shen, G. H., Alloy, L. B., Abramson, L. Y., & Sylvia, L. G. (2008). Social rhythm regularity and the onset of affective episodes in bipolar spectrum individuals. *Bipolar Disorders, 10*(4), 520–529. doi:10.1111/j.1399-5618.2008.00583.x

Suppes, T., Mintz, J., McElroy, S.L., Altshuler, L.L., Kupka, R.W., Frye, M.A., Keck, P.E. Jr., Nolen, W.A., Leverich, G.S., Grunze, H., Rush, A.J., & Post, RM. (2005). Mixed hypomania in 908 patients with bipolar disorder evaluated prospectively in the Stanley Foundation bipolar treatment network: A sex-specific phenomenon.. *Archives of General Psychiatry, 62*, 1089–1096. doi:10.1001/archpsyc.62.10.1089

Young, R. C., Biggs, J. T., Ziegler, V. E., & Meyer, D. A. (1978). A rating scale for mania: Reliability, validity and sensitivity. *British Journal of Psychiatry, 133*, 429–435. doi:10.1192/bjp.133.5.429

Sleep Duration and Child Well-Being: A Nonlinear Association

Sarah James

Lauren Hale

Although numerous studies among adults have shown a U-shaped association between sleep duration and health outcomes, fewer studies have investigated the theory that children also have an optimal sleep duration range, with both lower and upper limits. We evaluated whether children's sleep duration at ages 5 and 9 has a U-shaped association with both behavioral problems and physical health at age 9. We analyzed data from 1,965 participants in a longitudinal birth cohort, the Fragile Families and Child Wellbeing Study. This sample of children was 52% male and approximately 22% non-Hispanic White, 52% non-Hispanic Black, 23% Hispanic, and 3% some other race/ethnicity. The child's primary caregiver reported the predictor of interest: sleep duration at age 5 and age 9. Both children and primary caregivers reported on outcomes of the child's behavior problems (internalizing and externalizing) and overall physical health. We found that the association between children's sleep duration and well-being was typically nonlinear and U-shaped. Adjusting for their sleep duration at age 5, children who sleep either too much or too little at age 9 had higher levels of behavior problems and scored lower on a global measure of physical health. These nonlinear patterns were similar whether children or primary caregivers reported child outcomes, with the exception that there was a linear and increasing association of longer sleep duration and caregiver-rated child health. This study highlights that both short and long sleep duration may be risk factors for adverse behavioral and health outcomes in school-age children.

INTRODUCTION

Sleep is part of a complex internally regulated homeostatic system (Borbély & Achermann, 1999; Saper, Cano, & Scammell, 2005). Theoretically, therefore, there is an optimal duration of sleep to maintain the right balance between sleep and wakefulness. In such a model, any sleep duration that is outside of this optimal range would be either too short or too long for optimal health and well-being. Indeed, prior research has found a U-shaped association between habitual sleep duration and health in numerous studies of adults. For example, regularly sleeping either too little or too much has been associated with a higher risk of obesity, cardiovascular disease, and all-cause mortality in adults (Buxton & Marcelli, 2010; Grandner, Hale, Moore, & Patel, 2010; Taheri, Lin, Austin, Young, & Mignot, 2004). The mechanisms that have been suggested to explain the association between short sleep duration and poor health have included metabolic, immunological, and endocrine pathways (Grandner et al., 2010). However, the mechanisms though which overly long sleep duration has been associated with poor health are less well understood (Grandner & Drummond, 2007; Hossin, 2016). One possibility is that long sleep duration directly produces poor outcomes; alternatively, the association between long sleep and poor health may be due to reverse causality or underlying conditions producing both longer sleep duration and poor health.

If the association between sleep duration and well-being comes about through biological mechanisms that do not change over the life course, a U-shaped association of sleep and well-being should be found among both adults and children. To our knowledge, however, only a few studies have evaluated whether the association between sleep duration and children's outcomes takes this nonlinear form.

One study has modeled a nonlinear effect of sleep duration at ages 3–7.9 on children's body mass index (BMI) and overweight status 4–7 years later by measuring sleep duration with indicators of whether the child sleeps less than 8 hr, 8–8.9 hr, 9–9.9 hr (reference), 10–10.9 hr, or 11 hr or more each night (Snell, Adam, & Duncan, 2007). This study has found that children who sleep for 11 hr or more each night have an elevated risk of higher BMI and being overweight as compared to children who sleep 9–9.9 hr per night. Another study has allowed for nonlinearities in an exploratory graphical examination of the association of children's sleep duration with physical and mental health measures but has concluded there are no nonlinearities (Price, Quach, Wake, Bittman, & Hiscock, 2015).

Given the theoretical expectation of a nonlinear association of sleep duration with well-being, and the lack of studies evaluating such a pattern in children, in this article we asked whether sleep duration is associated with behavioral and physical health outcomes in a U-shaped pattern for a large sample of 9-year-old children. We measured sleep duration both contemporaneously to the outcomes (when children are age 9) and at the prior study wave (when children are age 5). We hypothesized that both current and prior measures of sleep duration might have independent associations with behavioral and physical health outcomes. The association between age 9 sleep duration and the outcomes may reflect short-term associations, whereas sleep duration from an earlier age may indicate the lasting effects of problematic sleep duration during an earlier developmental period.

Prior Research

School-Age Children's Sleep Duration and Behavioral Problems

Prior studies evaluating how children's sleep duration is associated with behavioral problems have shown mixed results. One study has indicated that the objectively measured sleep duration of a small sample of elementary school children was associated with conduct problems but not hyperactivity or emotional problems (Holley, Hill, & Stevenson, 2011). Another study has shown that sleeping for less than 9 hr per night was associated with higher emotional lability for a group of Australian 7-year-olds (Nixon et al., 2008). In addition, in a large sample of American children the odds of inadequate sleep have been shown to be higher among 6- to 11-year-olds with depressive symptoms than those without depressive symptoms (Smaldone, Honig, & Byrne, 2007). Finally, cross-sectional analyses of Australian children have shown that children with low psychosocial quality of life at ages 6–7 slept more than their peers without this clinical level of problematic behavior; there were no statistically significant associations of sleep duration with behavior at ages 4–5 or 8–9 (Price et al., 2015). Although the final study (Price et al., 2015) has included preliminary graphical exploration of raw data that could capture nonlinearities, these analyses were not adjusted for any confounders, and neither this study nor the others has tested whether a model that allows for a U-shaped relationship between children's sleep duration and behavior problems is supported by the data.

School-Age Children's Sleep Duration and Health Outcomes

A substantial literature has documented a significant negative—and, in some cases, U-shaped—association between children's sleep duration and weight gain, overweight, and obesity (Bagley, Kelly, & El-Sheikh, 2015; Cappuccio et al., 2008; Chen, Beydoun, & Wang, 2008; Magee & Hale, 2012; Nixon et al., 2008; Price et al., 2015; Snell et al., 2007). However, less research has considered the potential association between sleep duration and global measures of child health. One exception, which uses the same data set as the present study, has found that the sleep duration of 5-year-old children is not associated with having good, fair, or poor health relative to excellent or very good health after adjusting for the presence of language-based bedtime routines at age 3 and other family factors (Hale, Berger, LeBourgeois, & Brooks-Gunn, 2011). Similarly, Price et al. (2015) have found no association of sleep duration with low levels of physical health among 4- to 9-year-old Australian children. As with the literature on children's sleep durations and behavioral problems, none of these prior studies on the association between children's sleep duration and global measures of health have analyzed whether long sleep duration is associated with poorer health or if there is a U-shaped association of sleep with health.

Biological Pathways Between Sleep and Well-Being

Sleep duration has been theorized to relate to behavior and health via a number of biological pathways. For behavioral outcomes, sleep deprivation in adults has been shown to limit prefrontal cortex and amygdala connectivity and to make negative emotional stimuli more salient (Yoo, Gujar, Hu, Jolesz, & Walker, 2007). For physical health, the mechanisms through which insufficient sleep is problematic for overweight and obesity have been especially well documented. Sleep deprivation has been shown to decrease levels of leptin, an appetite-suppressing hormone, and increase levels of ghrelin, an appetite-enhancing hormone (Taheri et al., 2004); these hormonal changes have been associated with increased appetite and consuming more calories after a sleep-deprived night (Brondel, Romer, Nougues, Touyarou, & Davenne, 2010). Beyond weight status, short sleep duration (less than 7.7 hr) has been associated with higher waking and peak cortisol levels than those for average sleep duration (7.7–9.3 hr) in a sample of 8-year-old Finnish children (Räikkönen et al., 2010). In addition, emerging evidence has suggested that sleep and immune system function may have a circular relationship, whereby sickness impairs sleep and sleep problems contribute to illness (Bryant, Trinder, & Curtis, 2004). Relatively little of this research has been conducted on pediatric populations, however.

Contributions

We are unaware of any longitudinal, population-based studies that have investigated whether children's behavioral problems and physical health have a nonlinear association with sleep duration. Therefore, we tested a model of sleep homeostasis in which both short and long sleep durations are associated with poorer outcomes than sleep durations between these extremes. By leveraging a longitudinal design, we were able to evaluate to what extent children's sleep duration was associated with their well-being in middle childhood; we tested this association both when sleep duration was measured contemporaneously to the outcome and at a prior study wave. This study also improved upon prior work on sleep and child well-being by using a large and diverse sample of children. Finally, this study considered the behavior and physical health of children as assessed via both self-report and caregiver-report.

METHOD

We analyzed data from the Fragile Families and Child Wellbeing Study (FFCWS), a population-based longitudinal study of children born in large American cities (population > 200,000) between 1998 and 2000, with an oversample of nonmarital births.[1] Using a multistage probability sample procedure, participants were recruited in hospitals at the time of the child's birth. Interviews with mothers and fathers (or other primary caregivers)[2] occurred at the child's birth and again when the child was ages 1, 3, 5, and 9. Children were interviewed at age 9. Study topics included parental relationships, child outcomes, and the impact of contextual and policy conditions on families and children. FFCWS included child and primary caregiver reports of behavior problems and physical health, as well as the primary caregiver's report of the child's sleep duration.

Of the 4,898 participants enrolled in FFCWS at the child's birth, 2,503 participated in the three surveys beyond the baseline (in-home interview at age 5, primary caregiver interview at age 9, and child interview at age 9) necessary to provide the outcome and key predictor variables in these analyses. The analytic sample included 79% of these cases, or 1,965 participants in the FFCWS (see Table 1 for sample description). The 21% of missing cases who did participate in the relevant survey waves came from the following sources. First, 33 cases had unusable data on sleep duration: 21 cases were missing sleep duration at age 5, one other case was missing sleep duration at age 9, and an additional 12 cases had extreme sleep durations and were dropped from the analyses (see the Sleep Duration section under Measures). Second, 360 cases had missing values for one or more of the outcomes of interest. Third, an additional 144 cases were missing demographic or control variable information. Although we have presented the results of analyses employing listwise deletion to address this missing data, we have replicated the analyses using multiple imputation for missing control variables and find the results to be substantively unchanged in that sample ($N = 2{,}109$).

Compared to the baseline FFCWS cohort, children included in analyses were in somewhat better circumstances. Mothers of children in the analytic sample were more likely to be native-born non-Hispanic Blacks (52%) and less likely to be native-born Hispanics (23%), native-borns of some other race/ethnicity (3%), or foreign born (11%) than were mothers in the baseline cohort (48%, 27%, 4%, and 11%, respectively). In addition, mothers of children in the analytic sample had more education on average than do mothers in the baseline cohort; in the analytic sample, 31% had less than a high school education (35% in the baseline cohort), 31% had a high school diploma or GED (30% in the baseline cohort), 27% had some college education (24% in the baseline cohort), and 11% had a college degree (11% in the baseline cohort). However, there was no difference between our analytic sample and the baseline cohort in the proportion of children who were born with a low birth weight, were male, or have mothers and fathers of the same race/ethnicity. It is unclear whether the pattern of missing data will lead to under- or overestimates of the associations between sleep duration and well-being.

Measures

Child Behavior Problems and Health

Both children and primary caregivers reported child behavior problems and health at age 9.

Children evaluated their behavior problems using the Internalizing and Externalizing subscales of the Self-Description Questionnaire (SDQ; Marsh, 1990). Children rated to what extent a set of statements described their feelings and behaviors at school and home on a scale of 0 (*not at all true*), 1 (*a little bit true*), 2 (*mostly true*), and 3 (*very true*). Internalizing behavior included actions directed toward the self, such as depressive and anxious tendencies. There were eight items in the Internalizing subscale, with a potential score ranging from 0 to 24.[3] Externalizing behavior included other-directed actions, such as conduct disorder and acting out. There were six items in the Externalizing subscale, with a potential score ranging from 0

[1] Detailed information on study procedures is available at http://www.fragilefamilies.princeton.edu/

[2] Primary caregivers were mothers at both the age 5 and age 9 survey waves in 95% of cases in the analytic sample; mothers were assumed to be the primary caregiver where the child's mother and father lived together or for single mothers.

[3] In the FFCWS age 9 sample, the SDQ Internalizing subscale has a Cronbach's alpha of 0.78 and mean of 1.15 ($SD = 0.70$).

TABLE 1
Analytic Sample Description

	M *or Proportion*	*Range*
Child's Age in Months[a]	111.63	105–129
Child Low Birth Weight (< 2,500 g)	0.10	0–1
Child Male	0.52	0–1
Child's Puberty Score[a]	1.46	1.0–3.2
Mother Non-Hispanic White, Native Born	0.22	0–1
Mother Non-Hispanic Black, Native Born	0.52	0–1
Mother Hispanic, Native Born	0.23	0–1
Mother Other Race/Ethnicity, Native Born	0.03	0–1
Father Same Race/Ethnicity as Mother	0.86	0–1
Mother Foreign Born	0.11	0–1
Mother's Age[b]	30.05	19–50
Mother Has Less Than High School Education	0.31	0–1
Mother Has High School Diploma or GED	0.31	0–1
Mother Attended Some College	0.27	0–1
Mother Is a College Graduate	0.11	0–1
Household Income[b]	$38,045.22	$0–$688,444
Biological Parents Married[b]	0.32	0–1
Biological Parents Cohabiting[b]	0.12	0–1
No. of Children in Home[b]	2.50	0–10
Hours of Sleep, Age 9[a]	9.44	6–14
Hours of Sleep, Age 5[b]	8.95	6–15
Child's Self-Rated Internalizing Behavior (SDQ)[a]	9.25	0–24
PCG's Rating of Child's Internalizing Behavior (CBCL)[a]	3.73	0–42
Child's Self-Rated Externalizing Behavior (SDQ)[a]	5.53	0–18
PCG's Rating of Child's Externalizing Behavior (CBCL)[a]	6.28	0–70
Child's Self-Rated Physical Health[a]	4.10	1–5
PCG's Rating of Child's Physical Health[a]	4.40	1–5

Note: $N = 1,965$. SDQ = Self-Description Questionnaire; PCG = primary caregiver; CBCL = Child Behavior Checklist.
[a]Measured at age 9.
[b]Measured at age 5; other characteristics measured at baseline.

to 18.[4] Primary caregivers appraised children's behavior problems using the Child Behavior Checklist (CBCL). Primary caregivers rated how much a series of behaviors were representative of the child's typical behavior on a scale of 1 (*not true*), 2 (*somewhat or sometimes true*), and 3 (*very true or often true*). Internalizing behavior summed the Withdrawn/Depressed[5] and Anxious/Depressed[6] subscales for a total of 21 items with potential scores ranging from 21 to 63. Externalizing behavior summed the Aggressive[7] and Rule-Breaking[8] subscales for a total of 35 items with potential scores ranging from 35 to 105.

Both children and primary caregivers reported on the child's general physical health at the 9-year survey wave. Health ratings were 1 (*poor*), 2 (*fair*), 3 (*good*), 4 (*very good*), and 5 (*excellent*).

Sleep Duration

Primary caregivers reported how many hours of sleep their children typically got per night during the week in both the age 5 and age 9 survey waves. In the analytic sample, hours of sleep ranged from 0 to 17 at age 5 and 4 to 14 at age 9. To adjust for implausible sleep durations, we dropped the 12 cases with implausibly short (less than 6 hr) or long (more than 15 hr) nightly sleep durations using listwise deletion; this method has been previously used by Price et al. (2015). As an alternative, we also employed another method for dealing with the extreme cases in which we bottom- and top-coded extreme sleep durations such that less than 6 hr per night was recoded to 6 hr per night (bottom-coded) and more than 15 hr per night was recoded to 15 hr per night (top-coded). Results were similar with either approach, but for a conservative estimate we showed results from the models without the extreme cases.

Child Characteristics

Child characteristics included the child's age in months at the time of the 9-year interview, whether the child had a low birth weight (< 2,500 g, assessed at birth), and whether the child was male or female (recorded at birth). The child's pubertal development was reported at age 9 by the child's primary caregiver

[4] In the FFCWS age 9 sample, the SDQ Externalizing subscale has a Cronbach's alpha of 0.76 and mean of 0.92 (*SD* = 0.72).

[5] In the FFCWS age 9 sample, the CBCL Withdrawn/Depressed subscale has a Cronbach's alpha of 0.70.

[6] In the FFCWS age 9 sample, the CBCL Anxious/Depressed subscale has a Cronbach's alpha of 0.78.

[7] In the FFCWS age 9 sample, the CBCL Aggressive subscale has a Cronbach's alpha of 0.89.

[8] In the FFCWS age 9 sample, the CBCL Rule-Breaking subscale has a Cronbach's alpha of 0.77.

and was a scale ranging from 1 to 4 that indicated the degree to which the child had experienced a height growth spurt, hair growth, skin changes, a deepening voice (boys), facial hair growth (boys), breast growth (girls), or menarche (girls). We included these variables because they have been shown in prior studies to be associated with both child sleep and child well-being.

Parent Characteristics

Mothers reported their race/ethnicity, nativity, and educational attainment at the time of the child's birth. Whether the father was of the same race/ethnicity as the child's mother was also measured at the child's birth. Both parents' race/ethnicity was self-reported and included categories for White (non-Hispanic), Black (non-Hispanic), Hispanic, and some other race/ethnicity. Nativity indicated whether the mother was born in the United States. Maternal educational attainment was measured with categories for whether the mother had obtained less than high school education, a high school diploma or GED, some college education, or a college degree. Mothers reported their age, household income, relationship (married, cohabiting, or no relationship) with the biological father, and household composition at the 5-year interview. Household income, in dollars, was logged in analyses. Household composition indicated how many children, in addition to the focal child, live in the home at the 5-year interview. Again, these variables were included to avoid confounding influences of other variables known to be associated with both child sleep and child well-being.

Analytic Strategy

We estimated the extent to which children's sleep durations at ages 5 and 9 were associated with their self-rated and primary-caregiver-rated behavior problems and physical health at age 9. In the following analyses, alpha was the model intercept, X_1 was sleep duration, X_2 was a vector of child and family characteristics (control variables with the vector of coefficients β_2), and X_3 was a nonlinear, quadratic term for sleep duration (i.e., hours of sleep, squared).

$$E(Y|x) = \alpha + \beta_1 X_1 + \beta_2 X_2 + \beta_3 X_3$$

Behavior problems were evaluated using ordinary least squares regression. Physical health was modeled using ordered logit models. There were three outcomes—internalizing behavior, externalizing behavior, and physical health—reported separately by mothers and children for a total of six models (see Table 2). Each analysis had the same set of control variables, the measurement of which was described in the prior section: the child's age in months at age 9, whether the child was born with a low birth weight (< 2,500 g), child sex, the child's pubertal progression score at age 9, maternal race/ethnicity and nativity, whether the father was the of the same race/ethnicity as the mother, the mother's age at the 5-year interview, maternal educational attainment at the child's birth, household income at the 5-year interview, biological parents' relationship at the 5-year interview, and the number of children in the home at the 5-year interview.

TABLE 2
Selected Coefficients and Standard Errors (in Parentheses) From OLS Models of Child Behavior and Exponentiated Coefficients and Standard Errors (in Parentheses) From Ordered Logit Models of Child Health

	OLS				*Ordered Logit*	
	Internalizing Behavior		*Externalizing Behavior*		*Physical Health*	
	Child Report	*PCG Report*	*Child Report*	*PCG Report*	*Child Report*	*PCG Report*
	(1)	*(2)*	*(3)*	*(4)*	*(5)*	*(6)*
Intercept	26.536** (8.310)	14.074* (6.804)	29.192*** (6.391)	35.319** (10.897)		
Hours of Sleep, Age 9	−2.611* (1.220)	−2.084* (0.999)	−2.368* (0.938)	−5.495*** (1.600)	1.934* (0.332)	1.108* (0.043)
(Hours of Sleep, Age 9)^2	0.139* (0.067)	0.101† (0.055)	0.129* (0.051)	0.275** (0.088)	0.968† (0.018)	
Hours of Sleep, Age 5	0.515 (1.144)	−0.267 (0.937)	−0.978 (0.880)	0.161 (1.501)	1.427 (0.316)	1.022 (0.039)
(Hours of Sleep, Age 5)^2	−0.020 (0.060)	0.014 (0.049)	0.051 (0.046)	−0.018 (0.079)	0.982 (0.017)	
Control Variables	✓	✓	✓	✓	✓	✓
R^2	0.076	0.029	0.096	0.061		
AIC					4,888.678	4,038.714

Note: $N = 1{,}965$. These analyses also account for the child's age in months at age 9, whether the child was born with a low birth weight (< 2,500 g), child sex, the child's pubertal progression score at age 9, maternal race/ethnicity and nativity, whether the father is the of the same race/ethnicity as the mother, the mother's age at the 5-year interview, maternal educational attainment at the child's birth, maternal household income at the 5-year interview, biological parents' relationship at the 5-year interview, and the number of children in the home at the 5-year interview. OLS = ordinary least squares regression; PCG = primary caregiver; AIC = Akaike information criterion.

$^\dagger p < .10$. $^*p < .05$. $^{**}p < .01$. $^{***}p < .001$.

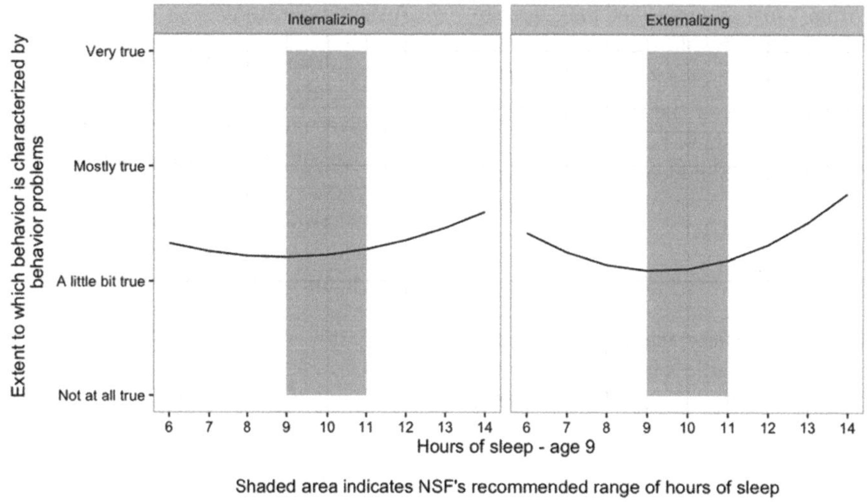

FIGURE 1 Hours of sleep and predicted self-reported behavior, age 9. *Note*: NSF = National Sleep Foundation.

RESULTS

Children's sleep durations in the primary school years were associated with their well-being, with both shorter and longer sleep durations associated with worse outcomes than sleep durations between these extremes. Using the child's sleep duration at ages 5 and 9 as predictors, Table 2 displays coefficients for ordinary least squares regression models, which tested the association of these variables with behavior problems at age 9, and exponentiated coefficients (odds ratios) for ordered logit models, which tested the association of these variables with physical health at age 9. These models allowed for both a linear effect of sleep duration and a nonlinear (quadratic or U-shaped) effect of sleep duration on the outcomes via the term hours of sleep, squared. (See Appendix Table A1 for full coefficients from these models.)

For internalizing behavior, there was a statistically significant association of behavior problems with the child's sleep duration and the nonlinear term for sleep duration even when models were adjusted for a number of control variables. This pattern was true whether the child reported his or her own internalizing behavior (Model 1) or the primary caregiver reported the child's internalizing behavior problems (Model 2). The pattern of findings was the same for the child's externalizing behavior problems, whether reported by the child (Model 3) or the child's primary caregiver (Model 4), as well as the child's own report of his or her physical health (Model 5). For the primary caregiver's report of the child's physical health (Model 6), the nonlinear terms for sleep duration were not significantly associated with the outcome. Therefore, these terms were not included in the model presented here.

None of the models of child behavior or physical health indicated that sleep duration when the child was 5 years old had a statistically significant association with behavior problems or health at age 9. Thus, concurrent sleep patterns were more strongly associated with the child's own and his or her primary caregiver's report of behavior problems and physical health than were the child's sleep duration in the previous survey wave.

Nonlinear Association Between Sleep Duration and Child Behavior

Figures 1 and 2 present predicted levels of behavior problems and physical health for children with different sleep durations, based on the models of child behavior presented in Table 2. These figures hold other covariates at their mean or modal levels.[9] For reference, the recommended range of 9–11 hr of sleep for school-age children, as recommended by the National Sleep Foundation (NSF; Hirshkowitz et al., 2015), is indicated by the shaded area.

Figures 1 and 2 display the nonlinear association of sleep duration at age 9 with the child's behavior problems, as reported by the child and the primary caregiver, respectively. For each reporter, the left column is internalizing behavior problems and the right column is externalizing behavior problems. The horizontal axis of these plots corresponds to the child's sleep duration. The shaded area indicates the NSF's range of recommended sleep duration for school-age children (9–11 hr; Hirshkowitz et al., 2015). The

[9] That is, these figures make predictions for a child who is 111.62 months old at the age 9 interview, is not low birth weight, is male, has a pubertal development score of 1.46 at age 9, and lives in a household with 2.5 other children at age 5; has a Black mother and father who are not coresident when the child is age 5; and whose mother is a native-born woman 30.05 years old at the age 5 interview with a high school diploma or GED whose household income was $38,0435.22 when the child was age 5.

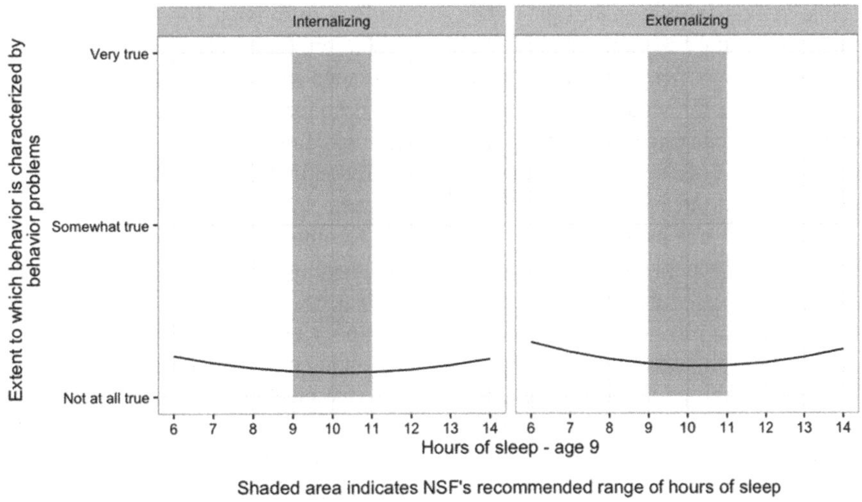

FIGURE 2 Hours of sleep and predicted primary-caregiver-reported behavior, age 9. *Note*: NSF = National Sleep Foundation.

vertical axis of these plots corresponds to the level of child behavior problems; higher scores indicate worse child behavior. Rather than showing the numeric value for levels of behavior problems, these axes denote to what extent the child's behavior was characterized by the given type of behavior problems, ranging from *not at all true* to *somewhat true* and *very true* in primary caregiver reports, and from *not at all true* to *a little bit true, mostly true*, and *very true* in child reports.

Overall, there was a U-shaped association between child's sleep duration at age 9 and behavior problems. Children who slept a very small or very large number of hours per night reported the highest levels of behavior problems. This broad effect held for both child- and primary-caregiver-reported internalizing and externalizing behavior problems, though there were small differences by reporter. Children reported on average higher levels of behavior problems than did their primary caregivers, and the most dramatic curvilinear associations were found for children's reported behavior problems and their sleep duration. The lowest levels of behavior problems mirrored the NSF's recommended sleep duration for school-age children (9–11 hr; Hirshkowitz et al., 2015) in primary caregiver reports. However, the lowest level of behavior problems as reported by the child corresponded to a slightly shorter sleep duration, in the range of 8–10 hr of sleep per night.

Nonlinear Association Between Sleep Duration and Physical Health

Figure 3 displays the association between sleep duration and the probability that the child was rated to have a given level of physical health, based on the models for child health in Table 2.

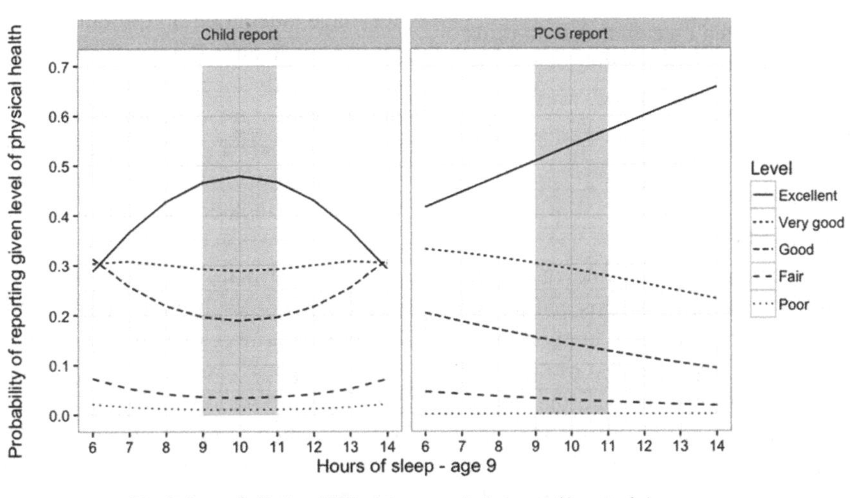

FIGURE 3 Hours of sleep and predicted child health, age 9. *Note*: PCG = primary caregiver; NSF = National Sleep Foundation.

The plot on the left is the child's rating, the plot on the right is the primary caregiver's rating, the horizontal axis corresponds to the child's nightly sleep duration at age 9, and the shaded area denotes recommended sleep duration for school-age children. The vertical axis is the probability of reporting that the child was rated to have a given level of physical health. As in the figures for child behavior, these figures hold other covariates at their mean or modal levels, and the shaded area indicates the recommended range of 9–11 hr of sleep for school-age children.

The association of sleep duration with physical health differed by who reported the child's physical health. When children reported their physical health, there was a U-shaped association with sleep duration, as shown in the solid line in Figure 3, which corresponds to a rating of excellent physical health. The highest probability of the child reporting excellent physical health was found within the NSF's recommended sleep duration for school age children (9–11 hr; Hirshkowitz et al., 2015), and children who sleep low or high numbers of hours each night had lower probabilities of reporting excellent physical health. In contrast, the primary caregiver's assessment of the child's physical health did not have the same nonlinear association; the best model of fit was a linear model that did not include the term for a nonlinear effect of the child's hours of sleep. Figure 3 shows that children who slept the least had the lowest probability of having a primary caregiver who reported excellent physical health. As the number of hours the child slept at age 9 increased, the probability that the primary caregiver rated the child as being in excellent physical health increased.

Robustness Checks

The results shown in the focal analyses were robust to an alternative specification that included a control for the child's having a bedtime in the prior (age 5) and current (age 9) survey waves. These bedtime indicators did not have a statistically significant association with the outcomes of interest, and the association of sleep duration and child outcomes did not differ meaningfully from models without these controls. Thus, for parsimony, the final results did not account for whether the child has a bedtime at ages 5 or 9.

DISCUSSION

There was a nonlinear association between children's sleep duration and their concurrent behavior problems and physical health even after adjusting for their sleep duration in an earlier study wave. Children who slept the least or the most had the highest levels of behavior problems and the lowest self-rated physical health. For behavior problems, this pattern was consistent regardless of whether the child or the parent reported the child's behavior problems—though the gradient was more dramatic when children report their behavior problems. In contrast, who evaluates child health made a difference for its association with sleep duration. When children rated their physical health, there was a U-shaped association of sleep duration with health. When the primary caregiver rated the child's health, the association was linear and increasing.

These findings suggest that future research on the association between children's sleep duration and well-being should follow two recommendations. First, future studies should consider the full range of child sleep durations. Measuring only whether the child sleeps more or less than a recommended number of hours does not capture the full range of child experiences, and grouping children who sleep an adequate amount with those who sleep too much may mask important differences in these groups. Analyses utilizing the full range of child sleep durations should also consider using a nonlinear specification when modeling the association between sleep duration and child well-being. Second, subsequent research should be particularly attentive to who reports child outcomes. This study finds that the association between a child's sleep duration and his or her behavior problems is largely consistent regardless of whether the outcome of interest is evaluated by the child or the primary caregiver. Thus, both reporters are reliable when considering how sleep duration is related to child behavior. In contrast, the association of sleep and health differs when the child and the primary caregiver report the child's physical health.

These analyses are among the first to use longitudinal, population-based data to evaluate the extent to which there is a nonlinear association between children's sleep duration and multiple reports of their behavior problems and physical health. However, this study does have several significant limitations. First, the study design did not allow us to rule out a reverse causal explanation or a bidirectional relationship between sleep duration and well-being. Not all outcomes are measured at multiple data waves, so we did not control for prior behavior problems or health status in the models. Second, the models explain a low but nontrivial portion of the variance in the outcomes of interest. Although we have attempted to produce models that adjust for a variety of factors known to be associated with both children's nightly sleep duration and well-being, child health and behavior are complex phenomena produced by many interactive social, psychological, and biological inputs. Other, unmeasured factors that may also matter for this association include additional health and behavior conditions, other stressful life experiences, and genetic factors. Third, the primary predictor—the report of children's sleep duration—comes from a report by their primary caregiver, rather than a more objective estimate (e.g., actigraphy, polysomnography). Any error in primary caregiver reports of child sleep duration, compared to the child's actual nightly sleep duration, may be influenced by the primary caregiver's impressions of the child's behavior problems and physical health. In general, the presence of this type of measurement error tends to attenuate the associations between observed variables and thus underestimate true effect sizes. In addition, our sleep measure included only one question about children's typical sleep duration, which does not indicate the variability of children's sleep across nights. Although these analyses were not able to address these biases directly, future work should integrate more objective estimates of sleep duration into population-based studies to improve accuracy and eliminate any underlying caregiver-specific factor that influences the report of the child's sleep duration. Finally, although FFCWS is a population-based sample of children born in large American cities, study participants are overall more disadvantaged than American children as a whole; it is not clear if these results would generalize to children from rural areas, born in a different time period, or who were more advantaged.

Despite its limitations, this research has important clinical implications and suggests potential areas for practitioner intervention. First, this study reiterates prior consensus that short sleep duration is associated with poor outcomes. Short sleep is more prevalent than long sleep in children, and practitioners should intervene to help families ensure that children get sufficient sleep for optimal health and well-being. Second, this study is the first to highlight that long sleep duration, already shown to be associated with adverse health outcomes in adults, is also potentially a concern for school-age children. As with adults, underlying factors that are in themselves problematic for behavior and health may be causing children to sleep for longer durations. Nevertheless, clinicians should take note of particularly long nightly sleep durations in children, which may be indicators of or precursors to an underlying condition. Finally, clinicians should be reassured by the finding that concurrent but not past sleep duration is associated with child outcomes, indicating that sleep and well-being have short-term but not long-term associations. This pattern suggests that the association of sleep duration with problematic behavior and health outcomes may be mitigated with contemporaneous interventions.

In conclusion, sleep duration is a risk factor for the well-being of children who sleep either too much or too little. Future research should investigate both the clinical implications and the broader social consequences of these findings.

FUNDING

Research reported in this publication was supported by the Eunice Kennedy Shriver National Institute of Child Health and Human Development of the National Institutes of Health under award numbers R01HD073352, R01HD36916, R01HD39135, R01HD40421, and P2CHD047879; and a consortium of private foundations. The content is solely the responsibility of the authors and does not necessarily represent the official views of the National Institutes of Health.

ORCID

Sarah James http://www.orcid.org/0000-0002-7761-8074

REFERENCES

Bagley, E. J., Kelly, R. J., & El-Sheikh, M. (2015). Longitudinal relations between children's sleep and body mass index: The moderating role of socioeconomic risk. *Sleep Health*, *1*(1), 44–49. doi:10.1016/j.sleh.2014.12.001

Borbély, A. A., & Achermann, P. (1999). Sleep homeostasis and models of sleep regulation. *Journal of Biological Rhythms*, *14*(6), 557–568.

Brondel, L., Romer, M. A., Nougues, P. M., Touyarou, P., & Davenne, D. (2010). Acute partial sleep deprivation increases food intake in healthy men. *American Journal of Clinical Nutrition*, *91*(6), 1550–1559. doi:10.3945/ajcn.2009.28523

Bryant, P. A., Trinder, J., & Curtis, N. (2004). Sick and tired: Does sleep have a vital role in the immune system? *Nature Reviews Immunology*, *4* (6), 457–467. doi:10.1038/nri1369

Buxton, O. M., & Marcelli, E. (2010). Short and long sleep are positively associated with obesity, diabetes, hypertension, and cardiovascular disease among adults in the United States. *Social Science & Medicine*, *71* (5), 1027–1036. doi:10.1016/j.socscimed.2010.05.041

Cappuccio, F. P., Taggart, F. M., Kandala, N.-B., Currie, A., Peile, E., Stranges, S., & Miller, M. A. (2008). Meta-analysis of short sleep duration and obesity in children and adults. *Sleep*, *31*(5), 619–626. Retrieved from http://wrap.warwick.ac.uk/30144/

Chen, X., Beydoun, M. A., & Wang, Y. (2008). Is sleep duration associated with childhood obesity? A systematic review and meta-analysis. *Obesity*, *16*(2), 265–274. doi:10.1038/oby.2007.63

Grandner, M. A., & Drummond, S. P. (2007). Who are the long sleepers? Towards an understanding of the mortality relationship. *Sleep Medicine Reviews*, *11*(5), 341–360. doi:10.1016/j.smrv.2007.03.010

Grandner, M. A., Hale, L., Moore, M., & Patel, N. P. (2010). Mortality associated with short sleep duration: The evidence, the possible mechanisms, and the future. *Sleep Medicine Reviews*, *14*(3), 191–203. doi:10.1016/j.smrv.2009.07.006

Hale, L., Berger, L. M., LeBourgeois, M. K., & Brooks-Gunn, J. (2011). A longitudinal study of preschoolers' language-based bedtime routines, sleep duration, and well-being. *Journal of Family Psychology*, *25*(3), 423–433. doi:10.1037/a0023564

Hirshkowitz, M., Whiton, K., Albert, S. M., Alessi, C., Bruni, O., DonCarlos, L., & Adams Hillard, P. J. (2015). National sleep foundation's sleep time duration recommendations: Methodology and results summary. *Sleep Health*, *1*(1), 40–43. http://doi.org/10.1016/j.sleh.2014.12.010

Holley, S., Hill, C. M., & Stevenson, J. (2011). An hour less sleep is a risk factor for childhood conduct problems. *Child: Care, Health and Development*, *37*(4), 563–570. http://doi.org/10.1111/j.1365-2214.2010.01203.x

Hossin, M. Z. (2016). From habitual sleep hours to morbidity and mortality: Existing evidence, potential mechanisms, and future agenda. *Sleep Health*, *2*(2), 146–153. doi:10.1016/j.sleh.2016.01.006

Magee, L., & Hale, L. (2012). Longitudinal associations between sleep duration and subsequent weight gain: A systematic review. *Sleep Medicine Reviews*, *16* (3), 231–241. doi:10.1016/j.smrv.2011.05.005

Marsh, H. W. (1990). *Self-description questionnaire manual*. Campbelltown, Australia: University of Western Sydney, Macarthur.

Nixon, G. M., Thompson, J. M. D., Han, D. Y., Becroft, D. M., Clark, P. M., Robinson, E., & Mitchell, E. A. (2008). Short sleep duration in middle childhood: Risk factors and consequences. *Sleep*, *31*(1), 71–78.

Price, A. M. H., Quach, J., Wake, M., Bittman, M., & Hiscock, H. (2015). Cross-sectional sleep thresholds for optimal health and well-being in Australian 4-9-year-olds. *Sleep Medicine*. http://doi.org/10.1016/j.sleep.2015.08.013

Räikkönen, K., Matthews, K. A., Pesonen, A.-K., Pyhälä, R., Paavonen, E. J., Feldt, K., & Kajantie, E. (2010). Poor sleep and altered hypothalamic-pituitary-adrenocortical and sympatho-adrenal-medullary system activity in children. *Journal of Clinical Endocrinology and Metabolism*, *95*(5), 2254–2261. http://doi.org/10.1210/jc.2009-0943

Saper, C. B., Cano, G., & Scammell, T. E. (2005). Homeostatic, circadian, and emotional regulation of sleep. *The Journal of Comparative Neurology*, *493*(1), 92–98. doi:10.1002/(ISSN)1096-9861

Smaldone, A., Honig, J. C., & Byrne, M. W. (2007). Sleepless in America: Inadequate sleep and relationships to health and well-being of our nation's children. *Pediatrics*, *119*(Suppl. 1), S29–S37. http://doi.org/10.1542/peds.2006-2089F

Snell, E. K., Adam, E. K., & Duncan, G. J. (2007). Sleep and the body mass index and overweight status of children and adolescents. *Child Development*, *78*(1), 309–323. doi:10.1111/cdev.2007.78.issue-1

Taheri, S., Lin, L., Austin, D., Young, T., & Mignot, E. (2004). Short sleep duration is associated with reduced leptin, elevated ghrelin, and increased body mass index. *PLoS Medicine*, *1*(3), e62. http://doi.org/10.1371/journal.pmed.0010062

Yoo, S.-S., Gujar, N., Hu, P., Jolesz, F. A., & Walker, M. P. (2007). The human emotional brain without sleep – a prefrontal amygdala disconnect. *Current Biology*, *17*(20), 877–878. http://doi.org/10.1016/j.cub.2007.08.007

APPENDIX

TABLE A1

Coefficients and Standard Deviations From OLS Models of Child Behavior and Exponentiated Coefficients and Standard Errors (in Parentheses) From Ordered Logit Models of Child Health

	OLS				*Ordered Logit*	
	Internalizing Behavior		*Externalizing Behavior*		*Physical Health*	
	Child Report	*PCG Report*	*Child Report*	*PCG Report*	*Child Report*	*PCG Report*
	(1)	*(2)*	*(3)*	*(4)*	*(5)*	*(6)*
Intercept	26.536** (8.310)	14.074* (6.804)	29.192*** (6.391)	35.319** (10.897)		
Hours of Sleep, age 9	−2.611* (1.220)	−2.084* (0.999)	−2.368* (0.938)	−5.495*** (1.600)	1.934* (0.332)	1.108* (0.043)
(Hours of Sleep, age 9)^2	0.139* (0.067)	0.101† (0.055)	0.129* (0.051)	0.275** (0.088)	0.968† (0.018)	
Hours of Sleep, age 5	0.515 (1.144)	−0.267 (0.937)	−0.978 (0.880)	0.161 (1.501)	1.427 (0.316)	1.022 (0.039)
(Hours of Sleep, age 5)^2	−0.020 (0.060)	0.014 (0.049)	0.051 (0.046)	−0.018 (0.079)	0.982 (0.017)	
Child's Age in Months	−0.030 (0.032)	0.031 (0.026)	−0.044† (0.025)	0.041 (0.042)	1.010 (0.010)	1.007 (0.012)
Child Low Birth Weight (ref: > 2,500 g)	0.812* (0.406)	−0.151 (0.332)	0.073 (0.312)	−0.752 (0.532)	0.941 (0.142)	0.908 (0.147)
Child Male (ref: Female)	0.403 (0.253)	0.250 (0.207)	1.328*** (0.194)	1.288*** (0.332)	1.026 (0.088)	0.852† (0.094)
Child's Puberty Score	0.215 (0.358)	0.747* (0.293)	0.341 (0.275)	0.368 (0.469)	0.680** (0.124)	0.958 (0.132)
Mother Non-Hispanic Black, Native Born (ref: White, Native Born)	1.134** (0.363)	−1.261*** (0.297)	0.869** (0.279)	−1.410** (0.476)	0.994 (0.123)	0.783+ (0.135)
Mother Hispanic, Native Born (Ref: White, Native Born)	0.551 (0.410)	−0.314 (0.336)	−0.325 (0.315)	−1.583** (0.538)	0.736* (0.140)	0.740* (0.152)
Mother Other Race/Ethnicity, Native Born (ref: White, Native Born)	−0.768 (0.820)	0.891 (0.672)	0.163 (0.631)	0.802 (1.076)	1.667† (0.285)	1.198 (0.317)
Father Same Race/Ethnicity as Mother (ref: Father Not Same Race/Ethnicity)	0.051 (0.370)	0.202 (0.303)	−0.098 (0.285)	−0.094 (0.486)	1.001 (0.126)	1.118 (0.136)
Mother Foreign Born	−0.370 (0.448)	0.091 (0.367)	−0.955** (0.345)	−0.846 (0.588)	0.921 (0.154)	0.724* (0.164)
Mother's Age	−0.080*** (0.023)	−0.003 (0.019)	−0.021 (0.018)	−0.053 + (0.031)	0.992 (0.008)	0.990 (0.009)
Mother Has High School Diploma or GED (ref: Less Than High School Education)	−0.531† (0.316)	−0.245 (0.259)	0.001 (0.243)	−0.230 (0.414)	1.053 (0.110)	0.765* (0.116)
Mother Attended Some College (ref: Less Than High School Education)	−0.901* (0.355)	−0.376 (0.291)	−0.329 (0.273)	−0.564 (0.465)	1.190 (0.124)	0.984 (0.132)
Mother Is a College Graduate (ref: Less Than High School Education)	−1.085* (0.534)	−0.018 (0.437)	−0.217 (0.411)	−0.173 (0.700)	1.165 (0.183)	0.933 (0.202)
Log of Household Income	−0.370** (0.113)	−0.251** (0.092)	−0.406*** (0.087)	−0.527*** (0.148)	0.988 (0.040)	1.078† (0.041)
Biological Parents Married (ref: No Relationship)	−0.241 (0.319)	−0.358 (0.261)	−0.237 (0.245)	−0.992* (0.418)	0.915 (0.110)	1.250† (0.118)
Biological Parents Cohabiting (ref: No Relationship)	−1.007** (0.390)	−0.086 (0.319)	−0.545† (0.300)	−0.697 (0.511)	0.990 (0.135)	1.084 (0.142)
No. of Children in Home	0.265** (0.095)	0.030 (0.078)	0.040 (0.073)	0.378** (0.125)	1.002 (0.033)	0.998 (0.035)
R^2	0.076	0.029	0.096	0.061		
AIC					4,888.678	4,038.714

Note: N = 1,965. OLS = ordinary least squares regression; PCG = primary caregiver; AIC = Akaike information criterion.

$^{\dagger}p < .10$. $^{*}p < .05$. $^{**}p < .01$. $^{***}p < .001$.

Tracking Effects of Problematic Social Networking on Adolescent Psychopathology: The Mediating Role of Sleep Disruptions

Lynette Vernon

Kathryn L. Modecki

Bonnie L. Barber

Concerns are growing about adolescents' problematic social networking and possible links to depressed mood and externalizing behavior. Yet there remains little understanding of underlying processes that may account for these associations, including the mediating role of sleep disruption. This study tests this putative mediating process and examines change in problematic social networking investment and disrupted sleep, in relation to change in depressed mood and externalizing behavior. A sample of 874 students (41% male; 57.2% Caucasian; baseline *M* age = 14.4 years) from 27 high schools were surveyed. Participants' problematic social networking, sleep disruption, and psychopathology (depressed mood, externalizing behaviors) were measured annually over 3 years. Longitudinal mediation was tested using latent trajectories of problematic social networking use, sleep disruption, and psychopathology. Both problematic social networking and sleep disruption underwent positive linear growth over time. Adolescents who increasingly invested in social networking reported increased depressed mood, with around 53% of this association explained by the indirect effect of increased sleep disruptions. Further, adolescents who increasingly invested in social networking also reported increased externalizing behavior; some of this relation was explained (13%) via increased sleep disruptions. However an alternative model in which increased externalizing was associated with increased social networking, mediated by sleep disruptions, indicated a reciprocal relation of similar magnitude. It is important for parents, teachers, and psychologists to minimize the negative effects of social networking on adolescents' psychopathology. Interventions should potentially target promoting healthy sleep habits through reductions in social networking investment and rescheduling usage away from bedtime.

Recognition of the importance of quality sleep in healthy adolescent development has led to increased concerns about technology and the role it could play in disrupting bedtime behaviors (Cain & Gradisar, 2010; Carskadon, 2011; Gradisar & Short, 2013; Suganuma et al., 2007; Van den Bulck, 2004, 2007; Zimmerman, 2008). Electronic media has become an integral part of adolescent lives, with a recent report finding that adolescents use an average of 9 hr of entertainment media per day, with slightly more than 1 hr of that time, on average, devoted to social media (Rideout, 2015). At nighttime, adolescents' engagement with electronic media can affect their sleep duration and quality, which can subsequently lead to problematic daytime functioning (Cain & Gradisar, 2010;

King, Delfabbro, Zwaans, & Kaptsis, 2013; Vernon, Barber, & Modecki, 2015). Indeed, risk of sleep disruption increases when youth are exposed to more than 2 hr of bright light from screens, due to the suppression of melatonin, a sleep-promoting hormone (Wood, Rea, Plitnick, & Figueiro, 2013). Although an increasing number of longitudinal studies have advanced our understanding of the importance of sleep and consequences of sleep deprivation (Buckhalt, El-Sheikh, Keller, & Kelly, 2009; Fredriksen, Rhodes, Reddy, & Way, 2004) and further studies have examined relations between electronic media use and sleep (Hale & Guan, 2015), few studies have examined specific media activities together with the consequences of sleep deprivation (Arora, Broglia, Thomas, & Taheri, 2014; Lemola, Perkinson-Gloor, Brand, Dewald-Kaufmann, & Grob, 2015). Thus, gaps remain in our understanding of the extent to which investment in social media couples with sleep disruption to affect youth psychopathology, including depressed mood and externalizing behaviors. This longitudinal study addresses these gaps by employing a series of latent growth curves, which allow for examination of individual change over time, as well as individual differences in trajectories, and models the mediational process of technology—sleep disruption—psychopathology (Cheong, MacKinnon, & Khoo, 2003).

SLEEP DEVELOPMENT

Most adolescents require slightly more than 9 hr of sleep per night but also prefer later bedtimes and wake-up times due to a shift in their biological clock (Carskadon, 2002; Hirshkowitz et al., 2015). To some extent, this developmental change is biologically based, and circadian changes are correlated with pubertal stages (Tate, Richardson, & Carskadon, 2004). Adolescents' preference for later bedtimes can become problematic when their schedules are dictated by external forces, such as on school nights when they must rise early, resulting in consistently fewer than 9 hr of sleep (Acebo & Carskadon, 2002; Kelley, Lockley, Foster, & Kelley, 2015; Warner, Murray, & Meyer, 2008). In addition to biological and environmental factors regulating adolescents' sleep, behaviors performed close to bedtime can potentially disturb their "wind-down" process and affect quality and amount of sleep. For example, in National Sleep Foundation's (2011) *2011 Sleep in America Poll*, 72% of youth reported using cell phones in the hour before bed, and there were similar rates for other electronic media devices. Further, media that was more interactive was associated with greater difficulty falling asleep. In all, reported school day total sleep time averaged 7½ hr, which is well below the recommended 8- to 10-hr requirement for teenagers (Hirshkowitz et al., 2015). Globally, similar patterns of reduced sleep duration and quality for adolescents using electronic media before bedtime have been reported (for review, see Bartel, Gradisar, & Williamson, 2015; Fredriksen et al., 2004; King et al., 2013; Lemola et al., 2015; Suganuma et al., 2007; Van den Bulck, 2004, 2007). Given the importance of adolescent sleep, and the role of electronic media use in its disruption, a development framework is required to assess how changes in sleep behaviors and electronic media are functionally linked to adolescent well-being.

SLEEP AND PSYCHOPATHOLOGY

There is a growing consensus that healthy development of sleep behaviors during adolescence contributes to improved cognitive performance and well-being, preventing later mental health problems and other manifestations of psychopathology (McCracken, 2002; Sadeh, Gruber, & Raviv, 2002; Talbot, McGlinchey, Kaplan, Dahl, & Harvey, 2010; Wolfson & Carskadon, 1998; Zimmerman, 2008). Extensive research into negative outcomes associated with poor-quality and insufficient sleep finds links to internalizing emotional difficulties such as mood disturbances and externalizing difficulties such as conduct and behavior problems (Dahl & Lewin, 2002; Fuligni & Hardway, 2006; Lemola et al., 2015; Talbot et al., 2010). For example, adolescents with adequate, good-quality sleep report lower levels of depressed mood and less tiredness during the day compared to adolescents with poor sleep habits (Acebo & Carskadon, 2002; Fuligni & Hardway, 2006; Wolfson & Carskadon, 1998). As well, adolescents who have inadequate sleep on a regular basis report adverse effects, including sleepiness during the day, irritability and low tolerance levels, less control of emotions and exaggerated affect, all of which can lead to increases in negative mood and risk taking (Carskadon, 2002, 2011; Talbot et al., 2010). Indeed Dahl and Lewin (2002) reported that too little sleep can impair adolescents' ability to do two important things at once, such as thinking and curbing emotions. As a result, tired adolescents are unable to regulate mood and negative emotions. Of importance, one major driver of such tiredness among adolescents may be their heavy use of technology, including computers, laptops, and mobile devices with Internet access. In this case, the *content* on these devices, including emotionally arousing posts on social networking sites (SNSs), and the *location* and *timing* of use before and after bedtime are especially salient (Zimmerman, 2008). In spite of the significance of these factors in relation to adolescent sleep, few studies have examined the developmental course of sleep and psychopathology over time, and none, to our knowledge, have considered the role of social networking investment as precursor to this relation.

HOW DOES SOCIAL NETWORKING USE AFFECT SLEEP AND PSYCHOPATHOLGY?

Adolescents use social media for shared interactions with their peers and to gather collectively online. Unfortunately, however, the pull of SNSs can readily encroach upon adolescents' sleep. In previous generations, social interactions took place in person or over landline telephones. Today adolescents have access to technology with real time contact 24 hr a day, 7 days a week (Calamaro, Mason, & Ratcliffe, 2009). As a result, social media use, including posting on or perusing SNSs, messaging, and instant updating of profile status, can facilitate (or strain) social relationships in ways never experienced by previous generations (Shapiro & Margolin, 2014). For instance, recent data from the Pew Research Center shows that 76% of adolescents use social media and 71% say they use Facebook (a major SNS platform) as their main form of social media contact (Lenhart, 2015). In addition to continuous access to social media during the day, an increasing number of adolescents also access SNSs via the Internet in their bedrooms at night (33% of 8- to 18-year-olds; Rideout, Foehr, & Roberts, 2010) via a variety of sources (computer, tablet, and cell phone/smartphone).

Because adolescents have access to technology in their bedrooms, lights-out for many of them may not signal intention to settle down to a quality night's sleep (Exelmans & Van den Bulck, 2015; Munezawa et al., 2011). Research on the technology-mediated activities of adolescents describes a high prevalence of mobile phone use after lights-out and subsequent tiredness the following day (Eggermont & Van den Bulck, 2006; Munezawa et al., 2011; Van den Bulck, 2007). Further, because of recent increased capability of smartphones to readily access the Internet and SNSs, concerns about the impact of technology after lights-out on healthy adolescent development are exacerbated (Nalwa & Anand, 2003). Illustratively, some research in this area has focused on the impact of SNS on sleep and finds that excessive use of social networking, classified as addiction to social networking, directly leads to later bedtimes and poor-quality sleep among college students (Andreassen, Torsheim, Brunborg, & Pallesen, 2012; Wolniczak et al., 2013).

In addition to displacing sleep time, engaging with technology can have consequences for adolescent well-being, including manifestations of psychopathology. In fact, there is a growing body of research pointing to the benefits and risks that result from the rapid rise in social media use by adolescents (see Kuss & Griffiths, 2011, for review). For example, the dramatic increase in social networking has been accompanied by adolescents' growing use of social media to foster connections to others and fulfil emotional needs. But whether heavy investment in SNSs negatively impacts well-being is not well understood. In one study investigating gambling addictions, researchers argued that any behavior that stimulates emotional arousal can become addictive (Brown, 1987). Following on from this conclusion, Young (1998) developed an Internet addiction scale to examine Internet behaviors of university students. She found that students who met the criteria for dependency on the Internet became more emotionally aroused and reported more negative well-being compared to nondependent students. More recently, scales have been developed to investigate addiction to social networking (Andreassen et al., 2012; Kuss & Griffiths, 2011; Wolniczak et al., 2013) with emerging evidence for excessive use of social networking being related to relationship problems. Little is known, however, about adolescent investment in SNS and associated manifestations of psychopathology.

One of the reasons SNS use tends to increase, and thus be potentially problematic, is that it can be highly rewarding. SNSs provide a cyber-place where people can connect with their friendship networks (Griffiths, 2013) and gain rewards for participation in activities such as posting or messaging through "likes" and comments. A number of studies suggest that there may be benefits to using SNSs to engage with friends, develop social self-concept (Barker, 2009; Blomfield-Neira & Barber, 2014), and build social connections and support, especially for those who are lonely (Ellison, Steinfield, & Lampe, 2007, 2011; Lee, Noh, & Koo, 2013; Liu & Yu, 2013). Such positive engagement can motivate users to invest heavily in SNSs.

Yet there may be costs associated with this highly appealing arena of participation, particularly in relation to adolescent mental health. A growing body of evidence suggests that for some adolescents SNS use can undermine well-being (Valkenburg, Peter, & Schouten, 2006), predicting higher levels of depressed mood (Blomfield-Neira & Barber, 2014; Steers, Wickham, & Acitelli, 2014) and increased behavior problems (Mikami, Szwedo, Allen, Evans, & Hare, 2010). The emotional salience of social media may account, in part, for these effects, for two primary reasons: unfavorable social comparisons with exacerbated feelings of worthlessness, and aggression victimization when online.

Discrepancies between adolescents' comparison group and appraisals of self can lead to internalizing and externalizing problems, especially if these comparisons undermine confidence in youth's relative abilities or attributes. For example, adolescents who compare themselves to others on social media report feelings of envy and higher levels of depression (Tandoc, Ferrucci, & Duffy, 2015). Similarly, Facebook social comparisons account for links between intensity of social networking (time spent, or number of times viewing) and depression (Steers et al., 2014). Given that the heaviest Internet users in adolescence may be those with lower self-concept (Israelashvili, Kim, & Bukobza, 2012), this ubiquitous platform for social comparison may be undermining mental health and well-being, particularly for more vulnerable adolescents. More needs to be understood about the consequences of personal dependence, or overinvestment in SNSs, in the development of symptoms of internalizing, especially with respect to the causal order of the investment–depressed mood link.

In addition to facilitating unfavorable self-driven comparisons, electronic media can also be a venue for cyber-aggression (Modecki, Minchin, Harbaugh, Guerra, & Runions, 2014). In fact, research suggests that adolescents manifest cross-situational stability in their interpersonal interactions, with continuity in adverse behaviors between their computer-mediated and face-to-face communication contexts (Mikami et al., 2010; Modecki et al., 2014). Adolescents' heavy use of the Internet is linked to poor coping and negative interpersonal relationships (Milani, Osualdella, & Di Blasio, 2009). Involvement in cyber-aggression, either as a perpetrator or victim, has also been linked to poor mental health, including elevated depressive and externalizing symptoms (Modecki, Barber, & Vernon, 2013; Wang, Nansel, & Iannotti, 2011). Moreover, adolescent bullying is associated with sleep difficulties (Hunter, Durkin, Boyle, Booth, & Rasmussen, 2014). One recent study of 19,436 school students in Japan reports that bullying is significantly linked to irregular bedtimes (Tochigi et al., 2012). In particular, using a mobile device for e-mail exchanges and calling after lights-out leads to emotional arousal and facilitates bullying. Notably, much of this bullying occurs on social media, but we know little about the developmental course of the links between SNS use and externalizing behaviors and about the possible mediating role of sleep disruption.

We posit that a process unfolds for many teens in which heavy SNS use leads to poor sleep. That is, SNS use has a displacement effect on sleep time, coupled with increased arousal and negative affect for teens, just before bedtime. For adolescents who are highly invested in social media, upsetting negative feedback received at night, prior to bedtime or after lights-out, likely activates emotional arousal (e.g., envy, anxiety) and hampers sleep onset (Tandoc et al., 2015). Indeed, emotional arousal before bed has been researched extensively (Beattie, Kyle, Espie, & Biello, 2015; Kahn, Sheppes, & Sadeh, 2013) and, in the context of viewing adult or violent media, has been linked to difficulties in falling asleep for children and adolescents (Eggermont & Van den Bulck, 2006; Munezawa et al., 2011; Van den Bulck, 2000). We suggest that similar emotional arousal from social networking activities prior to sleep may be an important factor in adolescents' sleep disruption. As a result, disturbed sleep could be a possible mechanism for the links between participating in social networking and negative well-being.

Despite growing interest in and research on adolescents' social networking experiences, there is little evidence of how investment in SNSs evolves over time or how this relates to changes in adolescent sleep, which could mediate links between SNS use and psychopathology. Because the development of healthy sleep habits is of paramount importance during adolescence (Shochat, Cohen-Zion, & Tzischinsky, 2014), identifying contexts that affect sleep competence, and subsequent outcomes associated with poor sleep, are important and understudied areas of research.

THE CURRENT STUDY

Recent findings document the negative impact of disrupted sleep on adolescent functioning (Carskadon, 2011). Further, a key feature in adolescents' lives is social networking, and for some youth, problematic SNS investment leads to poor quality sleep and daytime sleepiness (Wolniczak et al., 2013). Despite preliminary evidence of links between problematic social networking and poor sleep, and despite heavy interest in the impact of poor sleep on adolescent psychopathology, no research has yet examined these relations simultaneously, nor has research to date examined whether *change* in these aspects of adolescent lives are linked, as opposed to examining single snapshots of each construct at one point in time. Here, we hypothesize that increased investment in social networking is associated with sleep disruptions, which in turn may be associated with increases in both depressed mood and externalizing behavior. Thus, our analyses address two major questions: Are *changes* in problematic SNS use and *changes* in manifestations of psychopathology (i.e., depressed mood and externalizing behaviors) related to one another? Further, do increases in sleep disruptions mediate the relation between increased problematic social networking and increased psychopathology?

METHODS

Participants

Data were drawn from a longitudinal study on adolescent activity participation (Youth Activity Participation Study), including areas of well-being such as health correlates related to sleep and constructs related to technology use (see Blomfield-Neira & Barber, 2014; Vernon et al., 2015, for descriptions of the study). The sample comprised 874 high school students (41% male, baseline *M* age = 14.4 years) from metropolitan and regional areas across Western Australia. Of the sample, 57.2% were Caucasian, 7.2% Asian, and 1.6% Aboriginal or Torres Strait Islander, 23.3% other (e.g., Middle Eastern, African, Indian, and Maori); 10.6% did not nominate ethnicity. School-level socioeconomic status (SES) was obtained from Australian Curriculum, Assessment and Reporting Authority (2015), which computes the yearly Index of Community Socio-Educational Advantage for schools. The Index of Community Socio-Educational Advantage is calculated using Australian Bureau of Statistics data and draws on education, occupation, income, ethnicity, and location of student household (Australian Curriculum, Assessment and Reporting Authority, 2015). Schools were placed on a numerical scale that described their comparative socioeconomic advantage; 14 of the 27 schools were at or below the median with 48.3% of the students in these low-SES schools.

In Year 9, 85% of the students had a social networking profile, with 74% having access to the Internet in their bedrooms. This grew to 92% having a SNS profile in Year 11, of whom 92% had access to the Internet in their

TABLE 1
Correlations, Means, Standard Deviations, Cronbach's Alpha Coefficients of Youth Characteristics—Problematic Social Networking Use, Sleep Disruptions, Depressed Mood, Externalizing Behavior, Gender, Socioeconomic Status, and Puberty Maturation

Variable List		*1*	*2*	*3*	*4*	*5*	*6*	*7*	*8*	*9*	*10*	*11*	*12*
1. Problematic SNS Use	(T0)	1											
2. Problematic SNS Use	(T1)	.65**	1										
3. Problematic SNS Use	(T2)	.47**	.52**	1									
4. Sleep Disruption	(T0)	.35**	.25**	.16**	1								
5. Sleep Disruption	(T1)	.34**	.29**	.22**	.63**	1							
6. Sleep Disruption	(T2)	.26**	.22**	.18**	.48**	.59**	1						
7. Depressed Mood	(T0)	.31**	.26**	.21**	.46**	.42**	.32**	1					
8. Depressed Mood	(T1)	.31**	.33**	.20**	.33**	.46**	.38**	.54**	1				
9. Depressed Mood	(T2)	.24**	.25**	.24**	.36**	.40**	.50**	.51**	.60**	1			
10. Externalizing Behavior	(T0)	.37**	.20**	.20**	.24**	.20**	.15**	.24**	.19**	.19**	1		
11. Externalizing Behavior	(T1)	.29**	.32**	.21**	.16**	.21**	.21**	.18**	.23**	.23**	.55**	1	
12. Externalizing Behavior	(T2)	.22**	.24**	.28**	.11**	.19**	.14**	.21**	.22**	.18**	.45**	.57**	1
13. Gender		−.10**	−.12**	−.07*	−.17**	−.23**	−.18**	−.23**	−.28**	−.20**	.04	.09**	.13**
14. SES High–Low		−.04	.00	.03	−.02	−.04	−.05	−.07	−.05	−.07	−.10**	−.08*	−.07
15. Puberty Maturation	(T0)	−.01	.04	.07	.01	.00	.01	.01	.07	.03	.10**	.06	.13**
M		1.98	2.04	2.08	2.76	2.86	3.02	2.59	2.74	2.84	1.39	1.42	1.47
SD		1.22	1.17	1.09	.85	.86	.87	1.06	1.14	1.15	.67	.73	.63
α		.91	.90	.89	.76	.76	.75	.80	.83	.83	.81	.79	.79

Note: For gender, girls' (n = 515) values coded as 0 and boys' (n = 359) values coded as 1; For socioeconomic status (SES), lower SES's (n = 422) values coded as 0 and higher SES's (n = 452) values coded as 1; problematic SNS use range = 0–5; sleep disruptions range = 1–5; depressed mood range = 1–6; externalizing behavior range = 1–8. T = Time; SNS = social networking site.

$^*p < .05$. $^{**}p < .01$.

bedroom. As well, Year 9 students averaged 8.24 hr (*SD* = 1.02) of sleep on weeknights, with 32% indicating they go to bed after 10 p.m. Hours of sleep declined the following year to 8.11 hr (*SD* = 1.05), with 46% indicating they go to bed after 10 p.m. We did not collect sleep-hour data in Year 11.

Procedures

Ethical approval was obtained from the University Human Research Ethics Committee, the Education Department and Catholic Education Office. Study participation required active informed student and parent consent. Students were recruited from 27 high schools (16 government, 11 nongovernment), selected from schools across Western Australian and were surveyed annually for 3 years from 2011.[1] Students were informed that the survey was voluntary and confidential and that no information would be released to their teachers, school, or parents. The survey was administered using iPads via intranet over a 45-min session. Alternatively a paper survey could be administered at the school's request.

Measures

Scale internal consistency estimates are presented in Table 1.

Problematic SNS Use

The problematic use of social networking scale consisted of the mean score for four items measured across three waves. These items were adapted from Young's (1998) Internet Addiction Scale and used in previous research (adapted from Vernon et al., 2015). Items measured the degree to which adolescents invest emotionally in social networking and included "I prefer to spend time on Facebook/Myspace/Bebo rather than attend social activities/events"; "I use Facebook/Myspace/Bebo as a way of making me feel good"; "I get into arguments with other people about the amount of time I spend on Facebook/Myspace/Bebo." Possible responses ranged from 0 (*no SNS profile*) to 1 (*completely disagree*) and 5 (*completely agree*). In these data, the baseline problematic SNS scale was negatively correlated with amount of sleep (r = –.22, $p < .05$) and positively associated with later times to bed (r = .29, $p < .05$).

Sleep Disruptions

Sleep items were adapted from the School Sleep Habits Survey (Wolfson & Carskadon, 1998, 2003). Based on theory where sleep imbalance impairs

[1] The Australian education system is classified into two broad categories according to the source of funding: Government or state schools (also known as public schools) and nongovernmental schools (also known as private schools and include Catholic and Independent schools).

cognitive-emotional regulation (Dahl & Lewin, 2002), measures for perceived quality of sleep and daytime sleepiness were assessed using exploratory factor analysis with geomin rotation to determine the factorial structure of the eight sleep items included in our survey. A three-factor solution fit the data well; however, one factor was discounted due to cross-loadings. Therefore, a two-factor solution, which also fit the data well, was explored; one related to the affective domain and the other to the behavioral domain. The affective domain, used in the current analyses, tapped how students felt about their sleep. We chose the affective domain for this study because we theorized that adolescents who used SNSs into the night would report feeling less satisfied with their sleep. That is, youth who heavily invested in SNS use would ruminate over SNS content at night and experience difficulties getting to sleep and feelings of tiredness during the day. Therefore, the resulting affective scale tapped perceptions about sleep affect during the previous 2 weeks and included the following: How often have you: "felt tired or sleepy during the day"; "had an extremely hard time falling asleep"; "had a good night's sleep (reversed)"; "felt satisfied with your sleep" (reversed). Responses for all sleep indicators were 1 (*never*), 2 (*once*), 3 (*twice*), 4 (*several times*), and 5 (*every day/night*).

Depressed Mood

Depressed mood was measured using the mean of five items designed to tap emotional well-being, originally from the longitudinal Michigan Study of Adolescent Life Transitions. Scale items have been published in prior research (e.g., Barber, Eccles, & Stone, 2001; Durkin & Barber, 2002), and in our sample, validity of the full scale has also been supported (Modecki et al., 2013). In these data, the baseline scale was negatively correlated with self-esteem ($r = -.51, p < .05$), and social self-concept ($r = -.32, p < .05$). Items included "How often do you feel there is nothing nice you can look forward to?" and "How often do you feel unhappy, sad or depressed?" Responses ranged from 1 (*never*) to 6 (*daily*).

Externalizing Behavior

Externalizing behavior consisted of the mean of seven items drawn from Fredricks and Eccles (2006), which tapped delinquency and aggressive behaviors. Previous research shows that this measure is a valid indicator of status offenses, aggression, and delinquency. Although previous use of the scale has sometimes included substance abuse (Modecki et al., 2013), this was not included as substance use, and sleep should be considered separately (Acebo & Carskadon, 2002). The items were measured on an 8-point scale from 1 (*none*) to 8 (*31 or more times*) and include "In the past 6 months how often have you skipped school without parent permission?"; "... have you gotten in a physical fight with another person?" and "... have you taken something from a store without paying for it?"

Covariates

Relevant covariates were controlled for including gender (0 = female; 1 = male), SES (0 = equal to or below median; 1 = above median), and an adapted measure of pubertal timing (Dubas, Graber, & Petersen, 1991). Pubertal timing was assessed in Year 9 with the item "Teenagers' bodies change a lot as they grow up; this is referred to as your physical development. Compared to other people your age do you think your physical development has started?" with responses from 1 (*much later*) to 5 (*much earlier*). Previously published studies demonstrate validity of the measure (Modecki, Barber, & Eccles, 2014).

Analytic Procedure

Analyses were conducted using latent growth modeling (LGM) in *Mplus* 7.2 (Muthén & Muthén, 1998–2012). Latent changes in the independent variable (problematic social networking use), dependent variables (either depressed mood or externalizing behavior), and mediating variable (sleep disruption) were modeled (Cheong et al., 2003; MacKinnon, 2008; von Soest & Hagtvet, 2011). Previous research demonstrates use of LGM to estimate longitudinal mediation effects (see Littlefield, Sher, & Wood, 2010, for a comprehensive review of the procedure, and von Soest & Hagtvet, 2011, for a framework for analysis). For all models we used full information maximum likelihood procedure in order to use all available data from each participant (Yuan & Bentler, 2000). Bias-corrected bootstrapping was used to determine the mediated (i.e., indirect) effects using 95% asymmetric confidence intervals (CIs) to adjust for non-normality of data. Unstandardized parameter point estimates with 95% asymmetric CIs were reported for significance (MacKinnon, 2008; Muthén, 2007).

For all study variables (problematic SNS use, sleep disruption, depressed mood, and externalizing behavior), unconditional (with no covariates) univariate growth curve models were run individually. Next, conditional parallel process models were run to examine the direct effects between early levels of the constructs (intercepts) and change in each of the constructs (slopes), with gender, pubertal timing, and SES entered as covariates. This was followed by the conditional, multiple mediation parallel process models for each psychopathology indicator, as illustrated in Figure 1. For instance, for depressed mood, the steps of the analyses were as follows: First the direct effects between intercepts and slopes of problematic SNS use (the independent variable) with sleep disruption (the mediator) were modeled, then links between problematic SNS use

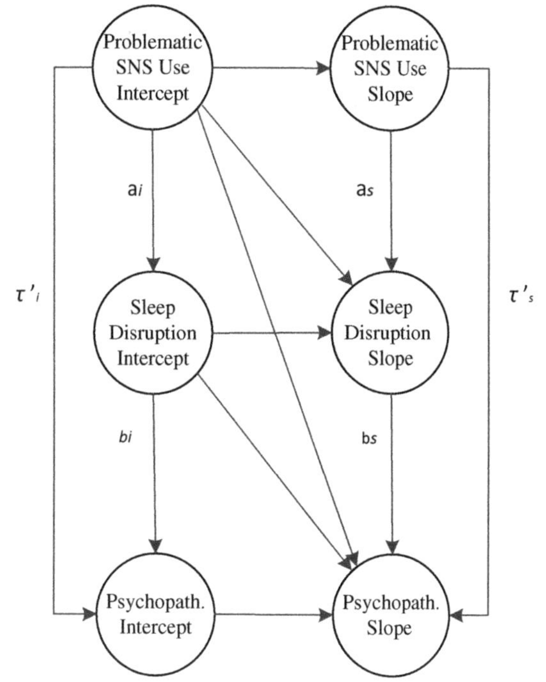

FIGURE 1 Latent growth curve mediation model. *Note*: Psychopathology modeled separately for depressed mood and externalizing behavior. Covariate paths for gender, socioeconomic status (SES) and pubertal maturation not included in the model. Direct effect of initial level (Year 9) of problematic social networking site (SNS) use on initial level of psychopathology = $\tau'i$. Indirect effect of initial level of problematic SNS use on initial level of sleep disruptions on initial level of psychopathology = ai bi. Total effect of initial level of problematic SNS use on initial level of psychopathology = $\tau'i + ai\ bi$. Direct effect of changes in problematic SNS use on change in psychopathology = $\tau's$. Indirect effect of change in problematic SNS use on changes in sleep disruptions on changes in psychopathology = as bs. Total effect of change in problematic SNS use on change in psychopathology = $\tau's + as\ bs$.

with depressed mood (the dependent variable) were modeled, followed by modeling the direct effects between sleep disruption, and the intercept and slopes of depressed mood. Finally, the multiple mediation models for problematic SNS use, sleep disruption, and depressed mood were run (Figure 1). The psychopathology intercept and psychopathology slope represent the LGM of the respective psychopathology constructs (i.e., depressed mood or externalizing behavior). Intercept factors represent the initial level (Year 9 at school, age roughly 14.5) for each construct, and slope factors represent change in the constructs from Year 9 to Year 11.

Because the temporal order of mediational models should be informed by strong theory, the order for the model was created a priori (Cheong et al., 2003). Thus, the relation of baseline levels of problematic SNS use (intercept) was modeled to predict baseline measures of sleep disruption. However, there is some early evidence that poor sleep can contribute to increased media use among adults (Tavernier & Willoughby, 2014) and as a more rigorous check of our theory, the reversed models were also tested. For our theorized model, Figure 1 indicates the directional paths, with the slopes controlled for their intercept (von Soest & Hagtvet, 2011). Bias-corrected bootstrap CIs were computed for indirect effects (the products of coefficients approach; Preacher & Hayes, 2008) by multiplying the path coefficient that links problematic SNS use intercept to depressed mood or externalizing behavior intercept through the mediator intercept of sleep disruption. Similarly, examination of the coefficients for the mediational processes for the associated slopes determined if changes in sleep schedules was the correct mechanism to account for changes in the associations between problematic SNS use and psychopathology.

RESULTS

Table 1 displays correlations, means, standard deviations, and scale reliabilities among problematic SNS use, sleep disruption, and psychopathology constructs over the three periods with covariates gender, SES, and pubertal maturation.

Univariate Growth Models

Overall the univariate model estimates of the growth trajectories for problematic SNS use, sleep disruptions, depressed mood, and externalizing behavior all provided good fit to the data, that is, comparative fit index (CFI) > .95, root mean square error of approximation (RMSEA) and standardized root mean square residual (SRMR) < .08 (Hu & Bentler, 1999). Slope parameters indicated that, overall, individuals increased in problematic SNS use, sleep disruptions, depressed mood, and externalizing behaviors from Year 9 to Year 11. The intercept and slope factor for each study variable exhibited significant variability (all $ps < .05$), suggesting variability initially and in the rate of change across participants.

Parallel Process Models

Next, conditional parallel process models were estimated. These models were run as a precursor to examining the potential mediating role of sleep disruptions in the relation between problematic SNS use and psychopathology. Initially, total effects (without the mediator) between SNS use and psychopathology were determined by examining the relation between the LGM for problematic SNS use and LGMs for each psychopathology construct in two separate parallel-process models. In these models, directional paths between intercepts and slopes (i.e., controlling the slope for its intercept) also enable clarification of mediational processes in the final model (von Soest & Hagtvet, 2011). Results for all parallel-process models are presented

TABLE 2

Parallel Process Latent Growth Models of Depressed Mood and Externalizing Behaviors With Problematic SNS Use and Sleep Disruptions

			B	*95% CI*	*β*
Problematic SNS Use and Depressed Mood Parallel Process Model					
Problematic SNS Use Intercept	→	Depressed Mood Intercept	0.32	[0.24, 0.40]	.43*
Problematic SNS Use Slope	→	Depressed Mood Slope	0.35	[0.12, 0.72]	.51*
Sleep Disruptions and Depressed Mood Parallel Process Model					
Sleep Disruptions Intercept	→	Depressed Mood Intercept	0.75	[0.63, 0.88]	.67*
Sleep Disruptions slope	→	Depressed Mood Slope	0.95	[0.68, 1.51]	.85*
Problematic SNS Use and Externalizing Behavior Parallel Process Model					
Problematic SNS Use Intercept	→	Externalizing Behavior Intercept	0.23	[0.18, 0.28]	.51*
Problematic SNS Use Slope	→	Externalizing Behavior Slope	0.28	[0.11, 0.65]	.48*
Sleep Disruptions and Externalizing Behavior Parallel Process Model					
Sleep Disruptions Intercept	→	Externalizing Behavior Intercept	0.27	[0.20, 0.35]	.39*
Sleep Disruptions Slope	→	Externalizing Behavior Slope	0.25	[0.10, 0.56]	.26*
Problematic SNS Use and Sleep Disruptions Parallel Process Model					
Problematic SNS Use Intercept	→	Sleep Disruptions Intercept	0.27	[0.21, 0.33]	.41*
Problematic SNS Use Slope	→	Sleep Disruptions slope	0.19	[0.07, 0.37]	.30*

Note: $n = 807$. All variables are controlled for gender, socioeconomic status, and pubertal maturation. CI = confidence interval; SNS = social networking site.
*$p < .05$.

in Table 2 and show good fit (i.e., CFI >.95, RMSEA and SRMR < .08; Hu & Bentler, 1999). Direct effects for the intercept-to-intercept and slope-to-slope models for problematic SNS use and psychopathology constructs were all statistically significant. Students with higher baseline levels of problematic SNS use also tended to have higher initial levels of depressed mood and externalizing behavior. Furthermore, changes in problematic SNS use were associated with changes in both depressed mood and externalizing behavior.

Further, to examine the relations between the independent variable (SNS use) and the mediator variable (sleep), we combined the LGM for problematic SNS use with the LGM for sleep disruptions, again controlling slope of the construct for its intercept. As seen in Table 2, the intercept and slope of problematic SNS use was positively associated with the intercept and slope of the mediator variable, sleep disruptions. That is, students with high initial levels of problematic SNS use tended to also have higher initial levels of sleep disruptions; as students' growth in problematic SNS use from Year 9 to Year 11 increased, so too did their sleep disruption. Finally, the mediator and dependent variables for psychopathology were run in two separate parallel-process models, one for depressed mood and the other for externalizing behavior. Again these models specified directional paths between intercepts and slopes, and values are reported in Table 2. In these models, the more frequent the sleep disruptions, the more depressed mood and externalizing behaviors reported in Year 9. Further, changes in sleep disruptions were positively associated with changes in depressed mood and externalizing behavior.

Mediation Models

Finally, multiple mediation models were estimated to determine if the effect of investment in SNS on the intercept and slope of each psychopathology variable (depressed mood and externalizing behavior) was due to early levels and change in the mediator (sleep disruption). The results of the two parallel-process models are presented in Figure 2.

Depressed Mood

Sleep disruptions intercept partially mediated the relation between initial levels of problematic SNS use and depressed mood with good fit, $\chi^2(30) = 83.98$, $p < .000$, CFI = .979, RMSEA = .047, 90% CI [0.035, 0.059], SRMR = .023. The indirect effect (IE) of problematic SNS use intercept on depressed mood intercept through sleep disruptions intercept was significant as tested by asymmetric CI method (IE = 0.181), 95% CI [0.132, 0.244]. Furthermore, although the direct relation between intercept of problematic SNS use and intercept of depressed mood remained statistically significant ($\beta = .167$, $p < .05$), the magnitude was lower than the total effects between the two constructs ($\beta = .413$, $p < .05$), suggesting partial mediation. The effect size ratio (indirect effect/total effect; MacKinnon, 2008) was 0.60, indicating that 60% of the intercept association between problematic SNS and depressed mood was explained by the indirect effect through sleep disruption intercept. Of principal interest, change in sleep disruptions mediated the association between change in problematic SNS use and change in depressed mood (IE = 0.181), 95% CI [0.049, 0.433], with the direct effects no longer significant in this

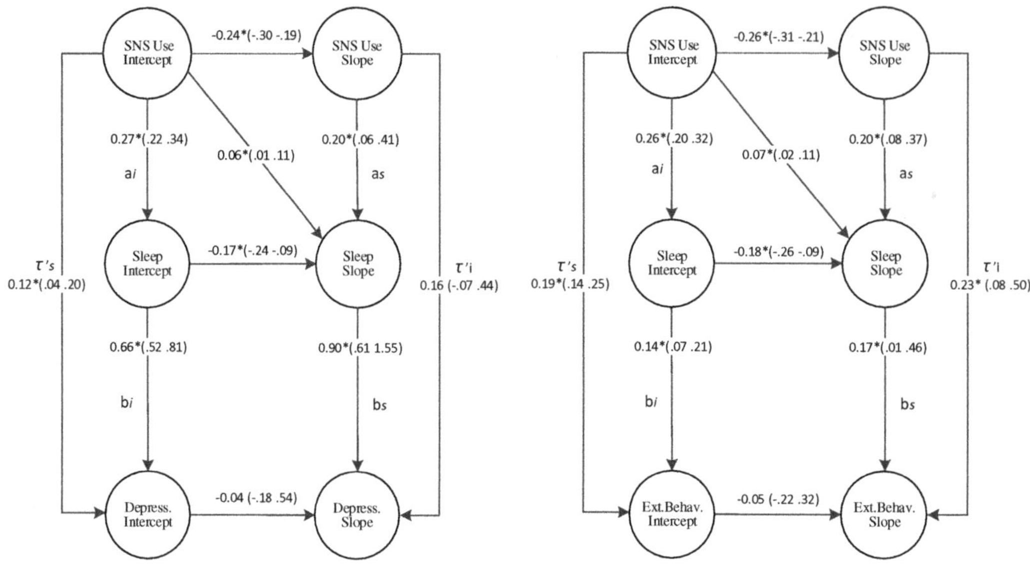

FIGURE 2 Latent growth curve mediation models (n = 807) for problematic social networking use, sleep disruptions, depressed mood, and externalizing behavior with unstandardized parameter estimates. *Note*: The 95% bias corrected bootstrap confidence interval is displayed in parentheses. All variables were controlled for gender, socioeconomic status, and pubertal maturation but are not displayed for clarity purposes as were 2 insignificant paths to dependent variable. Direct effects intercepts = τ '*i* ; Indirect effect intercepts = *ai bi*; Total effect intercepts = τ '*i* + *ai bi*; Direct effect Slopes = τ '*s* ; Indirect effect Slopes = *as bs*; Total effect Slopes = τ '*s* + *as bs*; SNS use = problematic social networking site use; Sleep = sleep disruptions; Depress = depressed mood; Ext. Behav. = externalizing behavior. *p <.05.

model. The effect size ratio was 0.53, so around 53% of the original slope relation was explained by the indirect effect through sleep disruption slope. Three other multiple mediation pathways were significant (for clarity, these pathways are not included in Figure 2; however, further information is available from the authors).

Externalizing Behavior

Sleep disruptions intercept partially mediated the relation between initial levels of problematic SNS use and externalizing behavior with good fit, $\chi^2(30) = 76.46$, $p < .000$, CFI = .979, RMSEA = .044, 90% CI [0.032, 0.056], SRMR = .024. The indirect effect of problematic SNS use intercept on externalizing behavior intercept through sleep disruptions intercept was significant (IE = 0.037), 95% CI [0.019, 0.060]. The direct relation between intercept problematic SNS use and externalizing behavior, although reduced, remained statistically significant, suggesting partial mediation. The effect size ratio was 0.17, so only around 17% of the intercept relation between problematic SNS and externalizing behavior was explained by the indirect effect through sleep disruption. Change in sleep disruptions partially mediated the effect of change in problematic SNS use on change in externalizing behavior (IE = 0.034), 95% CI [0.006, 0.131], with the direct effects ($\beta = .407$, $p < .05$) remaining significant and of similar magnitude to the total effects ($\beta = .468$, $p < .05$). The effect of the mediator variable (sleep disruption slope) on the outcome of externalizing behavior was small, with the effect size ratio being 0.13, indicating that only 13% of the original slope relation between problematic SNS use and externalizing behavior was explained by the indirect effect through sleep disruption slope. Three other multiple mediation pathways were significant, and for clarity, these pathways are not included in Figure 2 (see the note in the Figure 2 caption; further information is available from the authors).

Alternative Models

To determine if demonstrated directional effects worked in the opposite direction, alternative models were tested. That is, rather than change in problematic SNSs use predicting change in sleep disruption and in turn predicting changes of depressed mood or externalizing behavior, manifestations of psychopathology may be responsible for growth in sleep disruptions and problematic SNSs use. In fact, there is evidence of bidirectional relations between sleep and mood disorders (Carney & Moss, 2014). Examination of the alternative models allowed us to make relative evaluations of fit, as well as examine the significance of the indirect effects for intercept and slope.

The alternative models and results, in which problematic SNS use was the outcome variable, sleep was the mediator, and either depressed mood or externalizing behaviors was the predictor, are presented in Figure 3.

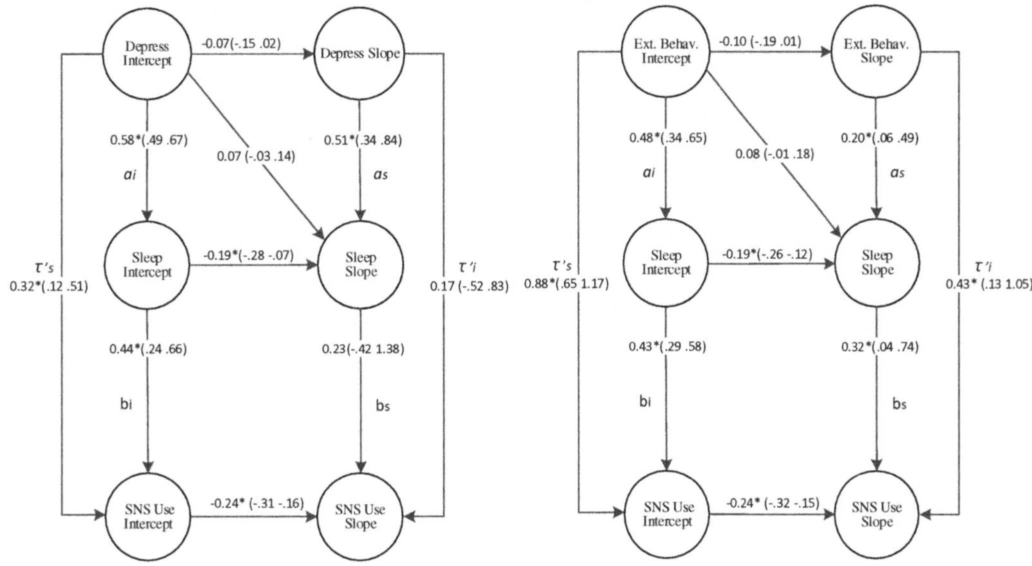

FIGURE 3 Alternative model for latent growth curve mediation models (n = 807) for depressed mood and externalizing behavior, sleep disruptions, problematic social networking use with unstandardized parameter estimates. *Note*: The 95% bias corrected bootstrap confidence interval is displayed in parentheses. All variables were controlled for gender, socioeconomic status, and pubertal maturation but are not displayed for clarity purposes, as were two insignificant paths to dependent variable. Direct effects intercepts = τ *'I*; Indirect effect intercepts = *ai* b*i*; Total effect intercepts = τ *'i* + *ai* b*i*; Direct effect Slopes = τ *'s* ; Indirect effect Slopes = *as* b*s*; Total effect Slopes = τ *'s* + *as* b*s*; SNS use = problematic social networking site use; Sleep = sleep disruptions; Depress = depressed mood; Ext. Behav. = externalizing behavior. **p* <.05.

Gender, SES, and pubertal timing were also included as covariates to these models. The alternative models were estimated and fit the data well: depressed mood, χ^2 (30) = 81.20, p < .000, RMSEA = .046; externalizing behavior, $\chi^2(30)$ = 76.78, p < .000, RMSEA = .044. When considering the model whereby depressed mood predicted sleep disruption, which in turn predicted problematic SNS use, only the indirect effects through the intercepts were significant (IE = 0.251), 95% CI [0.134, 0.400]. The effect size was lower than the original model (0.44), indicating that only 44% of the original intercept relation between depressed mood and problematic SNS use was being explained by the indirect effect through the intercept of sleep disruptions. As previously noted, the indirect effects through the intercepts and slopes for the original model were significant and greater in magnitude, so although there is a reciprocal relation through initial levels (intercepts), the trajectory for depressed mood was influenced by the trajectory of sleep, rather than vice versa.

However, this was not the case for externalizing behavior. In the alternative model for externalizing, the reciprocal relation was evident for both initial levels (intercepts) and trajectories (slopes). The indirect effects for the intercepts (IE = 0.206), 95% CI [0.126, 0.315], and for the slopes (IE = 0.064), 95% CI [0.012, 0.223], were both significant. The effect size ratio was similar in magnitude to the original model's association for both intercept (0.19) and slope (0.13).

DISCUSSION

The goal of this study was to examine links between adolescents' social networking use and psychopathology across 3 years of high school and to assess whether changes in disturbed sleep explained this relation. We hypothesized that adolescents who invested heavily in social media would have increased sleep disruption, leading to increased psychopathology in the form of elevated depressed mood and problem behavior. Although research has previously established links between adolescent sleep and well-being, and between SNS use and sleep, no study has assessed all three together, over time, to consider their developmental course and variability within-person. Across 3 years of high school, on average, youth increased their investment in SNSs, reported increased sleep disruptions, and increased levels of internalizing and externalizing symptoms. Of importance, our findings indicated that increasingly problematic SNS use predicted increases in sleep disruption, which in turn lead to increases in psychopathology. Thus, one way to help promote and maintain healthy sleep habits during adolescence is to help youth restrict their unhealthy use of SNS. As a result of improved sleep, youth may be buffered against increases in symptoms of psychopathology associated with too-heavy investment in SNS.

We were particularly interested in understanding whether adolescents' increasing sleep disruption was a plausible mechanism linking increases in their problematic SNS use to escalations in psychopathology over time. Notably, this relation existed only in our hypothesized direction for depressed mood; increasingly problematic SNS use predicted sleep disruption, which in turn was associated with increasing depressed mood. A considerable amount, slightly more than half, of the original relation between change in SNS use and change in depressed mood was explained by change in sleep disruption. Thus unhealthy SNS use appears to be especially salient to manifestations of internalizing, and programs to prevent depression during adolescence could consider including messages to reduce SNS use and encouraging youth to reschedule time online to well before bedtime.

Our mediating model for externalizing was slightly less clear-cut. Increasing problematic SNS use predicted more sleep disruptions, which in turn was associated with increasing externalizing behaviors, *and vice versa*. Thus, for externalizing behavior, relations seem to run in *both* directions; problematic SNS use lead to externalizing and vice versa, both mediated by sleep disruption. Further, the role of sleep as an operating mechanism in links between problematic SNS use and externalizing behavior was relatively smaller in comparison to models with depressed mood. Thus, although there was a significant indirect effect through sleep disruption, a significant direct effect still remained so that changes in problematic SNS use predicted changes in externalizing behaviors, even when the associated change in sleep disruption was controlled, and vice versa. Such tight links between SNS use and externalizing could be interpreted as consistent with previous evidence that social networking is just a new way of displaying the same patterns of behaviors (Mikami et al., 2010; Modecki et al., 2014). Thus, those who already have developing delinquent tendencies or aggressive behaviors may use social networking to manifest socially inept interactions. Furthermore, heavy use of social networking to facilitate aggressive behaviors arguably also interferes with sleep, leading to cyclical escalations of externalizing behaviors and poor quality sleep (Tochigi et al., 2012).

Of interest, although young people's immersion in technology is a growing concern for parents, teachers, psychologists, and policymakers generally the focus of those concerns is on the direct impact of strong emotional investment in technology on youth's psychological well-being. Relatively less attention has been paid to the displacing effect of heavy technology investment on key aspects of adolescents' routine, including sleep. However, an emerging body of evidence suggests that social networking is indeed associated with poor sleep quality (Wolniczak et al., 2013) and sleep displacement (Andreassen et al., 2012). Here, our findings echo this notion and highlight that much of the role of SNSs in the development of internalizing and externalizing symptoms may be attributed to sleep disruption.

Indeed, sleep disruption is a key concern for adolescents. Our research assessed sleep disruption, including how satisfied students were with their sleep, whether they had difficulty getting to sleep, and whether they felt tired and sleepy during the day. As a group, adolescents reported increases in these aspects of disturbed sleep across the high school years. These increases in sleep disruption were precipitated by increased engagement in social networking, which is consistent with more general findings that adolescents who use interactive media before bed are at risk of poor sleep (Gradisar & Short, 2013). The implications of this link between increases in SNS investment and sleep disruptions is that youth may need to be screened for and monitored about investment in, and use of, social networking. In particular, our results indicate that early (age 14) SNS investment is predictive of subsequent increases in problematic sleep, so that young adolescents who are heavy SNS users may especially benefit from intervention. In general, educating youth about the benefits of reducing and rescheduling their use of SNSs, as well as discussing its impact on sleep and subsequent psychopathology, could be a useful addition to prevention programming.

Educating youth about ways to protect their sleep is important, because disturbed sleep is linked to increases in psychopathology symptoms. Consistent with our prediction, adolescents who experienced higher levels of sleep disruption at the beginning of ninth grade also exhibited higher levels of depressed mood and externalizing behaviors. Further, we found that as sleep disruptions increased over time so did symptoms of psychopathology. Our finding of parallel increases in depressive symptoms and poor sleep is consistent with previous research (Fredriksen et al., 2004). However, our result indicating parallel increases between externalizing symptoms and poor sleep is novel and points to the importance of sleep for maintenance of psychological resources such as self-control and coping (Modecki, Zimmer-Gembeck, & Guerra, in press).

Study Limitations and Future Directions

This study is unique, as it uses latent growth modeling to examine growth trajectories over time in sleep disruptions, investment in social networking, depressed mood, and externalizing behaviors. Although using LGM to examine longitudinal mediation is superior to cross-sectional studies, the causal interpretations must be viewed with caution (Cheong et al., 2003). The proposed pathways between intercepts and slopes are correlational, and constructs were concurrently measured. However, causal conclusions regarding the associations can be based on strong theory (Cheong et al., 2003), and for this study, the temporal relation between heavy SNS use and sleep disruptions suggests that they are contemporaneously linked; heavy use of SNSs displaces sleep. In terms of the relation between sleep and the indicators of psychopathology, previous research using LGM has suggested a link from sleep to depressive symptoms (Fredriksen et al., 2004), and this rationale was used to test our mediational pathway for depressed mood. However, strong theory and research were less evident for predictions about the externalizing behavior pathway, and our results testing both causal directions suggest that the pathway for externalizing behavior is worthy of further investigation.

Future research should lag growth processes, perhaps using two-phase piecewise modeling in which earlier growth processes are modeled simultaneously with later growth process. In this case, change in the mediator would precede the change in the outcome, providing information about the direction for mediational hypotheses (Cheong et al., 2003). However, this suggestion requires more waves of data than we had available. Despite these limitations, we have improved the interpretability of the model by controlling the dependent variable's slope for its intercept so that the mediation analysis is not confounded by initial differences between individuals in the dependent variable (von Soest & Hagtvet, 2011).

Although this study used multiple items for each construct, we were not able to ascertain whether sleep quality, nighttime problems, or daytime sleepiness was the driver of symptoms of psychopathology. Further, the data were self-reported, and future research would benefit from collecting other measures around sleep duration, daytime functioning, and engagement online. Sleep and mood diaries (Short, Gradisar, Lack, Wright, & Chatburn, 2013) used in tandem with real-time monitoring of SNS activities would offer a substantial advance to our understanding, allowing for the consideration of both between-person comparisons of heavily invested and less invested SNS users and within-person differences in sleep displacement or disruption on nights when more time is spent on SNSs. Previous research suggests that pathological dependence on the Internet results in loss of sleep and excessive daytime fatigue (Nalwa & Anand, 2003). As our investment in the SNS scale taps a subjective sense of dependency on SNSs (e.g., feeling out of touch when one has not logged on, getting into arguments about time spent on SNS), we have made an assumption that those who are heavily invested in social networking are likely to be carrying out the activity not only during the day but also in the evening, (just before bed and possibly continuing after lights-out), both of which disrupt adolescents' sleep. Verification of this temporal aspect of the association is needed.

We note, however, that problematic investment in SNSs as we have defined it transcends solely temporal classification and reflects a psychological dependency, albeit linked to a felt need for constant access to respond and interact at any time of the day or night. This SNS constancy requirement can lead to arguments with family and friends about the time spent social networking. Sleep becomes a casualty, not only because time spent social networking displaces sleep but also because personal dependency on SNSs (feeling moody and irritable if one cannot access SNSs) increases emotional arousal and delays sleep onset (Eggermont & Van den Bulck, 2006). Research into the emotional valence of social media interactions during daytime compared to those at night may also inform about useful boundaries for healthy use of social media.

Conclusion

Sleep needs change over the course of adolescence, and identification of psychosocial and behavioral risk factors for impaired sleep offer a first step for promoting healthier adolescent development. This study has made two important contributions to the research into adolescent sleep and psychopathology. First our study suggests that for some adolescents, heavy investment in and problematic use of social networking is reflective of psychological dependency. This dependency on social networking manifests in adolescents searching for affirmative posts and making social comparisons as a way to feel good about themselves. The time and effort that adolescents devote to maintaining a socially acceptable online presence may come at the cost of a good night's sleep. The second important contribution of the study is that disturbed sleep has implications for psychopathology. Adolescents with increased sleep disruptions are at risk of developing depressed mood and engaging in externalizing behaviors during high school. These findings suggest that to guide healthy development, schools, teachers, and parents may need to focus on the role of adolescent sleep disruption, with heavy investment in social networking as a precursor. Educational guidelines to reduce social networking investment and reschedule use away from bedtimes could help to ensure that sleep is not a casualty of healthy development. In all, promoting healthy sleep hygiene among adolescents should positively impact their long-term well-being.

ACKNOWLEDGMENTS

We thank the high school principals, their staff, and the students who participated in the Youth Activity Participation–WA study. We are grateful to everyone in the Youth Activity Participation-WA team, with special thanks to Corey Blomfield-Neira, Bree Abbott, Catherine Drane, and Stuart Watson for their intellectual input, vital support, and contributions to data collection over the years.

FUNDING

Portions of this research were supported through three grants under the Australian Research Council's Discovery Projects funding scheme: DP0774125 and DP1095791 to Bonnie L. Barber and Jacquelynne Eccles, and

DP130104670 to Bonnie L. Barber, Kathryn L. Modecki, and Jacquelynne Eccles.

ORCID

Lynette Vernon http://orcid.org/0000-0003-1945-3176
Kathryn L. Modecki http://orcid.org/0000-0002-9937-9748
Bonnie L. Barber http://orcid.org/0000-0002-8799-8453

REFERENCES

Acebo, C., & Carskadon, M. A. (2002). Influence of irregular sleep patterns on waking behavior. In M. A. Carskadon (Ed.), *Adolescent sleep patterns: Biological, social, and psychological influence* (pp. 220–236). New York, NY: Cambridge University Press.

Andreassen, C. S., Torsheim, T., Brunborg, G. S., & Pallesen, S. (2012). Development of a Facebook addiction scale. *Psychological Reports, 110* (2), 501–517. doi:10.2466/02.09.18

Arora, T., Broglia, E., Thomas, G. N., & Taheri, S. (2014). Associations between specific technologies and adolescent sleep quantity, sleep quality, and parasomnias. *Sleep Medicine, 15*, 240–247. doi:10.1016/j.sleep.2013.08.799

Australian Curriculum, Assessment and Reporting Authority. (2015). *My school technical paper*. Sydney, Australia: ACARA. Retrieved from http://www.acara.edu.au

Barber, B. L., Eccles, J. S., & Stone, M. R. (2001). Whatever happened to the jock, the brain, and the princess? Young adult pathways linked to adolescent activity involvement and social identity. *Journal of Adolescent Research, 16*(5), 429–455. doi:10.1177/0743558401165002

Barker, V. (2009). Older adolescents' motivations for social network site use: The influence of gender, group identity, and collective self-esteem. *Cyberpsychology & Behavior, 12*(2), 209–213. doi:10.1089/cpb.2008.0228

Bartel, K. A., Gradisar, M., & Williamson, P. (2015). Protective and risk factors for adolescent sleep: A meta-analytic review. *Sleep Medicine Reviews, 21*, 72–85. doi:10.1016/j.smrv.2014.08.002

Beattie, L., Kyle, S., Espie, C., & Biello, S. (2015). Social interactions, emotion and sleep: A systematic review and research agenda. *Sleep Medicine Reviews, 24*, 83–100. doi:10.1016/j.smrv.2014.12.005

Blomfield-Neira, C. J., & Barber, B. L. (2014). Social networking site use: Linked to adolescents' social self-concept, self-esteem, and depressed mood. *Australian Journal of Psychology, 66*(1), 56–64. doi:10.1111/ajpy.12034

Brown, R. I. F. (1987). Classical and operant paradigms in the management of gambling addictions. *Behavioural Psychotherapy, 15*(02), 111–122. doi:10.1017/S0141347300011204

Buckhalt, J. A., El-Sheikh, M., Keller, P. S., & Kelly, R. J. (2009). Concurrent and longitudinal relations between children's sleep and cognitive functioning: The moderating role of parent education. *Child Development, 80*(3), 875–892. doi:10.1111/j.1467-8624.2009.01303.x

Cain, N., & Gradisar, M. (2010). Electronic media use and sleep in school-aged children and adolescents: A review. *Sleep Medicine, 11*(8), 735–742. doi:10.1016/j.sleep.2010.02.006

Calamaro, C. J., Mason, T. B., & Ratcliffe, S. J. (2009). Adolescents living the 24/7 lifestyle: Effects of caffeine and technology on sleep duration and daytime functioning. *Pediatrics, 123*(6), 1005–1010. doi:10.1542/peds.2008-3641

Carney, C. E., & Moss, T. G. (2014). Sleep disorders and depression. In C. S. Richards & M. W. O'Hara (Eds.), *The Oxford handbook of depression and comorbidity* (pp. 349–366). New York, NY: Oxford University Press. doi:10.1093/oxfordhb/9780199797004.013.012

Carskadon, M. A. (2002). Factors influencing sleep patterns of adolescents. In M. A. Carskadon (Ed.), *Adolescent sleep patterns: Biological, social, and psychological influences* (pp. 4–26). New York, NY: Cambridge University Press.

Carskadon, M. A. (2011). Sleep in adolescents: The perfect storm. *Pediatric Clinics of North America, 58*(3), 637–647. doi:10.1016/j.pcl.2011.03.003

Cheong, J., MacKinnon, D. P., & Khoo, S. T. (2003). Investigation of mediational processes using parallel process latent growth curve modeling. *Structural Equation Modeling: A Multidisciplinary Journal, 10*(2), 238–262. doi:10.1207/S15328007SEM1002_5

Dahl, R. E., & Lewin, D. S. (2002). Pathways to adolescent health sleep regulation and behavior. *Journal of Adolescent Health, 31*(6), 175–184. doi:10.1016/S1054139X(02)00506-2

Dubas, J. S., Graber, J. A., & Petersen, A. C. (1991). A longitudinal investigation of adolescents' changing perceptions of pubertal timing. *Developmental Psychology, 27*(4), 580–586. doi:10.1037/0012-1649.27.4.580

Durkin, K., & Barber, B. (2002). Not so doomed: Computer game play and positive adolescent development. *Journal of Applied Developmental Psychology, 23*(4), 373–392. doi:10.1016/S0193-3973(02)00124-7

Eggermont, S., & Van den Bulck, J. (2006). Nodding off or switching off? The use of popular media as a sleep aid in secondary-school children. *Journal of Paediatrics and Child Health, 42*, 428–433. doi:10.1111/j.14401754.2006.00892

Ellison, N. B., Steinfield, C., & Lampe, C. (2007). The benefits of Facebook "friends:" Social capital and college students' use of online social network sites. *Journal of Computer-Mediated Communication, 12* (4), 1143–1168. doi:10.1111/j.10836101.2007.00367

Ellison, N. B., Steinfield, C., & Lampe, C. (2011). Connection strategies: Social capital implications of Facebook-enabled communication practices. *New Media & Society, 14*, 1–10. doi:10.1177/1461444810385389

Exelmans, L., & Van den Bulck, J. (2015). Technology and sleep: How electronic media exposure has impacted core concepts of sleep medicine. *Behavioral Sleep Medicine, 13*(6), 439–441. doi:10.1080/15402002.2015.1083025

Fredricks, J. A., & Eccles, J. S. (2006). Is extracurricular participation associated with beneficial outcomes? Concurrent and longitudinal relations. *Developmental Psychology, 42*(4), 698–713. doi:10.1037/0012-1649.42.4.698

Fredriksen, K., Rhodes, J., Reddy, R., & Way, N. (2004). Sleepless in Chicago: Tracking the effects of adolescent sleep loss during the middle school years. *Child Development, 75*(1), 84–95. doi:10.1111/j.1467-8624.2004.00655

Fuligni, A. J., & Hardway, C. (2006). Daily variation in adolescents' sleep, activities, and psychological well-being. *Journal of Research on Adolescence, 16*(3), 353–378. doi:10.1111/j.1532-7795.2006.00498

Gradisar, M., & Short, M. A. (2013). Sleep hygiene and environment: The role of technology. In A. R. Wolfson & H. Montgomery-Downs (Eds.), *Oxford handbook of infant, child, and adolescent sleep and behavior* (pp. 113–126). Oxford, UK: Oxford University Press.

Griffiths, M. D. (2013). Social networking addiction: Emerging themes and issues. *Journal of Addiction Research & Therapy, 4*(5), 1–2. doi:10.4172/2155-6105.1000e118

Hale, L., & Guan, S. (2015). Screen time and sleep among school-aged children and adolescents: A systematic literature review. *Sleep Medicine Reviews, 21*, 50–58. doi:10.1016/j.smrv.2014.07.007

Hirshkowitz, M., Whiton, K., Albert, S. M., Alessi, C., Bruni, O., DonCarlos, L., … Adams Hillard, P. J. (2015). National Sleep Foundation's sleep time duration recommendations: Methodology and results summary. *Sleep Health, 1*, 40–43. doi:10.1016/j.sleh.2014.12.010

Hu, L. T., & Bentler, P. M. (1999). Cutoff criteria for fit indexes in covariance structure analysis: Conventional criteria versus new alternatives. *Structural Equation Modeling: A Multidisciplinary Journal*, *6*(1), 1–55. doi:10.1080/10705519909540118

Hunter, S. C., Durkin, K., Boyle, J. M. E., Booth, J. N., & Rasmussen, S. (2014). Adolescent bullying and sleep difficulties. *Europe's Journal of Psychology*, *10*(4), 740–755. doi:10.5964/ejop.v10i4.815

Israelashvili, M., Kim, T., & Bukobza, G. (2012). Adolescents' over-use of the cyber world–internet addiction or identity exploration? *Journal of Adolescence*, *35*(2), 417–424. doi:10.1016/j.adolescence.2011.07.015

Kahn, M., Sheppes, G., & Sadeh, A. (2013). Sleep and emotions: Bidirectional links and underlying mechanisms. *International Journal of Psychophysiology*, *89*(2), 218–228. doi:10.1016/j.ijpsycho.2013.05.010

Kelley, P., Lockley, S. W., Foster, R. G., & Kelley, J. (2015). Synchronizing education to adolescent biology: 'Let teens sleep, start school later'. *Learning, Media and Technology*, *40*(2), 210–226. doi:10.1080/17439884.2014.942666

King, D. L., Delfabbro, P. H., Zwaans, T., & Kaptsis, D. (2013). Clinical features and axis I comorbidity of Australian adolescent pathological Internet and video game users. *Australian & New Zealand Journal of Psychiatry*, *47*(11), 1058–1067. doi:10.1177/0004867413491159

Kuss, D. J., & Griffiths, M. D. (2011). Online social networking and addiction-a review of the psychological literature. *International Journal of Environmental Research and Public Health*, *8*(9), 3528–3552. doi:10.3390/ijerph8093528

Lee, K. T., Noh, M. J., & Koo, D. M. (2013). Lonely people are no longer lonely on social networking sites: The mediating role of self-disclosure and social support. *Cyberpsychology, Behavior, and Social Networking*, *16*(6), 413–418. doi:10.1089/cyber.2012.0553

Lemola, S., Perkinson-Gloor, N., Brand, S., Dewald-Kaufmann, J. F., & Grob, A. (2015). Adolescents' electronic media use at night, sleep disturbance, and depressive symptoms in the smartphone age. *Journal of Youth and Adolescence*, *44*(2), 405–418. doi:10.1007/s10964-014-0176-x

Lenhart, A. (2015). *Teens, social media & technology: Overview 2015*. Retrieved from http://www.pewinternet.org/2015/04/09/teens-social-media-technology-2015

Littlefield, A. K., Sher, K. J., & Wood, P. K. (2010). Do changes in drinking motives mediate the relation between personality change and "maturing out" of problem drinking? *Journal of Abnormal Psychology*, *119*(1), 93–105. doi:10.1037/a0017512

Liu, C., & Yu, C. (2013). Can Facebook use induce well-being? *Cyberpsychology, Behavior and Social Networking*, *16*(9), 674–678. doi:10.1089/cyber.2012.0301

MacKinnon, D. P. (2008). *Introduction to statistical mediation analysis*. New York, NY: Erlbaum.

McCracken, J. T. (2002). The search for vulnerability signatures for depression in high-risk adolescents: Mechanisms and significance. In M. A. Carskadon (Ed.), *Adolescent sleep patterns: Biological, social, and psychological influences* (pp. 254–268). New York, NY: Cambridge Press.

Mikami, A. Y., Szwedo, D. E., Allen, J. P., Evans, M. A., & Hare, A. L. (2010). Adolescent peer relationships and behavior problems predict young adults' communication on social networking websites. *Developmental Psychology*, *46*(1), 46–56. doi:10.1037/a0017420

Milani, L., Osualdella, D., & Di Blasio, P. (2009). Quality of interpersonal relationships and problematic Internet use in adolescence. *Cyberpsychology & Behavior*, *12*(6), 681–684. doi:10.1089/cpb.2009.0071

Modecki, K. L., Barber, B. L., & Eccles, J. S. (2014). Binge drinking trajectories across adolescence: For early maturing youth, extra-curricular activities are protective. *Journal of Adolescent Health*, *54*(1), 61–66. doi:10.1016/j.jadohealth.2013.07.032

Modecki, K. L., Barber, B. L., & Vernon, L. (2013). Mapping developmental precursors of cyber-aggression: Trajectories of risk predict perpetration and victimization. *Journal of Youth and Adolescence*, *42*(5), 651–661. doi:10.1007/s10964-012-9887-z

Modecki, K. L., Minchin, J., Harbaugh, G., Guerra, N., & Runions, K. C. (2014). Bullying prevalence across contexts: A meta-analysis measuring cyber and traditional bullying. *Journal of Adolescent Health*, *55*(5), 602–611. doi:10.1016/j.jadohealth.2014.06.007

Modecki, K. L., Zimmer-Gembeck, M., & Guerra, N. (in press). Emotion regulation, coping and decision-making: Three linked skills for preventing externalizing problems in adolescence. *Child Development*.

Munezawa, T., Kaneita, Y., Osaki, Y., Kanda, H., Minowa, M., Suzuki, K., ... Ohida, T. (2011). The association between use of mobile phones after lights out and sleep disruptions among Japanese adolescents: A nationwide cross-sectional survey. *Sleep*, *34*(8), 1013. doi:10.5665/SLEEP.1152

Muthén, B. O. (2007). Standardized coefficients in *Mplus*. Retrieved from http://statmodel2.com/download/StandardizedCoefficients.pdf

Muthén, L. K., & Muthén, B. O. (1998-2012). *Mplus user's guide*. Los Angeles, CA: Muthén & Muthén.

Nalwa, K., & Anand, A. P. (2003). Internet addiction in students: A cause of concern. *Cyberpsychology and Behavior*, *6*(6), 653–656. doi:10.1089/109493103322725441

National Sleep Foundation. (2011). *Sleep in America poll: Communications technology and sleep*. Washington, DC: Author. Retrieved from https://sleepfoundation.org/

Preacher, K. J., & Hayes, A. F. (2008). Asymptotic and resampling strategies for assessing and comparing indirect effects in multiple mediator models. *Behavior Research Methods*, *40*(3), 879–891. doi:10.3758/BRM.40.3.879

Rideout, V. J. (2015). *The common sense census: Media use by tweens and teens*. Retrieved from https://www.commonsensemedia.org/

Rideout, V. J., Foehr, U. G., & Roberts, D. F. (2010). *Generation* M^2*: Media in the lives of 8-to 18-year-olds* (ERIC No. 527859). Retrieved from: http://eric.ed.gov/?id=ED527859

Sadeh, A., Gruber, R., & Raviv, A. (2002). Sleep, neurobehavioral functioning, and behavior problems in school-age children. *Child Development*, *73*(2), 405–417. doi:10.1111/14678624.00414

Shapiro, L. A. S., & Margolin, G. (2014). Growing up wired: Social networking sites and adolescent psychosocial development. *Clinical Child and Family Psychology Review*, *17*(1), 1–18. doi:10.1007/s10567-013-0135-1

Shochat, T., Cohen-Zion, M., & Tzischinsky, O. (2014). Functional consequences of inadequate sleep in adolescents: A systematic review. *Sleep Medicine Reviews*, *18*(1), 75–87. doi:10.1016/j.smrv.2013.03.005

Short, M. A., Gradisar, M., Lack, L. C., Wright, H. R., & Chatburn, A. (2013). Estimating adolescent sleep patterns: Parent reports versus adolescent self-report surveys, sleep diaries, and actigraphy. *Nature and Science of Sleep*, *5*, 23–26. doi:10.2147/NSS.S38369

Steers, M. L. N., Wickham, R. E., & Acitelli, L. K. (2014). Seeing everyone else's highlight reels: How Facebook usage is linked to depressive symptoms. *Journal of Social and Clinical Psychology*, *33*, 701–731. doi:10.1521/jscp.2014.33.8.701

Suganuma, N., Kikuchi, T., Yanagi, K., Yamamura, S., Morishima, H., Adachi, H., ... Takeda, M. (2007). Using electronic media before sleep can curtail sleep time and result in self-perceived insufficient sleep. *Sleep and Biological Rhythms*, *5*, 204–214. doi:10.1111/j.1479-8425.2007.00276.x

Talbot, L. S., McGlinchey, E. L., Kaplan, K. A., Dahl, R. E., & Harvey, A. G. (2010). Sleep deprivation in adolescents and adults: Changes in affect. *Emotion*, *10*, 831–841. doi:10.1037/a0020138

Tandoc, E. C., Ferrucci, P., & Duffy, M. (2015). Facebook use, envy, and depression among college students: Is facebooking depressing? *Computers in Human Behavior*, *43*, 139–146. doi:10.1016/j.chb.2014.10.053

Tate, B. A., Richardson, G. S., & Carskadon, M. A. (2004). Maturational changes in sleep-wake timing: Longitudinal studies of the circadian activity rhythm of a diurnal rodent. In M. A. Carskadon (Ed.), *Adolescent sleep patterns: Biological, social, and psychological influences* (pp. 40–49). New York, NY: Cambridge University Press.

Tavernier, R., & Willoughby, T. (2014). Sleep problems: Predictor or outcome of media use among emerging adults at university? *Journal of Sleep Research*, *23*(4), 389–396. doi:10.1111/jsr.12132

Tochigi, M., Nishida, A., Shimodera, S., Oshima, N., Inoue, K., Okazaki, Y., & Sasaki, T. (2012). Irregular bedtime and nocturnal cellular phone usage as risk factors for being involved in bullying: A cross-sectional survey of Japanese adolescents. *PLoS One*, *7*, e45736. doi:10.1371/journal.pone.0045736

Valkenburg, P. M., Peter, J., & Schouten, A. P. (2006). Friend networking sites and their relationship to adolescents' well-being and social self-esteem. *Cyberpsychology & Behavior*, *9*(5), 584–590. doi:10.1089/cpb.2006.9.584

Van den Bulck, J. (2000). Is television bad for your health? Behavior and body image of the adolescent "couch potato". *Journal of Youth and Adolescence*, *29*(3), 273–288. doi:10.1023/A:1005102523848

Van den Bulck, J. (2004). Television viewing, computer game playing, and Internet use and self-reported time to bed and time out of bed in secondary-school children. *Sleep*, *27*(1), 101–104.

Van den Bulck, J. (2007). Adolescent use of mobile phones for calling and for sending text messages after lights out: Results from a prospective cohort study with a one-year follow-up. *Sleep*, *30*(9), 1220.

Vernon, L., Barber, B. L., & Modecki, K. L. (2015). Adolescent problematic social networking and school experiences: The mediating effects of sleep disruptions and sleep quality. *Cyberpsychology, Behavior and Social Networking*, *18*(7), 386–392. doi:10.1089/cyber.2015.0107

von Soest, T., & Hagtvet, K. A. (2011). Mediation analysis in a latent growth curve modeling framework. *Structural Equation Modeling: A Multidisciplinary Journal*, *18*(2), 289–314. doi:10.1080/10705511.2011.557344

Wang, J., Nansel, T. R., & Iannotti, R. J. (2011). Cyber and traditional bullying: Differential association with depression. *Journal of Adolescent Health*, *48*(4), 415–417. doi:10.1016/j.jadohealth.2010.07.012

Warner, S., Murray, G., & Meyer, D. (2008). Holiday and school-term sleep patterns of Australian adolescents. *Journal of Adolescence*, *31*(5), 595–608. doi:10.1016/j.adolescence.2007.10.005

Wolfson, A. R., & Carskadon, M. A. (1998). Sleep schedules and daytime functioning in adolescents. *Child Development*, *69*(4), 875–887. doi:10.2307/1132351

Wolfson, A. R., & Carskadon, M. A. (2003). Understanding adolescent's sleep patterns and school performance: A critical appraisal. *Sleep Medicine Reviews*, *7*(6), 491–506. doi:10.1016/S1087-0792(03)90003-7

Wolniczak, I., Cáceres-DelAguila, J. A., Palma-Ardiles, G., Arroyo, K. J., Solís-Visscher, R., Paredes-Yauri, S., ... Bernabe-Ortiz, A. (2013). Association between Facebook dependence and poor sleep quality: A study in a sample of undergraduate students in Peru. *PLoS One*, *8*(3), e59087. doi:10.1371/journal.pone.0059087

Wood, B., Rea, M. S., Plitnick, B., & Figueiro, M. G. (2013). Light level and duration of exposure determine the impact of self-luminous tablets on melatonin suppression. *Applied Ergonomics*, *44*(2), 237–240. doi:10.1016/j.apergo.2012.07.008

Young, K. S. (1998). Internet addiction: The emergence of a new clinical disorder. *CyberPsychology & Behavior*, *1*(3), 237–244. doi:10.1089/cpb.1998.1.237

Yuan, K., & Bentler, P. M. (2000). Three likelihood-based methods for mean and covariance structure analysis with nonnormal missing data. *Sociological Methodology*, *30*(1), 165–200. doi:10.1111/0081-1750.00078

Zimmerman, F. J. (2008). *Children's media use and sleep problems: Issues and unanswered questions* (Research Brief). Retrieved from http://files.eric.ed.gov/fulltext/ED527857.pdf

ADHD and Sleep Quality: Longitudinal Analyses From Childhood to Early Adulthood in a Twin Cohort

Alice M. Gregory

Jessica C. Agnew-Blais and Timothy Matthews

Terrie E. Moffitt

Louise Arseneault

Attention-deficit/hyperactivity disorder (ADHD) is associated with poor sleep quality, but there is more to learn about the longitudinal association and aetiology of this association. We investigated the following: (a) Is there an association between childhood ADHD and poor sleep quality in young adulthood? (b) Is this driven by the long-term effects of childhood ADHD or concurrent associations with ADHD in young adulthood? (c) To what extent do genetic and environmental influences explain the overlap between symptoms of ADHD and poor sleep quality? Participants were from the Environmental Risk Longitudinal Twin Study of 2,232 twin children born in the United Kingdom in 1994–1995. We ascertained ADHD diagnoses at ages 5, 7, 10, 12, and 18. We assessed sleep quality using the Pittsburgh Sleep Quality Index at age 18. We used regression models to examine longitudinal associations and bivariate twin modelling to test genetic and environmental influences. Children with ADHD had poorer sleep quality in young adulthood, but only if their ADHD persisted. Adults with ADHD had more sleep problems than those without ADHD, over and above psychiatric comorbidity and maternal insomnia. ADHD and sleep problems in young adulthood were associated because of genetic (55%) and nonshared environmental influences (45%). Should ADHD remit, children with ADHD do not appear to have an increased risk of later sleep problems. Good quality sleep is important for multiple areas of functioning, and a better understanding of why adults with ADHD have poorer sleep quality will further the goal of improving treatments.

INTRODUCTION

ADHD and Sleep Quality

Children with attention-deficit/hyperactivity disorder (ADHD) experience poorer sleep quality compared to those without this disorder (Sung, Hiscock, Sciberras, & Efron, 2008; Yoon, Jain, & Shapiro, 2012). Parents of children with ADHD can find sleep problems a particularly challenging feature of looking after their offspring (Cortese, 2015), and sleep problems in children with ADHD may be associated with poorer family functioning (Sung et al., 2008). Although historically sleep disturbances have often been overlooked and considered an unimportant secondary consequence of mental and physical health problems, this view is now outdated. Sleep is important, and poor sleep quality assessed at certain stages over the life course has been associated with multiple areas of psychological functioning including psychiatric disorders (Gregory & Sadeh, 2016) and poor academic performance (Curcio, Ferrara, & DeGennaro, 2006; Dewald, Meijer, Oort, Kerkhof, & Bogels, 2010). Atypical sleep length or poor sleep quality has also been associated with markers of physical health problems including obesity (e.g. Patel & Hu, 2008), metabolic syndrome (Jennings, Muldoon, Hall, Buysse, & Manuck, 2007), and even mortality (Cappuccio, D'Elia, Strazzullo, & Miller, 2010).

Although concurrent associations between childhood ADHD and sleep disturbances are well-established (Yoon et al., 2012), less is known about the longitudinal associations between these problems (Cortese, 2015). What little longitudinal research there is has proved informative (Gregory, Van den Ende, Willis, & Verhulst, 2008; Hansen, Skirbekk, Oerbeck, Wentzel-Larsen, & Kristensen, 2013; Scott et al., 2013; Touchette et al., 2007). For example, one study demonstrated that ADHD severity predicted persistent sleep problems in children (Lycett, Mensah, Hiscock, & Sciberras, 2014). Another revealed that severe sleep problems in infancy predicted ADHD at 5 years of age (Thunstrom, 2002). Our own work in this area showed bidirectional associations between ADHD symptoms and sleep disturbance at age 4 and preadolescence (Gregory & O'Connor, 2002). In another study, we found that adults 38 years of age with insomnia did not appear to have a developmental history of ADHD but were instead more likely to have suffered from anxiety and depression during their youth (Goldman-Mellor et al., 2014). Results focusing on different developmental periods produce mixed results, and there is scarce evidence of the longitudinal association between sleep quality and ADHD from childhood to adulthood, perhaps partially because ADHD has been extensively believed to be a childhood disorder.

Given the great significance of sleep quality for functioning in multiple domains in adulthood, one important question in need of further investigation is whether children with ADHD are likely to have poor sleep quality later in life. On one hand, we note that in many cases ADHD does not persist over time (Agnew-Blais et al., 2016; Faraone, Biederman, & Mick, 2006; Moffitt et al., 2015), and it is possible that once ADHD has remitted, sleep disturbances do as well. On the other hand, it is possible that sleep disturbances develop, or persist, independent of the course of ADHD. For example, children with sleep disturbances may develop negative associations with their bedrooms and bedtime that result in long-term sleep problems, regardless of change in ADHD status. Studies to date have not fully addressed this question due to typically short follow-up periods, and there have been calls to further examine associations between ADHD and sleep across developmental stages (Cortese, 2015). Although concurrent associations between ADHD and sleep quality have been reported in both children and adults (Yoon et al., 2012), the adult period is relatively underresearched and the question of whether children with ADHD have sleep disturbances in young adulthood has not been thoroughly tested.

Mechanisms Underlying Associations Between Sleep Quality and ADHD

Explanations for the associations between sleep quality and ADHD are plentiful (for a general discussion of comorbidity, see Angold, Costello, & Erkanli, 1999). For example, it is possible that ADHD could lead to poor sleep quality; indeed, stimulant medication prescribed for ADHD can lead to sleep difficulties (Cortese et al., 2013). Another explanation focuses on common pathways influencing both ADHD and sleep quality, including common neurobiological pathways involved in arousal (Yoon et al., 2012). Although shared genetic mechanisms between ADHD and sleep have been proposed, there is relatively little behavioural genetic research exploring this association (for a review of twin studies focusing on sleep and associated difficulties, see Barclay & Gregory, 2013). What little research there is has focused on childhood, with one study suggesting that early links between sleep disturbance and ADHD symptoms could be largely due to environmental influences (Van den Oord, Boomsma, & Verhulst, 2000). Another study suggested that a functional polymorphism of the catechol-O-methyltransferase gene may be involved in risk of poor sleep continuity (e.g., reduced sleep efficiency) in those with ADHD (Gruber et al., 2006).

Research Questions

The aim of this study was to examine the longitudinal association between ADHD and sleep quality and to explore the genetic and environmental underpinnings of this association. Specifically, we tested (a) whether childhood ADHD is associated with poor sleep quality in young adulthood, (b) if the association between childhood ADHD and poorer sleep quality at age 18 is explained by ADHD in adulthood, and (c) the extent to which genetic and environmental influences explain the overlap between ADHD and sleep quality.

METHODS

Study Cohort

Participants were members of the Environmental Risk (E-Risk) Longitudinal Twin Study, which tracks the development of a birth cohort of 2,232 British children. The sample was drawn from a larger birth register of twins born in England and Wales in 1994–1995 (Trouton, Spinath, &

Plomin, 2002). The E-Risk sample was constructed in 1999–2000, when 1,116 families (93% of those eligible) with same-sex 5-year-old twins participated in home-visit assessments. This sample comprised 55% monozygotic and 45% dizygotic twin pairs; sex was evenly distributed within zygosity (49% male). Families were recruited to represent the UK population with newborns in the 1990s, on the basis of residential location throughout England and Wales and mother's age. Teenage mothers with twins were overselected to replace high-risk families who were selectively lost to the register through nonresponse. Older mothers having twins via assisted reproduction were underselected to avoid an excess of well-educated older mothers. Full details about the sample are reported elsewhere (Moffitt & Erisk Study Team, 2002).

Follow-up home visits were conducted when the children were ages 7 (98% participation), 10 (96%), 12 (96%), and 18 years (93%). The families were contacted by phone to arrange visits and received vouchers to acknowledge the time they spent for the interview. With parents' permission, questionnaires were mailed to the children's teachers, who returned questionnaires for 94% of children at age 5, 93% of those followed up at age 7, 90% at age 10, and 83% at age 12. We interviewed 2,066 participants when they were age 18. There were no differences between those who did and did not take part at age 18 in socioeconomic status when the cohort was initially defined ($\chi^2 = .86$, $p = .65$), or age-5 IQ ($t = .98$, $p = .33$), internalizing or externalizing problems ($t = .40$, $p = .69$ and $t = .41$, $p = .68$, respectively). Home visits at ages 5, 7, 10, and 12 years included assessments with participants and their mothers; home visits at age 18 included interviews only with participants. We asked participants to identify individuals who know them well to act as coinformants; 99.3% had coinformant data. The Joint South London and Maudsley and the Institute of Psychiatry Research Ethics Committee approved each phase of the study. Parents gave informed consent and twins gave assent between 5 and 12 years and then informed consent at age 18.

At follow-up, the study sample represented the full range of socioeconomic conditions in the United Kingdom, as reflected in the families' distribution on a neighborhood-level socioeconomic index (ACORN [A Classification of Residential Neighbourhoods], developed by CACI Inc. for commercial use in Great Britain; Odgers, Caspi, Russell, et al., 2012). ACORN uses census and other survey-based geodemographic discriminators to classify enumeration districts (~150 households) into socioeconomic groups ranging from "wealthy achievers" (Category 1) with high incomes, large single-family houses, and access to many amenities, to "hard-pressed" neighborhoods (Category 5) dominated by government-subsidized housing estates, low incomes, high unemployment, and single parents. ACORN classifications were geocoded to match the location of each E-Risk Study family's home (Odgers, Caspi, Bates, Sampson, & Moffitt, 2012). E-Risk families' ACORN distribution closely matches that of households nationwide: 25.6% of E-Risk families live in "wealthy achiever" neighborhoods compared to 25.3% nationwide, 5.3% versus 11.6% live in "urban prosperity" neighborhoods, 29.6% versus 26.9% live in "comfortably off" neighborhoods, 13.4% versus 13.9% live in "moderate means" neighborhoods, and 26.1% versus 20.7% live in "hard-pressed" neighborhoods. E-Risk underrepresents "urban prosperity" neighborhoods because such households are likely to be childless. The majority of E-Risk Study participants consider themselves White (90.4%).

ADHD

We ascertained ADHD diagnosis in childhood on the basis of mother and teacher reports of 18 symptoms of inattention and hyperactivity-impulsivity according to the criteria outlined in the *Diagnostic and Statistical Manual of Mental Disorders* (4th ed. [*DSM-IV*]; American Psychiatric Association, 1994; Caspi et al., 2008; Kuntsi et al., 2004; Polanczyk et al., 2010).We considered participants to have a diagnosis of childhood ADHD if they met criteria at age 5, 7, 10, or 12. Participants who had ADHD information on at least two childhood assessments and did not meet diagnostic criteria at any available assessment were classified as not having childhood ADHD. In total, 247 participants (12.1%) met criteria for ADHD in childhood.

We ascertained ADHD diagnosis at age 18 based on private structured interviews with participants regarding 18 symptoms of inattention and hyperactivity-impulsivity according to *DSM-5* criteria (American Psychiatric Association, 2013). Symptoms were reported for the preceding 12 months. Participants had to endorse five or more inattentive and/or five or more hyperactivity–impulsivity symptoms to be diagnosed. We also required that symptoms interfered with individual's "life at home, or with family and friends" and "life at school or work" as rated 3 or higher on a scale from 1 (*mild interference*) to 5 (*severe*), thereby meeting criteria for impairment and pervasiveness. The *DSM-5* requirement of symptom onset prior to age 12 was met if parents or teachers reported more than 2 ADHD symptoms at ages 5, 7, 10, or 12.We identified 166 (8.1 %) participants with ADHD at age 18. We also collected information from coinformants (most frequently from participants' mothers and co-twins) who rated participants on 8 ADHD symptoms at age 18.

Combining information from childhood and adult ADHD, we identified three mutually exclusive groups (Agnew-Blais et al., 2016): persistent ADHD (ADHD in childhood and at age 18, $n = 54$), remitted ADHD (ADHD in childhood, but not at age 18, $n = 193$), and late-onset ADHD (ADHD at age 18 only, $n = 112$). A total of 1,681 (82.4%) participants did not meet criteria for ADHD in childhood or adulthood.

Sleep Quality

At 18 years of age, sleep disturbance over the past month was assessed using the Pittsburgh Sleep Quality Index (PSQI; Buysse, Reynolds, Monk, Berman, & Kupger, 1989), which is a questionnaire measure containing 18 items. Items include both open-ended questions (e.g., "During the past month, when have you usually gone to bed at night?") and fixed-choice questions ("During the past month, how would you rate your sleep quality overall? 'Very good; Fairly good; Fairly bad or Very bad'?"). Questions tap a range of aspects of sleep quality and can be used to derive seven component scores (subjective sleep quality, sleep latency, sleep duration, habitual sleep efficiency, sleep disturbances, use of sleep medications, and daytime dysfunction), as well as a global score. Higher scores on this measure reflect poorer sleep quality. The PSQI is reported to have internal consistency and test–retest reliability in the .8 range (Backhaus, Junghanns, Broocks, Riemann, & Hohagen, 2002; Buysse et al., 1989; Carpenter & Andrykowski, 1998). In the current sample, the mean was 5.39 (*SD* = 3.18), and the Cronbach's alpha was .69. A substantial proportion (39.9%) of the participants scored higher than 5 on the PSQI, which has been proposed as a clinical cutoff (Buysse et al., 1989). The PSQI score correlates highly with other measures of sleep such as sleep diary data (Backhaus et al., 2002).

Covariates

At age 12, participants' mothers were asked about insomnia. Mothers reported on their symptoms of insomnia in a private standardized interview. A diagnosis of insomnia was derived based largely on the criteria outlined by the *DSM-IV* (American Psychiatric Association, 1994). Specifically, mothers were asked if they themselves experienced difficulty falling asleep, difficulty staying asleep, or problems waking too early. Answers were provided on a 5-point scale: 0 (*none*), 1 (*mild*), 2 (*moderate*), 3 (*severe*), and 4 (*very severe*). Mothers were also asked, "How much do sleep problems interfere with your daily functioning?" from 1 (*not at all*) to 5 (*very much*). If mothers reported a sleep difficulty that they considered to be "severe" or "very severe" and reported an interference score at or greater than 3, they were considered to have insomnia. Based on these criteria, 9.6% of mothers reported themselves to have insomnia.

Participants were evaluated at the age-18 interview for the presence of depressive disorder, generalized anxiety disorder, alcohol dependence, cannabis dependence, and conduct disorder (at least moderate) over the previous 12 months according to *DSM-IV* criteria (American Psychiatric Association, 1994). For the generalized anxiety disorder diagnosis, we did not require the 6-month symptom duration criterion because of the youth of our study sample. Assessments were conducted in face-to-face interviews using the Diagnostic Interview Schedule (Robins, Cottler, Bucholz, & Compton, 1995). The assessment of conduct disorder was conducted as part of a computer-assisted module. In addition, at age 18, participants were asked whether they had young children (*N* = 41) and were queried about ADHD medication use (*N* = 13).

Statistical Analyses

To determine whether childhood ADHD was associated with poorer sleep quality at age 18, we used linear regression with childhood ADHD diagnosis predicting age-18 PSQI total score, adjusting for the participant's sex and childhood social class. To test whether the association between childhood ADHD and age-18 sleep quality was accounted for by young adult ADHD, we additionally adjusted for age-18 ADHD diagnosis in the prior model. To further illustrate these findings, we compared sleep quality among individuals with no ADHD, persistent, remitted, and late-onset ADHD at age 18. To investigate whether psychiatric comorbidities at age 18 explain the association between ADHD and poorer sleep quality, we additionally adjusted for age-18 mental health problems. Furthermore, we controlled for potential genetic confounding by adjusting for maternal insomnia. Finally, we performed sensitivity analyses excluding participants currently taking ADHD medication and those with young children, and conducted analyses using co-informant ratings of ADHD symptoms at age 18 in place of self-report. We did not find significant interactions between sex and either childhood or young adult ADHD in predicting sleep quality at age 18; therefore we present findings across both genders. Analyses were conducted in STATA (StataCorp, 2009) and accounted for nonindependence of the clustered twin observations using the Huber/White variance estimator (Williams, 2000).

We used twin modelling to examine the nature of the association between ADHD and sleep quality (Rijsdijk & Sham, 2002). Twin studies compare the similarity of MZ twin pairs to the similarity of DZ twin pairs to estimate genetic and environmental influences on traits. Because MZ twins share 100% of their genes and DZ twins share on average half of their segregating genes, the difference in the MZ versus DZ twin correlation is used to estimate the relative contribution of additive genetic influences (A; where alleles "add up" to influence behaviour), shared environmental influences (C; environmental influences that act to make individuals within a family alike), and nonshared environmental influences (E; environmental influences that act to make individuals within a family different; this source of variance also includes measurement error). If the correlation between MZ pairs is greater than that of DZ pairs, genetic influences are playing a role. DZ twin correlations greater than half the size of the MZ correlations suggest that shared environment is important, whereas MZ correlations below 1 indicate the influence of nonshared environment (see Plomin, DeFries, Knopik, & Neiderhiser, 2013).

Model-fitting was conducted in the program OpenMx, a widely used programme for analysing behavioural genetic data (Boker et al., 2011). For our twin analyses, we focused on a *symptom* count for both variables. This is considered to be the optimal method when running twin analyses in order to maximise power and for computational simplicity. A Cholesky decomposition was fitted to estimate the effects of A, C, and E on ADHD symptoms and sleep quality. This was interpreted as a correlated factors solution (Loehlin, 1996), which allows the genetic and environmental influences on these phenotypes to correlate. The fit of more parsimonious submodels can be tested by dropping parameters and comparing the fit statistic of the submodel, provided as minus twice the log-likelihood (−2LL), against that of the full ACE model. We tested a model containing genetic and nonshared environmental influences only (an AE model) to determine whether we could drop the C parameters without a significant deterioration in fit. Information about the precision of parameter estimates (and their explained variance) was obtained by likelihood-based 95% confidence intervals (CIs).

RESULTS

Longitudinal Associations Between ADHD and Sleep Quality

Individuals with a diagnosis of ADHD in childhood had poorer sleep quality in young adulthood ($\beta = .07$, 95% CIs [.02, .12], $p = .006$), (Table 1). After adjusting for ADHD diagnosis in adulthood, we found that childhood ADHD was no longer associated with age-18 sleep quality ($\beta = .03$, 95% CIs [–.01, .08], $p = .143$), whereas young adult ADHD was significantly associated with poorer sleep quality ($\beta = .19$, 95% CIs [.14, .25], $p < .001$). This indicates that the persistence of ADHD explains the association between childhood ADHD and later sleep quality: Children with ADHD have poor quality sleep when they reach young adulthood only if they have persistent ADHD. This finding is illustrated in Figure 1, which compares sleep quality among individuals with no ADHD, persistent, remitted, and late-onset ADHD. Compared to the group without ADHD, the persistent and late-onset groups had poorer sleep quality in adulthood; however, among those with remitted ADHD, sleep quality was not significantly different from individuals who never had ADHD.

The association between young adult ADHD and poor sleep quality remained after simultaneous adjustment for a wide range of comorbid mental health problems (Table 1). This is particularly noteworthy, as each of the mental health problems examined, with the exception of cannabis dependence, was associated with poor sleep quality (Table 1). Furthermore, we found the association remained when adjusting for maternal insomnia (Table 1). To explore the association between young adult ADHD and sleep quality further, we distinguished hyperactive/impulsive and inattentive symptoms to test whether sleep quality was associated with a

TABLE 1
Results of Regression Analyses Predicting Sleep Quality

	Sleep Quality			
	Model 1 (Childhood ADHD)	*Model 2 (+ Adult ADHD)*	*Model 3 (+ Psychiatric Comorbidity)*	*Model 4 (+ Maternal Insomnia)*
	β [95% CI]	β [95% CI]	β [95% CI]	β [95% CI]
Childhood ADHD Diagnosis	0.07** [0.02, 0.12]	0.03 [−0.01, 0.08]	0.01 [−0.03, 0.05]	0.01 [−0.03, 0.06]
Young Adult ADHD Diagnosis		0.19*** [0.14, 0.25]	0.12*** [0.06, 0.17]	0.12*** [0.06, 0.17]
Depression			0.23*** [0.18, 0.28]	0.22*** [0.17, 0.27]
Generalized Anxiety Disorder			0.10*** [0.05, 0.15]	0.11*** [0.06, 0.16]
Cannabis Dependence			0.04† [−0.01, 0.09]	0.04† [−0.01, 0.09]
Alcohol Abuse			0.06** [0.02, 0.10]	0.06** [0.02, 0.10]
Conduct Disorder			0.10*** [0.05, 0.15]	0.10*** [0.05, 0.16]
Maternal Insomnia				0.07** [0.03, 0.12]

Note: All models are adjusted for sex and social class; each regression model builds upon the last, adding additional variables. Childhood attention-deficit/hyperactivity disorder (ADHD) was assessed at ages 5, 7, 10, and 12 years. Sleep quality: higher score = poorer sleep. Adulthood ADHD and psychiatric comorbidity were assessed at 18 years of age. CI = confidence interval.

†$p < .10$. **$p < .01$. ***$p < .001$.

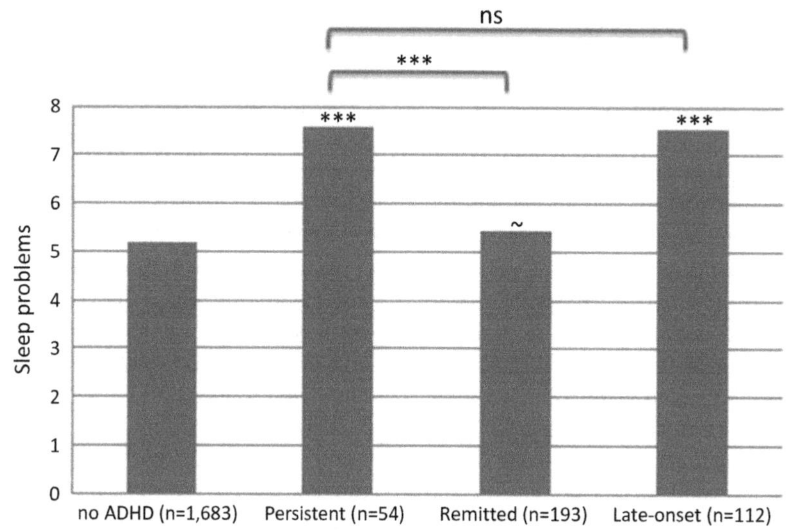

FIGURE 1 Sleep quality score among individuals without attention-deficit/hyperactivity disorder (ADHD) and with persistent, remitted, and late-onset ADHD. *Note.* Asterisks directly above the bars indicate the significance of tests comparing each ADHD group to individuals with no ADHD; asterisks above the brackets indicate significance of statistical comparisons between individuals with persistent and late-onset ADHD, and persistent and remitted ADHD. Sleep problems (higher score = poorer sleep quality). ~$p < 0.10$; ***$p < 0.001$.

specific type of ADHD symptoms. We found that both types of symptoms were independently associated (controlling for each other) with poorer sleep quality: hyperactive/impulsive ($\beta = .13$, 95% CIs [.07, .19], $p < .001$; inattentive ($\beta = .20$, 95% CIs [.14, .25], $p < .001$). Associations between young adult ADHD and sleep quality held in further analyses excluding participants taking ADHD medication at age 18 ($\beta = .12$, 95% CIs [.06, .17], $p < .001$), or who had young children by age 18 ($\beta = .12$, 95% CIs [.07, .17], $p < .001$). We also found that coinformant-reported ADHD symptoms at age 18 were significantly associated with PSQI score ($\beta = .16$, 95% CIs [.11, .22], $p < .001$) and that after including coinformant-rated ADHD symptoms in regression models, childhood ADHD diagnosis was again no longer significantly associated with PSQI score. This indicates that findings regarding ADHD at age 18 are not biased by participants reporting on their own symptoms.

TABLE 2
Correlations by Twin Group

	T1 ADHD	*T1 Sleep*	*T2 ADHD*	*T2 Sleep*
MZ twins				
T1 ADHD	1			
T1 Sleep	.27***	1		
T2 ADHD	.37***	.14**	1	
T2 Sleep	.16***	.34***	.31***	1
DZ twins				
T1 ADHD	1			
T1 Sleep	.32***	1		
T2 ADHD	.09	.12**	1	
T2 Sleep	.14**	.13**	.24***	1

Note: T1 = Twin 1; T2 = Twin 2; ADHD = attention-deficit/hyperactivity disorder symptoms (sum of inattentive and hyperactivity symptoms); sleep = sleep quality (higher score = poorer sleep quality); MZ = monozygotic twins; DZ = dizygotic twins.

**$p < .01$. ***$p < .001$.

Genetic and Environmental Influences on the Association Between ADHD and Sleep Quality

Given that the association between ADHD and poor sleep quality appeared to be driven by adulthood ADHD, we focused on the adulthood period exclusively in the behavioural genetic analyses. Twin correlations are presented in Table 2. The univariate correlations (e.g., correlation between ADHD symptoms for Twin 1 and Twin 2) for both ADHD and sleep quality are higher for MZ twins than DZ twins, suggesting genetic influence. For both ADHD symptoms and sleep quality, the MZ twin correlation was much less than unity, suggesting a substantial role for nonshared environment and/or measurement error. The cross-twin cross-trait correlations (e.g., ADHD symptoms in Twin 1 and sleep quality in Twin 2) were all larger for MZ twins as compared to DZ (Table 2), suggesting genetic influence on this association.

For the behavioural genetic model, the shared environment (C) component could be dropped without a significant loss of fit (Δ–2LL = .02; $\Delta df = 3$, $p = 1$) and the AE model is presented and the AE bivariate model is presented in Figure 2. First, we present the univariate estimates for ADHD and sleep quality from the bivariate model. Individual differences in ADHD symptoms could be explained by influences that were both genetic (.34), 95% CIs [.27, .41], and nonshared environmental (.66), 95% CIs

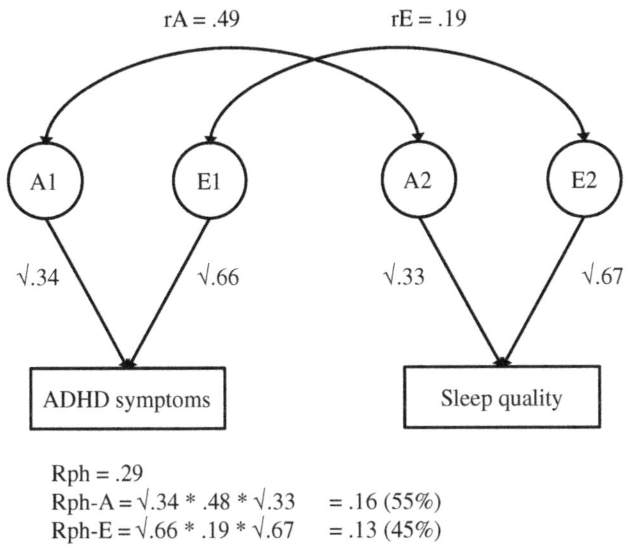

FIGURE 2 AE correlated factors model.

Note. A = genetic; E = nonshared environmental; rA = genetic correlation; rE = nonshared environmental correlation; Rph = phenotypic correlation; ADHD = attention-deficit/hyperactivity symptoms (sum of inattentive and hyperactivity symptoms); sleep = sleep quality (higher score = poorer sleep quality).

[.59, .73]. Individual differences in sleep quality were also explained by genetic (.33), 95% CIs [.26, .39], and nonshared environmental (.67), 95% CIs [.61, .74] influences. Second, we observed a moderate genetic overlap between ADHD symptoms and sleep quality (rA = .49), 95% CIs [.35, .64]. The nonshared environmental correlation was smaller (rE = .19), 95% CIs [.11, .26]. The phenotypic correlation was explained roughly equally by genetic influences (55%) and nonshared environmental influences (45%).

DISCUSSION

ADHD in Childhood and Sleep Quality in Adulthood

The importance of good quality sleep for multiple areas of functioning in adulthood is increasingly evident. Therefore, understanding more about the established association with ADHD is essential. Here we report longitudinal data from early childhood to young adulthood in a twin sample representative of the general U.K. population in terms of socioeconomic status. Children with ADHD have an increased risk for experiencing poor sleep quality in early adulthood, but only if their ADHD persists. If ADHD remits over time, individuals are not more likely than those who had never been diagnosed with ADHD to have poorer sleep quality in young adulthood. Together with the finding that ADHD remits in a substantial proportion of the population, this provides the positive message that when ADHD in childhood remits, these people do not show poorer sleep than others as they move into adulthood. These findings have clinical significance, as they can reassure parents and children with ADHD.

Childhood ADHD was not associated with later sleep problems after taking into account the persistence of ADHD symptoms in young adulthood. This suggests that *concurrent* ADHD symptoms explain the longitudinal association between childhood ADHD and young adult sleep. Indeed, it is possible that certain characteristics of ADHD such as being easily distracted by extraneous stimuli reduce good quality sleep (e.g., by delaying sleep onset). A further possibility is that ADHD medication disrupts sleep (Cortese et al., 2013). However, medication use is unlikely to explain our results, as when we excluded those taking ADHD medication from our concurrent analyses, the association was substantively unchanged.

It is also possible that disturbed sleep leads to ADHD symptoms. It is clear that those experiencing poor sleep quality may display symptoms typical of ADHD (e.g. Owens, 2005). Furthermore, previous research has shown that when certain sleep-related problems are improved (e.g., an adenotonsillectomy is performed to reduce sleep-disordered breathing), ADHD symptoms may also decrease (Sedky, Bennett, & Carvalho, 2014). An explanation for the association between *persistent* ADHD and sleep difficulties is that underlying brain vulnerability may be driving this association. Future work aimed at explaining the association between ADHD and sleep difficulties may benefit from a greater focus on the key brain centres involved in the regulation of arousal, attention, and sleep (Owens et al., 2013). Our current results are consistent with studies on childhood and adolescence emotional difficulties that showed sleep disturbances predict later difficulties, but perhaps not the reverse (Gregory & O'Connor, 2002; for a review, see Alvaro, Roberts, & Harris, 2013).

The association between ADHD and poor sleep quality during adulthood was robust controlling for many potential confounders. We observed that ADHD was independently associated with poor sleep quality, over and above several mental health problems in young adulthood. Indeed, although not a central aim of our study, it is noteworthy that except for cannabis dependence, all other adult psychiatric disorders examined in this study were associated with adult sleep quality. Furthermore, depression showed the strongest association with sleep quality. These findings are consistent with a growing body of literature showing links between sleep quality and psychopathology (and particularly internalising problems; Goldman-Mellor et al., 2014; Riemann, 2007). It is unsurprising that sleep quality is associated with internalising problems, given that insomnia or hypersomnia is listed as a symptom of major depressive disorder in the *DSM-5* (American Psychiatric Association, 2013). Furthermore, the association we observed was not accounted for by the few parents in our sample with young children. These current analyses, however, do not tell us about the direction of the association (young adult ADHD leading to poorer sleep vs. poorer sleep leading to ADHD symptoms). We were not able to examine the possibility that sleep disturbances in childhood predicted later ADHD, and it is well-established that inadequate sleep can result in symptoms that mimic those of ADHD in children (Dahl, 1996). This argument is applicable also to adults (e.g., poor sleep in adults could result in symptoms of ADHD such as difficulty sustaining attention or remembering daily tasks).

Genetic and Environmental Influences

Our genetic estimate for ADHD is similar to those from other twin studies investigating ADHD in adulthood (Franke et al., 2012). Similarly, the genetic estimate for sleep quality reported here was similar to the ones in other samples using exactly the same measure reported by us (Gregory et al., 2011; Taylor, Gregory, Freeman, & Ronald, 2015) and by others (Genderson et al., 2013). More generally, this fits well with robust evidence that genes are important for all complex traits (Polderman et al., 2015). We observed substantial genetic overlap between ADHD and sleep quality, and overall, genes explained roughly half of the association between these variables. This is in line with the generalist genes hypothesis, which proposes that specific genes may confer a general risk but that the development of specific symptom clusters may be determined by the environment (Eley, 1997). Our finding here is unsurprising given a recent review of behavioural genetics (Plomin, DeFries, Knopik, & Neiderhiser, 2016). Indeed, the authors proposed that one of the top 10 replicated findings from the field is that correlations between traits are substantially influenced by genes. Although the estimate reported here differs from certain others focusing on younger populations (Van den Oord et al., 2000), it is important to note that heritability is a population statistic, so changes in estimates at different developmental stages are unsurprising (Plomin et al., 2013).

Our finding of substantial genetic and environmental influences on the overlap between sleep disturbances and ADHD opens the door to some hypotheses for future research. First, attention has been directed to elucidating whether sleep problems lead to mental health problems or vice versa. Our findings indicate that both sleep problems and ADHD have common origins, partly genetically influenced. Investigations into elucidating the co-occurrence of poor sleep quality and mental health problems may shift focus in the direction of influences predating both problems. Second, in the future, polygenic risk score analyses could be used to understand the genetic overlap of these two disorders. For example, it will be possible to examine whether ADHD polygenic risk score explains variation in young adult sleep problems. Such an approach would use genome-wide information to consider whether common risk alleles associated with childhood ADHD are also associated with sleep quality. This new approach may offer better chances of explaining genetic covariance for the phenotypes (Hamshere et al., 2013). As we continue to identify genes involved in complex traits, we expect to find genetic variants associated with both ADHD and sleep disturbances. Third, our findings indicate that influences from the environment are not to be neglected for a better understanding of the association between ADHD and sleep problems in adulthood. The omnipresence of new technologies, communication devices and social media, and how people use these, may have an effect on the co-occurrence of both problems. The use of illicit substances, including alcohol and drugs, may also play a role in the development of ADHD and sleep problems in young adulthood. Indeed, it is known that ADHD is a risk for alcohol use (Molina & Pelham, 2003), and drinking alcohol can impact negatively upon sleep quality (Ebrahim, Shapiro, Williams, & Fenwick, 2013). We predict that these environmental influences may therefore help to account for some of the overlap between ADHD and sleep disturbance.

Limitations

Certain limitations must be acknowledged. First, we collected self-report of both ADHD and sleep quality, which may have artificially inflated the associations. However, we found very similar results when using co-informant rated ADHD symptoms at age 18, rather than self-report. Furthermore, the use of polysomnography has been considered the gold-standard method of assessing sleep. Although we acknowledge the clear value of polysomnography, we note that each method used to assess sleep provides a unique insight into aspects of sleep that other techniques may not capture and that assessing sleep using multiple methods provides the most comprehensive picture (Gregory & Sadeh, 2016). It is interesting that some studies in adulthood (but not all; see Philipsen et al., 2005) have reported links between ADHD and objectively assessed sleep quality (e.g., Boonstra et al., 2007; Sobanski, Schredl, Kettler, & Alm, 2008).

Second, we collected information on sleep quality in young adulthood but not prior during childhood. As a consequence, we could not test the direction of the association between sleep quality and ADHD. Based on previous literature examining different time spans, it is possible that such an association would have been found (Gregory & O'Connor, 2002; Thunstrom, 2002). Relatedly, research suggests that attempts to improve sleep may have a positive impact upon ADHD symptoms within childhood (see Hiscock et al., 2015), and further research needs to extend this interesting work.

Third, we focused on sleep quality in the full range rather than sleep disorders. Given that ADHD has been associated with a whole host of sleep disorders, such as sleep-disordered breathing and periodic limb movement disorder (Yoon et al., 2012), it is possible that such disorders may have been underlying the association reported here.

Fourth, is it important to note limitations that have been levelled at the twin design. It has been proposed that twins may not be representative of the wider nontwin population. Here, however, we found that the prevalence rates of ADHD and mean PSQI scores were within the range of other studies focusing on nontwin populations (Buysse et al., 2008; Centers for Disease Control and Prevention, 2010; Hayashino et al., 2010; Polanczyk, Salum, Sugaya, Caye, & Rohde, 2015). Replications of our results using other genetically informative designs would be of value.

Conclusion

In conclusion, our results provide the positive message that ADHD does not predict later sleep quality over and above the persistence of ADHD into adulthood. The concurrent association between ADHD and poor sleep quality in the young adult years, which in comparison to the childhood years has received limited attention, was robust and influenced by genetic and nonshared environmental factors. Replication is now essential before the full implications of these results are clear. Taking this work further, we acknowledge that a next step is to elucidate the pathways by which shared genes and environmental factors may influence the association between ADHD and sleep disturbances with the longer term aim of reducing the likelihood of this association, which can cause such suffering and impairment.

ACKNOWLEDGMENTS

We are grateful to the study mothers, fathers, twins, and teachers for their participation. Our thanks to Avshalom Caspi and to the members of the E-Risk Study team for their dedication, hard work, and insights.

FUNDING

The E-Risk Study is funded by the Medical Research Council (G1002190). Additional support was provided by NICHD grant HD077482, and by the Jacobs Foundation.

REFERENCES

Agnew-Blais, J. C., Polanczyk, G. V., Danese, A., Wertz, J., Moffitt, T. E., & Arseneault, L. (2016). Evaluation of the persistence, remission, and emergence of attention-deficit/ hyperactivity disorder in young adulthood. *JAMA Psychiatry*. Advance online publication. doi:10.1001/jamapsychiatry.2016.0465

Alvaro, P. K., Roberts, R. M., & Harris, J. K. (2013). A systematic review assessing bidirectionality between sleep disturbances, anxiety, and depression. *Sleep*, *36*, 1059–1068.

American Psychiatric Association. (1994). *Diagnostic and statistical manual of mental disorders* (4th ed.) Washington, DC: Author.

American Psychiatric Association. (2013). *Diagnostic and statistical manual of mental disorders* (5th ed.). Washington, DC: Author.

Angold, A., Costello, E. J., & Erkanli, A. (1999). Comorbidity. *Journal of Child Psychology & Psychiatry*, *40*, 57–87. doi:10.1111/jcpp.1999.40.issue-1

Backhaus, J., Junghanns, K., Broocks, A., Riemann, D., & Hohagen, F. (2002). Test-retest reliability and validity of the Pittsburgh Sleep Quality Index in primary insomnia. *Journal of Psychosomatic Research*, *53*, 737–740. doi:10.1016/S0022-3999(02)00330-6

Barclay, N. L., & Gregory, A. M. (2013). Quantitative genetic research on sleep: A review of normal sleep, sleep disturbances and associated emotional, behavioural, and health-related difficulties. *Sleep Medicine Reviews*, *17*, 29–40. doi:10.1016/j.smrv.2012.01.008

Boker, S., Neale, M., Maes, H., Wilde, M., Spiegel, M., Brick, T., … Fox, J. (2011). OpenMx: An open source extended structural equation modelling framework. *Psychometrika*, *76*, 306–317. doi:10.1007/s11336-010-9200-6

Boonstra, A. M., Kooij, J. S., Oosterlaan, J., Sergeant, J. A., Buitelaar, J. K., & Van Someren, E. J. W. (2007). Hyperactive night and day? Actigraphy studies in adult ADHD: A baseline comparison and the effect of methylphenidate. *Sleep*, *30*, 433–442.

Buysse, D. J., Hall, M. L., Strollo, P. J., Kamarck, T. W., Owens, J., Lee, L., … Matthews, K. A. (2008). Relationships between the Pittsburgh Sleep Quality Index (PSQI), Epworth Sleepiness Scale (ESS), and clinical/polysomnographic measures in a community sample. *Journal of Clinical Sleep Medicine*, *4*, 563–571.

Buysse, D. J., Reynolds, C. F., Monk, T. H., Berman, S. R., & Kupger, D. J. (1989). The Pittsburgh Sleep Quality Index: A new instrument for psychiatric practice and research. *Psychiatry Research*, *28*, 193–213. doi:10.1016/0165-1781(89)90047-4

Cappuccio, F. P., D'Elia, L., Strazzullo, P., & Miller, M. A. (2010). Sleep duration and all-cause mortality: A systematic review and meta-analysis of prospective studies. *Sleep*, *33*, 585–592.

Carpenter, J. S., & Andrykowski, M. A. (1998). Psychometric evaluation of the Pittsburgh Sleep Quality Index. *Journal of Psychosomatic Research*, *45*, 5–13. doi:10.1016/S0022-3999(97)00298-5

Caspi, A., Langley, K., Milne, B., Moffitt, T. E., O'Donovan, M., Owen, M. J., … Thapar, A. (2008). A replicated molecular genetic basis for subtyping antisocial behavior in children with attention-deficit/hyperactivity disorder. *Archives of General Psychiatry*, *65*, 203–210. doi:10.1001/archgenpsychiatry.2007.24

Centers for Disease Control and Prevention. (2010). Increasing prevalence of parent-reported attention-deficit/hyperactivity disorder among children—United States, 2003 and 2007. *Morbidity and Mortality Weekly Report*, *59*, 1439–1443.

Cortese, S. (2015). Sleep and ADHD: What we know and what we do not know. *Sleep Medicine*, *16*, 5–6. doi:10.1016/j.sleep.2014.10.003

Cortese, S., Brown, T. E., Corkum, P., Gruber, R., O'Brien, L. M., Stein, M., … Owens, J. (2013). Assessment and management of sleep problems in youths with attention-deficit/hyperactivity disorder. *Journal of the American Academy of Child & Adolescent Psychiatry*, *52*, 784–796. doi:10.1016/j.jaac.2013.06.001

Curcio, G., Ferrara, M., & DeGennaro, L. (2006). Sleep loss, learning capacity and academic performance. *Sleep Medicine Reviews*, *10*, 323–337. doi:10.1016/j.smrv.2005.11.001

Dahl, R. E. (1996). The regulation of sleep and arousal: Development and psychopathology. *Development and Psychopathology*, *8*, 3–27. doi:10.1017/S0954579400006945

Dewald, J. F., Meijer, A. M., Oort, F. J., Kerkhof, G. A., & Bogels, S. M. (2010). The influence of sleep quality, sleep duration and sleepiness on school performance in children and adolescents: A meta-analytic review. *Sleep Medicine Reviews*, *14*, 179–189. doi:10.1016/j.smrv.2009.10.004

Ebrahim, I. O., Shapiro, C. M., Williams, A. J., & Fenwick, P. B. (2013). Alcohol and sleep I: Effects on normal sleep. *Alcoholism, Clinical and Experimental Research*, *37*, 539–549. doi:10.1111/acer.12006

Eley, T. C. (1997). General genes: A new theme in developmental psychopathology. *Current Directions in Psychological Science*, *6*, 90–95. doi:10.1111/cdir.1997.6.issue-4

Faraone, S. V., Biederman, J., & Mick, E. (2006). The age-dependent decline of attention deficit hyperactivity disorder: A meta-analysis of follow-up studies. *Psychological Medicine*, *36*, 159–165. doi:10.1017/S003329170500471X

Franke, B., Faraone, S. V., Asherson, P., Buitelaar, J., Bau, C. H. D., Ramos-Quiroga, J. A., ... Reif, A. (2012). The genetics of attention deficit/hyperactivity disorder in adults, a review. *Molecular Psychiatry, 17*, 960–987. doi:10.1038/mp.2011.138

Genderson, M. R., Rana, B. K., Panizzon, M. S., Grant, M. D., Toomey, R., Jacobson, K. C., ... Lyons, M. J. (2013). Genetic and environmental influences on sleep quality in middle-aged men: A twin study. *Journal of Sleep Research, 22*, 519–526. doi:10.1111/jsr.2013.22.issue-5

Goldman-Mellor, S., Gregory, A. M., Caspi, A., Harrington, H., Parsons, M., Poulton, R., & Moffitt, T. E. (2014). Mental health antecedents of early midlife insomnia: Evidence from a four-decade longitudinal study. *Sleep, 37*, 1767–1775.

Gregory, A. M., Buysse, D. J., Willis, T. A., Rijsdijk, F. V., Maughan, B., Rowe, R., ... Eley, T. C. (2011). Associations between sleep quality and anxiety and depression symptoms in a sample of young adult twins and siblings. *Journal of Psychosomatic Research, 71*, 250–255. doi:10.1016/j.jpsychores.2011.03.011

Gregory, A. M., & O'Connor, T. G. (2002). Sleep problems in childhood: A longitudinal study of developmental change and association with behavioral problems. *Journal of the American Academy of Child and Adolescent Psychiatry, 41*, 964–971. doi:10.1097/00004583-200208000-00015

Gregory, A. M., & Sadeh, A. (2016). Annual research review: Sleep problems in childhood psychiatric disorders—A review of the latest science. *Journal of Child Psychology & Psychiatry, 57*, 296–317. doi:10.1111/jcpp.12469

Gregory, A. M., Van den Ende, J., Willis, T. A., & Verhulst, F. C. (2008). Parent-reported sleep problems during development and self-reported anxiety/depression, attention problems and aggression later in life. *Archives of Pediatrics & Adolescent Medicine, 162*, 330–335. doi:10.1001/archpedi.162.4.330

Gruber, R., Grizenko, N., Schwartz, G., Ben Amor, L., Gauthier, J., De Guzman, R., & Joober, R. (2006). Sleep and COMT polymorphism in ADHD children: Preliminary actigraphic data. *Journal of the American Academy of Child and Adolescent Psychiatry, 45*, 982–989. doi:10.1097/01.chi.0000220848.48650.10

Hamshere, M. L., Stergiakouli, E., Langley, K., Martin, J., Holmans, P., Kent, L. N., ... Craddock, N. (2013). Shared polygenic contribution between childhood attention-deficit hyperactivity disorder and adult schizophrenia. *The British Journal of Psychiatry, 203*, 107–111. doi:10.1192/bjp.bp.112.117432

Hansen, B. H., Skirbekk, B., Oerbeck, B., Wentzel-Larsen, T., & Kristensen, H. (2013). Persistence of sleep problems in children with anxiety and attention deficit hyperactivity disorders. *Child Psychiatry & Human Development, 44*, 290–304. doi:10.1007/s10578-012-0325-y

Hayashino, Y., Yamazaki, S., Takegami, M., Nakayama, T., Sokejima, S., & Fukuhara, S. (2010). Association between number of comorbid conditions, depression, and sleep quality using the Pittsburgh Sleep Quality Index: Results from a population-based survey. *Sleep Medicine, 11*, 366–371. doi:10.1016/j.sleep.2009.05.021

Hiscock, H., Sciberras, E., Mensah, F., Gerner, B., Efron, D., Khano, S., & Oberklaid, F. (2015). Impact of a behavioural sleep intervention on symptoms and sleep in children with attention deficit hyperactivity disorder, and parental mental health: Randomised controlled trial. *British Medical Journal, 350*, h68. doi:10.1136/bmj.h68

Jennings, J. R., Muldoon, M. F., Hall, M., Buysse, D. J., & Manuck, S. B. (2007). Self-reported sleep quality is associated with the metabolic syndrome. *Sleep, 30*, 219–223.

Kuntsi, J., Eley, T. C., Taylor, A., Hughes, C., Asherson, P., Caspi, A., & Moffitt, T. E. (2004). Co-occurrence of ADHD and low IQ has genetic origins. *American Journal of Medical Genetics Part B-Neuropsychiatric Genetics, 124B*, 41–47. doi:10.1002/(ISSN)1096-8628

Loehlin, J. C. (1996). The Cholesky approach: A cautionary note. *Behavior Genetics, 26*, 65–69. doi:10.1007/BF02361160

Lycett, K., Mensah, F. K., Hiscock, H., & Sciberras, E. (2014). A prospective study of sleep problems in children with ADHD. *Sleep Medicine, 15*, 1354–1361. doi:10.1016/j.sleep.2014.06.004

Moffitt, T. E., & E-Risk Study Team. (2002). Teen-aged mothers in contemporary Britain. *Journal of Child Psychology and Psychiatry, 43*, 727–742. doi:10.1111/jcpp.2002.43.issue-6

Moffitt, T. E., Houts, R., Asherson, P., Belsky, D. W., Corcoran, D. L., Hammerle, M., ... Caspi, A. (2015). Is adult ADHD a childhood-onset neurodevelopmental disorder? Evidence from a four-decade longitudinal cohort study. *American Journal of Psychiatry, 172*, 967–977. doi:10.1176/appi.ajp.2015.14101266

Molina, B. S. G., & Pelham, W. E. (2003). Childhood predictors of adolescent substance use in a longitudinal study of children with ADHD. *Journal of Abnormal Psychology, 112*, 497–507. doi:10.1037/0021-843X.112.3.497

Odgers, C. L., Caspi, A., Bates, C. J., Sampson, R. J., & Moffitt, T. E. (2012). Systematic social observation of children's neighborhoods using Google street view: A reliable and cost-effective method. *Journal of Child Psychology and Psychiatry, 53*, 1009–1017. doi:10.1111/jcpp.2012.53.issue-10

Odgers, C. L., Caspi, A., Russell, M. A., Sampson, R. J., Arseneault, L., & Moffitt, T. E. (2012). Supportive parenting mediates neighborhood socioeconomic disparities in children's antisocial behavior from ages 5 to 12. *Development and Psychopathology, 24*, 705–721. doi:10.1017/S0954579412000326

Owens, J. A. (2005). The ADHD and sleep conundrum: A review. *Journal of Developmental and Behavioral Pediatrics, 26*, 312–322. doi:10.1097/00004703-200508000-00011

Owens, J., Gruber, R., Brown, T., Corkum, P., Cortese, S., O'Brien, L. M., ...Weiss, M. (2013). Future research directions in sleep and ADHD: Report of a consensus working group. *Journal of Attention Disorders, 17*, 550–564. doi:10.1177/1087054712457992

Patel, S. R., & Hu, F. B. (2008). Short sleep duration and weight gain: A systematic review. *Obesity, 16*, 643–653. doi:10.1038/oby.2007.118

Philipsen, A., Feige, B., Hesslinger, B., Ebert, D., Carl, C., Hornyak, M. D., ... Riemann, D. (2005). Sleep in adults with attention-deficit/hyperactivity disorder: A controlled polysomnographic study including spectral analysis of the sleep EEG. *Sleep, 28*, 877–884.

Plomin, R., DeFries, J. C., Knopik, V. S., & Neiderhiser, J. M. (2013). *Behavioral genetics* (6th ed.). New York, NY: Worth.

Plomin, R., DeFries, J. C., Knopik, V. S., & Neiderhiser, J. M. (2016). Top 10 replicated findings from behavioral genetics. *Perspectives on Psychological Science, 11*, 3–23. doi:10.1177/1745691615617439

Polanczyk, G., Caspi, A., Houts, R., Kollins, S. H., Rohde, L. A., & Moffitt, T. E. (2010). Implications of extending the ADHD age-of-onset criterion to age 12: Results from a prospectively studied birth cohort. *Journal of the American Academy of Child and Adolescent Psychiatry, 49*, 210–216.

Polanczyk, G. V., Salum, G. A., Sugaya, L. S., Caye, A., & Rohde, L. A. (2015). Annual research review: A meta-analysis of the worldwide prevalence of mental disorders in children and adolescents. *Journal of Child Psychology and Psychiatry, 56*, 345–365. doi:10.1111/jcpp.12381

Polderman, T. J. C., Benyamin, B., de Leeuw, C. A., Sullivan, P. F., van Bochoven, A., Visscher, P. M., & Posthuman, D. (2015). Meta-analysis of the heritability of human traits based on fifty years of twin studies. *Nature Genetics, 47*, 702–709. doi:10.1038/ng.3285

Riemann, D. (2007). Insomnia and comorbid psychiatric disorders. *Sleep Medicine, 8*, S15–S20. doi:10.1016/S1389-9457(08)70004-2

Rijsdijk, F. V., & Sham, P. C. (2002). Analytic approaches to twin data using structural equation models. *Briefings in Bioinformatics, 3*, 119–133. doi:10.1093/bib/3.2.119

Robins, L. N., Cottler, L., Bucholz, K., & Compton, W. (1995). *Diagnostic interview schedule for DSM-IV.* St Louis, MO: Washington University Press.

Scott, N., Blair, P. S., Emond, A. M., Fleming, P. J., Humphreys, J. S., Henderson, J., & Gringras, P. (2013). Sleep patterns in children with ADHD: A population-based cohort study from birth to 11years. *Journal of Sleep Research, 22*, 121–128. doi:10.1111/j.1365-2869.2012.01054.x

Sedky, K., Bennett, D. S., & Carvalho, K. S. (2014). Attention deficit hyperactivity disorder and sleep disordered breathing in pediatric populations: A meta-analysis. *Sleep Medicine Reviews*, *18*, 349–356. doi:10.1016/j.smrv.2013.12.003

Sobanski, E., Schredl, M., Kettler, N., & Alm, B. (2008). Sleep in adults with attention deficit hyperactivity disorder (ADHD) before and during treatment with methylphenidate: A controlled polysomnographic study. *Sleep*, *31*, 375–381.

StataCorp (2009). Stata statistical software: Release 11. College Station, TX: StataCorp LP.

Sung, V., Hiscock, H., Sciberras, E., & Efron, D. (2008). Sleep problems in children with attention-deficit/hyperactivity disorder - Prevalence and the effect on the child and family. *Archives of Pediatrics & Adolescent Medicine*, *162*, 336–342. doi:10.1001/archpedi.162.4.336

Taylor, M. J., Gregory, A. M., Freeman, D., & Ronald, A. (2015). Do sleep disturbances and psychotic-like experiences in adolescence share genetic and environmental influences? *Journal of Abnormal Psychology*, *124*, 674–684. doi:10.1037/abn0000057

Thunstrom, M. (2002). Severe sleep problems in infancy associated with subsequent development of attention-deficit/hyperactivity disorder at 5.5 years of age. *Acta Paediatrica*, *91*, 584–592. doi:10.1111/j.1651-2227.2002.tb03281.x

Touchette, E., Petit, D., Seguin, J. R., Boivin, M., Tremblay, R. E., & Montplaisir, J. Y. (2007). Associations between sleep duration patterns and behavioral/cognitive functioning at school entry. *Sleep*, *30*, 1213–1219.

Trouton, A., Spinath, F. M., & Plomin, R. (2002). Twins Early Development Study (TEDS): A multivariate, longitudinal genetic investigation of language, cognition and behavior problems in childhood. *Twin Research*, *5*, 444–448. doi:10.1375/136905202320906255

Van den Oord, E. J. C. G., Boomsma, D. I., & Verhulst, F. C. (2000). A study of genetic and environmental effects on the co-occurrence of problem behaviors in three-year-old twins. *Journal of Abnormal Psychology*, *109*, 360–372. doi:10.1037/0021-843X.109.3.360

Williams, R. L. (2000). A note on robust variance estimation for cluster-correlated data. *Biometrics*, *56*, 645–646. doi:10.1111/j.0006-341X.2000.00645.x

Yoon, S. Y. R., Jain, U., & Shapiro, C. (2012). Sleep in attention-deficit/hyperactivity disorder in children and adults: Past, present, and future. *Sleep Medicine Reviews*, *16*, 371–388. doi:10.1016/j.smrv.2011.07.001

Future Directions in Sleep and Developmental Psychopathology

Lisa J. Meltzer

It is critical for psychologists to gain a better understanding about the intersection between sleep and developmental psychopathology. However, while many strive to answer the question of whether sleep causes developmental psychopathology, or vice versa, ultimately the relationship between sleep and developmental psychopathology is complex and dynamic. This article considers future directions in the field of clinical child and adolescent psychology that go beyond this mechanistic question, highlighting areas important to address for clinicians and researchers who strive to better understand how best to serve children and adolescents with developmental psychopathology. Questions are presented about what is normal in terms of sleep across development, the role of individual variability in terms of sleep needs and vulnerability to sleep loss, and how sleep may serve as a risk or resilience factor for developmental psychopathology, concluding with considerations for interventions.

There is a growing literature demonstrating the complex and dynamic relationship between sleep and developmental psychopathology (Gregory & Sadeh, 2016). Yet this is just the tip of the iceberg in terms of what both researchers and clinicians need to know. It would be nice to answer the overarching question of whether sleep causes developmental psychopathology, or vice versa, but ultimately the relationship between sleep and developmental psychopathology is complex and dynamic. To begin to disentangle these issues, more research is needed, including longitudinal population-based studies, experimental sleep manipulation protocols, genetic studies, neuroimaging studies, and intervention studies. But that is the obvious statement included in every review paper or Discussion section. So in this article I attempt to go beyond the obvious and provide some thoughts on factors that should be considered by researchers and clinicians interested in better understanding and addressing the interaction between sleep and developmental psychopathology in children and adolescents.

WHAT IS NORMAL?

Although the field of pediatric sleep research has grown rapidly over the past 25 years, much remains to be learned about sleep and circadian rhythms in children and adolescents. At the most basic level more information is needed about normal sleep, including sleep need and sleep disturbances across development, inter- and intra-individual differences in sleep, and the relationship between circadian rhythms and development. To understand how sleep serves as a mechanism for the development and/or maintenance of psychopathology, we first need to learn more about the role of sleep and typical development.

How Much Sleep Is Just Right?

Sleep duration is the amount of sleep one obtains, typically overnight, or in the case of younger children, over a 24-hr period (including naps). The American Academy of Sleep Medicine recently published guidelines for normal sleep duration (Paruthi et al., 2016), with recommended ranges of sleep duration for each developmental period. Yet these recommended ranges are relatively broad, highlighting that actual individual sleep need can be highly variable. Some children clearly need more sleep, and others need less sleep.

But the factors that contribute to a child's sleep need have not been well defined. Is it possible that the same mechanisms that drive individual sleep need also factor into the development of psychopathology?

Deficient sleep is common among youth, especially adolescents, thus a number of studies have examined the association between sleep deprivation and social and emotional consequences of deficient sleep (Beebe, 2011; Owens, 2014; Shochat, Cohen-Zion, & Tzischinsky, 2014). But only a few have examined this question prospectively or with a controlled sleep manipulation trial. For example, in a large sample of community-dwelling youth, Roberts and Duong (2014) examined reciprocal relationship between sleep duration and depression. Study results showed that deficient sleep (≤ 6 hr per night) predicted both depressive symptoms and *Diagnostic and Statistical Manual of Mental Disorders* (4th ed.; American Psychiatric Association, 1994) major depression 1 year later, even when controlling for baseline major depression, whereas major depression, but not depressive symptoms, predicted deficient sleep 1 year later (Roberts & Duong, 2014).

Other studies have used sleep manipulation protocols with children and adolescents to examine the role of sleep duration. When comparing 5 nights of sleep restriction (6.5 hr in bed per night) to healthy sleep opportunity (10 hr in bed per night), adolescents reported increased tension, anger, anxiety, and irritability following sleep restriction, as well as poorer emotion regulation (Baum et al., 2014). For children, 7–11 years of age, increasing or decreasing a child's typical sleep duration by 1 hr for 5 nights impacted child behavior in school (Gruber, Cassoff, Frenette, Wiebe, & Carrier, 2012). Specifically, sleep extension was found to improve emotional lability and restless-impulsive behaviors, whereas sleep restriction worsened these outcomes. Together these studies provide preliminary evidence of how insufficient sleep duration can result in negative mood and behavioral functioning among children and adolescents.

But deficient sleep is only half of the story, as much remains to be learned about long sleepers. Data from the Youth Risk Behavior Surveys showed that adolescents with either short (≤ 5 hr) or long (≥ 10 hr) sleep were at increased risk for suicidality (Fitzgerald, Messias, & Buysse, 2011). James and Hale (2016) also reported the importance of considering the full range of sleep duration in children, as long sleepers may also be at increased risk for poor health outcomes. But does obtaining the "right" amount of sleep protect youth from the development of psychopathology? When considering the interaction between genetics and environment (both for sleep problems and psychopathology), is it possible that healthy sleep duration can prevent or delay the onset of psychiatric symptoms or disorders?

Answering the questions of individual sleep need is not easy. In adults, self-reported sleep duration has been described as a function of lifestyle choices (e.g., staying up late or getting up early to work; Van Dongen, Vitellaro, & Dinges, 2005). For older children and adolescent, lifestyle choices are often dictated by homework or activities, combined with early school start times. For younger children, sleep schedules are often set by parents. Neither of these situations allows for one to measure a youth's true sleep need. The ideal way to identify a child's sleep need is to monitor him or her in a controlled lab environment, where there are no pressures to wake up early, complete homework, or participate in extracurricular activities. Once youth are allowed to catch up on their sleep (assuming they enter the lab sleep deprived), one could then measure their actual sleep duration needs over several nights. In addition, performance and mood could also be captured with changes in their sleep duration (e.g., actual sleep need; then following nights of sleep need minus 1, 2, or 3 hr). However, few labs in the United States are equipped to handle such an experimental protocol. So in the interim, additional longitudinal studies are needed that allow for an examination of predictors and outcomes, as well as experimental trials that manipulate sleep duration in small doses in the home environment.

Night-to-Night Variability

Along with the inter-individual differences, it is important to consider the intra-individual differences in sleep, specifically night-to-night variability. Many children and adolescents have different sleep schedules (and different sleep durations) for school nights and weekend nights, and even within a school week can have significant variability in their night-to-night sleep patterns. Night-to-night variability in sleep is often seen in mood disorders (Harvey, 2011); and in adults, night-to-night variability in sleep has been shown to be a consistent predictor of subjective well-being, including life satisfaction and positive affect, as well as symptoms of depression and anxiety (Lemola, Ledermann, Friedman, & Gamble, 2013).

A recent review highlights a small number of studies that have demonstrated an association between night-to-night variability and increased symptoms of anxiety and depression, as well as increased externalizing behaviors, aggression, and inattention (Becker, Sidol, Van Dyk, Epstein, & Beebe, 2016). One study with adolescents found that sleep variability was associated with more anxiety, depression, and fatigue, above and beyond mean total sleep time (Fuligni & Hardway, 2006). A more recent study using diffusion tensor imaging showed an association between bedtime variability and white matter integrity in adolescents, with the authors concluding that inconsistent sleep schedules may have a long-term impact on the developing brain (Telzer, Goldenberg, Fuligni, Lieberman, & Galvan, 2015). Thus relying on "average" sleep duration, or asking a single question about "typical" sleep routines, is not sufficient to determine how sleep variability within an individual contributes to the development of psychopathology. In addition to the experimental, longitudinal, and treatment trials that are needed to further examine the role of night-to-night variability on sleep, there is a role for more advanced statistical approaches to analysis, as well as mathematical modeling that may help shed light on sleep variability and changes across development (Becker, Sidol, et al., 2016; Skeldon, Derks, & Dijk, 2016).

The Role of Circadian Rhythm

Along with sleep duration, it is important to consider sleep timing, or the role of the circadian rhythm. The suprachiasmatic nucleus controls circadian rhythms and is regulated by the light/dark cycle. It has been suggested that a person's circadian preference or chronotype (e.g., most alert and awake in the morning vs. most alert and awake in the evening) is strongly influenced by genetics (Gehrman, Keenan, Byrne, & Pack, 2015); however, a number of behavioral factors, including inconsistent sleep schedules, can disrupt the circadian system. As circadian rhythms and sleep are intertwined processes, circadian preference and the timing of sleep is another area for investigation. This is especially important for adolescents, who experience a normal delay in their circadian rhythm with puberty (Carskadon & Acebo, 2002). When combined with early school start times, a delayed circadian rhythm contributes to insufficient sleep (Moore & Meltzer, 2008).

But what (if anything) does a strong circadian preference tell us about a child's vulnerability to psychiatric illness? Alternatively, if we alter a youth's circadian preference (which can be challenging but feasible), will this have a significant impact on his or her well-being? This last question is most notable, as light therapy is often use to regulate circadian rhythms, with periods of bright light in the morning used to advance (or make earlier) one's sleep schedule, whereas bright light late in the day can serve to delay sleep onset (Wyatt, 2011). For youth with inconsistent daily routines (as may occur, e.g., with mood disorders), inconsistent light timing may further exacerbate problems with circadian rhythm sleep-wake disturbances (Harvey, 2011). Interestingly, Richardson and colleagues (2016) reviewed the small evidence base that exercise may play a role in the circadian timing of sleep. However, few studies have been done in this area with adolescents, and the authors suggest the importance of considering multiple factors related to exercise, including timing, duration, dose, intensity, and/or modality (Richardson et al., 2016). Finally, although circadian factors play an important role in bipolar disorder, there are a number of ethical and feasibility issues that may prevent future studies from better identifying the relationship between circadian rhythms and psychiatric disorders (Harvey, 2011; Harvey, Mullin, & Hinshaw, 2006).

Sleep by Any Other Name

Beyond sleep duration, how "sleep" is defined varies greatly across studies. For example, sleep quality is a subjective report of one's sleep. But studies differ in their approaches to sleep quality. The most common approach is to simply ask a person to rate his or her sleep quality, but the time frame can be anything from last night, the previous month, or simply "in general." In addition, any time the focus of a study is a school-age child or adolescent, it is critical to capture the youth's self-report. Studies have consistently shown that as children get older parents are less involved with bedtime routines and are often not aware of sleep disturbances (Amschler & McKenzie, 2005; Meltzer et al., 2013; Paavonen et al., 2000). In addition, sleep quality and sleepiness/fatigue are subjective measures (similar to internalizing behaviors) that are often difficult for parents to report on. Most studies of subjective sleep quality to date have relied heavily on parent report (Lewandowski, Toliver-Sokol, & Palermo, 2011; Spruyt & Gozal, 2011). But even with child/adolescent report, it is important to remember that reporter bias may result when querying youth with anxiety or mood disorders (Mullin et al., 2016). It is possible that some of the conflicting results about the relationship between sleep and psychopathology in the literature are a result of using different measurement approaches and/or different reporters.

Similarly, "sleep disturbances" are often broadly defined, with results relying on a single question ("Do you have problems sleeping?") to more specific queries about reasons about why someone has trouble sleeping. But sleep disturbances can encompass difficulties falling asleep, multiple night wakings, early sleep termination, difficulties waking in the morning, and/or daytime sleepiness. Each of these "disturbances" highlights distinct aspects of sleep that can be addressed in treatment. But the individual contribution of each of these "disturbances" for the development and/or maintenance of psychopathology is unclear. Notably both insomnia (difficulties falling asleep or staying asleep) and hypersomnia (sleeping too much) are included as diagnostic criteria for many mood disorders in childhood and adolescence (American Psychiatric Association, 2014).

Thus, future studies should take care to use validated measures of sleep, in particular ones that include multiple domains of sleep, as well as self-report whenever possible. In addition, these subjective measures should be combined with actigraphy, an objective estimate of sleep–wake patterns, whenever possible. For example, a recent meta-analysis highlighted the benefits of using actigraphy not only for the measure of sleep in children with attention deficit/hyperactivity disorder (ADHD) but also for the detection of motor activity (De Crescenzo et al., 2016).

There are also a number of common physiological sleep disorders seen in children and adolescents (American Academy of Sleep Medicine, 2014), but more information is needed about the relationship between sleep disorders and developmental psychopathology. A recent meta-analysis found a significant relationship between obstructive sleep apnea (OSA) and depressive symptoms in youth, with a significant improvement in depressive symptoms after adenotonsillectomy for the treatment of OSA (Yilmaz, Sedky, & Bennett, 2013). However, the authors highlighted that little is known about the underlying mechanisms that contribute to the relationship between depressive symptoms and OSA.

Another recent meta-analysis found mild OSA to be associated with increased symptoms of ADHD, with treatment of OSA with adenotonsillectomy resulting in decreased ADHD symptoms (Sedky, Bennett, & Carvalho, 2014). Together these reviews highlight the importance of screening for sleep disordered breathing (e.g., regular and loud snoring, witnessed pauses in breathing) among all pediatric patients, in particular those with mood or behavior problems.

Finally, a number of modifiable behaviors can have a significant impact on sleep, daytime mood, and functioning. Along with insufficient sleep duration (which has already been mentioned), the most common sleep "problem" among youth is poor sleep hygiene (Mindell, Meltzer, Carskadon, & Chervin, 2009). These unhealthy sleep habits include irregular sleep schedules, the consumption of caffeine in the late afternoon or evening, and technology in the bedroom. Because these "sleep stealers" play an important role in a youth's sleep and daytime functioning, they should regularly be considered in research studies, as well as addressed in clinical practice.

RISK AND RESILIENCE FACTORS

Along with a better understanding of what is "normal" in terms of sleep, it is critical to have a better grasp of how sleep serves as a risk or resilience factor for developmental psychopathology in youth. Genetics have been shown to play a role in both the development of psychopathology and sleep and circadian problems. But genetics don't tell the full story, so what other factors play a role in this complex relationship between sleep and psychopathology?

Critical Periods of Development?

Just as developmental psychopathology encompasses a lifespan perspective, a better understanding of the impact of sleep across development is essential. Is ensuring sufficient and high-quality sleep during infancy as critical as during adolescence? Is there a stage of development where sleep is more critical in terms of sleep's impact on psychopathology? One emerging area of work that may help shed light on the role of sleep and development is through the examination of slow-wave activity (SWA) as measured by sleep EEG. Two studies have found that the pattern of changes in SWA reflects typical cortical maturation, with a shift from posterior to anterior regions across childhood and adolescence (Kurth et al., 2010, 2012). For example, a predominance of SWA in the occipital lobe in early childhood corresponds with the development of visual acuity, whereas a predominance of SWA in the frontal lobes is seen in adolescence, corresponding to the development of executive functioning. Thus it is likely that sleep plays an important role at each developmental stage in terms of normative development.

Beyond sleep and normal development, recent preliminary studies from the same group have examined sleep EEG in adolescents with major depression or early onset schizophrenia. In one study, differences in SWA were found between adolescents with and without major depression (Tesler et al., 2016). The authors suggest that the increased SWA over the frontal regions in adolescents with major depression may reflect altered pruning of synapses in this area and represent a deviant neurodevelopmental pattern. In addition, it is possible that the differences could reflect maladaptive repetitive thinking. A smaller study found that although there were no differences in overall sleep efficiency or sleep architecture, sleep spindle density differed between adolescents with and without early onset schizophrenia (Tesler et al., 2015). The authors discussed how spindle density may be a promising marker to aid in the diagnosis of early onset schizophrenia in adolescents.

Individual Vulnerability to Sleep Loss?

Along with individual sleep need (discussed earlier), it is possible that sleep loss has a differential identical impact on daytime functioning across individuals. Some children and adolescents may be more sensitive to sleep loss, in particular youth with anxiety disorders, as suggested by Mullin and colleagues (2016). How to determine one's individual vulnerability to sleep loss is an area requiring additional investigation that would require either the controlled laboratory scenario previously described or experimental studies that tightly control sleep duration and serially measure how an individual responds to different doses of sleep duration.

Clearly, more research is needed to elucidate if there is a certain amount of sleep loss that serves as a risk factor for psychopathology. A single night of significant sleep loss (3 hr) has been shown to negatively impact outcomes in preschoolers (Schumacher et al., 2016). But it is more common for youth to chronically experience small amount of sleep loss (e.g., 30–60 min) every night across the school week, especially if there is technology in the bedroom (Buxton et al., 2015; Mindell et al., 2009). What role does this cumulative sleep debt have on the onset and/or maintenance of developmental psychopathology? Considered the other direction, a recent study found that youth with ADHD obtained 40 min less sleep by overnight polysomnography (PSG) compared to youth without ADHD (Virring, Lambek, Thomsen, Moller, & Jennum, 2016). Is it possible that prolonged cumulative sleep loss (which may be due to a number of different factors) contributes to daytime behavior problems? However, to intentionally subject a youth (with or without a psychiatric disorder) to chronic sleep deprivation for long periods to answer this question raises significant ethical concerns; thus, population-based studies that follow youths over development are needed to begin answering this question.

Children Don't Live in a Vacuum

Anytime risk and resilience factors are considered, it is important to also focus on the family and environment in which the child lives. Twin studies have shown the role of both genetics and the shared environment for sleep (e.g., Barclay & Gregory, 2013) and psychopathology (e.g., Barclay & Gregory, 2013; Dunn et al., 2011; Pinto, Soares, Carvalho-Correia, & Mesquita, 2015; Scaini, Belotti, & Ogliari, 2014). But to help disentangle the complex relationship between sleep and psychopathology, more research is needed to determine the overlap versus unique contribution of and interaction between genes and the environment. Finally, when considering treatments that address sleep and/or developmental psychopathology, the environment in which the child lives and attends school, and the broader community, should be considered to ensure treatment success.

INTERVENTIONS

Just as the relationship between sleep and developmental psychopathology is complex and dynamic, so are the questions about how to best treat children and adolescents with comorbid sleep and psychiatric concerns. For example, which should be addressed first, sleep or psychopathology? Or perhaps they should be treated concurrently? Although there are a number of treatment approaches shown to be effective for behavior, mood, and/or anxiety disorders in youth, there are few randomized controlled trials that examine treatment of sleep disturbances in school-age children and adolescents, and even fewer studies that focus on youth with comorbid sleep and psychiatric disorders (Meltzer & Mindell, 2014). Further, Harvey and colleagues (2011) have proposed that sleep disturbance is linked to psychopathology through genetics and both dopaminergic and serotonergic function. Thus they suggested that sleep disturbance is transdiagnostic and perhaps a single treatment could be used to reduce sleep disturbance for different psychiatric disorders (Harvey et al., 2011).

One recent study examined a brief behavioral sleep intervention for youth with comorbid ADHD and autism (Papadopoulos et al., 2015). The treatment included two in-person consultations that provided psychoeducation about sleep and a basic plan to improve sleep-related behaviors, followed by one telephone call. School-age children who participated in the treatment had fewer sleep problems 3 months posttreatment (primarily due to improvements in sleep onset delay), as well as greater improvements in quality of life, ADHD symptom severity, and overall behavior. The efficacy of this relatively simple intervention is promising for clinicians as either a stand-alone treatment or one that can be integrated into other treatment plans.

More information is also needed about the role of pharmacotherapy, both in terms of how psychiatric medications impact sleep in youth and how to best integrate pharmacotherapy and nonpharmacological approaches for the concurrent treatment of sleep and developmental psychopathology. Two recent studies considered the impact of medications to treat ADHD on children's sleep. Becker, Froehlich, and colleagues (2016) examined long-acting metheylphenidate (MPH) on 163 school-age children. Similar to previous studies, increased doses of MPH were associated with increased sleep problems. But for children with sleep problems prior to medication initiation, sleep problems actually decreased after taking MPH (Becker, Froehlich, & Epstein, 2016). Morash-Conway and colleagues (2016) also examined the impact of long-acting MPH on school-age children with ADHD, with sleep measured by overnight PSG. In this study, total sleep time was decreased by 40 minutes on MPH compared to placebo (Morash-Conway et al., 2016). However, they also found that children who were considered "good sleepers" prior to medication were more likely to have improvements in attention accuracy with medication than "poor sleepers." Although both studies provide encouraging results, the Becker study was limited by measurement issues (the use of a single item: "trouble sleeping"), and the Morash-Conway study was limited by a small sample size. Thus to truly answer questions about the impact on sleep of pharmacological treatments for ADHD (or other psychiatric disorders), future studies need to include multiple domains of sleep, an objective measure of sleep (PSG or actigraphy), and larger sample sizes.

There are no FDA-approved medications for insomnia in youth; however, a number of psychiatric drugs are used off-label to improve sleep quantity and quality in children and adolescents, even for children without comorbid psychiatric conditions (Owens et al., 2005; Owens, Rosen, & Mindell, 2003; Owens, Rosen, Mindell, & Kirchner, 2010). When children do have comorbid psychiatric conditions, medications may be chosen with the goal of targeting both the sleep and psychiatric symptoms, but again, more trials are needed that rigorously evaluate these empirical approaches.

Finally, there are a number of nonpharmacological approaches that utilize sleep mechanisms (i.e., sleep deprivation, bright light therapy [BLT], and/or social rhythms therapy), in particular for the treatment of mood disorders (Harvey, 2011). Unfortunately there have been few studies in children or adolescents that have examined these interventions. One recent study is among the first to examine the impact of chronotherapeutic techniques on adolescents with depression in an inpatient setting. Specifically this study compared 2 weeks of BLT plus a single night of sleep deprivation to BLT alone for 2 weeks. The study found that BLT served to stabilize and further reduce depressive symptoms 2 weeks after treatment, but a single night of sleep deprivation had no additive effect (Gest et al., 2016). Although this preliminary study leaves many questions unanswered, the authors suggest the potential value of BLT, a noninvasive chronotherapeutic treatment, for adolescents with depression.

CONCLUSION

The intersection between sleep and developmental psychopathology is exciting and deserving of more attention by researchers to help elucidate mechanisms and treatment options. Although my consideration of future directions asks more questions than it answers, I hope these questions encourage you to further consider the role of sleep in children and adolescents in your own research and clinical practice.

REFERENCES

American Academy of Sleep Medicine. (2014). *International classification of sleep disorders, 3rd ed.: Diagnostic and coding manual.* Westchester, IL: American Academy of Sleep Medicine.

American Psychiatric Association. (1994). *Diagnostic and statistical manual of mental disorders* (4th ed.).;

American Psychiatric Association. (2014). *Diagnostic and statistical manual of mental disorders, fifth edition* (5th ed.). Washington, DC: American Psychiatric Association.

Amschler, D. H., & McKenzie, J. F. (2005). Elementary students' sleep habits and teacher observations of sleep-related problems. *Journal of School Health, 75*(2), 50–56. doi:10.1111/josh.2005.75.issue-2

Barclay, N. L., & Gregory, A. M. (2013). Quantitative genetic research on sleep: A review of normal sleep, sleep disturbances and associated emotional, behavioural, and health-related difficulties. *Sleep Medicine Reviews, 17*(1), 29–40. doi: 10.1016/j.smrv.2012.01.008

Baum, K. T., Desai, A., Field, J., Miller, L. E., Rausch, J., & Beebe, D. W. (2014). Sleep restriction worsens mood and emotion regulation in adolescents. *Journal of Child Psychology and Psychiatry and Allied Disciplines, 55*, 180–190. doi:10.1111/jcpp.12125

Becker, S. P., Froehlich, T. E., & Epstein, J. N. (2016). Effects of methylphenidate on sleep functioning in children with attention-deficit/hyperactivity disorder. *Journal of Developmental and Behavioral Pediatrics, 37*(5), 395–404. doi:10.1097/DBP.0000000000000285

Becker, S. P., Sidol, C. A., Van Dyk, T. R., Epstein, J. N., & Beebe, D. W. (2016). Intraindividual variability of sleep/wake patterns in relation to child and adolescent functioning: A systematic review. *Sleep Medicine Reviews*. Advance online publication. doi:10.1016/j.smrv.2016.07.004

Beebe, D. W. (2011). Cognitive, behavioral, and functional consequences of inadequate sleep in children and adolescents. *Pediatric Clinics of North America, 58*(3), 649–665. doi:10.1016/j.pcl.2011.03.002

Buxton, O. M., Chang, A. M., Spilsbury, J. C., Bos, T., Emsellem, H., & Knutson, K. L. (2015). Sleep in the modern family: Protective family routines for child and adolescent sleep. *Sleep Health, 1*(1), 15–27. doi:10.1016/j.sleh.2014.12.002

Carskadon, M. A., & Acebo, C. (2002). Regulation of sleepiness in adolescents: Update, insights, and speculation. *Sleep, 25*(6), 606–614.

De Crescenzo, F., Licchelli, S., Ciabattini, M., Menghini, D., Armando, M., Alfieri, P., ... Vicari, S. (2016). The use of actigraphy in the monitoring of sleep and activity in ADHD: A meta-analysis. *Sleep Medicine Reviews, 26*, 9–20. doi:10.1016/j.smrv.2015.04.002

Dunn, E. C., Uddin, M., Subramanian, S. V., Smoller, J. W., Galea, S., & Koenen, K. C. (2011). Research review: Gene–environment interaction research in youth depression - a systematic review with recommendations for future research. *Journal of Child Psychology and Psychiatry and Allied Disciplines, 52*(12), 1223–1238. doi:10.1111/j.1469-7610.2011.02466.x

Fitzgerald, C. T., Messias, E., & Buysse, D. J. (2011). Teen sleep and suicidality: Results from the youth risk behavior surveys of 2007 and 2009. *Journal of Clinical Sleep Medicine, 7*(4), 351–356. doi:10.5664/JCSM.1188

Fuligni, A. J., & Hardway, C. (2006). Daily variation in adolescents' sleep, activities, and psychological well-being. *Journal of Research on Adolescence, 16*(3), 353–378. doi:10.1111/jora.2006.16.issue-3

Gehrman, P. R., Keenan, B. T., Byrne, E. M., & Pack, A. I. (2015). Genetics of sleep disorders. *Psychiatric Clinics of North America, 38*(4), 667–681. doi:10.1016/j.psc.2015.07.004

Gest, S., Holtmann, M., Bogen, S., Schulz, C., Pniewski, B., & Legenbauer, T. (2016). Chronotherapeutic treatments for depression in youth. *European Child & Adolescent Psychiatry, 25*(2), 151–161. doi:10.1007/s00787-015-0720-6;10.1007/s00787-015-0720-6[pii]

Gregory, A. M., & Sadeh, A. (2016). Annual Research Review: Sleep problems in childhood psychiatric disorders: A review of the latest science. *Journal of Child Psychology and Psychiatry and Allied Disciplines, 57*(3), 296–317. doi:10.1111/jcpp.12469

Gruber, R., Cassoff, J., Frenette, S., Wiebe, S., & Carrier, J. (2012). Impact of sleep extension and restriction on children's emotional lability and impulsivity. *Pediatrics, 130*(5), e1155–e1161. doi:10.1542/peds.2012-0564

Harvey, A. G. (2011). Sleep and circadian functioning: Critical mechanisms in the mood disorders? *Annual Review of Clinical Psychology, 7*, 297–319. doi:10.1146/annurev-clinpsy-032210-104550

Harvey, A. G., Mullin, B. C., & Hinshaw, S. P. (2006). Sleep and circadian rhythms in children and adolescents with bipolar disorder. *Developmental Psychopathology, 18*(4), 1147–1168. doi:10.1017/S095457940606055X

Harvey, A. G., Murray, G., Chandler, R. A., & Soehner, A. (2011). Sleep disturbance as transdiagnostic: Consideration of neurobiological mechanisms. *Clinical Psychology Reviews, 31*(2), 225–235. doi:10.1016/j.cpr.2010.04.003

James, S., & Hale, L. (2016). Sleep duration and child wellbeing: A nonlinear association. *Journal of Clinical Child and Adolescent Psychology*, 1–11. doi:10.1080/15374416.2016.1204920

Kurth, S., Ringli, M., Geiger, A., LeBourgeois, M., Jenni, O. G., & Huber, R. (2010). Mapping of cortical activity in the first two decades of life: A high-density sleep electroencephalogram study. *Journal of Neuroscience, 30*(40), 13211–13219. doi:10.1523/JNEUROSCI.2532-10.2010

Kurth, S., Ringli, M., LeBourgeois, M. K., Geiger, A., Buchmann, A., Jenni, O. G., & Huber, R. (2012). Mapping the electrophysiological marker of sleep depth reveals skill maturation in children and adolescents. *Neuroimage, 63*, 959–965. doi:10.1016/j.neuroimage.2012.03.053

Lemola, S., Ledermann, T., Friedman, E. M., & Gamble, K. L. (2013). Variability of sleep duration is related to subjective sleep quality and subjective well-being: An actigraphy study. *PLoS One, 8*(8), e71292. doi:10.1371/journal.pone.0071292

Lewandowski, A. S., Toliver-Sokol, M., & Palermo, T. M. (2011). Evidence-based review of subjective pediatric sleep measures. *Journal of Pediatric Psychology, 36*(7), 780–793. doi:10.1093/jpepsy/jsq119

Meltzer, L. J., Avis, K. T., Biggs, S., Reynolds, A. C., Crabtree, V. M., & Bevans, K. B. (2013). The Children's Report of Sleep Patterns (CRSP):

A self-report measure of sleep for school-aged children. *Journal of Clinical Sleep Medicine*, *9*(3), 235–245. doi:10.5664/jcsm.2486

Meltzer, L. J., & Mindell, J. A. (2014). Systematic review and meta-analysis of behavioral interventions for pediatric insomnia. *Journal of Pediatric Psychology*, *39*(8), 932–948. doi:10.1093/jpepsy/jsu041

Mindell, J. A., Meltzer, L. J., Carskadon, M. A., & Chervin, R. D. (2009). Developmental aspects of sleep hygiene: Findings from the 2004 National Sleep Foundation Sleep in America Poll. *Sleep Medicine*, *10* (7), 771–779. doi:10.1016/j.sleep.2008.07.016

Moore, M., & Meltzer, L. J. (2008). The sleepy adolescent: Causes and consequences of sleepiness in teens. *Paediatric Respiratory Reviews*, *9* (2), 114–121. doi:10.1016/j.prrv.2008.01.001

Morash-Conway, J., Gendron, M., & Corkum, P. (2016). The role of sleep quality and quantity in moderating the effectiveness of medication in the treatment of children with ADHD. *Attention Deficit and Hyperactivity Disorders*. Advance online publication. doi:10.1007/s12402-016-0204-7

Mullin, B. C., Pyle, L., Haraden, D., Riederer, J., Brim, N., Kaplan, D., & Novins, D. (2016). A preliminary multimethod comparison of sleep among adolescents with and without generalized anxiety disorder. *Journal of Clinical Child and Adolescent Psychology*. Advance online publication. doi:10.1080/15374416.2016.1220312

Owens, J. (2014). Insufficient sleep in adolescents and young adults: An update on causes and consequences. *Pediatrics*, *134*(3), e921–e932. doi:10.1542/peds.2014-1696

Owens, J. A., Babcock, D., Blumer, J., Chervin, R. D., Ferber, R., Goetting, M., … Sheldon, S. (2005). The use of pharmacotherapy in the treatment of pediatric insomnia in primary care: Rational approaches. A consensus meeting summary. *Journal of Clinical Sleep Medicine*, *1*, 49–59.

Owens, J. A., Rosen, C. L., & Mindell, J. A. (2003). Medication use in the treatment of pediatric insomnia: Results of a survey of community-based pediatricians. *Pediatrics*, *111*(5, Pt. 1), e628–e635.

Owens, J. A., Rosen, C. L., Mindell, J. A., & Kirchner, L. H. (2010). Use of pharmacotherapy for in child psychiatry practice: A national survey. *Sleep Medicine*, *11*(7), 692–700. doi:10.1016/j.sleep.2009.11.015

Paavonen, E. J., Aronen, E. T., Moilanen, I., Piha, J., Rasanen, E., Tamminen, T., & Almqvist, F. (2000). Sleep problems of school-aged children: A complementary view. *Acta Paediatrica*, *89*(2), 223–228. doi:10.1111/j.1651-2227.2000.tb01220.x.

Papadopoulos, N., Sciberras, E., Hiscock, H., Mulraney, M., McGillivray, J., & Rinehart, N. (2015). The efficacy of a brief behavioral sleep intervention in school-aged children with ADHD and comorbid autism spectrum disorder. *Journal of Attention Disorders*. Advance online publication. doi:10.1177/1087054714568565

Paruthi, S., Brooks, L. J., D'Ambrosio, C., Hall, W., Kotagal, S., Lloyd, R. M. … Wise, M. S. (2016). Recommended Amount of Sleep for Pediatric Populations: A Consensus Statement of the American Academy of Sleep Medicine. *Journal of Clinical Sleep Medicine*, *12*, 785–786. doi:10.5664/jcsm.5866

Pinto, R. Q., Soares, I., Carvalho-Correia, E., & Mesquita, A. R. (2015). Gene-environment interactions in psychopathology throughout early childhood: A systematic review. *Psychiatric Genetics*, *25*(6), 223–233. doi:10.1097/YPG.0000000000000106

Richardson, C. E., Gradisar, M., Short, M. A., & Lang, C. (2016). Can exercise regulate the circadian system of adolescents? Novel implications for the treatment of delayed sleep-wake phase disorder. *Sleep Medicine Reviews*. doi:10.1016/j.smrv.2016.06.010

Roberts, R. E., & Duong, H. T. (2014). The prospective association between sleep deprivation and depression among adolescents. *Sleep*, *37* (2), 239–244. doi:10.5665/sleep.3388

Scaini, S., Belotti, R., & Ogliari, A. (2014). Genetic and environmental contributions to social anxiety across different ages: A meta-analytic approach to twin data. *Journal of Anxiety Disorders*, *28*(7), 650–656. doi:10.1016/j.janxdis.2014.07.002

Schumacher, A. M., Miller, A. L., Watamura, S. A., Kurth, S., Lassonde, J. M., & LeBourgeois, M. K. (2016). Sleep moderates the association between response inhibition and self-regulation in early childhood. *Journal of Clinical Child and Adolescent Psychology*. Advance online publication. doi:10.1080/15374416.2016.1204921

Sedky, K., Bennett, D. S., & Carvalho, K. S. (2014). Attention deficit hyperactivity disorder and sleep disordered breathing in pediatric populations: A meta-analysis. *Sleep Medicine Reviews*, *18*(4), 349–356. doi:10.1016/j.smrv.2013.12.003

Shochat, T., Cohen-Zion, M., & Tzischinsky, O. (2014). Functional consequences of inadequate sleep in adolescents: A systematic review. *Sleep Medicine Reviews*, *18*(1), 75–87. doi:10.1016/j.smrv.2013.03.005

Skeldon, A. C., Derks, G., & Dijk, D. J. (2016). Modelling changes in sleep timing and duration across the lifespan: Changes in circadian rhythmicity or sleep homeostasis? *Sleep Medicine Reviews*, *28*, 96–107. doi:10.1016/j.smrv.2015.05.011

Spruyt, K., & Gozal, D. (2011). Pediatric sleep questionnaires as diagnostic or epidemiological tools: A review of currently available instruments. *Sleep Medicine Reviews*, *15*(1), 19–32. doi:10.1016/j.smrv.2010.07.005

Telzer, E. H., Goldenberg, D., Fuligni, A. J., Lieberman, M. D., & Galvan, A. (2015). Sleep variability in adolescence is associated with altered brain development. *Developmental Cognitive Neuroscience*, *14*, 16–22. doi:10.1016/j.dcn.2015.05.007

Tesler, N., Gerstenberg, M., Franscini, M., Jenni, O. G., Walitza, S., & Huber, R. (2015). Reduced sleep spindle density in early onset schizophrenia: A preliminary finding. *Schizophrenia Research*, *166*(1–3), 355–357. doi:10.1016/j.schres.2015.04.042

Tesler, N., Gerstenberg, M., Franscini, M., Jenni, O. G., Walitza, S., & Huber, R. (2016). Increased frontal sleep slow wave activity in adolescents with major depression. *Neuroimage: Clinical*, *10*, 250–256. doi:10.1016/j.nicl.2015.10.014

Van Dongen, H. P., Vitellaro, K. M., & Dinges, D. F. (2005). Individual differences in adult human sleep and wakefulness: Leitmotif for a research agenda. *Sleep*, *28*(4), 479–496.

Virring, A., Lambek, R., Thomsen, P. H., Moller, L. R., & Jennum, P. J. (2016). Disturbed sleep in attention-deficit hyperactivity disorder (ADHD) is not a question of psychiatric comorbidity or ADHD presentation. *Journal of Sleep Research*, *25*(3), 333–340. doi:10.1111/jsr.12377

Wyatt, J. K. (2011). Circadian rhythm sleep disorders. *Pediatric Clinics of North America*, *58*(3), 621–635. doi:10.1016/j.pcl.2011.03.014

Yilmaz, E., Sedky, K., & Bennett, D. S. (2013). The relationship between depressive symptoms and obstructive sleep apnea in pediatric populations: A meta-analysis. *Journal of Clinical Sleep Medicine*, *9*(11), 1213–1220. doi:10.5664/jcsm.3178

Index

For Product Safety Concerns and Information please contact our EU representative GPSR@taylorandfrancis.com Taylor & Francis Verlag GmbH, Kaufingerstraße 24, 80331 München, Germany

Batch number: 10733608

Printed by Printforce, the Netherlands